MW00808712

ISBN: 978-0-8132-3719-0
eISBN: 9780-8132-3720-6

Cataloging-in-Publication Data on File at the Library of Congress

First publication: *Liturgische Bibelhermeneutik. Die Heilige Schrift im Horizont des Gottesdienstes,*
Liturgiewissenschaftliche Quellen und Forschungen, 109 (Münster: Aschendorff Verlag, 2020).
The translation is made from an abridged version prepared by the author.

Printed in the United States.
Book design by Burt&Burt
Interior set with Minion Pro and Astoria

LITURGICAL HERMENUETICS
OF SACRED SCRIPTURE

Liturgical Hermenueutics of Sacred Scripture

MARCO BENINI

Translated by
BRIAN McNEIL

Foreword by
MICHAEL G. WITCZAK

The Catholic University of America Press
Washington, D.C.

Contents

Translator's Note

Biblical citations are from the New American Bible Revised Edition.

Texts of the Church's magisterium are quoted from official Vatican English-language translations.

When "Word" (in German: *Wort*) refers to Christ as the Word of God or to Scripture as the Word of God, it is always capitalized in the text of the book itself. In quotations from official Vatican texts and from Scripture, however, their capitalization is retained.

I wish to emphasize that the use of masculine terms and pronouns, as well as expressions such as "the kingdom of God," is due *exclusively* to stylistic considerations.

Abbreviations

AAS	*Acta Apostolicae Sedis*
AHMA	*Analecta hymnica medii aevi*
ALw	*Archiv für Liturgiewissenschaft*
An.Li	Analecta liturgica
BEL.H	Bibliotheca „Ephemerides liturgicae". Sectio Historica
BEL.S	Bibliotheca „Ephemerides liturgicae". Subsidia
BiKi	*Bibel und Kirche*
BiLi	*Bibel und Liturgie*
BN	*Biblische Notizen*
ByZ	*Byzantinische Zeitschrift*
CCC	*Catechism of the Catholic Church*
CChr.SL	Corpus Christianorum. Series Latina
CSEL	Corpus Scriptorum Ecclesiasticorum Latinorum
DACL	*Dictionnaire d'archéologie chrétienne et de liturgie*
DH	*Enchiridion symbolorum definitionum et declarationum de rebus fidei et morum. Lateinisch-Deutsch = Kompendium der Glaubensbekenntnisse und kirchlichen Lehrentscheidungen*, edited by H. Denzinger and P. Hünermann, 43rd ed. Freiburg/Br.: Herder, 2010.
Diss.T	Dissertationen. Theologische Reihe
DOP	*Dumbarton Oaks Papers*
DV	*Dei Verbum* (see magisterium)

EDIL	*Enchiridion documentorum instaurationis liturgicae.* 4 vols, edited by R. Kaczynski. Rome: CLV-Edizioni Liturgiche, 1976–2018.
EHS	Europäische Hochschulschrift
EL	*Ephemerides liturgicae*
EO	*Ecclesia orans*
EThL	Ephemerides theologicae Lovanienses
FontC	Fontes Christiani
FThSt	Freiburger theologische Studien
FZPhTh	*Freiburger Zeitschrift für Philosophie und Theologie*
GCS	Die griechischen christlichen Schriftsteller der ersten Jahrhunderte
GdK	Gottesdienst der Kirche
GeV	Gelasianum Vetus / Sacramentarium Gelasianum = *Liber sacramentorum romanae aeclesiae ordinis anni circuli* […] (see liturgical sources)
GILH	General Introduction to the Liturgy of the Hours: *Liturgy of the Hours* 1:21–98 (see liturgical sources)
GILM	General Introduction to the Lectionary for Mass
GIRM	General Instruction of the Roman Missal (*Missal,* 17–87)
HerKorr	*Herder Korrespondenz*
HlD	*Heiliger Dienst*
HThKAT	Herders theologischer Kommentar zum Alten Testament
HWP	Historisches Wörterbuch der Philosophie
IKaZ	*Internationale Katholische Zeitschrift Communio*
IThS	Innsbrucker theologische Studien
JbAC	*Jahrbuch für Antike und Christentum*
JBTh	*Jahrbuch für Biblische Theologie*
JLw	*Jahrbuch für Liturgiewissenschaft*
JRGS	Joseph Ratzinger, *Gesammelte Schriften*
JThF	Jerusalemer Theologisches Forum
KKTS	Konfessionskundliche und kontroverstheologische Studien
LC	Liturgia condenda

LiZs	*Liturgische Zeitschrift*
LJ	*Liturgisches Jahrbuch*
LQF	Liturgiegeschichtliche Quellen und Forschungen
LThK	*Lexikon für Theologie und Kirche. Durchgesehene Ausgabe der 3. Auflage 1993 – 2001*, edited by W. Kasper. 3rd ed., 11 vols. Freiburg/Br.: Herder, 2006.
MBTh	Münsterische Beiträge zur Theologie
MD	*La Maison-Dieu*
MLCT	Monumenta liturgica Concilii Tridentini
MRom	Missale Romanum (see liturgical sources)
MSIL	Monumenta, studia, instrumenta liturgica
OCA	Orientalia Christiana Analecta
OCP	*Orientalia Christiana Periodica*
ÖBS	Österreichische Biblische Studien
ÖSLS	Österreichische Studien zur Liturgiewissenschaft und Sakramententheologie
OLM	Ordo Lectionum Missae
PG	Patrologia Graeca
PL	Patrologia Latina
PiLi	Pietas liturgica
PiLi.S	Pietas liturgica. Studia
PLA	Premesse al Lezionario Ambrosiano: *Lezionario Ambrosiano* 1, XIII–LVI. (see liturgical sources)
PRG	Pontificale Romano–Germanicum: *Le Pontifical Romano-Germanique* (see liturgical sources)
PPSt	Pius-Parsch-Studien
PTS	Patristische Texte und Studien
QD	Quaestiones disputatae
QL	*Questions Liturgiques*
QVetChr	Vetera Christianorum / Quaderni
RAC	*Reallexikon für Antike und Christentum*
RED.F	Rerum ecclesiasticarum documenta. Series maior. Fontes
RivLi	*Rivista liturgica*
RRom	Rituale Romanum (see liturgical sources)
RSPhTh	*Revue des sciences philosophiques et théologiques*
SC	*Sacrosanctum Concilium* (see magisterium)

SChr	Sources chrétiennes
SL	*Studia liturgica*
SÖAW.PH	Sitzungsberichte der Österreichischen Akademie der Wissenschaften. Philosophisch-Historische Klasse
SSL	Spicilegium sacrum Lovaniense
StA	Studia Anselmiana
StPaLi	Studien zur Pastoralliturgie
StZ	*Stimmen der Zeit*
TAB	Texte und Arbeiten
TC	Traditio christiana
ThGL	*Theologie und Glaube*
ThPh	*Theologie und Philosophie*
ThPQ	*Theologisch-praktische Quartalschrift*
ThQ	Theologische Quartalschrift
TRE	*Theologische Realenzyklopädie*
TThS	Trierer theologische Studien
TThZ	*Trierer theologische Zeitschrift*
UTB	Universitätstaschenbücher
VD	Benedict XVI, *Verbum Domini* (see magisterium)
WEC	*Worship in the Early Church: An Anthology of Historical Sources*, edited by L. J. Johnson. Dublin: Columbia, 2010;
WUNT	Wissenschaftliche Untersuchungen zum Neuen Testament

Foreword

MICHAEL G. WITCZAK

Scripture and Liturgy have been in a close relationship since the earliest days of Christianity. The account of the disciples on the road to Emmaus has served as a rediscovery of this reality in recent years. Jesus walked with two disciples on the road but they did not recognize him. They were distraught at the death of Jesus and the stranger broke the scriptures open for them: "Then beginning with Moses and all the prophets, he interpreted to them what referred to him in all the scriptures" (Lk 24:27). So taken were they with his words that they invited him to join them for supper.

> And it happened that, while he was with them at table, he took bread, said the blessing, broke it, and gave it to them. With that their eyes were opened and they recognized him, but he vanished from their sight. Then they said to each other, "Were not our hearts burning [within us] while he spoke to us on the way and opened the scriptures to us?" So they set out at once and returned to Jerusalem where they found gathered together the eleven and those with them who were saying, "The Lord has truly been raised and has appeared to Simon!" Then the two recounted what had taken place on the way and how he was made known to them in the breaking of the bread (Lk 24:30–35).

This dual recognition of the presence of Christ, in the breaking of the bread and in the word, both in a moment of insight, lies at the heart of the recent attention of the intimate relationship between the presence of Christ in the word proclaimed in Scripture and within the eucharistic action. The Constitution on the Sacred Liturgy explores the relationship in several places (e.g., SC 7 and 56).

The understanding of the relationship between Scripture and the Liturgy as a single action of manifestation of the presence of Christ has had a long development. The patristic record of hundreds of scripturally-based sermons proclaimed within the liturgy is copious, with a wealth of sermons both in the East and the West. This tradition is maintained through the pontificate of Gregory the Great (+604), but seems slowly to die out in the seventh century. The Ordo Romanus Primus (ca. 700) does not mention a sermon by the pope in the Easter liturgy. Preaching never dies out, but it seems to move from within the liturgical context to outside it. The scriptures are proclaimed but the homiletic breaking open of it migrates to different times and places. The lack of a homily is a hint that the scripture is a rubrical requirement but not a pastoral reality. The development of the liturgy of the prone (the reading of the gospel in the vernacular, announcements of fast days and holy days, proclamation of wedding banns, a sermon in the vernacular) shows a renewed pastoral instinct, but liturgically it is an insertion into the liturgy and not an organic part of it: it is not mentioned in the rubrics.

Even as recently as the great history of the development of the Mass of the Roman Rite by Joseph Jungmann (1948; 5th ed. 1962), he spoke of the first part of the Mass as the *Vormesse*, the "Fore-Mass," not integral to the Mass properly so-called. The usual way to explain the Mass was that it was in two parts, the Mass of the Catechumens and the Mass of the Faithful. The common understanding of how one fulfilled one's Sunday obligation to attend Mass was by being present at the Offertory, Consecration, and Communion of the Mass of the Faithful.

The teaching of the Constitution of the Sacred Liturgy shifts this understanding: "The two parts which, in a certain sense, go to make up the Mass, namely, the liturgy of the word and the eucharistic liturgy, are so closely connected with each other that they form but one single act of worship. Accordingly this sacred Synod strongly urges pastors of souls that, when instructing the faithful, they insistently teach them to take their part in the entire Mass, especially on Sundays and feasts of obligation" (SC 56).

This change in the understanding of the integrality of word and sacrament developed over one hundred fifty years from the early nineteenth century to the years of the Second Vatican Council. The biblical movement and the liturgical movement developed side by side, energized by the same dynamics of a rediscovery of the long history of the Church and its rich heritage, finally brought together in a single series by J. P. Migne in the *Patrologia Latina* and the *Patrologia Graeca* (ca. 1840–65). For the first time all the extant literature from Christian theologians from the years 100 to 1100 were available in a convenient edition. This wealth of resources led to general reevaluations of the tradition. The emergence of history as an academic discipline likewise gave additional tools to scholars to trace the narrative of Christian scripture study and liturgical study separately and then eventually together.

By the time of the Second Vatican Council there was a desire that the Word of God play a more prominent role of Church life and worship. The fathers at Vatican II expressed the desire that more scripture be read in the liturgy (SC 24; 35), both in the Mass (51–52) and in the Liturgy of the Hours (91–92). A multi-year lectionary was envisaged (51), as well as the reintegration of a homily into the Mass (52).

In the years since the Council, a number of studies have been made on the role of the Bible in the Liturgy. The book in your hands, by Marco Benini, a priest of the Diocese of Eichstätt, and professor of liturgy in the Theological Faculty Trier, is a reworking of his *Habilitationsschrift* and makes available to an English-speaking audience the fruits of his research and reflection. He explores how Scripture read in the context of the liturgical celebration takes on meanings not discovered when the scripture is read during one's own private prayer or during scripture study done at one's desk. The reading of the word of God within the gathered assembly of the faithful, from a lectionary, by liturgical ministers, and reflected on in a homily, brings out dimensions of the Word not found in private study or private prayer.

As you read this work, you will encounter a detailed exegesis of the conciliar recognition of the key role of the scriptures. The post-conciliar development of the lectionary is a concrete manifestation of this conviction. The lectionary for Mass, for the Liturgy of the Hours, and for sacramental liturgies is explored in relationship to the liturgical year. The particular role of the psalms is highlighted, and then the scriptural basis of prayers (both the great consecratory prayers like the Eucharistic Prayer and the shorter orations), songs, and hymns are explored at some length. In addition, the scriptural basis of the symbols and gestures received detailed treatment.

The laying out of the riches of the scriptures, organized into lectionaries, and informing the whole structure of the liturgical act, leads to a theological analysis of the liturgical hermeneutics of the Word of God. Specific theological themes come up for particular attention, such as the memorial quality of Scripture: That what was done once for all by Christ is available in power in the current celebration. That word is a form of sacrament revealing dimensions of God's presence and action in our midst. The Holy Spirit is present and active in the liturgy, in the word proclaimed and in the scripturally inspired prayers, such as in the epiclesis of the Eucharistic Prayer.

The last part of the book looks at the reception of this renewed understanding of the Word within the Liturgy and its impact on the spirituality of the Church.

All in all, this book will lead to a deeper understanding and appreciation of the scriptures in the liturgy and its importance in the life of the Church. I commend to you the joy and work that this book presents to you. Fr. Benini has done us a service that we will continue to pay dividends to us for the years ahead.

Preface

Understanding the Bible through the Liturgy—this is a summary of my approach in the present book. After being accepted in 2018 as my Habilitation thesis by the Theological Faculty of the Catholic University of Eichstätt–Ingolstadt, Germany, the German original was published in 2020 (see the copyright page).

On the occasion of the publication of this abridged English translation, I would like to express my sincere thanks first of all to Bishop Dr. Gregor Maria Hanke, OSB, who made my academic path possible, has given me his explicit support, and followed my progress with interest. I am likewise grateful to my professor, Dr. Jürgen Bärsch, who supervised my doctoral thesis as well as my Habilitation. It was my distinct pleasure to be awarded both the Habilitation Prize of the Catholic University of Eichstätt–Ingolstadt and the Pius Parsch Prize (Klosterneuburg/Vienna, Austria).

The 2017 conference of the *Societas Liturgica* in Louvain proved decisive for my further path. Dr. Mark Morozowich, Dean of the School of Theology and Religious Studies at The Catholic University of America (CUA) in Washington, D.C., attended my lecture on the sacramentality of the Word and opened the door to a visiting professorship (and then a research professorship) in the USA, where I have taught for six semesters. I am profoundly grateful to him and to my colleagues in the Liturgy Area, Dr. Michael Witczak, Dr. Stefanos Alexopoulos, Dr. Dominic Serra, and Dr. Paul McPartlan, for the marvelous collaboration and many valuable experiences, both academic and personal.

I am especially grateful to the Confraternity of Christian Doctrine (USCCB) for making possible an English translation of my work. It accepted the application via the Catholic Biblical Association and generously bore the translation costs. I am grateful to Dr. Brian McNeil for his careful translation, to Mr. John Martino for good collaboration with The CUA Press and to the editors, especially Dr. Pablo T. Gadenz, for including the book in the Verbum

Domini series. American students participating in a summer school course on "Understanding the Bible from the Liturgy" in Trier, Germany, helped review the book. Nils Thomas adjusted all the footnotes. Helene Schmidt provided the index. Janosch Dörfel proofread the text.

The study has been considerably shortened in comparison to the German version. Some subsections, for example on signs and actions, or reflections on the structure of the lectionary, were omitted. In order to keep as much of the content as possible, I have concentrated on reducing the bibliography and the footnotes. It is still worth consulting the original text!

The English translation makes this work available to a far wider readership. By taking the Liturgy as starting point and basis, may this book contribute—both in praxis and in academic reflection—to a deeper understanding of Scripture as the living Word of God.

Marco Benini
September 30, 2023, Memorial of Saint Jerome
Washington, D.C.

Introduction

"And the Word became flesh." This verse from the Johannine prologue (Jn 1:14) might serve as a theological-substantial title for the profound oil painting by Dosso Dossi (1480/90-1542), which art history has given the classical title: "The Holy Family" (see book cover). The painting, probably dating to 1527/28, can be seen today in the Capitoline Museum in Rome. Mary points with the index finger of her left hand to illegible passages. Turning around, she directs a questioning look to Jesus, whom Joseph holds out toward her. Jesus responds to her gaze and begins to embrace her.

The painting can be interpreted in various ways and opens up an interpretive sphere that leads well to the theme of the present work of liturgical scholarship. As the illegible passages illustrate, Scripture is not completely comprehensible on its own. We need to look to Jesus. In other words, we need a relationship with Christ that is lived in faith if we are to understand the Scriptures aright. This relationship must be concrete and requires forms in which it can express itself and come alive—and this is precisely what happens in the celebration of the Liturgy, where Christ's presence and his attention can be experienced. The painting can thus lead to the question of how access to sacred Scripture is opened up through liturgy and how Scripture is understood through the celebration of worship.

A "historical" way of looking at the painting indicates that Mary can have only the Old Testament in her hands. When she looks at her Son, this also raises the question of the relationship between the Old and New Testaments, a question that is highly significant for biblical theology and on which every lectionary system must take a position.

Christ is the center of the composition. Light seems to radiate from him, illuminating both Mary and Joseph as well as the book of Scripture (this can be seen in the shadow cast across Mary's right arm). One could interpret the image to mean that Christ is the inner center of the meaning of Scripture, and that it is from him that the message of the whole of Scripture and the life of believers are illuminated.

Besides this, the depiction of the book and the child Jesus accentuates the two aspects of "Word" and "flesh" that John 1:14 links, that is to say, the two aspects of the Word of God in Scripture and of the incarnate Word of God in his human-bodily form. When we carry this idea further to the Liturgy, it evokes a relatedness of the presence of Christ in the proclaimed Word and in his eucharistic Body and Blood, and hence the interconnection of Word and sacrament.[1]

Dosso Dossi's painting points us to fundamental theological aspects that in the celebration of liturgy reach the concrete everyday life of both the individual and of the Church as a whole. The present study explores the relatedness of Scripture and Liturgy. More precisely, it seeks to investigate sacred Scripture within the horizon of worship as well as its implications for the theology of the Liturgy. In so doing, this study presents a liturgical hermeneutics of sacred Scripture.

---

1 See Second Vatican Council, *Sacrosanctum Concilium* (December 4, 1963), 7.

Foundational Overview

CHAPTER ONE

The Significance of the Theme of "Sacred Scripture in Liturgical Worship"

S everal passages of *Sacrosanctum Concilium,* the *Constitution on the Sacred Liturgy,* make explicit what our reflection on Dossi's painting has only indicated. The significance of the topics on which we have touched here can be seen especially in the programmatic statement: "Sacred Scripture is of the greatest importance in the celebration of the liturgy" (*SC* 24).

A historical overview, presenting snapshots that recall individual aspects, will make the relevance of such a formulation even clearer. The close connection between Liturgy and Sacred Scripture goes back to Judaism and the beginnings of Christianity. Not only has worship always drawn on Scripture, but the Liturgy also made an essential contribution to the formation of the canon, since only those texts that were publicly read aloud in worship were counted as the Word of God and received into the canon.[1] This elementary relatedness, to which (for example) the homilies of the Church fathers bear witness, moved in practice into the background during the age

---

1 See Tobias Nicklas, "Zum Verhältnis von Liturgie und Neuem Testament: Rezeption oder Kreation," in *Liturgische Bibelrezeption. Dimensionen und Perspektiven interdisziplinärer Forschung / Liturgical Reception of the Bible. Dimensions and Perspectives of Interdisciplinary Research,* ed. H. Buchinger and C. Leonhard (Göttingen: Vandenhoeck & Ruprecht, 2022), 39–56; Yves-Marie Blanchard, "Interdépendance entre la formulation du Canon biblique chrétien et la lecture liturgique," in *Présence et rôle de la Bible dans la liturgie,* ed. M. Klöckener (Fribourg: Academic Press, 2006); Klaus-Peter Jörns, "Liturgie – Wiege der Heiligen Schrift?" *ALw* 34, no. 3 (1992): 313-32; Gordon W. Lathrop, *Saving Images: The Presence of the Bible in Christian Liturgy* (Minneapolis: Fortress Press, 2017), 6-19; Louis-Marie Chauvet, "What makes Liturgy biblical? – Texts," *SL* 22, no. 2 (1992): 128. On the relationship between Jewish Scripture and liturgy, see Louis-Marie Chauvet, *Symbol and Sacrament: A Sacramental Reinterpretation of Christian Existence* (Collegeville, MN: Liturgical Press, 1995), 191-95. The Pontifical Biblical Commission likewise mentions the liturgy as a factor in the formation of the canon; see *The Interpretation of the Bible in the Church* (Vatican City: Libreria Editrice Vaticana, 1993), 28. See also B.IX.33.2.

of confessionalization, thanks to polemical theology: the ecclesial communities that were brought forth by the Reformation were described in an eye-catching but imprecise way as the "Church of the Word," while Catholics understood themselves primarily as the "Church of the sacraments." In the age of the Enlightenment, when the attempt was made to renew the "Liturgy in accordance with the principles of reason and of sacred Scripture,"[2] greater importance was attributed to the biblical model and to the reading of Scripture since the Bible served as the source of instruction and edification. The twentieth-century biblical and liturgical movements reawakened a clearer consciousness of the significance of Sacred Scripture both for the Christian existence and for the Church's worship. Pius Parsch (1884-1954) united both these concerns in his popular-liturgical apostolate in Klosterneuburg.[3] He founded the periodical *Bibel und Liturgie* in 1926, and was convinced that "The Bible and the Liturgy are two gifts of God that have been given from on high to Christians in this century for the renewal of the religious life."[4] Even before the Second Vatican Council, in the so-called "Betsingmesse" (pray-and-sing-Mass) developed in Germany and Austria, the Epistle and the Gospel were read in the vernacular. Moreover, there were reflections on a revision of the order of readings[5] and on the relationship between the Liturgy and the Bible.[6]

The Council Fathers were then able to reap the fruits of these developments, thereby displaying a new esteem for the Word of God, as the conciliar documents attest. In addition to no. 24 of the *Constitution on the Sacred Liturgy*, which we have already mentioned, the insight into the presence of

---

2 Benedikt Kranemann, "Liturgie nach den Grundsätzen der Vernunft und der Heiligen Schrift. Überlegungen zur Prägung der Liturgie des deutschen Aufklärungskatholizismus durch die Bibel," *ALw* 37, no. 1 (1995): 45-67.

3 See Anton W. Höslinger, "Bibel und Liturgie," in *Liturgie lernen und leben – zwischen Tradition und Innovation. Pius-Parsch-Symposion 2014*, PPSt 12, ed. A. Redtenbacher (Freiburg/Br.: Herder, 2015), 225-34; Norbert Höslinger and Theodor Maas-Ewerd, eds., *Mit sanfter Zähigkeit: Pius Parsch und die biblisch-liturgische Erneuerung*, Schriften des Pius-Parsch-Instituts Klosterneuburg 4 (Klosterneuburg: Pius-Parsch-Institut, 1979). It is characteristic that he begins his explanation of the Mass with the chapter "The Mass and Holy Scripture": Pius Parsch, *The Liturgy of the Mass*, 3rd ed., trans. H. E. Winstone (London: St Louis, 1957).

4 Pius Parsch, *Wie halte ich Bibelstunde?*, 2nd ed., ed. F. Röhrig, (Klosterneuburg: Pius-Parsch-Institut, 1957), 53-54.

5 See Elmar Nübold, *Entstehung und Bewertung der neuen Perikopenordnung des römischen Ritus für die Messfeier and Sonn- und Festtagen* (Paderborn: Bonifatius, 1986), 21-81.

6 I mention here Jean Daniélou, *The Bible and the Liturgy* (Notre Dame, IN.: University of Notre Dame Press, 1956); Divo Barsotti, *Il mistero cristiano e la parola di Dio* (Florence: Fiorentina, 1953).

Christ in the Word that is proclaimed (cf. *SC* 7; 33) is a theological rediscovery of particular importance. This was, indeed, often expounded by the
Church Fathers, but there was, in general, little awareness of it.[7] In order that
the faithful may "be instructed by God's word" (*SC* 48), "In sacred celebrations there is to be more reading from holy Scripture, and it is to be more
varied and suitable" (*SC* 35,1). In the case of the scriptural readings at Mass,
the following image is used: "The treasures of the Bible are to be opened up
more lavishly, so that richer fare may be provided for the faithful at the table
of God's word" (*SC* 51). The homily is now regarded as "part of the liturgy
itself" (*SC* 52; 35,2). The reflection on Scripture in liturgy and on its pastoral
importance, as well as the recovered insight into the unity of the Liturgy of
the Word and the Liturgy of the Eucharist (cf. *SC* 56),[8] also found expression in *Dei Verbum*, the *Constitution on Divine Revelation*: "The Church has
always venerated the divine Scriptures just as she venerates the body of the
Lord, since, especially in the eucharistic liturgy, she unceasingly receives and
offers to the faithful the bread of life from the table both of God's word and
of Christ's body" (*DV* 21).[9] This underlines as clearly as possible the dignity of
the Word of God, and thus definitively puts an end to confessional disputes
on this point.

In addition to the Council and the subsequent liturgical reform with the
reestablishing of the ambo[10] and the considerable expansion of the order of
readings[11] which, apart from some points of criticism, is generally regarded
as a theological and spiritual gain, the Church's magisterium down to the

---

7 See Otto Nußbaum, "Von der Gegenwart Gottes/Christi im Wort der Schriftlesungen und
zur Auswirkung dieser Gegenwart auf das Buch der Schriftlesungen," in *Wort und Buch in
der Liturgie: Interdisziplinäre Beiträge zur Wirkmächtigkeit des Wortes und Zeichenhaftigkeit
des Buches*, ed. H. P. Neuheuser (St. Ottilien: EOS, 1995), 65–92, on the patristic writers 72–77;
Franziskus Eisenbach, *Die Gegenwart Jesu Christi im Gottesdienst: Systematische Studien zur
Liturgiekonstitution des II. Vatikanischen Konzils* (Mainz: Grünewald, 1982), 496–557.

8 See Hanns Peter Neuheuser, "Das Bild vom Tisch des Wortes und des Brotes: Kernaussagen
der Liturgiekonstitution zum Verhältnis von Wortliturgie und Eucharistiefeier," in Neuheuser,
Wort und Buch, 133–69.

9 Second Vatican Council, *Dei Verbum* (November 15, 1965), 21. On the translation, see
B.VIII.29.2.

10 See Marco Benini, "Der Ambo – 'Tisch des Gotteswortes' (SC 51)," in *"Zeichen und Symbol
überirdischer Wirklichkeit": Liturgische Orte und ihre künstlerische Gestaltung: Eine Festschrift
für den Künstler Friedrich Koller*, ed. S. Kopp and J. Werz, 25–33 (Regensburg: Friedrich Pustet,
2019).

11 See Manlio Sodi, *La parola di Dio nella celebrazione eucaristica: The Word of God in the
Eucharistic Celebration: Tavole sinottiche – Synoptic Tables*, MSIL 7 (Vatican City: Libreria
Editrice Vaticana, 2000).

present day has taken up the topic of the Bible and the Liturgy. The Pontifical Biblical Commission devoted a special section to the Liturgy in its document *Interpretation of the Bible in the Church* (1993) and spoke about the homily in the context of the use of the Bible in pastoral ministry.[12] Pope Benedict XVI made "The Word of God in the Life and Mission of the Church" the theme of the General Assembly of the Synod of Bishops in 2008, and presented liturgy in the Postsynodal Apostolic Exhortation *Verbum Domini* as the "privileged setting for the Word of God."[13] In his Apostolic Exhortation *Evangelii Gaudium,* Pope Francis specifically discussed the homily and its preparation.[14] The Congregation for Divine Worship and the Discipline of the Sacraments took up the insights from these two Apostolic Exhortations and published the Homiletic Directory in 2015, which attaches particular value to the liturgical context of the homily.[15] In 2019, Pope Francis instituted the Sunday of the Word of God.[16]

Like the magisterium, academic theology studies the reception of Scripture in liturgy and sees this as a field for future work; the present book belongs in this context.[17] For example, the papers delivered at a broad international conference on the "Liturgical Reception of the Bible: Dimensions and Perspectives for Interdisciplinary Research," which also included the liturgies of the Eastern Churches, have recently been published.[18] Biblical scholars appear to have taken a greater interest in recent years in the reception of

---

12 See Pontifical Biblical Commission, *Interpretation of the Bible,* 37–39; see also Pontifical Biblical Commission, *Inspiration and Truth of Sacred Scripture* (Collegeville, MN: Liturgical Press, 2014), xviii–xix, 66–68.

13 See Benedict XVI, Postsynodal Apostolic Exhortation *Verbum Domini* (September 30, 2010), 52–71. See Nikola Eterović, ed., *La parola di Dio nella vita e nella missione della Chiesa: XII assemblea generale ordinaria del sinodo dei vescovi: Esortazione apostolica Verbum Domini,* Sinodo dei vescovi 2 (Vatican City: Libreria Editrice Vaticana, 2011); Martin Klöckener, "Bibel und Liturgie: Anmerkungen zu ihrer inneren Beziehung nach dem apostolischen Schreiben 'Verbum Domini,'" *LJ* 62, no. 3 (2012): 157–80.

14 See Francis, Apostolic Exhortation *Evangelii Gaudium* (November 24, 2013), 135–39.

15 See Congregation for Divine Worship and the Discipline of the Sacraments, *Homiletic Directory* (June 29, 2014).

16 See Francis, Motu proprio *Aperuit illis* (September 30, 2019).

17 See David N. Power, *"The Word of the Lord": Liturgy's Use of Scripture* (Maryknoll, NY: Orbis Books, 2001).

18 See Harald Buchinger and Clemens Leonhard, eds., *Liturgische Bibelrezeption,* Forschungen zur Kirchen- und Dogmengeschichte 108 (Göttingen: Vandenhoeck & Ruprecht, 2022).

the Bible in worship, thereby making it more possible to envisage a bridge between biblical and liturgical scholarship.[19]

Besides this, theological reflection on Scripture in worship and on the way in which the Word is proclaimed is of ecumenical interest. It is well known that the Catholic order of readings with its rich selection of pericopes has been an important influence also on Protestant orders of readings: on the North American Common Lectionary (1983) and its revision, the Revised Common Lectionary (1992), as well as on the British Four-Year Lectionary (1990).[20] We also note that Protestant liturgical scholars take an interest in the reading of Scripture during worship.[21]

We can affirm that Scripture influences the Liturgy and that, on the other hand, the Liturgy contributes to the understanding of Scripture. What we have indicated up to this point makes it clear that the two "directions"—from Scripture to Liturgy and from Liturgy to Scripture—permeate each other. We shall now identify the object, the goal, and the structure of the present study and give an account of the methodology employed.

---

19 See Georg Braulik and Norbert Lohfink, eds., *Liturgie und Bibel: Gesammelte Aufsätze*, ÖBS 28 (Frankfurt/M.: Lang, 2005); Georg Braulik and Norbert Lohfink, eds., *Osternacht und Altes Testament. Studien und Vorschläge: Mit einer Exsultetvertonung von Erwin Bücken*, ÖBS 22 (Frankfurt/M.: Lang, 2003); Georg Steins, "'Wort des lebendigen Gottes': Neue Brücken zwischen Bibelauslegung und Liturgie," in *Kanonisch-intertextuelle Studien zum Alten Testament*, Stuttgarter Biblische Aufsatzbände 48. Altes Testament, ed. G. Steins (Stuttgart: Katholisches Bibelwerk, 2009), 131-44; Georg Braulik, *L'esegesi anticotestamentaria e la liturgia: Nuovi sviluppi negli ultimi decenni*, Leiturgia – Lectiones Vagagginianae 5 (Assisi: Citadella Editrice, 2014). See C.39.

20 See Fritz West, *Scripture and Memory: The Ecumenical Hermeneutic of the Three-Year Lectionaries*. A Pueblo Book (Collegeville, MN: Liturgical Press, 1997); Ansgar Franz, *Wortgottesdienst der Messe und Altes Testament: Katholische und ökumenische Lektionarreform nach dem II. Vatikanum im Spiegel von Ordo Lectionum Missae, Revised Common Lectionary and Four-Year Lectionary: Positionen, Probleme, Perspektiven*, PiLi.S 14 (Tübingen/Basel: Francke, 2002), esp. 99-165.

21 See Lathrop, *Saving Images*; Alexander Deeg, *Das äußere Wort und seine liturgische Gestalt: Überlegungen zu einer evangelischen Fundamentalliturgik*, Arbeiten zur Pastoraltheologie, Liturgik und Hymnologie 68 (Göttingen: Vandenhoeck & Ruprecht, 2012), 309; Alexander Deeg, "Heilige Schrift und Gottesdienst: Evangelische Überlegungen zur Bibel in der Liturgie," in *Wort des lebendigen Gottes*, ed. A. Franz and A. Zerfaß, PiLi 16 (Tübingen: Narr Francke Attempto, 2016), 63-66; Thomas Melzl, *Die Schriftlesung im Gottesdienst: Eine liturgiewissenschaftliche Betrachtung* (Leipzig: Evangelische Verlagsanstalt, 2011).

CHAPTER TWO

Liturgical Hermeneutics
of Sacred Scripture
Object, Structure, Methodology,
and the Goal of this Study

1. OBJECT: LITURGICAL HERMENEUTICS
OF SACRED SCRIPTURE

If, as I have just shown, Scripture plays such a large role in liturgy, we must ask the fundamental question about the liturgical use of Scripture: How does the Liturgy deal with Sacred Scripture?— and above all, What is the significance of the fact that it does so in this way? There are undoubtedly no small differences between meditating on Scripture alone "in one's inner room," the study of Scripture with academic methodologies, and the encounter with Scripture in the celebration of liturgy.[22] This reality makes the question of hermeneutics central. An initial clarification of concepts, therefore, is helpful.

Hermeneutics,[23] as is well known, is the art and the theory of understanding, which attempts to identify meaning and significance and forms a "theory

---

22 See Hanns Peter Neuheuser, "Wortliturgie und Bibellektüre – Zur Prävalenz der liturgischen Wortverkündigung vor dem privaten Bibelstudium," *LJ* 60, no. 1 (2010): 21-40.

23 See Claus v. Bormann, "Hermeneutik: I. Philosophisch-theologisch," in *TRE 25*, ed. G. Krause and G. Müller (Berlin: De Gruyter, 1995), 108-37; Ulrich H. J. Körtner, *Einführung in die theologische Hermeneutik*, Einführung Theologie (Darmstadt: Wissenschaftliche Buchgesellschaft, 2006), 11-21; Ingolf U. Dalferth, *Die Kunst des Verstehens: Grundzüge einer Hermeneutik der Kommunikation durch Texte* (Tübingen: Mohr Siebeck, 2018).

of interpretation."[24] Biblical hermeneutics[25] is concerned with understanding the Bible and is already found in Scripture itself. In the Old Testament, older texts were updated and given a new interpretation in new contexts. In the New Testament, what "was said to those of old" was read anew in the light of the Christ event; some texts "can actually have been understood as a biblical hermeneutics of the Old Testament."[26] Interpretation of Scripture has continued throughout history down to the present day.[27] Depending on the starting point one chooses for looking at the Bible, or the interest which guides the questions one asks, various kinds of biblical hermeneutics can be established. Manfred Oeming has articulated the contemporary plurality of interpretive methods in a kind of "hermeneutical square":

1. Methods oriented to the *authors* and their worlds;
2. Methods oriented to the *texts* and their worlds;
3. Methods oriented to the *readers* (the recipients) and their worlds;
4. Methods oriented to the *issues* and their worlds.[28]

A *liturgical* biblical hermeneutics belongs under the third point in this classification since it concerns the question of how the Bible is received in the celebration of liturgy and understood by those who take part in worship. This means that the immediate interest here is not the Bible as a book, as the canon of the Old and New Testaments printed in a single volume. Neither does the primary interest lie in identifying the original situation or the historical genesis of the books of the Bible. Nor is the focus primarily on particular issues, themes, or realities addressed in the Bible, or on dogmatic propositions of faith that can be derived from Scripture.

The starting point here, rather, is the *Liturgy itself*. For this reason, the present work begins by observing and describing how the various forms of liturgical celebrations (e.g., the Mass, the sacraments, the Liturgy of the Hours) both employ and bear the imprint of Sacred Scripture. This involves the question of ritual actions in connection with the Word of God— in proclamation and in the implementation of actions and signs—that is to say, how Scripture is "staged" and celebrated. Secondly, our observations are

---

24 Georg Wieland, "Hermeneutik: I. Begriff und Geschichte," in *LThK 5*, ed. W. Kasper (Freiburg/Br.: Herder, 1996), 1.

25 See Manfred Oeming, *Contemporary Biblical Hermeneutics: An Introduction*, trans. Joachim F. Vette (New York: Ashgate, 2006).

26 Oeming, 2. He mentions Matthew, Luke, Romans, and Hebrews in particular.

27 See Oeming, 9-27.

28 See Oeming, 7-8, 131-38.

accompanied by a reflection that is aimed at the guiding question: What is the nature of a liturgical hermeneutics of Sacred Scripture, a hermeneutics generated by the celebration of the Liturgy itself?

Naturally, this guiding question unites several dimensions, such as: What are the hermeneutical consequences for the understanding of Sacred Scripture, when it is employed in the Liturgy in the ways described here? How does the liturgical celebration influence the interpretation of Scripture or of the specific pericope? What theological aspects can be discerned behind the phenomenon of the liturgical reception of Scripture—aspects that are therefore also hermeneutically significant? The question of the unity of Scripture is also central to its understanding: what relationship between the Old Testament and New is mediated by the Liturgy? Since Liturgy is the celebration of the paschal mystery of Christ, we must examine the extent to which a Christological interpretation of Old Testament texts is prescribed (so to speak) by the liturgical framework, or to what extent liturgy allows the individual to interpret them freely. The relationship between the canonical Bible and the "liturgical Bible" (that is, those parts of the Bible that have been admitted to the Liturgy) is not unimportant. Posed as a question: What is the reciprocal relationship between Bible and celebration? What accents do the liturgical year and the liturgical setting, or the selection and combination of scriptural passages in readings, prayers, and hymns, introduce into the understanding of Scripture and of individual pericopes, and what accents are thereby blurred? We must also reflect on how the Liturgy gives paths of access to Scripture on the one hand, and how, on the other hand, Scripture is received in the celebration of worship. A liturgical biblical hermeneutics asks how the act of worship creates a bridge between the text and the participants; ultimately, it is this bridge that makes it possible to understand the Scriptures. In terms of reception theory, we must see how ritual "staging" underlines and mediates the sacrality of Scripture as the revealed Word of God. Naturally, the reception is carried out both by the Church as the community of faith and by the individual participant in liturgical celebration. Spiritual aspects linked to this process likewise belong to a liturgical biblical hermeneutics.

The magisterium emphasizes the relevance of such questions: *Verbum Domini* 52 ascribes an "essential meaning" to the question of a hermeneutics that has its origin in the Liturgy. Indeed, the "correct approach to sacred Scripture" depends on this:

> To understand the word of God, then, we need to appreciate and experience the essential meaning and value of the liturgical action. *A faith-filled understanding of sacred Scripture must always refer back to the liturgy*, in which the word of God is celebrated as a timely and living word.

> …I encourage the Church's Pastors and all engaged in pastoral work to see that all the faithful learn to savor the deep meaning of the word of God which unfolds each year in the liturgy, revealing the fundamental mysteries of our faith. This is in turn the basis for a [the][29] correct approach to sacred Scripture.[30]

The demand that one must "appreciate and experience" the importance of the liturgical action for the understanding of Scripture links the reflection and the praxis of the liturgical celebration. This is in accord with the two-step procedure of this book, which aims, through observation ("to experience") and theological reflection ("to appreciate"), to analyze the use made of Scripture in worship, in order to elaborate the various dimensions of a liturgical hermeneutics of Sacred Scripture. This quotation makes it clear that such reflection also has pastoral implications for the concrete celebration of the Liturgy.

2. STRUCTURE

Every act of reflecting is preceded by an act of perceiving. The present book thus consists of two larger parts: the first emphasizes the observation of how Scripture is employed, and the second attempts a systematic overview that focuses primarily on reflection. The first section, "Part A. The Liturgical Use of Sacred Scripture," is structured according to article 24 of the *Constitution on the Liturgy*:

> Sacred Scripture is of the greatest importance in the celebration of the liturgy. For it is from Scripture that *lessons* are read and explained in the homily, and *psalms* are sung; the *prayers, collects,* and *liturgical songs* are scriptural in their inspiration and their force, and it is from the scriptures that *actions and signs* derive their meaning. Thus to achieve the restoration, progress, and adaptation of the sacred liturgy, it is essential to promote that warm and living love for Scripture to which the venerable tradition of both *eastern and western rites* gives testimony.

There is a substantial reason for the orientation to *SC* 24, since it is here that the Conciliar Fathers emphasize the role of Scripture in shaping the Liturgy as a whole, and then refer to the use made of Scripture in the various

---

29 The original document, presumably written in German or Italian, has here the definite article "der/il." This lends additional emphasis to the affirmation.

30 Italics original.

liturgical areas. At the same time, they take into account the different kinds of liturgical texts. The article thus offers a meaningful structure for a differentiated observation.

It is understandable that the readings are mentioned first because it is in them that the texts of Sacred Scripture are directly proclaimed and affirmed to be the Word of God (Section A. I). The homily, which expounds the Scripture and relates it to the life of the believers, is mentioned briefly, but it is not given a place of its own in the structure of this book, because it is the part of the Liturgy that is least determined by liturgical regulations, so that the concrete use made of Scripture is up to the individual preacher. Section A. II studies the Psalms, which are mentioned specifically in *SC* 24 because of their frequent and varied use in liturgy. Scripture also shapes the prayers, such as the central prayers in the celebration of the sacraments, or the orations that are mentioned explicitly in *SC* 24 and will be discussed together in Section A. III. The "songs" mentioned here (such as those in the Liturgy of the Hours or the hymns at Mass) are discussed separately in Section A.IV, because they differ from the prayers in character and function. Moreover, Scripture is employed to make many liturgical signs and actions meaningful, which Section A.V will exemplify by treating the washing of the feet on Holy Thursday and the white baptismal garment. In this way, a kind of "commentary" on *SC* 24 emerges.

Part B studies the "Dimensions of a Liturgical Hermeneutics of Sacred Scripture." It brings together, from systematic perspectives, the wide field that has been illuminated in Part A. This means that the insights from the first part, which are gleaned from the Liturgy itself, lead to the articulation of the second part,[31] where they are taken to a deeper level and further elaborated. Thus, Section B.VI reflects on the approaches to Scripture that have been presented in Part A and clarifies the extent to which the Liturgy opens up the "correct approach" (*Verbum Domini* 52) to Scripture. Section B.VII investigates how the liturgical context is an important hermeneutical key to the Word of God and distinguishes how the Liturgy offers or prescribes interpretations through the assigning of various texts or through the entire liturgical context of a celebration ("intertextuality"). The rites of the Liturgy of the Word—that is, how liturgy "stages" Sacred Scripture, generating a framework for its understanding—are likewise hermeneutically

---

31 Benedikt Kranemann, "Wort Gottes in der Liturgie," *LJ* 63, no. 3 (2012): 172 n. 23 rightly asks whether up to now "only the hermeneutics of the Eucharist has been transposed onto the liturgy of the Word," and whether this does justice to the liturgy of the Word. Accordingly, great importance is attached here to allowing the reflections of Part B to emerge from the liturgical use of Sacred Scripture itself, and to connect these reflections to this use.

significant. Here, the comparison with other Christian rites and with the synagogue is illuminating. Section B.VIII ("Theological Aspects of the Liturgical Hermeneutics of the Bible"), the substantial focus of this part, seeks to systematize the implications that are indicated or brought to light in Part A, so that here a contribution is made to a *liturgical theology* on the basis of the celebrated Word of God. The sacramentality of the Word will be of particular interest here. The following section, B.IX, takes up the question of reception in the strict sense, that is, how the community and the individual receive and understand Sacred Scripture in the Liturgy and are able to interpret it for themselves. No empirical investigations are carried out; conclusions are drawn from the varied use of Scripture (Part A). The two shorter sections on "Approaches" (VI) and "Reception" (IX) frame the more detailed sections VII and V [VII and VIII] and present what we might call two complementary and opposite directions: the Liturgy leads to Scripture and is at the same time the medium of its reception.

Part C, entitled "A Liturgical Approach," attempts a synthesis of the liturgical hermeneutics of the Bible and offers the prospect of a dialogue between biblical and liturgical scholarship, a prospect that is directly evoked by the theme of this book.

3. METHODOLOGY AND AIM

The methodology too is oriented to *SC* 24, which speaks in its final section of "that warm and living love for Scripture to which the venerable tradition of *both eastern and western rites* gives testimony." Accordingly, the book undertakes a comparison of rites that takes due account not only of the Roman rite, but also of particularly widespread rites from both East and West. In the case of the West, the rite of Milan (Ambrosian) has been chosen, because it is the most widespread after the Roman rite, and a new order of readings was introduced in 2008. This is of great hermeneutical interest, because it was revised explicitly in reaction to the criticism of the Ordo Lectionum Missae (OLM) and follows other principles of selection. The reform of the Milanese order of readings has received scant attention in liturgical scholarship up to now.

In the case of the East, we draw on the most widespread Eastern rite, the Byzantine rite, which is used by ca. 85% of all the eastern Churches.[32] This is

---

32 See Basilius J. Groen and Christian Gastgeber, eds., *Die Liturgie der Ostkirche. Ein Führer zu Gottesdienst und Glaubensleben der orthodoxen und orientalischen Kirchen*, 2nd ed. (Freiburg/ Br.: Herder, 2013), 17.

also of interest because up to now, there has been no systematic reform like that following the Second Vatican Council. The comparison with respect to the order of readings can thus be expanded to look both at a consciously renewed ordering and at a traditional ordering. This comparison allows us to recognize points in common and, above all, to display more clearly the particularities of each tradition. The comparison is not made for every example, but only where it is especially illuminating.[33]

The investigation has a synchronous structure, so that the starting point is always the contemporary form of the celebration. But since (in the words of Josef Andreas Jungmann, 1889-1975) liturgy is always "liturgy that has come into existence,"[34] or is always "in process,"[35] many things can be explained only by reference to history. Where necessary, therefore, the historical development will be taken into account.

This study aims to combine breadth and depth. In such a wide field, one can work only through exemplification. However, this limitation also makes it possible to look more closely at individual issues. The examples are chosen in such a way that Part A covers the various fields, such as the celebration of the Mass and the sacraments, the Liturgy of the Hours, and the liturgical year, thereby guaranteeing the breadth—which is further expanded through the specific comparisons of the rites. This too influences the selection, because examples are presented that shed additional light through the differences of the rites. The examples give information about the matters they are meant to present, but are not so singular that they would prevent the reader from recognizing fundamental traits.

This book aims to employ examples to build up a total picture. There are many individual studies that take up aspects of the order of readings, the use of Scripture in the prayers and hymns, the Psalms in liturgy, or the hermeneutics of the reading of Scripture in the Liturgy of the Word in the Mass,[36] and similar topics, but there has not yet been an explicit attempt to present a total vision (collections of essays likewise bring together only individual aspects). This book does not claim to be able to present completely new insights into the use of Scripture in the Liturgy. But no earlier monograph

---

33 For example, there is no corresponding equivalent in the Byzantine rite to the brief Roman collect or to the Ephphetha rite at baptism.

34 Josef Andreas Jungmann, *Gewordene Liturgie: Studien und Durchblicke* (Innsbruck: Rauch, 1941).

35 See Jürgen Barsch, *Liturgie im Prozess: Studien zur Geschichte des religiösen Lebens*, ed. Marco Benini (Münster: Aschendorff, 2019).

36 See Alexander Zerfaß, *Auf dem Weg nach Emmaus: Die Hermeneutik der Schriftlesung im Wortgottesdienst der Messe*, PiLi.S 24 (Tübingen/Basel: Narr Francke Attempto, 2016).

has offered a holistic vision that demonstrates with greater depth and clarity the nature of a liturgical hermeneutics of Sacred Scripture.

It is striking in this context that the Liturgy is not mentioned at all, or only briefly, in studies of biblical hermeneutics that seek to identify approaches and methodologies oriented to the readers.[37] Since most of the faithful come into contact with Scripture precisely in liturgy, the present book takes this experience as its starting point and seeks to present a decidedly *liturgical* hermeneutics of the Bible. The study is also intended to demonstrate that a *liturgical approach* to Scripture deserves a place in the wider academic discussion.

---

37 See Oeming, *Contemporary Biblical Hermeneutics* (which does not pay attention to the liturgy). But see also Manfred Oeming, "Die verborgene Nähe: Zum Verhältnis von liturgischer und exegetischer Schrifthermeneutik (mit besonderer Berücksichtigung des Alten Testaments in der christlichen Predigt)," in Franz and Zerfaß, *Wort des lebendigen Gottes*, 181-203.

PART A

The Liturgical Use
of Sacred Scripture

SECTION I
Readings

CHAPTER THREE

The Readings at Mass in the Liturgical Year
Principles of Selection

The Word of God is heard directly in the readings from Scripture during the Liturgy. In addition to the pericopes[1] that are proclaimed, it is the principles of selection and the relation between the readings that are of prime importance. The examples we shall investigate are taken from two different periods in the Roman, Milanese, and Byzantine order of readings at Mass: the Sundays between the festal cycles which do not have a specific character and are called "Sundays in Ordinary Time" in the Roman Liturgy, and the Sundays of Lent.

There are substantial reasons for this restriction. Whereas Ordinary Time is traditionally free of any specific content, Lent has *a priori* a thematic character as a period of preparation for Easter which affects the choice of pericopes. Secondly, the compilations of readings in these periods also differ in terms of their historical genesis. In the Roman and Milanese orders of readings, the period corresponding to Ordinary Time was given a new shape after the liturgical reform (in 1969 and 2008 respectively), whereas in Lent, traditional western elements from the early Church were retained or revitalized in the proclamation of the Gospel. The relationship between the Old and New Testament readings in the Lenten season of the Roman rite has been organized more consciously, so that they align with each other. This is

---

1 The Greek noun *perikopē* means something cut out and detached. The concept is already found in Justin, *Dial.* 72.3, 110.1-2. See Balthasar Fischer, "Formen der Verkündigung," in *Gestalt des Gottesdienstes: Sprachliche und nichtsprachliche Ausdrucksformen*, 2nd ed., GdK 3, ed. R. Berger (Regensburg: Pustet, 1990), 78; Christoph Markschies, "Liturgisches Lesen und Hermeneutik der Schrift," in *Patristica et Oecumenica (FS Wolfgang A. Bienert)*, Marburger Theologische Studien 85, ed. P. Gemeinhardt (Marburg: Elwert, 2004), 83.

a third reason for choosing Lent. Fourthly, it is remarkable how greatly the content of the non-festal period in Rome differs from the content in Milan. A comparison with the Byzantine selections is helpful because it differs clearly from the West in both periods. Since the shared motif is the preparation for Easter, we must pay all the more attention to the completely different pericopes in East and West and keep our eyes open for both common motifs and differentiating expressions. The concentration on these two seasons allows us to make more intensive observations.

We shall then look, in summary fashion, at other aspects of the selection of readings outside these two periods that are striking and that give us further hermeneutical insights.

1. THE NON-FESTAL SUNDAYS IN THE ROMAN, MILANESE, AND BYZANTINE LITURGY
1.1 The Ordo Lectionum Missae (1969; 2nd ed.1981)

In keeping with the instruction of the Council that "there is to be more reading from holy Scripture, and it is to be more varied and suitable" (*SC* 35,1) and that in the Mass, "a more representative portion [*praestantior pars*] of the holy scriptures will be read to the people in the course of a prescribed number of years" (*SC* 51), the Coetus XI "De lectionibus in Missa" elaborated over four years a new order of readings for the Roman rite, the *Ordo Lectionum Missae* (*OLM*),[2] which came into force on the First Sunday of Advent in 1969. A second edition of the *OLM*, expanded principally through a theological introduction to the proclamation of Scripture, appeared in 1981.[3] It was "above all a pastoral goal" that guided the order of readings "in accordance with the Second Vatican Council."[4] This goal is defined in concrete terms especially as spreading the knowledge of the scriptures, as understanding

---

2 Latin text: *EDIL* 1, 1858-91. English: *Documents on the Liturgy 1963-1979: Conciliar, Papal and Curial Texts*, ed. and trans. Thomas C. O'Brien (Collegeville, MN: Liturgical Press, 1982), 1843-69. See Gaston Fontaine, "Commentarium ad Ordinem Lectionum Missae," *Notitiae* 5, no. 47 (1969): 256-82; Annibale Bugnini, *The Reform of the Liturgy, 1948-1975*, trans. Matthew J. O'Connell (Collegeville, MN: Liturgical Press, 1990), 406-25; Paul Turner, *Words without Alloy. A Biography of the Lectionary for Mass* (Collegeville, MN: Liturgical Press, 2022).

3 See *GILM: EDIL* 2, 4055-181; *The Liturgy Documents; A Parish Resource*, ed. David Lysik, 4th ed., vol. 1 (Chicago: Liturgy Training Publications, 2004), 119-62. See Nübold, *Perikopenordnung*; Normand Bonneau, *The Sunday Lectionary: Ritual Word, Paschal Shape* (Collegeville, MN: Liturgical Press, 1998).

4 *GILM*, 58.

the salvation history that continues into the "today" of the celebration,[5] and as the spiritual profit of believers.[6]

There are two basic possibilities in the principles of selection with which we are concerned here:

1. The *lectio continua,* which distributes the complete contents of a Book over a specific space of time, so that the sequence follows the biblical text and hence the inherent structure of the Book.[7] When (as on the Sundays in Ordinary Time) some pericopes are omitted, one speaks of a *lectio semicontinua.*

2. The *lectio selecta,* which chooses the pericopes not with regard to the Book of the Bible, but in keeping with other specific categories.

The reading of the Gospel[8] is organized as a *lectio semicontinua.* As is well known, it follows one of the three synoptic Gospels in the three-year cycle, so that "the theology that is specific to each Gospel finds expression."[9] This establishes an interlinking between the course of the liturgical year and the life of Jesus not only in the Christmas and Easter cycles, but also in Ordinary Time. Besides this, sections that the evangelist already envisaged as connected passages can be read "in one piece." In a homily, one can refer back to the previous Sunday and draw attention to references that go beyond the individual pericope, those that are partly concealed by the division into pericopes but are nevertheless necessary for a better understanding of the Gospel that is proclaimed.[10] It is usually necessary to remind the congregation of this, and one must not assume that they still remember the Gospel

---

5 See *GILM,* 60-61.

6 See *GILM,* 80-81, 83; also 38, 45, 75-78, 88.

7 In the Mass, this is the case only with the readings from 1 John on the weekdays of Christmastide.

8 See *GILM,* 105; Nübold, *Perikopenordnung,* 235-43.

9 *GILM,* 105.

10 Consider, for example, the 21st/22nd Sundays A (Mt 16:13-27; see Nübold, *Perikopenordnung,* 237): On one Sunday, after Peter confesses that Jesus is the Messiah, he says to him: "Blessed are you, Simon son of Jonah [...] You are Peter, and upon this rock I will build my church." But when Jesus predicts his suffering, Peter rebukes him, and Jesus sternly says: "Get behind me, Satan!" In Jesus' discourse about bread (18th Sunday B), the words: "You are looking for me [...] because you ate the loaves and were filled" (Jn 6:26) can be understood only thanks to the narrative of the multiplication of the loaves, which was read on the preceding Sunday. The fact that Mk 1:21-39 is divided between two separate Sundays (4th and 5th Sundays B) obscures the fact that this passage depicts a Sabbath full of activity for Jesus, but the homily can usefully explain this.

of the preceding Sunday. One problem that has often been pointed out is that the variation in the date of Easter means that Matthew's Sermon on the Mount (4th-9th Sundays A) and Luke's Sermon on the Plain (6th-8th Sundays C) are torn asunder, and various sections are omitted in many years. The result is the exact opposite of what was intended.[11]

For a concrete celebration, the relationship of the individual readings to one another on one and the same Sunday (their vertical relationship, so to speak) is more decisive than the horizontal distribution of a book across the liturgical year, especially because the sequence of Old and New Testament readings replicates the canon.[12] The Old Testament reading was selected in view of the Gospel pericope (the principle of consonance),[13] in order to emphasize "the unity between the Old and New Testament."[14] That is a significant point for the hermeneutics of the Bible. These links, which sometimes appear truly appropriate, but at other times seem very formal, have varying degrees of value for the understanding of the Gospel, for the homily, and for the elucidation of the unity of Scripture. This process of selection is criticized from the perspective of the Old Testament, because it does not take seriously the intrinsic value of the Old Testament, but instead uses it as a "quarry" from which to extract only those passages that allow one to establish a link to the Gospel pericope. The consequence is that the Sunday readings also include less important texts, while passages that are more important within the context of Scripture itself are omitted.[15] Besides this, the "straitjacket of their correlation" means that they are "no longer able to say everything that they would wish to say."[16]

The *lectio semicontinua* from the Letters of the Apostles is inserted between the first reading and the Gospel. This is independent of the two

11 See Nübold, *Perikopenordnung*, 240-41; Franz, *Wortgottesdienst*, 90-91; Paul De Clerck, "'L'Ordo lectionum missae' de l'Église romaine," in *Présence et rôle de la Bible dans la liturgie*, ed. M. Klöckener (Fribourg: Academic Press, 2006), 247.

12 See Zerfaß, *Hermeneutik*, 163. Moreover, since Sunday is the "weekly anamnesis of the Paschal mystery," it possesses "a dignity antecedent to that of the developed Liturgical (and lectionary) year" (Franz, *Wortgottesdienst*, 303).

13 See Franz, 292-305.

14 *GILM*, 106.

15 See Norbert Lohfink, "Altes Testament und Liturgie: Unsere Schwierigkeiten und unsere Chancen," *LJ* 47, no. 1 (1997): 18; Norbert Lohfink, "Zur Perikopenordnung für die Sonntage im Jahreskreis," in *Liturgie und Bibel: Aufsätze*. ÖBS 28, ed. G. Braulik and N. Lohfink (Frankfurt/M.: Lang, 2005), 207-8.

16 Lohfink, "AT und Liturgie," 19; on the criticisms of the *OLM* and some counterarguments, see Elmar Nübold, "Das Alte Testament in der gegenwärtigen Perikopenordnung—Offene Wünsche," *LJ* 47, no. 3 (1997): 174-89.

other readings.[17] Accordingly, it sometimes has the appearance of a "foreign body"[18] that expresses such a completely different idea from the Gospel and the Old Testament reading that it is difficult to integrate it into a homily. Ansgar Franz identifies the *lectio semicontinua* of the Epistles as "by far the greatest structural problem of the *OLM*."[19] In retrospect, the pastoral difficulties led Adrien Nocent and Heinz Schürmann, both of whom had been members of the Coetus XI and had collaborated in drawing up the order of readings, to recognize this as an "error" that had to be corrected[20] and to offer suggestions for consonant Epistle readings.[21] It is, however, occasionally possible to discover a common theme in all three readings and to bring this fruitfully into the homily. If a thematic link appears without any conscious act of selection, it goes deeper than any mere association of words or

17 See *GILM*, 67-68, 107; Nübold, *Perikopenordnung*, 359-70.

18 Heinz Schürmann, "Das apostolische Kerygma als Interpretationshilfe für das vierfache Evangelium. Konsonante Episteln für die Sonntage im Jahreskreis," in *Surrexit Dominus vere. Die Gegenwart des Auferstandenen in seiner Kirche (FS Johannes Joachim Degenhardt),* ed. J. Ernst and S. Leingruber (Paderborn: Bonifatius, 1996), 173-87, at 178.

19 Franz, *Wortgottesdienst*, 91; he also points out the practical difficulty of noting the content of the second reading. This is already difficult in the context of one single Sunday formula, because it is inserted into a different context; *a fortiori,* the fact that people do not remember the Epistle readings of the past Sundays means that the intention behind a *lectio semicontinua* does not function (see Franz, 91-95, 276-80).

20 Adrien Nocent, "Eine 'kleine Geschichte am Rande'. Zum Lektionar für die Messe der 'gewöhnlichen' Sonntage," in *Streit am Tisch des Wortes? Zur Deutung und Bedeutung des Alten Testaments und seiner Verwendung in der Liturgie,* ed. A. Franz, PiLi 7 (St. Ottilien: EOS, 1997), 656.

21 See Adrien Nocent, "Les deuxièmes lectures des dimanches ordinaires," in *EO* 8 (1991): 125-36; Adrien Nocent, *Le renouveau liturgique. Une relecture,* Le point théologique 58 (Paris: Beauchesne, 1993), 24-34; Schürmann, "Das apostolische Kerygma," 177-80 (backed up by biblical-theological, liturgical, homiletic, and pastoral arguments); Heinz Schürmann, "Konsonante Episteln für die Sonntage im Jahreskreis. Eine Vergleichstabelle mit Reformvorschlägen zum Ordo Lectionum Missae," in *Schrift und Tradition (FS Josef Ernst),* ed. K. Backhaus and F. G. Untergaßmair (Paderborn: Schöningh, 1996), 395-441. See Franz, *Wortgottesdienst,* 241-48. Heinrich Kahlefeld had earlier pleaded at the international conferences of liturgical studies for a consonant orientation of all the readings to the Gospel; see Siegfried Schmitt, *Die internationalen liturgischen Studientreffen 1951-1960. Zur Vorgeschichte der Liturgiekonstitution,* TThS 53 (Trier: Paulinus, 1992), 354. – One can, of course, make the same criticism here as in the case of the Old Testament reading, namely, that the epistolary texts are selected only with a view to their convergence with the Gospels, excluding thereby precisely those texts that deal with other questions than the Gospels, and that thus present a genuine complement; see Winfried Haunerland, "'Lebendig ist das Wort Gottes' (Hebr 4,12). Die Liturgie als Sitz im Leben der Schrift," *ThPQ* 149, no. 2 (2001): 119.

intentional construction. This then makes the unity of Scripture visible in an even more comprehensive sense.[22]

These points of criticism—which are not intended to obscure the significant progress made in comparison to the order of readings in the preconciliar missal—show that an order of readings time and again needs a revision, especially because a "perfect" order of readings cannot exist. No order can do justice to every desirable principle of selection. It will always give preference to particular theological and pragmatic motivations, thereby deciding against other guiding principles that are equally justified. This is why Elmar Nübold was correct to speak of the "*Ordo lectionum semper reformandus*."[23] An example of this is the Milanese order of readings.

1.2. The Ambrosian Lectionary (2008)

A look at the new Ambrosian lectionary will enrich our perspectives with respect to a liturgical biblical hermeneutics. We shall investigate the principles of selection and the hermeneutical consequences that these entail because they differ clearly from the Roman order of readings. It is well known that the Archdiocese of Milan (together with some parishes outside the diocesan borders) cultivates a liturgical tradition of its own.[24] After the liturgical reform of the Second Vatican Council, the *OLM* was adopted provisionally *ad experimentum*, with the addition of a supplementary volume (1976) for the specific features of the Ambrosian rite.[25] In 2008, the Congregation of the Ambrosian Rite published a separate order of readings with the corresponding

---

22 See *Homiletic Directory*, 19.

23 Elmar Nübold, "Der Stellenwert des Alten Testaments in der nachvatikanischen Liturgiereform unter besonderer Berücksichtigung des Meßperikopen der Sonn- und Festtage," in Franz, *Streit am Tisch des Wortes?*, 617.

24 The Ambrosian rite is celebrated in 1,063 parishes of the archdiocese (out of 1,107; 44 use the Roman rite) and in some parishes of the dioceses of Bergamo (30), Novara (13), Lodi (2), and Lugano in Switzerland (55). See Claudio Magnoli, "Il Lezionario Ambrosiano per i tempi liturgici," *RivLi* 96, no. 4 (2009): 488 n. 8. On the Ambrosian rite (a historical presentation from Ambrose to the present day), see Cesare Alzati, *Ambrosianum mysterium. La Chiesa di Milano e la sua tradizione liturgica*, Archivio Ambrosiano 81 (Milan: Ambrosiana, 2000), on the readings 40-42, 75-78, 152-80; on the Liturgy in Ambrose, see Josef Schmitz, *Gottesdienst im altchristlichen Mailand. Eine liturgiewissenschaftliche Untersuchung über Initiation und Meßfeier während des Jahres zu Zeit des Bischof Ambrosius († 397)*, Theophaneia 25 (Bonn: Hanstein, 1975), on the readings Schmitz, 316-52, 440-41.

25 See *Lezionario Ambrosiano. Edito per ordine del Sig. Cardinale Giovanni Colombo*. Milan: Centro Ambrosiano di documentazione e studi religiosi, 1976.

lectionaries.[26] Liturgical scholarship up to now seems scarcely to have taken notice of this. The "premesse" (*PLA* refers to the *Premesse al Lezionario Ambrosiano,* that is the *General Introduction to the Ambrosian Lectionary*)[27] are oriented to the *OLM* (1981), with an analogous structure. They adapt it, in considerably greater detail, to the Ambrosian Rite.[28]

On the Sundays that interest us here, we encounter the first difference in the structuring of the liturgical year.[29] There is no "Ordinary Time" in the Ambrosian calendar because the year is articulated in three "Misteri" ("mysteries"). The "Mystery of the Incarnation of the Lord" encompasses not only the six weeks of Advent and Christmastide but also the "Time after the Epiphany," which corresponds to the first part of the Roman "Ordinary Time." After the Easter season ("Mystery of the Pascha of the Lord") until Advent, there is the analogous third Mystery, "The Mystery of Pentecost." This concept[30] is meant to express not only the chronological aspect (the time after Pentecost), but also a deeper theological-spiritual motif: namely, that this time draws "its *raison d'être* from the feast of Pentecost."[31] This is explained as follows in the *PLA*: the time after Pentecost "celebrates the presence of the Spirit who makes effective in history the salvation that has been accomplished in the person of Christ, and makes it present in the Church through the divine mysteries."[32] In accordance with the ancient Milanese

---

26 See *Lezionario Ambrosiano secondo il rito della Santa Chiesa di Milano. Riformato a norma dei decreti del Concilio Vaticano II promulgato dal Signor Cardinal Dionigi Tettamanzi* [...]. 7 vols. (Milan: ITL Arcidiocesi di Milano, 2008-2009). An exact list of the pericopes with key words about their content can be found in Cesare Alzati, *Il Lezionario della chiesa Ambrosiana. La tradizione liturgica e il rinnovato "ordo lectionum",* MSIL 50 (Vatican City: Libreria Editrice Vaticana, 2009), 241-45; with the addition of the Psalm and the Gospel acclamation, http://www.chiesadimilano.it/lezionario-ambrosiano (retrieved 7/11/2022). See also the special fascicle of *Ambrosius* 85, no. 1 (2009).

27 See *Lezionario ambrosiano,* 1, XIII-LVI.

28 See Claudio Magnoli, "Il quadro generale e le scelte qualificanti," *Ambrosius* 85, no. 1 (2009): 79.

29 See Magnoli, "Il Lezionario Ambrosiano per i tempi liturgici," *PLA,* 96-221.

30 The concept of the "Mistero *della* Pentecoste," which is found only in the superscription, is somewhat misleading because it could lead to seeing Pentecost (once again, one must add, from the perspective of the history of the Liturgy) not as the close of the fifty days of Eastertide, but rather as the beginning of the time which follows. Besides this, the liturgical color for the time from Pentecost to the Dedication of the Cathedral is the same as at Pentecost, namely red (this was already the case before 2008); see Marco Navoni, "Colori liturgici," in *Dizionario di liturgia Ambrosiana,* ed. M. Navoni, 147-48 (Milan: NED, 1996).

31 Magnoli, "Quadro generale," 84.

32 *PLA,* 195.

tradition, the time of the Mystery of Pentecost is subdivided into three sections which are marked by the feasts of the Beheading of John the Baptist (August 29) and the Dedication of the Cathedral of Milan on the third Sunday in October.[33] For each Mystery, there is one lectionary for the Sundays, with a three-year cycle of readings (ABC), and one lectionary for the weekdays with two cycles of readings.

Regarding the question of a liturgical biblical hermeneutics, it is significant that *PLA* 79 states that the aim for every Sunday, including those outside the festal cycles, is a consonance of all three readings, in order to achieve through "the criterion of a certain thematic unity […] a uniform understanding of the Mystery that is celebrated." This criterion, which finds its "principal point of application" on the Sundays and feasts of Advent, Christmastide, Lent, and Eastertide, is then "developed organically" on the Sundays after the Epiphany and after Pentecost.[34]

The Sundays after the Epiphany[35]

As in *OLM*, the Sunday after Epiphany, commemorates the Baptism of the Lord and still belongs to Christmastide. The 2nd to the 7th Sundays after Epiphany all have the "appearing" of Christ as their theme, the epiphany/manifestation of his messiahship and lordship in various signs and wonders. With his first sign at the wedding feast in Cana, "he revealed his glory" (Jn 2:11; as on the 2nd Sunday in Ordinary Time C in *OLM*). The multiplication of the loaves follows, which, like the baptism of Jesus and the miracle at Cana, St. Ambrose († 397) had already mentioned in *Illuminans altissimus*, the hymn for the Epiphany. This pericope is often omitted because the fourth Sunday in January is celebrated in Milan as the Feast of the Holy Family with proper readings. The 4th Sunday after Epiphany manifests Christ's lordship over the creation with the stilling of the storm on the sea (A/B) or Jesus' walking on the water (C). The 5th Sunday makes clear his lordship over

---

33 This articulation is already found in the Gospel Book of Busto Arsizio, the contents of which go back to the seventh century; see Patrizia Carmassi, *Libri liturgici e istituzioni ecclesiastiche a Milano in età medioevale. Studio sulla formazione del lezionario Ambrosiano*, LQF 85 (Münster: Aschendorff, 2001), 90, 115; Alzati, *Lezionario*, 75.

34 *PLA*, 79. See Claudio Magnoli, "Una certa unità tematica. Il n. 79 delle 'Premesse' al Lezionario ambrosiano," in *Sacrificium et canticum laudis. Parola, eucaristia, liturgia delle ore, vita della Chiesa (FS Manlio Sodi)*, Pontificia Academia Theologica. Itineraria 10, ed. D. Medeiros, 79–88 (Vatican City: Libreria Editrice Vaticana, 2015).

35 See Norberto Valli, "Libro I – Mistero dell'incarnazione," *Ambrosius* 85 (2009): 145–51; Valli, "'Redemptionis enim nostrae magna mysteria celebramus'. Il ciclo de tempore nella liturgia ambrosiana," *RivLi* 96, no. 4 (2009): 522–23.

life by means of three healing miracles (A: the son of the royal official; B: the daughter of a Gentile Canaanite woman; C: the servant of the officer at Capernaum). Besides this, another aspect of the Epiphany, namely, the turning of the peoples to the Lord, is made clear here, since all these healed persons were foreigners (non-Jews). Similarly, the 6th Sunday underlines Christ's miraculous power and his love of human beings: the healing of the man with the withered hand (A), of the woman with the flow of blood (B), and of the ten lepers (C). The Seventh Sunday amplifies Jesus' healing power by means of the expulsion of demons (A/B) and the forgiveness of sins (C).

Depending on the date of Easter, a greater or lesser number of these Sunday readings will be heard. But every year, the formulas for the second-last and last Sundays before Lent are taken, thematically setting the tone for Lent. In terms of the liturgical book, they belong to the period after the Epiphany, but they have striking parallels to the Byzantine pre-Lenten period; accordingly, we shall speak of them below. In principle, the Old Testament reading and the epistle[36] in the period after the Epiphany are both coordinated with the Gospel. In the case of the wedding feast at Cana, which is identical on the 2nd Sunday in all three lectionary years, the readings (and the Responsorial Psalm) lead in each year to a different aspect of the Gospel.[37]

The Sundays of the period after Pentecost[38]

After Epiphany, the thematic unity of the scriptural readings is substantially prescribed by the idea of the appearing of Christ, and thus in formal terms by the Gospel pericope. On the other hand, on the Sundays in the "period after Pentecost" from Trinity Sunday to the Sunday before the Beheading of John the Baptist, it is the first reading that has the leading position. This is the basis of the choice of epistle and Gospel, so that we make our way by stages through the Old Testament history of salvation, which is read in the light of the Christ event.

The first Sundays begin with the creation of the world (2nd Sunday with sapiential texts from Sirach 16–18); the creation of the human being (3rd Sunday AB with Genesis 2); the mystery of sin (3rd Sunday C with Genesis

---

36 The second reading is called "epistle," and is taken from the Letters of Paul and the Letter to the Hebrews (cf. *PLA*, 66).

37 The central ideas are: A: trust in the effectiveness of the word ("Do whatever he tells you"); B: the identity of Jesus Christ, in whom the entire fullness of God dwells; C: the intercession of the Mother of God. See Valli, "Mistero dell'Incarnazione," 146–47.

38 See Fontana, "Libro III," 204–10.

3; 4th Sunday exemplified by Noah [A], Sodom and Gomorrah [B], and Cain and Abel [C]); and the covenant with Abraham (5th Sunday).[39] The following Sundays each take one character (*figura*) from the history of Israel, which is interpreted as salvation history, and present (on most Sundays) the path God takes with humankind by means of what we might call "faces": Moses (6th Sunday), Joshua (7th Sunday), the judges and Samuel (8th Sunday), David (9th Sunday), Solomon (10th Sunday), Elijah (11th Sunday), Jeremiah and the destruction of the Temple (12th Sunday), Nehemiah and the rebuilding of the Temple (13th Sunday), and finally Ezra (14th Sunday). Depending on the date of Easter, up to four of the last Sundays can be omitted, but the last Sunday before the Beheading of John the Precursor is always kept. On this Sunday, the reading is from the martyrdom of the Maccabees, commemorated in the Milanese tradition at the end of August.

God's salvific action in history is thus proclaimed by means of selected examples from the Old Testament and is, at the same time, placed in the horizon of the New Testament by making links to the Epistle and the Gospel that display a thematic unity. Let us take the 3rd Sunday (creation) as our example. In year A, the creation of the human being Adam and his happy life in paradise (Gn 2:4b-17) is complemented with the aspect of sin and redemption by means of the antithesis between Adam and Christ (Rom 5:12-17). The Gospel presents the salvific will of the Father with the goal of eternal life, which appears in this combination of texts as the reestablishing of the paradisiac state: "God so loved the world that he gave his only Son, so that everyone who believes in him [...] might have eternal life" (Jn 3:16). The common theme of marriage unites the texts in year B: creation as man and woman (Gn 2:18-25), marriage as image of Christ's love for his Church (Eph 5:21-33), and the commandment of indissolubility (Mk 10:1-12). Year C again links the fall (Gn 3:1-20) with the parallel between Adam and Christ (Rom 5:18-21) and, in an original manner, with the Annunciation of the birth of Jesus, who "will save his people from their sins" (Mt 1:20b-24b). These are examples of a successful combination that demonstrates the advantages of a consonance for both the hearers and the homily. It is, however, not particularly difficult to point to examples of less successful combinations.

---

39 Fontana, 205 summarizes Sundays 2–5 and interprets them as God's self-revelation.

The Sundays after the Martyrdom of John the Precursor[40]

The second part of the Mystery of Pentecost encompasses the six or seven Sundays after the Beheading of the Baptist down to the Sunday of the Dedication of the Cathedral on the third Sunday in October. Following ancient Milanese tradition, the pericope Lk 9:7–11 (Herod's question about the identity of Jesus) is read on the Sunday after the Martyrdom of the Baptist, because it mentions the beheading of John. This pericope was assigned to year A. In year B we see John as the friend of the bridegroom, who decreases in order that Jesus may increase. The Gospel in year C describes the beginning of Jesus' preaching after the arrest of the Baptist. In all three years, therefore, the theme is the transition from the Precursor to Christ. The interruption that the martyrdom of the Baptist makes in the period of the Mystery of Pentecost thus has a biblical basis, and has consequences for the choice of pericopes. In accordance with Jesus' words, "The law and the prophets lasted until John; but from then on the kingdom of God is proclaimed" (Lk 16:16ab), the Old Testament had guided the order of readings in the first part of the Mystery of Pentecost, but now, it is once again the Gospel that serves as guide. The feast shows "the deep unity between the old covenant and the new, and also presents the new economy of salvation, in which, in the Church, everyone [...] is called to participate."[41]

On the following Sundays, we have "a series of Christological themes that are unfolding in an ecclesiological sense, the closer the Sunday of the Dedication [of the Cathedral] draws."[42] The 2nd and 3rd Sundays circle broadly around Christ, the only-begotten of the Father, to whom the Father has entrusted the judgment, to whom the Scriptures bear witness, the Christ whom Peter confesses. We also find the rebirth from water and the Spirit. The 4th Sunday celebrates the abiding presence of Christ in his Church as the bread of life, so that the theme of the Eucharist is determinative; the bread of life discourse (John 6) is distributed among the three lectionary years. On the 5th Sunday, the central theme is Christ's principal commandment of love. After this, the attention turns more strongly to the Church. The 6th Sunday recalls the sending out of the disciples, and thus of the believers, as servants of the Gospel (in A, Lk 17:7–10, "We have done what we were obliged to do"; in B, Mt 20:1–16, workers at the eleventh hour; and in C, Mt 10:40–42, "Whoever receives you receives me"). The parables of the kingdom of heaven

---

40 See Fontana, "Libro III," 210-16.

41 *PLA*, 209.

42 *PLA*, 211.

in Matthew 13 are distributed among the lectionary years with the aim of presenting the Church as the sign of the kingdom of God

The Sundays after the Dedication of the Cathedral[43]

The first Sunday after the Dedication of the Cathedral, the fourth in October, has the title "*Domenica del mandato missionario*," "Sunday of the missionary commission," coinciding with the World Mission Sunday of the universal Church. The Gospels speak of the missionary commission given by the risen Lord, and the readings from the Acts of the Apostles (instead of from the Old Testament) give examples of how this was carried out. The Epistle is chosen on the basis of consonance.

As a kind of answer or result, the lectionary places the following Sunday under the title "Participation of the Peoples in Salvation." The scriptural readings combine appropriate prophecies from Isaiah, Pauline texts addressed to the local communities in Rome, Philippi, and Ephesus who had come to the Christian faith from among the Gentiles, and the parables of the net full of fish (Mt 13:47–52), the banqueting hall that must be filled (Lk 14:1a, 15–24), and the royal wedding feast (Mt 22:1–14), which underline Christ's salvific will and announce the final judgment. As in *OLM*, the liturgical year concludes with the feast of Christ the King (but two weeks earlier, because Advent lasts for six weeks). The Gospel pericopes align with *OLM*, and the readings do so in part.

If one examines the three parts of the Mystery of Pentecost in order to identify the guiding hermeneutical concept, the idea of salvation history proves to be the common theme. The first part offers, by way of example, figures from the Old Testament; after the Beheading of John, there is a thematic switch to Christ and the Church; and finally, at the close of the third part, we enter an eschatological perspective.[44] The weekday readings, which we do not discuss here in detail, follow this basic concept as well and take the Sunday pericopes to a deeper level.[45] The *PLA* states that the path constructed in this way is meant to be both "*celebrativo e catechetico.*"[46]

There is another striking feature of the Milanese Sunday lectionary: namely, that the Vigil Mass of Sunday is understood as the "solemn opening

---

43 See Fontana, "Libro III," 216–23.

44 See Fontana, "Libro III," 203.

45 See *PLA*, 199, 202–08, 212–13, 218–21; see Fontana, "Libro III"; Magnoli, "Tempi liturgici," 505–07.

46 *PLA*, 199.

of the Day of the Lord,"[47] which can also be celebrated as a "*celebrazione vigiliare vespertina*"[48] in combination with First Vespers and a *lucernarium* (lamp-lighting ceremony). Even if this developed form is not chosen, it is always characterized by the additional proclamation of one of twelve resurrection Gospels in the introductory rites of the Mass, in order to highlight Sunday as the day of Christ's resurrection. This brief note brings us to the Byzantine order of readings which has eleven resurrection Gospels (*eōthina*) in the Orthros of Sunday.[49] In what follows, we shall look at the readings of the Divine Liturgy.

1.3. The Byzantine Order of Readings

We can compare the Roman Ordinary Time to the Byzantine liturgical period of the *Octoechos* (which means "eight tones"), which runs from All Saints (the Sunday after Pentecost) to the Sunday of the Pharisee and the Publican in the following year exclusive, when the pre-Lenten period begins. Three mutually independent cycles run here, for weekdays, Saturdays, and Sundays. It is only the last group, which are enumerated as Sundays after Pentecost (2–32), that interest us here. In principle, the Gospels and the readings are conceived as far as possible[50] as a *lectio semicontinua,* so that no consciously constructed relationship between the two is envisaged. Texts from Matthew are read until the Sunday before the Exaltation of the Cross (September 14) and thereafter texts from Luke.[51] With two exceptions, the omissions between the Sundays are so large that no pericopes follow each

---

47 *PLA*, 73.

48 Magnoli, "Quadro generale," 90–92; Claudio Magnoli, "Il Lezionario ambrosiano a norma dei decreti del Concilio Vaticano II," in *L'omelia* [...], BEL.S 160, ed. P. Chiaramello (Rome: CLV-Edizioni Liturgiche, 2012), 251–53; Cesare Alzati, "Il Libro della Liturgia Vigiliare Vespertina," *Ambrosius* 85 (2009): 111–17. In common parish praxis, however, this celebration has not yet found the place that was hoped for.

49 See Bebastià Janeras, "I vangeli domenicali della resurrezione nelle tradizioni liturgiche agiapolita e bizantina," in *Paschale mysterium. Studi in memoria dell'Abate Prof. Salvatore Marsili (1910-1983),* StA 91, An.Li 10, ed. G. Farnedi (Rome: Abbazia S. Paolo, 1986), 55–69; Stefano Rosso, *La celebrazione della storia della salvezza nel rito bizantino. Misteri sacramentali, feste e tempi liturgici,* MSIL 60 (Vatican City: Libreria Editrice Vaticana, 2010), 662–63, 891.

50 Only the Gospel of the 17th Matthew-Sunday is an exception to this schema.

51 Since the Gospel is taken from Matthew on All Saints too (the 1st Sunday after Pentecost), this is also the first Matthew-Sunday. There are 17 Matthew-Sundays and 15 Luke-Sundays (without counting the two Lukan Gospels of the pre-Lenten period). On the Sunday pericopes, see Rosso, *Celebrazione*, 893–95, 908–9.

other in the immediate sequence of the evangelist.[52] In terms of content, the emphasis lies on the miracles of Jesus (fifteen times), and especially on the healings of sick and possessed persons, as well as on the parables (nine times).[53]

During the *Octoechos*, the first reading is always taken as a *lectio semi-continua* from the Letters of the Apostle Paul in the sequence of the biblical canon. The Revelation of John is not found at all in the Byzantine order of readings.[54] The Old Testament may have disappeared from the Divine Liturgy as early as the seventh or eighth century.[55] It is read now only in the Vigils of Christmas, Epiphany, and Easter, in Holy Week, in the Liturgy of the Hours during Lent (also in the Liturgy of the Presanctified Gifts on Wednesday and Friday), and in some Great Vespers on the eve of a feast or solemnity.[56] This means that many Old Testament books are never read during liturgy.[57]

1.4. Results of Comparison

In comparing the three systems of readings, one must bear in mind that the two western orders of readings are recent and were conceived anew in a comprehensive manner, whereas the Byzantine lectionary grew historically out of the systems of readings in Jerusalem and Constantinople. They may have been combined in the tenth century in Constantinople, and then handed on down through the centuries.[58] For this reason alone, a complete comparison in all aspects is impossible, especially in the non-festal periods.

---

[52] The exceptions are the 8th/9th Matthew-Sunday and the 6th/7th Luke-Sunday.

[53] The numbers are in fact smaller, because in the immovable cycle the two Sundays before Christmas (Sunday of the Holy Ancestors of Christ and Sunday of the Fathers), the Sunday after Christmas, and the Sundays before and after the Epiphany have their own readings. It is also possible for feasts with proper readings to fall on a Sunday.

[54] See Rosso, *Celebrazione*, 607, 886; Alexis Kniazeff, "La lecture de l'Ancien et du Nouveau Testament dans le rite byzantin," in *La prière des heures*, ed. K. Bezobrazov and B. Botte (Paris: Éditions du Cerf, 1963), 201-51.

[55] See Juan Mateos and Steve Hawkes-Teeples, *The Liturgy of the Word*, History of the Liturgy of St. John Chrysostom 1 (Fairfax, VA: Jack Figel, Eastern Christian Publications, 2016), 48-49, 217-20.

[56] See Kniazeff, "Lecture," 204-5, 207-8; Hans-Joachim Schulz, "Liturgie, Tagzeiten und Kirchenjahr des byzantinischen Ritus," in *Handbuch der Ostkirchenkunde* 2, eds. W. Nyssen (Düsseldorf: Patmos, 1989), 30-100, 76. The Great Vespers before the feasts of apostles also have a New Testament reading.

[57] See Kniazeff, "Lecture," 250-51.

[58] See Rosso, *Celebrazione*, 886; Kniazeff, "Lecture," 214.

Accordingly, we shall compare above all the Roman and the Milanese orders of readings, complementing this with a look at the Byzantine order. We shall select four points that are important for a liturgical hermeneutics of Scripture.

Use of the Old Testament

In comparison to *OLM*, the Old Testament has a greater importance in the Ambrosian lectionary. This is true quantitatively, since the pericopes are often longer, and the Gospel is preceded on the weekdays of Advent and Lent by two Old Testament readings. (One can ask whether this is not too much for a weekday Mass, and whether it brings a genuine pastoral gain).[59] At the same time, and more significantly in terms of hermeneutics, one can also speak of a qualitative upgrade, because in the Ambrosian Rite the first reading on the Sundays after Pentecost functions as the guiding pericope, and the order of readings highlights important pericopes and significant figures from salvation history. In the Byzantine liturgy, on the other hand, the scanty use of Old Testament readings and their complete absence from the Divine Liturgy, from today's perspective, must certainly be seen as a loss which cannot be compensated by the use of the Old Testament in poetical compositions[60] or by the feasts of Old Testament saints.[61]

On Old Testament Salvation History

In the Milanese "Period after Pentecost" (from Pentecost to the Beheading of the Baptist), there are striking similarities to the principles of selection of the *OLM* for Lent. There one can likewise observe a thematic concordance among the three readings that is due both to the selection from the letters of the Apostles and, above all, to the use of Old Testament "readings with the

---

59 The principal point of criticism of the new lectionary is that it was drawn up with too little consideration for the reality in the parishes.

60 On this, see the numerous marginal indications of the biblical passages that are used in *Antologhion di tutto l'anno. Contenente l'ufficio quotidiano dall'Orológhion, dal Parakliti e dai Minéi [...]*. 4 vols (Rome: Lipa Edizioni, 1999-2000).

61 See, for example, Eliane Poirot, "La fête du saint prophète Elie dans la liturgie byzantine," *EO* 9 (1992): 173-200. Rosso gives a useful overview of the Old Testament saints (*Celebrazione*, 914-41). See Nikodemus C. Schnabel, "Die liturgische Verehrung der Heiligen des Alten Testaments in der lateinischen Kirche. Ein vergessenes Desiderat der Konzilsgeneration," in *Liturgies in East and West. Ecumenical Relevance of Early Liturgical Development. Acts of the International Symposium Vindobonense I, Vienna, November 17-20, 2007*, ed. H.-J. Feulner, ÖSLS 6 (Münster: Lit-Verlag, 2013), 319-31.

most important stages of salvation history from its beginning to the promise of the new covenant."[62] However, the time available in Lent is much too short for a genuine presentation of salvation history. Besides this, the important Gospels and the basic guiding idea of "Lent" mean that the Old Testament reading does not get the attention it deserves. Accordingly, this aim is in fact realized better in the Milanese order of readings.

The Ambrosian lectionary appears to have reacted to the criticism of the *OLM* by refraining from employing the Old Testament as a "quarry" for the Gospel. Instead, it respects the specific value of the Old Testament and seeks to create a certain overview, or a kind of "picture," of the Old Testament—something that cannot be achieved through the Sunday readings of the *OLM*. Since the other readings are selected on the basis of the Old Testament, the orientation takes the direction opposite to the *OLM*. It is significant for biblical hermeneutics that this corresponds exactly to the direction in which the Scriptures came into being.

Without going into detail here, we may note that the selection of readings from Old Testament salvation history matches the schema proposed by the Benedictine monastery of Maredsous in 1965. Adrien Nocent, a member of that community, submitted it to the Coetus XI when the *OLM* was being drawn up, but it was not taken into consideration.[63]

Thematic Arrangement in Longer Time Periods

A thematic assigning of the readings on a feast or festal cycle is based on the content of the celebration itself and can look back on a tradition that is already tangible in Egeria's account of her Holy Land pilgrimage (381-383).[64] This does not, however, apply to the other Sundays. The *OLM* employs this distinction to justify the absence of a thematic arrangement on the Sundays in Ordinary Time, declaring that the Liturgy is "always the celebration of the mystery of Christ"[65] (and not of some theme or another). The Milanese lectionary makes use of this absence of feast-days in order to fill these Sundays thematically. In principle, one cannot object to a thematic orientation; the only question is *how* to fill the Sundays thematically. Ultimately, it is

---

62 *GILM*, 97.

63 See Franz, *Wortgottesdienst*, 41-70, esp. 43-52.

64 See, e.g., Egeria, *Itinerarium* 32,1 (FontC 20:240; WEC 2:350): "*lectiones etiam aptae diei et loco leguntur.*" See Anne McGowan and Paul F. Bradshaw, *The Pilgrimage of Egeria. A New Translation of the Itinerarium Egeriae with Introduction and Commentary* (Collegeville: Liturgical Press, 2018), 170.

65 *GILM*, 68.

a matter of various answers to the question that is relevant to a liturgical hermeneutics of the Bible: namely, how and when the liturgical order may, should, or must dictate the themes—or how the Liturgy allows itself to be guided thematically by Scripture.[66]

Consonance within a Sunday Formula

A thematic allocation or orientation of readings that covers a longer period of time is not the same thing as consonance, since this aims at the harmony (*con-sonare*) of the pericopes within one single celebration. The three orders of readings that we discuss here display the various possibilities. The Byzantine order knows no consciously determined consonance; the Roman order knows a consonance between the Old Testament reading and the Gospel; and the Milanese order knows a consonance among all three readings. The Ambrosian lectionary clearly took account of the criticism made of the *OLM*: the "certain thematic unity" (*PLA* 79) corresponds to the demand for consonance that was made with regard to the second reading.

With regard to biblical hermeneutics, consonance can set limits, since it tempts us to see only the "common theme" of the compilers rather than the richness of the individual texts themselves. On the other hand, it can also contribute to a deeper and broader understanding of the pericopes, make them easier to remember, and promote the unity of the liturgical celebration.[67] Above all, it draws attention to the unity of Scripture and to the fact that the two Testaments belong together.[68]

2. THE SUNDAYS OF LENT IN THE ROMAN, MILANESE, AND BYZANTINE LITURGY

Our next step is the investigation of how Sacred Scripture is used in the Sunday Eucharist in Lent, an important period in the liturgical year, in order to garner further aspects of a liturgical hermeneutics of Scripture. In all three rites, the readings form an interesting biblical program that was composed in accord with theological criteria.

---

66 For further details and a proposal about an order of readings that takes account of the advantages of both the Roman and the Ambrosian principles, see Benini, *Liturgische Bibelhermeneutik*, 270-87.

67 On the advantages and the risks of consonance, see Franz, *Wortgottesdienst*, 296-305.

68 See B.VIII.30.

2.1. Overview of the Liturgies

Sunday	Roman	Milanese (Years A-B-C)	Byzantine
1st Lent	Jesus fasts for 40 days and is tempted A: Mt 4:1–11 B: Mk 1:12–15 C: Lk 4:1–13	*Sunday at the Beginning of Lent* Jesus fasts for 40 days and is tempted (Mt 4:1–11)	*Sunday of Orthodoxy / Feast of Icons* Heb 11:24–26, 32–40: Old Testament witnesses of faith (Moses etc.) did not attain the promise. Jn 1:43–51: Jesus calls the first disciples / Nathanael
2nd Lent	**Transfiguration** A: Mt 17:1–9 B: Mk 9:2–10 C: Lk 9:28b-36	*Sunday of the Samaritan Woman* Samaritan woman (Jn 4:5–42)	*Commemoration of Gregory Palamas* Heb 1:19-2:3: Listening to the Son of God leads to salvation. Mk 2:1–12: Healing of the lame man and authority of the Son of Man to forgive sins
3rd Lent	Samaritan woman (Jn 4:5–42) B: Cleansing of the Temple (Jn 2:13–25) C: Exhortation to repentance / parable of fig tree (Lk 13:1–9)	*Sunday of Abraham* Abraham (Jn 8:31–59)	*Veneration of the Cross* Heb 4:14-5:6: Jesus, the Son of God, as exalted high priest who is able to feel compassion Mk 8:34-9:1: Following Jesus in bearing the cross and self-denial, in order to save one's life

Table continued on next page.

4th Lent	The man born blind (Jn 9:1–41)	*Sunday of the Blind Man*	*Commemoration of John Climacus*
	B: Lifting up of the Son of Man (Jn 3:14–21)	The man born blind (Jn 9:1–38b)	Heb 6:13–20: Trustworthy promise through Jesus the high priest, who has gone as our forerunner into the holy of holies
	C: Parable of prodigal son (Lk 15:1–3, 11–32)		Mk 9:17–31: Healing of a young man who was possessed and prediction of Jesus' suffering
5th Lent	Lazarus (Jn 11:1–45)	*Sunday of Lazarus* Lazarus (Jn 11:1–53)[69]	*Commemoration of Mary of Egypt*
	B: Grain of wheat (Jn 12:20–33)		Heb 9:11–14: Christ the high priest brings salvation through his blood
	C: Woman caught in adultery (Jn 8:1–11)		Mk 10:32–45: Prediction of Jesus' suffering and request for the best places in the kingdom of God (reference to baptism and chalice)
			[Saturday of Lazarus (Jn 11:1–45)]
Palm Sunday	Jesus enters Jerusalem Passion according to Mt / Mk / Lk	*Mass for the Blessing of Palms:* Jesus enters Jerusalem (Jn 12:12–16) *Mass of the day:* Anointing in Bethany (Jn 11:55–12:11)	Phil 4:4–9: "Rejoice! The Lord is near." Jn 12:1–18: Jesus is anointed in Bethany and enters Jerusalem.

69 In Milan, the pericope is seven verses longer than in *OLM*. This longer text includes the decision of the Sanhedrin to kill Jesus and the prophetic words of the high priest Caiaphas that Jesus will die "for the people," thereby creating a theological-narrative "bridge" to Holy Week; see Francesco Braschi, "Libro II. Mistero della Pasqua," *Ambrosius* 85 (2009): 169.

2.2. The Western Orders of Readings (Rome / Milan)

In the Western orders of readings, the common elements in the Gospel readings are striking. The first Sunday of Lent links the Church's period of fasting to the model of Jesus, whose victory over temptation is proclaimed as an encouragement at the beginning of the Forty Days. By means of the order of readings, the Church accompanies Jesus on his path to Jerusalem, so that the believers participate in his journey or, more precisely, so that their path to Easter bears the imprint of Jesus' way to Jerusalem, to his death and resurrection—that is to say, the imprint of the paschal mystery.

The ensuing agreement of the Gospels of the Samaritan woman, the man born blind, and Lazarus is a fruit of the postconciliar liturgical reform, which draws on patristic traditions and gives these texts once more a prominent position as Gospels of the preparation or the commemoration of Baptism. They can also be chosen in the other years of readings.[70] The third Sunday establishes a mystagogical relationship between the symbol of water and baptism: whoever receives in the unrepeatable sacrament of Baptism the water that Christ gives will no longer thirst, since this water will become in him or her the source of eternal life. Baptism opens the eyes to Christ (just as the eyes of the man born blind were opened), thus making us "the enlightened" (as the baptized were called in the early Church). In the same way, the raising of Lazarus is an image of God's salvific action in baptism. Just as Christ, who proclaims himself to be the resurrection and the life, led Martha to faith and called Lazarus to life commanding that the burial bands be untied, so Baptism frees from entanglement in sin and death, and leads through faith to the new, eternal life in Christ. Besides this, the three Johannine pericopes show us exemplary figures who grow in faith, and an ascending path of the revelation of Christ.

Milan, following the Gospel of John, has also preserved the ancient Lenten pericope about Abraham,[71] which was probably read in Rome too, instead of the transfiguration of Jesus.[72] Naturally, the Gospel of the

---

70 See Balthasar Fischer, "Der patristische Hintergrund der drei großen johanneischen Tauf-perikopen von der Samariterin, der Heilung des Blindgeborenen und der Auferweckung des Lazarus am dritten, vierten und fünften Sonntag der Quadragesima," in Fischer, *Redemptionis mysterium. Studien zur Osterfeier und zur christlichen Initiation*, ed. A. Gerhards and A. Heinz (Paderborn: Schöningh, 1992/1983), 172–85. Fischer himself played an active role in this work of restoration (see Fischer, 173).

71 On the Abraham pericope in the Milanese tradition, see Carmassi, *Libri liturgici*, 311.

72 See Jean-Paul Bouhot, "Le choix des lectures liturgiques dans l'église romaine: quelques exemples," in *Präsenz und Verwendung der Heiligen Schrift im christlichen Frühmittelalter. Exegetische Literatur und liturgische Texte*, ed. P. Carmassi, Wolfenbütteler Mittelalter-Studien 20 (Wiesbaden: Harrasowitz, 2008), 245–46 (with reference to Antoine Chavasse).

transfiguration, as a stage on Jesus' path toward Jerusalem with the look ahead to his transfigured paschal glory, fits Lent well, and it is prescribed in the renewed Milanese lectionary as the Gospel of the Resurrection in the vigil Masses (*celebrazione vigiliare*) from the 2nd to the 5th Sundays.[73] In Year B, the *OLM* prescribes a "text from John about Christ's coming glorification through his cross and resurrection," and in C "a text from Luke about conversion,"[74] in order to offer a richer spiritual program in preparation for Easter. On the other hand, the same Gospels are employed in Milan each of the three reading years, thereby emphasizing their importance.

We must also look at the Old and New Testament readings, first in the Roman[75] and then in the Milanese rite. As *GILM* 97 states with regard to the first reading, a "series of texts for each Year presents the main elements of salvation history from its beginning until the promise of the New Covenant." Thus, on the 1st Sunday, there is a reading from the prehistory or a reference to the Exodus (A: the fall; B: Noah; C: salvation-historical creed in Deuteronomy 26). On the 2nd Sunday, there is an important passage about Abraham, and on the 3rd, the reading concerns Moses. On the 4th Sunday, the theme is Joshua or the kings (B: anointing of David: C: the end of Judah). Finally, on the 5th Sunday, we have the prophets who proclaim the eschatological salvation. The second reading was chosen to harmonize with the first reading and the Gospel, in order to achieve as close a unity as possible.

The same basic orientation of understanding Scripture is implied on both the vertical and the horizontal levels. Within the Mass formula of one Sunday, the conscious selection of the second reading and the "link"—very open, but nevertheless recognizable—between the first reading and the Gospel point to the path from the Old Testament to the New, and more concretely, to Christ. As Lent proceeds, the Old Testament reading makes its way through significant stages of salvation history and leads us to Holy Week and then to Easter. (The Song of the Suffering Servant, Is 50:4–7, which is obviously to be understood as pointing to Christ, is read each year on Palm Sunday.) This marks the paschal mystery of Christ as the goal of salvation history, and thus as an orientation for the interpretation of Scripture.[76]

Two principles guide the choice of the Old and New Testament readings in Milan.[77] First, there is the fundamental consonance in the Mass formula.

---

73 See *PLA*, 75; B.VIII.27.2.

74 *GILM*, 97 (the text on the 5th Sunday C is, however, taken from John).

75 See Nübold, *Perikopenordnung*, 248–53, 302–7, 348–49.

76 See B.VIII.30.

77 See Braschi, "Libro II," 165–70; Alzati, "Lezionario," 294–97.

The *PLA* speaks explicitly of the "coherence" (*coerenza*) between the themes of the individual Sundays and the respective Gospels.[78] This shows that the orientation to the Gospel guides the selection both in Milan and in Rome. A second principle of selection is noteworthy. From the 2nd to the 5th Sunday, the first reading is always taken from the Books of Exodus or Deuteronomy. The *PLA* points out that nodal points of the Old Testament salvation history are recalled in the chosen pericopes and are lived through once again.[79] The reasoning is thus similar to that in the *OLM*, but the period of salvation history is narrower in Milan by limiting it to the wandering in the desert. This may also contain an allusion to Jesus' forty-days fasting in the wilderness, which has been proclaimed on the 1st Sunday.

2.3. The Byzantine Order of Readings

The order of readings on the Sundays in Lent in the Byzantine liturgy has a completely different structure. Today's order deviates only in a few instances from the system of readings in Constantinople, transmitted through the so-called Typikon of the Great Church[80] (Hagia Sophia) from 950-959, though it is older. This system prevailed over the order in Jerusalem.[81] Since the chants in the Triodion mostly follow the old Jerusalem order of Gospels,[82] they are independent of today's Sunday readings. This means that we need not look at them in detail in what follows, (even when there are also unintended intertextual references).

One initial formal aspect we notice is that on the 1st Sunday of Lent and on Palm Sunday there are readings from John, while the intervening Sundays have readings from Mark in a canonically ascending order.[83] The Gospels

---

78 See *PLA*, 134.

79 *PLA*, 132.

80 See Juan Mateos (ed.), *Le Typicon de la Grande Église. Ms. Sainte-Croix no 40, Xe siècle*, 2 vols., OCA 165-66 (Rome: Pontificium Institutum Orientalium Studiorum, 1962-63).

81 See Gabriel Bertonière, *The Sundays of Lent in the Tridion [sic!]. The Sundays Without a Commemoration*, OCA 253 (Rome. Pontificium Institutum Orientalium Studiorum, 1997), 45-50.

82 See Bertonière, 97; Job Getcha, "Système des lectures bibliques du rite byzantin," in *Les lectures bibliques pour les dimanches et fêtes*, vol. 1 of *Liturgie, interprète de l'écriture*, ed. M. Triacca and A. Pistoia, BEL.S 119 (Rome: CLV-Edizioni Liturgiche, 2002), 36-37.

83 On this, and for the following section, see Nicolas Cernokrak, "La narratologie liturgique byzantine selon les pericopes dominicales du Grand Carême de l'évangile de saint Marc," in Triacca and Pistoia, *Liturgie, interprète de l'écriture* 1:183-200. It is possible that Jn 1:43–52 on the 1st Sunday is a remnant of an older Jerusalem system (see Cernokrak, 187 with n. 18).

from the 1st to the 5th Sundays are all linked by the term "Son of Man" (Jn 1:51; Mk 2:10; 8:38; 9:31; 10:33); on Palm Sunday, the designation of Jesus as "King of Israel" (Jn 1:49; 12:13) is a link back to the 1st Sunday, where the title "Son of God" (Jn 1:49) also occurs. The Johannine pericopes complement each other and thematize Jesus' public ministry at its beginning and end— from his calling of the disciples to his last path to Bethany and Jerusalem. Together with the ascending order within the Markan pericopes, the last two of which contain the prediction of Jesus' suffering and of his resurrection, this enables Lent—in a similar manner as in the West—to make present of the path Jesus takes toward his glorification.

The readings from the Apostolos on the first five Sundays are all taken from the Letter to the Hebrews, choosing passages that speak in various ways of the sovereignty of Christ, who is given the title "priest" on the 3rd, 4th, and 5th Sundays (Heb 4:14–5:6 [4 times]; 6:20; 9:11). The deviation of the reading on the 1st Sunday from this ascending order can be explained from the history of liturgy. This reading was selected for the commemoration of the prophets Moses, Aaron, and Samuel (cf. Heb 11:24–26, 32), which was celebrated on the 1st Sunday before it became the "Sunday of Orthodoxy" or "Feast of the Icons" in remembrance of the victory over Iconoclasm and the reintroduction of the veneration of icons in Constantinople in 843.[84]

The order of readings thus communicates a Christology of sovereignty through the reading and the Gospel with messianic titles. While it posits spiritual accents distinct from the West, it is impossible to overlook the common concern of a spiritual path that the Church offers through the scriptural readings both to the catechumens and to those already baptized, in order to lead them to the celebration of the paschal mystery of Christ. Alexander Schmemann sketches this path vividly by means of the pericopes.[85] The 1st Sunday places the promise at the very beginning: although the righteous of the Old Covenant are already acknowledged in a special manner because of their faith, they have not attained what was promised (Heb 11:39). The promise to Nathanael, who is newly come to Christ, that he will see something greater—heaven opened and the Son of Man among the angels (Jn 1:50–51)— is, so to speak, the continuation of the reading. This is why it is important to pay all the more attention to the exhortation of the 2nd Sunday and not to fall

---

84 See Cernokrak, 187; Job Getcha, *The Typikon Decoded. An Explanation of Byzantine Liturgical Practice*, Orthodox Liturgy Series 3 (Yonkers, NY: St Vladimir's Seminary Press, 2012), 65, 184–85; Alexander Schmemann, *Great Lent: A School of Repentance. Its Meaning for Orthodox Christians* (Crestwood, NY: St Vladimir's Seminary Press, 1984), 73. The first victory of Orthodoxy had taken place on the 1st Sunday of Lent.

85 See Schmemann, 73–85; Cernokrak, "Narratologie," 189–99.

away from the path of exalted salvation (Heb 2:1). This endeavor is illustrated by the Gospel of the lame man who is lowered through the roof, the man whose sins Christ absolves in order to demonstrate his divinity (Mk 2:1–12).

On the 2nd and 3rd Sundays, the Typikon of the Great Church of Constantinople has also preserved the summons to the catechumens to enroll for baptism.[86] This took place from the Monday of the 3rd week, when a cross was made on the brow of catechumens.[87] The Gospel about following Jesus by bearing the cross (Mk 8:34–9:1) seems to be meaningfully connected to this ceremony; the imitation of Christ is linked to the promise of saving one's life (Mk 8:35). When the praxis of infant baptism made the adult catechumenate obsolete, the veneration of the cross was introduced on this Sunday in commemoration of the solemn return of the holy Cross to Jerusalem under Emperor Heraclius († 641) in 631.[88] This Gospel now received an additional point of reference, for which it was equally appropriate. In mid-Lent, the cross already appears—also independently of historical background—in the light of the Resurrection. The hymnography and the synaxarion[89] interpret it as a sign of victory, as the tree of life in the midst of paradise—corresponding to the middle both of Lent and of the church's interior, in which the cross is exposed for veneration—as well as insignia borne before the victorious King, the risen Christ.

The Gospel of the 4th Sunday is likewise appropriate to the catechumenate because it describes the healing of a possessed boy as a transition from death to life (Mk 9:26–27). This could be linked to the baptismal exorcisms. In addition, this narrative incidentally contains an instruction about faith, prayer, and fasting.[90] The terms "baptism" and "chalice" on the 5th Sunday (Mk 10:32–45) have a clear reference to the paschal mystery of Christ and to initiation. The Gospels of the 4th and 5th Sundays look, by means of the prediction of Jesus' dying and rising, not so much at our own endeavors, as at what Christ has accomplished for the salvation of human beings.[91] The readings from Hebrews speak of Christ as the eternal High Priest who has

86 See Cernokrak, 193, 196; Mateos, *Typicon de la Grande Église*, 1:2, 20, 38.

87 See Getcha, *Typikon Decoded*, 191.

88 See Stefano Parenti and Elena Velkovska, "La croce nel rito bizantino," in *La croce nella Liturgia*, vol. 3 of *La Croce. Iconografia e interpretazione (secoli I-inizio XVI)*, ed. B. Ulianich (Naples: Elio de Rosa, 2007), 61-62; Joseph Hallit, "La croix dans le rite byzantin. Histoire et théologie," *Parole de l'Orient* 3, no. 2 (1972): 299-302.

89 See Schmemann, *Great Lent*, 77–78.

90 See Cernokrak, "Narratologie," 197. The words "and fasting" in the biblical text are a later addition.

91 See Schmemann, *Great Lent*, 77.

brought about salvation through his own blood and has entered as our pre-cursor into the Holy of Holies. In this way, they point to the paschal mystery.

The pre-Lenten season also belongs to the Triodion.[92] Because of their similarities to the two last Sundays after the Epiphany in the Milanese lectionary (see the italics and underscore), we shall briefly present them in a table.

Rite	Roman	Ambrosian	Byzantine
1	–	–	Sunday of the Pharisee and the Publican (Lk 18:10–14)
2	–	–	Sunday of the Prodigal Son (Lk 15:11–32)
3	–	Second-last Sunday after Epiphany: Sunday of the Divine Clemency A: Woman caught in adultery (Jn 8:1–11) B: Sinful woman in the house of Simon the Pharisee (Lk 7:36–50) C: Jesus calls the tax collector Levi (Mk 2:13–17)	Sunday of Judgment (Mt 25:31–46: Parable of the universal judgment) Or: Sunday of Abstaining from Meat (1 Cor 8:8–9:2: Abstaining from meat sacrificed to idols)
4	Ash Wednesday: *Mt 6:1–6, 16–18*: Almsgiving, prayer, and fasting	Last Sunday after Epiphany: Sunday of Pardon A: Prodigal Son (Lk 15:11–32) B: Pharisee and Publican (Lk 18:10–14) C: Zacchaeus (Lk 19:1–10)[93]	Before this day: Saturday of the Ascetics: *Mt 6:1–13: Almsgiving and prayer* Sunday of Pardon / of abstaining from milk / of eating cheese *Mt 6:14–21: Fasting*

92 See Schmemann, 16–30; Getcha, *Typikon Decoded*, 141-61.

93 The Gospel of Zacchaeus is read on the Byzantine 32nd Sunday after Pentecost.

2.4. The Results of Comparison

If one now compares the Western and the Byzantine orders of read-ings for Lent, one notes, despite differing pericopes, a common concern: Scripture is to become spiritual nourishment for both the catechumens and those already baptized on their path toward Easter, which thus becomes a way to accompany Christ toward his dying and rising. The primary function of Scripture here is not didactic, but anamnetic. It opens up an access to the paschal mystery that is made present in the liturgical celebration, the mystery that furthers faith in Christ and the Christian way of life.[94]

The same pericopes can be used in similar places (e.g., the Prodigal Son: Roman 4th Sunday C; Milanese 1st Sunday of Pardon; Byzantine 2nd Sunday of the pre-Lenten period) or in other contexts. Since the Gospels of the Samaritan woman and the man born blind speak of water,[95] they are employed in the Roman and the Milanese liturgy in Lent to prepare for the initiation into the Paschal Mystery. In the Byzantine liturgy, however, the same pericopes are prescribed for the Easter season, in order to point to the paschal event (of Baptism) and the working of the Spirit, which are contin-ued in the Church's "today." Accordingly, the place in the liturgical year also influences the interpretation of one and the same pericope.

It is also striking that biblical figures (the Samaritan woman, the man born blind, Martha) are increasingly presented as models of faith with whom the hearer can identify, in order to take on their role and receive inspirations for one's own path of faith.[96] Something similar can be said of the parables of the Prodigal Son or the Pharisee in the Temple, who embody spiritual attitudes such as repentance or humility, which are particularly appropriate to Lent. Such examples also display God's action, after which the Sundays of Divine Clemency or of Pardon are named. Scripture preserves the experience of faith in these exemplary figures and offers them for personal orientation and encouragement. When the faithful draw on Scripture in the celebration of liturgy, it can bear fruit as a spiritual resource for their Christian identity. The fact that the orders of readings posit differing spiritual accents, as we see (for example) in the Byzantine selection in accord with messianic titles, shows the differing characters of the rites.

In the case of the West, the consonant arrangement in both the Roman and the Ambrosian rites is striking. The selection in Rome of the second

---

94 See B.VIII.26.

95 Naturally, one factor here is the choice to follow the narrative sequence of the Gospel of John.

96 See B.IX.34.

reading, and in Milan of the reading and the epistle, in view of the Gospel, intends to undergird hermeneutically the orientation of the Old Testament to Christ. In a manner appropriate to Lent, the intensifying drama in the Gospel of John displays, Sunday by Sunday, the orientation to the paschal mystery.

3. FURTHER ASPECTS OF THE SELECTION OF READINGS

Up to this point, we have investigated the principles of selecting the readings for the Sundays in Ordinary Time and in Lent. We shall now summarize further aspects of the selection of readings that are relevant to a liturgical hermeneutics of the Bible.

Logically, the readings on feast days (and more broadly in festal cycles) are chosen for their thematic appropriateness, so that where possible the "chronology" of the Bible is taken over into the sequence of the liturgical year. (For example, the Gospel of the encounter between the risen Jesus and the apostle Thomas appears on the Sunday after Easter). However, this principle is not always consistently maintained.[97] Specific books were always assigned to certain periods in the liturgical year, such as the Acts of the Apostles to the Easter season in both East and West,[98] or especially Isaiah and other prophetic messianic texts in Advent.[99] The choice of certain books is usually obvious on the basis of the texts themselves, so that the Liturgy has been oriented to the text and a corresponding liturgical tradition has emerged. Besides this, the Milanese lectionary, partly with recourse to the sermons of Ambrose,[100] has a detailed list of the Books that are prescribed for a specific

---

97 One such exception is the Epiphany of the Lord on January 6. The Holy Family certainly did not go back to Bethlehem after the circumcision on the eighth day, and then wait for the Wise Men, as the liturgical chronology would suggest. Rather, this date was taken over by Rome from the East.

98 For exact references to the *lectio continua* from Acts, see Harald Buchinger, "Pentekoste, II. Alte Kirche. III. Zusammenfassende Interpretation," in *RAC* 27 (Stuttgart: Hiersemann, 2015), 94-108, esp. 95, 97-100, 105-6; Buchinger, "Pentekoste, Pfingsten und Himmelfahrt. Grunddaten und Fragen zur Frühgeschichte," in *Preaching after Easter. Mid-Pentecost, Ascension and Pentecost in Late Antiquity.* Supplements to Vigiliae Christinae 136, eds. R. W. Bishop (Leiden: Brill, 2016), 15-84, 19, 25-26, 41, 49-50, 53, 60, 74, 76.

99 See *GILM*, 74.

100 See Schmitz, *Gottesdienst Mailand*, 324-41, e.g., Genesis and Proverbs for Lent (today for the weekdays in Lent). See Ernst Dassmann, *Ambrosius von Mailand. Leben und Werk* (Stuttgart: Kohlhamer, 2004), 140.

period.[101] Here, the selection was motivated by the tradition. It is also clear that the liturgical year has a significant influence on the selection and the understanding of the biblical texts.

The sanctoral lectionary looks for pericopes that are as appropriate as possible to the life of a saint.[102] The selection follows a number of principles. In the case of biblical saints, a choice is made from the passages in which they are mentioned,[103] and/or one reads from their own writings. It frequently occurs that a reading about a biblical figure draws attention to details or contexts of which one is otherwise less conscious.[104] On Marian feasts in both West and East, in addition to the Gospels or Letters of Paul that mention her, readings are also taken from the Old Testament or from the Revelation of John. These are interpreted typologically with reference to Mary.[105]

For postbiblical saints, the choice often fell on passages that the saints had lived in a particularly exemplary manner, so that the saints bear witness to the continued impact of the scriptural message in their lifetime. In this way, the saints can appear as interpreters of a pericope that they explain or illustrate through the testimony of their own lives. This can be a matter of individual verses (e.g., Maximilian Kolbe [† 1941]: "No one has greater love than this, to lay down one's life for one's friends")[106] or of basic

---

101 See *PLA*, 77.

102 The quality of the selection is variable, especially when little is known for certain about the life of a saint. Before the Council, when no proper readings were available, recourse was very frequently to texts from the Common. On this point, the renewed lectionary is a genuine improvement. Nevertheless, some pericopes occur relatively frequently. – The following examples are taken from the Roman rite. On the Ambrosian sanctoral lectionary, see Magnoli, "Lezionario a norma," 260–64; *PLA*, 83.

103 See, e.g., Saint Peter (2/22; 6/29 on the day): "You are Peter, the rock …" (Mt 16:13–19); Saint Andrew (11/30): the calling of the first disciples (Mt 4:18–22). On memorials, a reading can be prescribed if this is a text proper to the day.

104 See, e.g., Saints Timothy and Titus (1/26) with the biographical or personal information in 2 Tim 1:1–8 or Titus 1:1–5.

105 According to Getcha, "Système des lectures," 30, 52–53, the typological selection occurs in the Byzantine lectionary especially on Marian feasts. His examples are the pericope about the ladder between heaven and earth (Gn 28:10–17), the burning bush (Ex 3:1–8), or the closed gate of the Temple (Ez 43:27–44:4), as well as the story of Martha and Mary (Lk 10:38–42), both of whom are types of the Mother of God. In the Roman rite too, especially in the lectionary for Masses of the Virgin Mary, the selection can be typologically motivated. In addition to the schema "promise – fulfillment" (e.g., Is 7:14), an interesting salvation-historical framework is sometimes opened up: cf. the use of Ex 19:3–8a (v. 8a: "Everything the Lord has said, we will do") in the Mass formula "Our Lady of Cana" in combination with Jn 2:1–11, esp. v. 5: "Do whatever he tells you."

106 Jn 15:13.

characteristics of a saint (e.g., John Bosco [† 1888]: "Rejoice in the Lord! [...] Your kindness should be known to all"; Jesus "called a child over and placed it in their midst").[107] Sometimes, passages are chosen that inspired and influenced the saints themselves; when these texts are read, in a certain sense, the saint keeps instructing today's hearers (e.g., Ignatius of Loyola [† 1556]: "Do everything for the glory of God").[108] At times, the readings have a reference to the writings of a saint (e.g., Ignatius of Antioch [†108]: the grain of wheat).[109] Another principle projects biblical persons onto a saint (e.g., Mary of Bethany onto Scholastica [† 542][110] or Peter onto popes),[111] or similar scenes from Scripture onto the *vita* of a saint (or one episode from it; see Monica [†387]: the story of the widow of Nain – "Do not weep! [...] Young man, I tell you, arise!" – echoed in the words of a bishop to Monica, "A son of so many tears cannot be lost").[112] One can observe something similar in the Byzantine liturgy, when on the feast of John Chrysostom († 402) the readings portray Christ, the high priest (Heb 7:26–8:2) and good shepherd *par excellence* (Jn 10:9–16), as the model of the Church's pastors, thereby implicitly affirming that the saint worked in a manner similar to Christ.[113]

These examples make it clear that the readings for postbiblical saints manifest a fundamental concern of the liturgical proclamation of Scripture: God's Word is translated into the dimension of life. The readings do not attest only to God's action in biblical times. In the focus on the saints who have actualized in their own lives the selected pericopes, the readings attest above all the continuing effect of this Word down through the ages. They show how salvation with its biblical foundation becomes effective in concrete persons,[114] thereby underlining the performative character of the Word of God.[115]

---

107 Phil 4:4–9; Mt 18:1–5.

108 1 Cor 10:31.

109 See Jn 12:24–26 and Ignatius, *To the Romans* 4.1–2; 6.1-8.3 (*Liturgy of the Hours*, 4:1490-92).

110 See Lk 10:38–42.

111 Cf. Jn 21:1, 15–17 for Fabian, Pius V, and Pius X; and Mt 16:13–19 for Silvester, Gregory VII, Leo the Great, and Clement.

112 See Augustine, *Confessions* 3.12.21; cf. 6.1.1; Lk 7:11–19.

113 These are also the Common readings for pastors of the Church.

114 See Hansjörg Auf der Maur, "Feste und Gedenktage der Heiligen," in *Feiern im Rhythmus der Zeit II/1*, ed. P. Harnoncourt and H. Auf der Maur, GdK 6,1 (Regensburg: Pustet, 1994), 267: "The feasts of the saints point, on the basis of particular saints, to the mystery of salvation as the origin of their holiness, and celebrate the concrete impact made by this mystery."

115 See B.VIII.28.3.

A thematic selection of readings is also made on the so-called devotional/idea feasts (e.g., the feasts of the Trinity, Corpus Christi, the Sacred Heart of Jesus, Christ the King, etc.). The Votive Masses, the Masses for Various Needs and Occasions, and the Masses for the Dead also have appropriate readings, which in the last case speak of the Resurrection of Christ or Christian hope. However, Rome has opposed efforts to secure the introduction of further thematic feasts (such as "Christ the Worker"),[116] and Coetus XI, which was responsible for the order of readings, has stated its fundamental opposition to a thematization of the readings for catechetical or other purposes[117] since the Liturgy is always the celebration of the entire Paschal Mystery. The Bible must not be reduced to a quarry for specific themes.

Another criterion of selection in the Byzantine order of readings (and in the past also in the Roman order of pericopes, especially during Lent)[118] comes from the sites of the old stational liturgy. For example, on the second Monday of the Easter season, the miracle of Cana (Jn 2:1–11) is read, which one would have expected to hear on Thursday of the first week. It is clear that the Gospels of these two days were exchanged in order to highlight the intercession of the Mother of God in the Chalkoprateia church in Constantinople, which was dedicated to her.[119]

The selection of a reading also involves the question of the length of a pericope, that is, where it begins and ends, and whether verses are omitted.[120] Such omissions are undertaken for "pastoral reasons," either to prevent a pericope from becoming too long (otherwise, a pericope would perhaps have had to be omitted completely) or to avoid difficulties in comprehension.[121]

The Byzantine order of readings has developed in some places a greater "freedom" in the selection. In some cases, one can no longer speak of omissions in the pericopes, but rather of combinations of passages taken from various chapters of the same Book (centonization, from *cento*, "patchwork"). This occurs especially in the Liturgy of the Hours—on the Feast of the Birth

---

116 See Hansjörg Auf der Maur, *Feiern im Rhythmus der Zeit 1. Herrenfeste in Woche und Jahr*, GdK 5 (Regensburg: Pustet, 1983), 221.

117 See Nübold, *Perikopenordnung*, 365-66 with n. 130.

118 See Hartman Grisar, *Das Missale im Lichte römischer Stadtgeschichte. Stationen, Perikopen, Gebräuche* (Freiburg/Br.: Herder, 1925), 19-35.

119 See Getcha, "Système des lectures," 30, 42-43, 51; John F. Baldovin, *The Urban Character of Christian Worship. The Origins, Development and Meaning of Stational Liturgy*, OCA 228 (Rome: Pontificium Institutum Orientalium, 1987), 154-57, 240-41, 251.

120 See Renato L. De Zan, "Bible and Liturgy," in *Introduction to the Liturgy*, vol. 1 of *Handbook for Liturgical Studies*, ed. A. J. Chupungco (Collegeville: Liturgical Press, 1997), 46-47.

121 See *GILM*, 76-77.

of John the Baptist, for example, the reading at Vespers consists of Is 40:1–3, 9; 41:17–18; 45:8; 48:20–21; 54:1—but is also found in the Divine Liturgy.[122] Combinations of parallel passages to a Gospel are prescribed in Holy Week, e.g., when on Holy Thursday the Gospel of Matthew is expanded through the washing of the feet (Jn 13:3–17) and the prayer on the Mount of Olives (Lk 22:43–45).[123] Clearly, with the same cycle of readings recurring every year, there was a wish to take account of the passages proper to other evangelists. However, the Gospel harmonies, such as the Diatessaron of Tatian († after 172), have an ambivalent role with regard to the liturgical proclamation of Scripture, given the existence of the canonical (and hence authoritative) Bible with its own structure and with the theological accents of the individual Books.

---

122 For example, on the feast of the Great Martyr Procopius: Lk 6:17–19; 9:1; 10:16–22.

123 Cf. Mt 26:1–20; Jn 13:3–17; Mt 26:21–39; Lk 22:43–45; Mt 26:40–27:2. See the similar procedure on Good Friday: Mt 27:1–38; Lk 23:39–43; Mt 27:39–54; Jn 19:31–37; Mt 27:55–61, or at the Orthros of the Great Saturday: 1 Cor 5:6–8; Gal 3:13–14.

CHAPTER FOUR

The Readings in the Celebration of the Sacraments

S ince the liturgical reform of the Second Vatican Council, the proclamation of the Word of God is an integral dimension of the celebration of
the sacraments too. The *Rituale Romanum* of 1614,[124] and most diocesan
rituals down to the *Collectio Rituum* (Germany: 1950; US: 1954), scarcely
envisaged scriptural readings at these celebrations. Now, however, a specific
Liturgy of the Word and a list of alternative readings are provided. It is only
at the celebration of the reconciliation of individual penitents (confession)
that the reading of Scripture is optional. As a matter of principle, *Verbum
Domini* 61 underlines the importance of Sacred Scripture for the sacraments,
especially in the sacraments of reconciliation and the Anointing of the Sick,
where Scripture is often neglected. We shall now explore the readings for the
Anointing of the Sick in the Roman and the Byzantine rites and examine
their function and the theological affirmations they make.

We choose the Anointing of the Sick because of the reference to it in
Verbum Domini but above all because the Byzantine rite prescribes a large
number of readings, which form an adequate basis for a comparison with
the choice of readings in the Roman rite today. Since the methodological
approach of the present study seeks to establish a dialogue between "eastern
and western rites" (*SC* 24) with regard to their use of Scripture, we choose a
sacramental celebration that offers sufficient texts for comparison.

A second argument for the choice of the Anointing of the Sick is the
breadth of the liturgical use of Scripture that this study seeks to cover. This

---

124 Cf. *Rituale Romanum. Editio Princeps (1614). Edizione anastatica, Introduzione e Appendice*, ed. M. Sodi and J. J. Flores Arcas, MLCT 5 (Vatican City: Libreria Editrice Vaticana,
2004), esp. 439. In the history of liturgy, the lack of a proclamation of Scripture (for example)
at Baptism is probably due to the separation of Baptism from the Easter Vigil with its own
Liturgy of the Word. This meant that Baptism had no readings of its own.

means that, if possible, all the sacraments should be discussed. The Eucharist has already been discussed by means of the order of readings at Mass and it will be addressed again with reference to the Communion antiphons.[125] Ordination will be discussed when we look at the prayers, and Baptism when we delve into the signs and actions.[126] An adequate comparison is impossible in the case of Confirmation, because the anointing with Myron (Chrism) takes place at Baptism, and thus has no specific readings of its own.[127] We only touch on the celebration of Penance because, as we have mentioned, the reading of Scripture in individual confession is optional, and a celebration in common is not suitable for comparison. We choose the Anointing of the Sick rather than the celebration of Matrimony[128] because of the Byzantine program of readings, since this contributes more to our investigation of a biblical hermeneutics.

1. THE READINGS IN THE CELEBRATION OF THE ANOINTING OF THE SICK

It is well known that the central foundational passage for the Anointing of the Sick is found in James 5:14-15, which always has a prominent place in the introductory rites in today's Roman celebration. What the Bible formulates, takes place in this celebration: "Are there any who are sick among you? Let them send for the priests of the Church, and let the priests pray over them, anointing them with oil in the name of the Lord; and the prayer of faith will save the sick persons, and the Lord will raise them up; and if they have committed any sins, their sins will be forgiven them."[129] The verbs in verse 15 (save, raise up, forgive) are taken up in the sacramental formula of the anointing.[130] The introductory rites make it clear that the ensuing

---

125 See A.IV.15.

126 See A.III.11 and A.V.

127 See the brief remarks in B.VIII.29.1.

128 See the brief remarks in B.VIII.29.1.

129 *The Rites of the Catholic Church as Revised by the Second Vatican Ecumenical Council*, prepared by International Commission on English in the Liturgy, 2 vols. (New York: Pueblo, 1990–91), 1:820.

130 See Charles W. Gusmer, *And You Visited Me: Sacramental Ministry to the Sick and the Dying* (Collegeville, MN: Pueblo, 1990), 7-11.

administering of the sacrament is linked to Sacred Scripture, to the early praxis of the Church, and to the commission given by the Lord.[131]

The following Liturgy of the Word seeks the most suitable pericope possible. The intention is not merely to communicate the historical information that Jesus showed his care for the sick in a comparable situation in the past. Rather, the Word of God is proclaimed as a *present* Word, so that Jesus' work of healing is made present in the one who receives the anointing. The first text suggested in the ritual is Mt 11:25-30, "Come to me, all you who labor and are burdened." The sense is that with these words, Jesus is addressing the sick person directly: they are an invitation to entrust oneself to the Lord. The reading appositely addresses the physical and emotional suffering of the sick person, and the promise—"I will give you rest"—is now made to the one who receives the sacrament. In the third option, the rite emphasizes the anamnetic understanding: "The healing hand of Christ is a sign of the presence of God; that same hand is extended to us in this sacrament now, to console and strengthen us."[132]

The ritual and the Mass lectionary contain a large number of pericopes that can be chosen for the Anointing of the Sick.[133] Some describe Jesus' healing of concrete persons; others present this in a general form or in prophetic announcements; others again speak of Jesus' charge to the disciples to take care of the sick, and pericopes from the Acts of the Apostles illustrate how the disciples carry out this task by healing "in the name of the Lord." Still other pericopes do not speak of illness, but describe the working of God or of Christ, in order to kindle the faith and trust that are important for a fruitful reception of the sacrament. Other readings speak of the suffering of the Servant of the Lord and of the union between the sick person and the suffering Christ or apostle, in order to show that he or she is not alone in this situation. Other pericopes seek to offer spiritual help to the sick for understanding their illness. Two readings speak of Christian *caritas* (Mt 25:31-40, "I was ill and you cared for me"; Lk 10:25-37: the Good Samaritan) and address the family more than the individual who is sick. Suitable readings are proposed for the situation of dying persons. These offer consolation and hope in view of eternal life. Four texts from Job bring lamentation to God.

---

131 The introductory rites present the words from the Letter of James as words of Christ himself: "Through the apostle James, he [Christ] has commanded us ..." (*Rites*, 1:820).

132 *Rites*, 1:822.

133 See *Rites*, 1:896-904.

Let us now look at the Byzantine liturgy of the Sick, the *euchelaion* (literally: "oil of prayer").[134] In the course of the historical development of the rite, the number of scriptural readings was repeatedly expanded,[135] until seven pairs of readings (Apostolos and Gospel) were established from the thirteenth century onward. In the full form, these belong to the anointings carried out by seven priests.[136] In the context of the present study, it is above all interesting to note that different Gospels were provided as options for men and women. For example, a Middle-Byzantine patriarchal Gospel book from the eleventh or twelfth century gives the choice between the healing of the royal official's son (Jn 4:46-54) for men and the healing of Peter's mother-in-law (Mt 8:14-23) for women.[137] This made it easier for the sick person to identify with the character in the Gospel and to transpose Jesus' healing to one's own self. This is an indicator of an anamnetic understanding of Sacred Scripture: just as, in the past, Jesus cared for the sick person, so he does this now in the celebration of the Anointing of the Sick.

An optional possibility of this kind in accordance with gender has not survived in today's seven pairs of readings, which we find from the fourteenth century in Greek euchologies (printing eliminated local differences in the readings).[138] However, both women and men appear in the readings. In practice, only one priest administers the anointing, so that usually only the first pair of readings is taken. In other places, the prayers are abbreviated so that time is left for the seven pairs of readings.[139] The combination allows us to discern a biblical theology of the Anointing of the Sick.

---

134 See Paul Meyendorff, *The Anointing of the Sick*, Orthodox Liturgy Series 1 (New York: SVS Press, 2009); Rosso, *Celebrazione*, 413-40.

135 On the liturgical history of the Byzantine anointing of the sick, see Tinatin Chrontz, *Die Feier des Heiligen Öles nach Jerusalemer Ordnung mit dem Text des slavischen Codex Hilferding 21 der Russischen Nationalbibliothek in Sankt Petersburg sowie georgischen Übersetzungen palästinischer und konstantinopolitanischer Quellen. Einführung – Edition – Kommentar*, JThF 18 (Münster: Aschendorff, 2012), 37-64, on the scriptural readings 362-77. See Stefano Parenti, "Care and Anointing of the Sick in the East," in *Sacraments and Sacramentals*, vol. 4 of *Handbook for Liturgical Studies*, ed. A. J. Chupungco (Collegeville, MN: Liturgical Press, 2000), 161-69; Meyendorff, *Anointing*, 31-62.

136 See Chronz, *Feier des Heiligen Öles*, 371, 376-77. According to James 5:14 too, a sick person is to summon "the presbyters" (plural) of the community. The participation by seven priests probably has its origin in a privilege of the aristocracy (cf. Chronz, 45-46).

137 See Chronz, 368-69, 371-75.

138 See Chronz, 374, 376.

139 See Bert Groen, "Die Krankensalbung im orthodoxen Griechenland," *LJ* 45, no. 3 (1995): 179.

	Apostolos (A)	Gospel (G)
1	Jas 5:10–16: Patience, if anyone is sick, let him summon the elders; prayers; anointing with oil	Lk 10:25–27: Good Samaritan (as a type of Christ / oil)
2	Rom 15:1–7: "We who are strong ought to put up with the failings of the weak"; patience and consolation: Christ too did not live for himself; mutual acceptance	Lk 19:1–10: Zacchaeus: "Today salvation has come to this house."
3	1 Cor 12:27-13:8: gift of healing; hymn in praise of love	Mt 10:1, 5–10 (or 5–8): the disciples are sent out to heal the sick
4	2 Cor 6:16-7:1: striving for perfect sanctification	Mt 8:14–23: healing of Peter's mother-in-law and of other possessed and sick persons (with Is 53:4: "He bore our diseases"); words about discipleship
5	2 Cor 1:8–11: Paul is rescued from "the sentence of death"; exhortation to prayer and to trust in God	Mt 25:13: parable of the ten virgins (oil): exhortation to vigilance; promise of the heavenly wedding feast
6	Gal 5:25-6:2: life by the Spirit; in cases of misconduct, bring people gently to the right path	Mt 15:21–28: Insistent request of the Canaanite woman: "Great is your faith!"
7	1 Thes 5:14–23: Support the weak. Rejoice. Pray. Give thanks. "May the God of peace himself make you perfectly holy and may you entirely, spirit, soul, and body, be preserved blameless for the coming of our Lord Jesus Christ."	Mt 9:9–13: The calling of Matthew: "Those who are well do not need a physician, but the sick do." Jesus "did not come to call the righteous but sinners."

We shall not comment on the individual pericopes, but only point out the clusters of motifs found in more than one reading. While obviously healings by Jesus and his commission to the disciples to heal are read (G3/G4/G6/A1/A3), health is understood in a broader sense which includes the forgiveness of sins (G2/G7/A4/A6/A7), so that the focus is on both physical and spiritual healing. There are also striking pericopes that mention oil and thereby establish a link to the anointing (A1/G1/G5). The Good Samaritan, who cleanses the wounds of the injured man with oil and wine[140] and binds them up, appears here, drawing on the patristic interpretation,[141] as a type of Christ (G1). This makes it clear that it is Christ himself who acts for the sick person through the anointing by the priests. Some pericopes kindle trust in Christ's loving care (G1/G2/G4) and exhort to prayer (G6/A1/A5), vigilance (G5), and the correct following of Christ (G1/G4); there is no narrow concentration in the readings on the hour of death. The readings that speak of the duty to take care of the weak are addressed to the fellowship of the Church and to the family members (A2/A6/A7). The scriptural readings thus generate an interpretative framework for the celebration and the understanding of the sacrament. The sinfulness and the request for forgiveness that are in the foreground in the Anointing of the Sick, which all participants in the service on Wednesday in Holy Week receive, is more strongly emphasized in the prayers than in the readings, but without reducing the focus to this aspect.[142] The *de facto* extension of the Anointing of the Sick to the forgiveness of sins, with the prayer of absolution at the end of the celebration. The emphasis in the East (also in the Eastern Churches united to Rome)[143] on spiritual healing, and likewise the narrowing down of the Anointing of the Sick to the sacrament of the dying ("extreme unction") in the West, cannot— and could not—be inferred either from the readings or from the texts of the prayers. Both of these have their origin in the historical development of pastoral care and of dogma.[144] While this shows the limited influence of the scriptural texts, it also shows their critical or corrective function[145] and their necessary contribution to the correct understanding of the sacrament of the Anointing of the Sick.

---

140 Before the *euchelaion*, a vessel of oil is to be made ready on a table before the icons of Christ and of the Mother of God. Oil and wine are poured into this vessel – a clear reference to the Good Samaritan; see Reiner Kaczynski, "Die Feier der Krankensalbung," in *Sakramentliche Liturgie*, ed. R. Meßner and R. Kaczynski, GdK 7/2 (Regensburg: Pustet, 1992), 318.

141 Cf. Origen, *In Lucam homiliae* 34.3 (FontC 4/2:338); Chronz, *Feier des Heiligen Öles*, 38 with n. 2.

142 Sin is seen as a sickness of the soul. Since all have sinned (see Rom 3:23), all need healing, and this is why they can receive the anointing of the sick. See Meyendorff, *Anointing*, 56, 68, 92, 98-101. In practice, this often leads to the anointing being understood as a replacement of confession (see Meyendorff, 56, 92, 101-03).

143 On the differentiation between Greek and Slav praxis, and their coalescence when they are adopted by the Orthodox Christians who live in the West (Europe, America): Meyendorff, 56-61.

144 On the West, see Kaczynski, "Krankensalbung," 274-97, esp. 274, 281-85.

145 Cf. B.VIII.26.

2. BIBLICAL-HERMENEUTICAL REFLECTIONS

What we have said about the Anointing of the Sick can be applied to other sacramental celebrations too. This leads to fundamental reflections on a liturgical hermeneutics of the Bible. The sacraments indicate in a particular way that God's salvific action, as attested to in the Bible, continues and can be experienced through the ministry of the Church. The reading from Scripture not only proclaims this—it also has an anamnetic function that aims to make salvation present.[146] The Liturgy of the Word in the celebrations of the sacraments also opens our eyes to the important common bond between Scripture and sacrament and to their inherent relatedness.[147]

Besides this, the optional readings give the individual an access to Scripture that is related to one's specific situation and show that it is relevant to one's own life, since one's own circumstances are linked to the revelation of God. The treasury of experience in Scripture gives help for the orientation and the interpretation of one's own life. While the optional readings indicate only special aspects, and hence various theological motifs (e.g., in the case of Baptism, Rom 6:3–5 [dying and rising with Christ] and Jn 3:1–6 ["born of water and the Spirit"]), the total corpus of the suggested readings articulates a theology of each sacrament, which the other texts of the liturgical celebration complement. The optional readings thus demonstrate the inherent link between access to Scripture and the reception of Scripture through liturgy.[148] These reflections on the sacramental celebrations can also be applied *mutatis mutandis* to the sacramentals.

---

146 Cf. B.VIII.27.

147 Cf. B.VIII.29.

148 See B.VI; B.IX.

CHAPTER FIVE

The Readings in the Celebration of the Liturgy of the Hours

After looking at the celebration of the Mass and the sacraments, we shall now consider the (Roman) Liturgy of the Hours, which is profoundly marked by the Word of God. It is the Church's "prayer of praise and supplication," "enriched with readings."[149] In the early traces of the Liturgy of the Hours, it is possible that the readings were adopted by the cathedral form only because of influence from monasticism,[150] but today they are an indispensable element. Through the postconciliar liturgical reform, the readings in the Liturgy of the Hours too were improved both quantitatively and qualitatively.[151] In what follows, our concern will not be with the principles of selection, since this was discussed with reference to the Mass, and scarcely any significantly new perspectives emerge here. But the differentiation between the short and the long readings[152] is a striking difference from the eucharistic celebration and has hermeneutical consequences.

---

149 *GILH*, 2.

150 See Rolf Zerfaß, *Die Schriftlesung im Kathedraloffizium Jerusalems*, LQF 48 (Münster: Aschendorff, 1968), 14, 40-43, 54-55, 177; Rolf Zerfaß, "Die Rolle der Lesung im Stundengebet," *LJ* 13, no. 3 (1963): 161-63.

151 See *SC* 89; 92; Emil Joseph Lengeling, "Liturgia Horarum. Die Lesungen und Responsorien im neuen Stundegebet," *LJ* 20, no. 4 (1970): 231-49.

152 We find such a distinction already in the Rule of Benedict: The short readings were to be pronounced "memoriter" (9.3) or "ex corde" (13.11), that is to say, from memory or by heart, whereas the readings at the Vigils were read from the lectern ("in codice super analogium," 9.5). See Angelus A. Häußling, "Verkündigung in den Tageshoren," *LJ* 13, no. 2 (1963): 92; *WEC* 4:28-29.

1. THE READINGS OF THE OFFICE OF READINGS

The first aim of the readings in the Office of Readings is to complement the readings of the Mass and make us familiar with the Bible in its entire breadth. For this reason, a two-year cycle was envisaged for this Office, but reasons of space meant that it was compressed into a one-year cycle in the Latin *editio typica* of the *Liturgia Horarum*. The intention was to publish the two-year cycle in an additional volume, which however has not yet happened. The lectionary fascicles of the German-language Office have adopted the two-year order of readings. "Passages from the Old Testament books are chosen for their greater importance in the understanding of the history of salvation and for their devotional value."[153] The New Testament is read (almost) completely[154] each year in the Mass and the Liturgy of the Hours. In keeping with tradition, the reading of the Gospel is reserved to the Mass.[155] The primary goal is thus to broaden the knowledge of Scripture, and passages were included that found no place in the *OLM* either because of their length or because of difficulties of comprehension.[156] In some cases, the familiar Mass readings, which are kept as brief as possible and are often detached from their immediate context, are read in the Office of Readings in the context of the Book as a whole. This contributes to a better understanding of the Mass texts.

The above quotation from *GILH* 146 speaks not only of the didactic function, but also of a spiritual function that is repeatedly emphasized in this document: "the treasuries of revelation [1st reading] and tradition [2nd reading] contained in the Office of Readings greatly assist spiritual progress."[157] If the intention of the readings from the fathers and Church writers, which are often related to the preceding reading, are thus meant to promote meditation on the Word of God,[158] one can also attribute a meditative function

---

153 *GILH*, 146.

154 See B.IX.35.1.

155 See Angelus A. Häußling, "Die Bibel in der Liturgie der Tagzeiten," in *Präsenz der Schrift im Frühmittelalter*, ed. P. Carmassi, Wolfenbütteler Mittelalter-Studien 20 (Wiesbaden: Harrassowitz, 2008), 312–15. While the preconciliar breviary included 13.9 % of the Old Testament and 33.5 % of the New Testament, 38.6 % of the Old Testament is now present: 33.9 % of the Pentateuch, 31.2 % of the other historical books, 40 % of the sapiential books, and 52.3 % of the prophets (see Lengeling, "Liturgia Horarum," 232, 236–37).

156 See *GILH*, 146.

157 *GILH*, 55.

158 See *GILH*, 163–64.

to the scriptural readings themselves[159] because their content is not simply registered as information, but is reflected upon in the presence of God. This meditative component stems above all from the integration of the scriptural reading into prayer, so that each bears fruit in the other.[160] The readings of the Office of Readings also have a pastoral goal: "Priests especially should explore these riches. They will then be able to teach everyone the word of God they themselves have received and make their doctrine 'the food of the people of God.'"[161] The fundamental anamnetic function of the reading of Scripture, which is important in the Liturgy, is not in the foreground in the Office of Readings, but it is just as much present there, because (especially in the great seasons of the year) God's saving activity, to which the readings bear witness, continues today.

2. THE SHORT READINGS

We must draw a distinction between the readings in the Office of Readings and the nearly five hundred short readings not only because of their brevity, but also in terms of their function. In keeping with the Ignatian dictum *non multa, sed multum,* the point here is not knowledge of the breadth of Scripture, but rather savoring its spiritual depth. It is an invitation to let oneself be permeated existentially by a word of God. The *GILH* states: "it emphasizes certain short passages which may receive less attention in the continuous reading of the scriptures."[162] Precisely its brevity can allow those who pray to experience its message as addressed directly to them, so that it makes an impact. In particular, the link to the time of day (e.g., in morning prayer: "It is now the hour for you to wake from sleep …")[163] or a temporal reference to daily life (e.g., at the beginning of work on Monday: "we urge them strongly in the name of the Lord Jesus Christ to earn their food by working quietly")[164] gives a word of Scripture additional concreteness. The repetition gradually imprints it on the one who prays; it is joined to various moods and experiences and can thus speak anew each time it is

---

159 See B.VIII.26.d.

160 See *GILH*, 140.

161 *GILH*, 55; cf. 165.

162 *GILH*, 45.

163 See Lauds on Tuesday of the 1st week (Rom 13:11b-13a), with an additional connotation when this text is read on the four Sundays of Advent.

164 See Lauds on Monday of the 1st week (2 Thes 3:10–12).

read. According to *GILH* 45, the short reading "is to be read and heard as the true proclamation of the word of God."

The proclamation of the message of salvation—of what God/Christ has done for the human being—lets us perceive above all an anamnetic function. This applies especially to the great seasons of the year. But even in Ordinary Time, the readings on Fridays and to some extent on Sundays also make present (more or less clearly) the paschal mystery of Christ. It is, however, difficult to describe in isolation the functions of the short reading, since this is always correlated to the content of the texts and more than one function is involved. Scriptural passages with a directive for conduct are often chosen, above all in Ordinary Time, usually accompanied by an encouragement, so that the short readings provide an inspiration for the day and have a paraenetic intention. The short readings also further one's spiritual edification. Together with the silence that follows them[165] and the responsory, they deepen the meditative function that has already been mentioned in connection with the Office of Readings and that leads from the scriptural text into prayer. Directly doxological short readings also exist.[166]

One who prays with knowledge and attentiveness will hear more than what is written in the few verses or words, because they evoke further connotations. Let us take one example at random, the short reading from Ezekiel 34:31, "You, my sheep, you are the sheep of my pasture, and I am your God, says the Lord God."[167] This can remind us of Psalm 23, of the activity of the good shepherd in Ezekiel 34, of Jesus' parable of the Good Shepherd that he himself is in John 10, and of similar passages. This, of course, presupposes familiarity with Scripture.

---

165 See *GILH*, 202.

166 See, as one prominent example, Rom 11:33–36 in the First Vespers on Sunday of the 1st week in Ordinary Time. See also Am 4:13; 5:8; 9:6 in the Little Hours on Thursday of the 1st week.

167 See None on Monday of the 2nd week.

CHAPTER SIX

Hermeneutical Insights

At the end of each section of Part A, we shall note the results of our investigation and the hermeneutical insights gained, briefly noting once again some perspectives attained from the what we have examined. These will form the basis for Part B, where we will reflect on and systematically develop them.

Our study of the order of readings of the Mass drew attention to the relatedness both of the individual texts (intertextuality)[168] and of the two Testaments (unity of Scripture).[169] In particular, the Milanese (Ambrosian) lectionary displays various possibilities of combining texts, each of which has hermeneutical consequences. Naturally, every preliminary theological decision has advantages and disadvantages, and excludes other principles. It is a good idea to pay attention to the reception of Sacred Scripture by the faithful[170] as well as to homiletic aspects. Besides this, the first section demonstrated the importance of the liturgical year, or of the specific celebration, for the selection and interpretation of the pericopes. The liturgical context functions as a hermeneutical key (so to speak) to the reading from Scripture.[171]

As we have seen several times in this section, the biblically attested working of God or Christ becomes present in the liturgical celebration through the proclamation of Scripture and is thus actualized and perpetuated. The identification with persons who act in Scripture plays an important role here.[172] It has become clear that the anamnesis of salvation is a fundamental

---

168 See B.VII.23.

169 See B.VIII.30.

170 See B.IX.

171 See B.VII.(23).

172 See B.IX.34.

dimension of the liturgical use of Scripture.[173] This also finds theological expression in the close union between Word and sacrament.[174] In addition to the didactic function of the readings, the meditative, the paraenetic, and also the corrective functions of such proclamation have emerged.[175]

We have touched on several kinds of access to Scripture that are mediated by the Liturgy: through the liturgical year (e.g., Lent as an accompanying of Christ to his dying and rising), through a biographical situation in the celebration of the sacrament, through the examples of the saints who illustrate a pericope in exemplary fashion with their lives, or through the repetition of identical scriptural texts (e.g., in the short readings in the Liturgy of the Hours), which creates familiarity.[176] It has become clear that Scripture is a spiritual resource in which experiences and models of faith are "stored up." These can be "called up" through the celebration of liturgy, so that they can be put into practice in life and can strengthen one's own identity in faith.[177]

173 See B.VIII.27.
174 See B.VIII.29.
175 See B.VIII.26.
176 See B.VI.21.
177 See B.IX.36.

SECTION II
The Psalms

The Psalms play an important role in the Liturgy, since, on the one hand, they are a word of the human being to God or in the presence of God; and, on the other hand, they are God's Word to the human being. This means that a divine-human dialogue unfolds in the Psalms, which also belongs to the essence of the Liturgy. They thus seem predestined for use in worship. In the Psalms, human beings bring their own situation to God—anabatically, that is, in an upward motion. They are "theo-poetry,"[1] a poetic expression of human life *coram Deo*, "in the presence of God." The variety of psalms reflects the variety of daily human experience: joy and suffering, good health and sickness, praise and petition, lamentation and thanksgiving, guilt and repentance, closeness to God and distance from God.

All this is found in the Psalms both as the experience of the individual and collectively as the experience of the people of Israel. Despite the foreignness of some expressions and existential contexts, indeed despite the unaccustomed way in which the Psalms relate everything to God as a matter

---

1 Erich Zenger, "'Du thronst auf den Psalmen Israels' (Ps 22,4). Von der Unverzichtbarkeit der jüdischen Psalmen im christlichen Wortgottesdienst," in *Wie das Wort Gottes feiern? Der Wortgottesdienst als theologische Herausforderung*, ed. B. Kranemann and T. Sternberg, QD 194 (Freiburg/Br.: Herder, 2002), 18-25.

of course,[2] their language is concrete and true to life, and open to a variety of actualizations, so that one can often discover oneself in them. When one repeats them again and again, the Psalms can help one pray or stand before God, even if not every psalm is addressed to God or is directly prayer.[3] For Christians, praying the Psalms is also rooted in the praxis of Jesus, who himself made the words of the Psalms his own. The existential reference is surely one basic reason for their popularity, as (for example) Athanasius (†373) underlines in his letter to Marcellinus:

> He who takes up this book—the Psalter—goes through the prophecies about the Savior as is customary in the other Scriptures, with admiration and adoration, but the other psalms he recognizes as being his own words. And the one who hears is deeply moved, as though he himself were speaking, and is affected by the words of the songs, as if they were his own songs [...], if they were written concerning him. [...T]hese words become like a mirror to the person singing them, so that he might perceive himself and the emotions of his soul, and thus affected, he might recite them.[4]
>
> For I believe that the whole of human existence, both the dispositions of the soul and the movement of the thoughts, have been measured out and encompassed in those very words of the Psalter. And nothing beyond these is found among men. [...] For any such eventuality he has instruction in the divine psalms.[5]

In the same letter, we also find the katabatic dimension: the Psalter is God's Word. It is a "miniature Bible" with many references within Sacred Scripture as a whole.[6]

> Yet the Book of Psalms is like a garden containing things of all these kinds, and it sets them to music.[7] [...] In this way the Book of Psalms, possessing the characteristic feature of the songs, itself chants those things in modulated voice that have been said in the other books in the form of detailed narrative. [...And sometimes at least, it also legislates: Cease from anger

---

2 See Zenger, 20.

3 See Adalbert de Vogüé, "Psalmodier n'est pas prier," *EO* 6 (1989): 7–32.

4 *Athanasius. The Life of Antony and the Letter to Marcellinus*, trans. Robert C. Gregg (New York: Paulist, 1980), 109–11 (Chs. 11–12). The importance of this letter is illustrated by the fact that, as early as one century after it was written, it was prefixed to the Psalter in the Codex Alexandrinus.

5 Gregg, *Athanasius*, 126 (Ch. 30).

6 See Zenger, "Unverzichtbarkeit," 26.

7 Gregg, *Athanasius*, 102 (Ch. 2).

[…]. And it narrates at times about the journeying of Israel, and prophesies concerning the Savior.[8]

The admission of the Psalter to the Old Testament canon clearly testifies that it is not merely human poetry but is at the same time the divinely inspired Word of God. It is structured in five books in analogy to the Pentateuch. Christians adopted the canonical Psalter as Sacred Scripture,[9] and regarded it as their "favorite book": the Psalms are mentioned explicitly in the New Testament (e.g., Lk 24:44) and roughly one-third of all the Old Testament quotations are taken from them.[10]

Moreover, "the narrative New Testament Christology" is "to a large degree a Christology of the psalms."[11] Through the redaction of the Psalter, a prophetization, Davidization, and Messianization of the Psalter was already undertaken within the Old Testament, so that the path to a Christologization, and beyond that, to an ecclesial interpretation of the people of God, had already been indicated.[12] Since the Psalter did not function in contemporary Judaism as a book of hymns or prayers for the Temple (only some individual psalms were selected for this purpose) or for the synagogue, the early Christians probably followed Jewish praxis and used it primarily as a text for meditation.[13] It was probably only at the end of the second century that the psalms made their way into Christian liturgy.[14]

---

8 Gregg, *Athanasius*, 108 (Ch. 9).

9 See Notker Füglister, "Die Verwendung und das Verständnis der Psalmen und des Psalters um die Zeitenwende," in *Beiträge zur Psalmenforschung. Psalm 2 und 22*, ed. J. Schreiner, Forschung zur Bibel 60 (Würzburg: Echter, 1988), 352-54.

10 See Frank-Lothar Hossfeld and Erich Zenger, *Die Psalmen. Kommentar zum Alten Testament mit der Einheitsübersetzung: 1. Psalm 1-50*, Die neue Echter-Bibel. Altes Testament 23,1 (Würzburg: Echter, 1993), 8.

11 Zenger, "Unverzichtbarkeit," 24; see Georg Braulik, "Psalter und Messias. Zum christologischen Verständnis der Psalmen im Alten Testament und bei den Kirchenvätern," in Braulik und Lofink, *Liturgie und Bibel*, 481. One may recall here the use of the Psalms in the Letter to the Hebrews, of Ps 110 in Mt 22:44 par. and Mt 26:64 par., of Ps 22 in the passion narratives, or of the Psalms in Acts 2.

12 See Füglister, "Psalter um die Zeitenwende," 365-77; Braulik, "Psalter und Messias,"; Georg Braulik, "Christologisches Verständnis der Psalmen – schon im Alten Testament?," in *Christologie der Liturgie. Der Gottesdienst der Kirche – Christusbekenntnis und Sinaibund*, ed. K. Richter and B. Kranemann, QD 159 (Freiburg/Br.: Herder, 1995), 57-86.

13 See Füglister, "Psalmen um die Zeitenwende," esp. 329-34; Norbert Lohfink, "Psalmengebet und Psalterredkation," in Braulik and Lohfink, *Bibel und Liturgie*, 438-43.

14 See Lohfink, "Psalmengebet," 439-40; for evidence from the third century, see Harald Buchinger, "Die älteste erhaltene christliche Psalmenhomilie. Zu Verwendung und Verständnis des Psalters bei Hippolyt," *TThZ* 104, no. 4 (1995): 274-75.

A "Psalter renaissance" occurred especially after the Constantinian shift,[15] as Athanasius' letter (quoted above) and sermons by other Church Fathers attest.[16] The popularity of the Psalms that finds expression there also influenced their use in the Liturgy. Since heretics like Arius spread their erroneous doctrinal views through songs they themselves had composed, the provincial Synod of Laodicea (ca. 364) forbade such poems and henceforth admitted only the canonical books for use in the Liturgy.[17] This strengthened the importance of the Psalms.

In the present chapter, we shall analyze Psalm 24 in its diverse liturgical contexts in order to bring to light various hermeneutical implications. We shall then turn our attention to the Responsorial Psalm and to the psalms in the Liturgy of the Hours.

15 Zenger, "Unverzichtbarkeit," 18. See James McKinnon, "Desert Monasticism and the Later Fourth-Century Psalmodic Movement," in *The Temple, the Church Fathers and Early Western Chant*, ed. J. McKinnon, Variorum Collected Studies Series 606 (Aldershot: Ashgate, 1998), 505–21; Joseph Dyer, "The Desert, the City and Psalmody in the Late Fourth Century," in *Western Plainchant in the First Millennium. Studies in the Medieval Liturgy and its Music*, ed. S. Gallagher (Aldershot: Ashgate, 2003), 11–43.

16 See, e.g., Ambrose, *Explanatio in psalmum* 1.4-12 (CSEL 64:4-10; *Liturgy of the Hours*, 3:343–44). See Marie-Josèphe Rondeau, *Les commentaires patristiques du Psautier (IIIe-Ve siècles)*, 2 vols., OCA 219-20 (Rome: Pontificium Institutum Studiorum Orientalium, 1982, 1985); Hermann Josef Sieben, *Schlüssel zum Psalter. Sechzehn Kirchenvätereinführungen von Hippolyt bis Cassiodor* (Paderborn et al.: Schöningh, 2011).

17 See can. 59; Text: *Enchiridion biblicum. Documenta ecclesiastica sacram scripturam spectantia*, ed. The Pontifical Biblical Commission, 4th ed. (Naples: d'Auria, 1965), 6 (no. 11).

CHAPTER SEVEN

The Spectrum of Interpretation of the Psalms

The openness of the psalms to a variety of interpretations can be seen in liturgy too, because the liturgical context is an important contributor to their interpretation. We shall investigate this with regard to Psalm 24, because its use in both East and West (cf. *SC* 24) covers a wide spectrum.

1. THE VARIED LITURGICAL USE OF PSALM 24 (23)

¹The earth is the LORD's and all it holds,
the world and those who dwell in it.
²For he founded it on the seas,
established it over the rivers.
³Who may go up the mountain of the LORD?
Who can stand in his holy place?
⁴"The clean of hand and pure of heart,
who has not given his soul to useless things,
what is vain.
⁵He will receive blessings from the LORD,
and justice from his saving God.
⁶Such is the generation that seeks him,
that seeks the face of the God of Jacob." *Selah*
⁷Lift up your heads, O gates;
be lifted, you ancient portals,
that the king of glory may enter,
⁸Who is this king of glory?
The LORD, strong and mighty,
the LORD, mighty in war.

[9]Lift up your heads, O gates;
rise up, you ancient portals,
that the king of glory may enter,
[10]Who is this king of glory? The LORD of hosts, he is the king of glory.
Selah

The Psalm[18] consists of three parts, and this leads to differing usages in the Liturgy. Verses 1–2 form a hymnic introduction with the confession that YHWH is the creator and possessor of the earth. The section vv. 3–6 comprises the conditions of admission to the mountain of the Lord and thus is speaking about the human being. Vv. 7–10 describe YHWH's entrance into the sanctuary and the "liturgy at the gates."[19]

The patristic interpretations of Psalm 24 refer primarily to the last part. They recognize Christ in the "king of glory" and illustrate three mysteries of salvation depending on how they understand the gates: the Incarnation, the descent of Christ into the realm of the dead, and the Ascension.[20] This is reflected even today in the liturgical use of the psalm.

a) In the Context of Advent and Christmas

Psalm 24:1–6 is prescribed as the Responsorial Psalm on the 4th Sunday in Advent A and on December 20. The response "Let the Lord enter; he is king of glory" (see vv. 7c, 10b) is related to the proclamation of the birth of Immanuel (Is 7:14) in the first reading, and the futuristic formulation "Let …enter" is related to Advent. This means that the doors to be opened are

18 See Jerzy Seremak, *Psalm 24 als Text zwischen den Texten*, ÖBS 26 (Frankfurt/M: Peter Lang, 2004); Dieter Böhler, *Psalmen 1-50*, HThKAT (Freiburg/Br.: Herder, 2021), 438–58; Frank-Lothar Hossfeld and Erich Zenger, *Psalm 1-50*, 37-38, 156-61; on the contextualization of Ps 24 in the Psalter, Lohfink, "Psalmengebet und Psalterredaktion," 454-58.

19 Frank-Lothar Hossfeld and Erich Zenger, *Psalm 1-50*, 156-67.

20 See André Rose, "'Attolite portas, principes, vestras …'. Aperçus sur la lecture chrétienne du Ps. 24 (23) B," in *Miscellanea liturgica in onore di Sua Eminenza il Cardinale Giacomo Lercaro, arcivescovo di Bologna, presidente del "Consilium" per l'applicazione della costituzione sulla sacra liturgia*, ed. G. Bevilacqua, 2 vols., (Rome: Desclée de Brouwer, 1966), 1:458-68; André Rose, *Les psaumes. Voix du Christ et de l'Église*, Bible et vie chrétienne. Référence (Paris: Lethielleux, 1982), 63, 70-71, 78, 118-19, 128, 216; Christiana Reemts, "Psalm 23. Öffnet ihm die Tore," in *Die Psalmen bei den Kirchenvätern. Psalm 1-30*, ed. T. Heither and Ch. Reemts (Münster: Aschendorff, 2017), 361-373; Franz-Rudolf Weinart, *Christi Himmelfahrt, neutestamentliches Fest im Spiegel alttestamentlicher Psalmen. Zur Entstehung des römischen Himmelfahrtsoffiziums*, Diss.T 25 (St. Ottilien: EOS, 1987), 143-47. See also: *Biblia patristica. Index des citations et allusions bibliques dans la littérature patristique*, ed. Centre d'Analyse et de Documentation Patristiques, 7 vols. (Paris: Centre National de la Recherche Scientifique, 1975-2000).

the world. In the Ambrosian liturgy, the 4th Sunday in Advent (which cor-responds in the date of celebration to the 2nd Roman Sunday) is dedicated to the entry of the Messiah, with the synoptic Gospels of Jesus' entrance into Jerusalem; here too, in Year C, Ps 24:3–6, 9–10 is used, with v. 7 as refrain.[21]

On the Solemnity of the Mother of God (January 1), Psalm 24 is framed in the Office of Readings by the antiphon from v. 7.[22] The psalm is chosen because of the Christological interpretation, but there may be a Marian aspect here too, which is more strongly present in Eastern liturgy and the-ology.[23] The psalm is given a clearly Marian reference in the Common of the Blessed Virgin Mary in the antiphon at the Office of Readings, which alludes to v. 5: "Mary received a blessing from the Lord and loving kindness from God her savior."[24] Mary is thus the answer to the question: "Who may go up the mountain of the Lord?" She is the gate through which the king of glory makes his entrance into the world.

On the feast of the Presentation of the Lord, vv. 7–10 are appropriately chosen as the Responsorial Psalm after Mal 3:1–4 ("And suddenly there will come to the temple the LORD whom you seek").[25] The "gates" of the psalm now recall the gates of the Temple in Jerusalem, taking up the original Sitz-im-Leben of Psalm 24:7–10 with reference to entering the Temple; the church —as the procession makes especially clear—becomes mimetically the image of the Temple.

b) On Palm Sunday

Ps 24 is used in a similar way, with the same interpretation, on Palm Sunday, where it is proposed as a processional song on the way to the church. The response takes up the children's song "Hosanna in the highest"[26] and

---

21 Accessible under http://www.chiesadimilano.it/lezionario-ambrosiano (retrieved 7/11/2022). V. 9 is prescribed as *salmello* in the Christmas Vigil between the fourth reading and the Epistle.

22 *Liturgy of the Hours*, 1:480–81.

23 See Harald Buchinger, "Lebensraum des Wortes. Zur Bibelverwendung der römischen Liturgie am Beispiel ihrer Gesänge," *LJ* 62, no. 3 (2012): 194.

24 *Liturgy of the Hours*, 1:1328.

25 The response is taken from v. 10b. On the feast of the Presentation in Milan, Ps 24:1–4a, 6–7,10 is chosen as response to the same reading.

26 *The Roman Missal. Renewed by Decree of the Most Holy Second Ecumenical Council of the Vatican, Promulgated by Authority of Pope Paul VI and Revised at the Direction of Pope John Paul II. English Translation according to the Third Typical Edition* (Collegeville: Liturgical Press, 2013), 280–81.

links the procession to the Gospel. The psalm interprets Jesus, who entered Jerusalem on that day, as the "king of glory"; it likewise gives an interpretation of this day's procession of the faithful to the church ("Who may go up the mountain of the LORD …"), thereby linking these two temporal levels. Moreover, the eschatological perspective of the heavenly Jerusalem is also present on Palm Sunday.[27] In a simple entry, without a procession, vv. 9–10 are a part of the entrance antiphon.

c) In the Context of Easter: Christ's Descent into the Realm of the Dead

Here, we must begin by pointing out an important interpretative variation between vv. 7 and 9 in the Septuagint (ἄρατε πύλας οἱ ἄρχοντες ὑμῶν) and in the Vulgate (*adtollite portas principes vestras*). In the Masoretic text, the gates themselves are addressed: they are to lift up their "heads" (i.e., the lintels). But here, the princes are told to open their gates. This personification opened the path to a dialogical elaboration of the scene. And the concept ἄρχοντες in the LXX, especially in combination with the κύριος τῶν δυνάμεων, suggested angels and demons.[28]

Accordingly, in the apocryphal Gospel according to Nicodemus, it was possible to interpret the psalm as speaking of Christ's descent into the realm of the dead. In a dialogue with the devil, Christ demands entry, and after the gates are opened, he rescues the captive souls from the nether world.[29] This was and is the background to the use of Psalm 24 at the Office of Readings on Holy Saturday with the antiphon from v. 7b; it suggests a Christological-soteriological understanding, although this is not specified.[30] This interpretation

---

27 This is clear, e.g., in the prayer of blessing of the palm branches ("may reach the eternal Jerusalem through him"; *Missal*, 275), and it is expressed in Psalm 24 through the motif of the pilgrimage of the peoples.

28 See Ralph Brucker, "'Wer ist der König der Herrlichkeit?' Ps 23[24] – Text, Wirkung, Rezeption," in *Die Septuaginta – Text, Wirkung, Rezeption. 4. Internationale Fachtagung veranstaltet von Septuaginta Deutsch (LXX.D) […]*, ed. W. Kraus and S. Kreuzer, WUNT 325 (Tübingen: Mohr Siebeck, 2014), 412-15, 420-26; Rose, "Attollite portas," 454-56.

29 See Marco Benini, *Die Feier des Osterfestkreises im Ingolstädter Pfarrbuch des Johannes Eck*, LQF 105 (Münster: Aschendorff, 2016), 320-21 (with bibliography); Marco Benini, "Johannes Eck als achtsamer Liturge. Sein Ingolstädter Pfarrbuch als liturgiehistorische Quelle unter besonderer Berücksichtigung der szenischen Liturgie des Osterfestkreises," ALw 57 (2015): 83-84; Rose, "'Attollite portas," 464-67; *The Apocryphal Gospels: Texts and Translations*, ed. Bart D. Ehrman and Zlatko Plešee (New York: Oxford University Press, 2011), 482-85 (Ch. 21-24).

30 *Liturgy of the Hours*, 2:494.

lies behind the so-called *Attollite portas* rite, which, from the late middle ages onward, often formed a part of the celebration of the Resurrection (instead of the Easter Vigil, which was moved forward to Holy Saturday morning).[31] It is still in use today in the diocese of Trier in Germany[32] and in the Byzantine Easter Vigil at the beginning of the Orthros.[33] With the same psalm dialogue as in the Gospel of Nicodemus, the church door is struck with the cross, thereby making present in a scenic-dramatic form Christ's redemptive descent.

d) On the Ascension of Christ

In patristic exegesis, Psalm 24 was already read in reference to the Lord's *ascensio*. In the Roman rite, it was included in its totality on this feast in the German-language Monastic Office.[34] Only echoes are found in the *Liturgia Horarum*.[35] There are likewise allusions to vv. 7–10 in some Byzantine troparia for the feast of the Ascension.[36]

e) As Sunday Psalm in the Four-Week Psalter

The schema of the commission for the distribution of the psalms for the *Liturgia Horarum* states, "Zion Psalm 23, a hymn for the entry of the Lord into the heavenly Jerusalem."[37] Hence, the commission selected Psalm 24, on the basis of patristic interpretation with reference to the Ascension of Christ, for the Office of Readings on the Sunday of the 4th week.[38]

---

31 See Benini, *Osterfestkreis*, 320-24; Balthasar Fischer, "Die Auferstehungsfeier am Ostermorgen. Altchristliches Gedankengut in mittelalterlicher Fassung," in Fischer, *Redemptionis mysterium*, 13-27.

32 See Benini, *Osterfestkreis*, 310 n. 6.

33 See *Anthologhion*, 3:154; Rosso, *Celebrazione*, 786, 788.

34 *Monastisches Stundenbuch für die Benediktiner des deutschen Sprachgebietes. Authentische Ausgabe für den liturgischen Gebrauch*, 3 vols. (St. Ottilien: EOS, 1-2; 2nd ed., 1993; 3: 3rd ed., 2011), 2:524 with the antiphon: "He who descended has also ascended to the highest heaven, in order to reign over all things. Alleluia."

35 There is only one allusion to Ps 24:10 in the Magnificat antiphon at Second Vespers (*Liturgy of the Hours*, 2:933).

36 *Anthologhion*, 3:441, 444-45, 449, 451-52, 457, 459; Rose, *Psaumes*, 128.

37 Vitus Huonder, *Die Psalmen in der Liturgia Horarum*, Studia Friburgensia 74 (Freiburg/Switz.: Universitätsverlag, 1991), 67, 213.

38 According to the title in the Septuagint and the Vulgate, Psalm 24 was sung on the first day after the Sabbath: "ψαλμὸς τῷ Δαυιδ τῆς μιᾶς σαββάτων / *Psalmus David prima sabbati*" (Hossfeld and Zenger, *Psalm 1-50*, 6, 156).

f) On All Saints and on the Commemorations of Saints

Psalm 24 is given another interpretation on All Saints, where vv. 1–6 as the Responsorial Psalm are linked to the vision of the 144,000 from all nations and races, peoples, and languages (Rev 7:2–4, 9–14), as the refrain makes clear: "Lord, this is the people that longs to see your face" (cf. v. 6). The saints appear as those who ascend to the place of the Lord, who have clean hands and a pure heart, who have sought God, and have received his salvation. The affirmations of the psalm thus take the reading to a deeper level, expand it, and apply it to the hearers too, who are still making their way to the mountain of the Lord. The focus here lies on human beings, on those who have been made perfect and those who are called thereto—and thus on an ecclesial dimension.

g) In the Context of the Consecration of a Church

In the rite of the consecration of a church, the Temple in Jerusalem from the psalm is linked subtly to the church building. After the solemn opening of the church door and the bishop's invitation, "Go within his gates giving thanks, enter his courts with songs of praise," Psalm 24 is sung with the antiphon "Lift high the ancient portals. The King of glory enters" (or another suitable hymn may be sung).[39] The psalm speaks both of the human beings who enter and of the entry of Christ/God. The church thus appears as the "mountain of the Lord" to which people are making their way; and through the "king of glory," it becomes his "holy place." The psalm also interprets the church as the place in which the human being "will receive blessings from the Lord, and justice from his saving God." This, of course, entails an ethical demand ("clean of hand and pure of heart"). The psalm presents the church as the place of encounter where those who ask after God receive the answer to their search. Since Psalm 24 also contains the motif of the eschatological pilgrimage of the peoples, the individual local community is integrated into the context of the worldwide Church and of God's universal plan of salvation.

Psalm 24 was used already in this way at the consecration of Hagia Sophia in Constantinople in 562, and this was probably adopted from the East.[40] In today's Byzantine rite of the consecration of a church, the bishop, holding the relics in his hand, calls out Psalm 24:7–10 at the doors of the

---

39 *Rites*, 2:370.

40 See Fischer, "Auferstehungsfeier," 15–16.

narthex, which are then opened.[41] Psalm 24 also has its place in the Office of Readings in the Commons of the Liturgy of the Hours for the feast of the dedication of a church.[42]

h) As Invitatory Psalm of the Liturgy of the Hours

Psalm 24 can also be taken as the invitatory.[43] As in the classical invitatory psalm 95 (94), praise of the Creator stands at the beginning. The situation of those who pray is envisaged: the ascent to the holy place marks the beginning of the prayer, and they recognize themselves in the ones who seek the face of the Lord. The gates of one's own self ought to open.

i) In the Byzantine Preparation for Communion

The use of Psalm 24 in the Byzantine preparation of the people to receive Communion moves in the same direction.[44] The communicant appears as the one who ascends with a pure heart to the Lord and receives his blessing and salvation in Holy Communion, because he opens the doors of his heart to Christ. Psalm 24 was probably sung originally also at the Great Entrance of the Divine Liturgy; the focus shifted here from the human being making his or her entrance to Christ.[45]

j) At the Byzantine Burial (of a Priest)

One characteristic element of the Byzantine burial of a priest (in comparison to the funeral rites for laypersons and for monks) is the three antiphons that each contain a psalm (23, 24, 84), other chants, and a reading

---

41 See Ioan Bizău, "Les psaumes et leur interprétation dans le rituel orthodoxe de la consécration de l'Eglise," in Braga and Pistoia, *Liturgie, interprète de l'écriture*, 2:159-62.

42 *Liturgy of the Hours*, 1:1299-1300.

43 *Liturgy of the Hours*, 1:649.

44 See P. Galadza, ed., *The Divine Liturgy. An Anthology for Worship*, 2nd ed. (Ottawa: Metropolitan Andrey Sheptytsky Institute of Eastern Christian Studies, 2005), 35.

45 On the development, see Robert F. Taft and Stefano Parenti, *Storia della liturgia di S. Giovanni Crisostomo. 2: Il grande ingresso. Edizione italiana rivista, aggiornata e ampliata*, Analekta Kryptopherrês 10 (Grottaferrata: Monastero Esarchico, 2014), 228-256. The original vv. 3-4 were probably expanded with vv. 7-10, or replaced by these verses. This, of course, brings a substantial shift in the interpretation of the Psalm. From the sixth century onwards, the Hymn of the Cherubim was added here ("King of all things" could suitably follow vv. 7-10 of the Psalm), and finally displaced the Psalm verses completely.

from the Apostolos and from the Gospel. The entrance into the sanctuary presumably motivated the choice of Psalm 24.[46]

In all the Byzantine funeral rites, after the corpse is lowered into the grave, the priest speaks Psalm 24:1, "The earth is the LORD'S and all it holds …," while he lets earth fall in the form of a cross onto the corpse.[47] Thus, he affirms that the dead person too, who now lies in the earth, belongs to the Lord.

2. HERMENEUTICS OF THE LITURGICAL USE OF THE PSALMS

We shall now systematize the liturgical occasions listed above, because they not only display the varied use and interpretation of this Psalm, but also expose differing hermeneutics that the Liturgy generally employs. Thus, they continue the trajectory of the "multi-perspectivity"[48] of the psalms, which is already established in the Psalter itself through the rereading by the various redactions within the Old Testament, and points beyond the Old Testament:

> In their original cultic use, the Psalms were already "formulas." A variety of persons could pray them. The reference of the words changed, depending on the one who prayed. In the Psalter as a whole, it is clear that even in psalms that are individual in their wording, the individuality of the one who prays is opened out onto Israel. […] The Israel that prays can, of course, be present in compact form in every praying assembly and in every individual Israelite, and all the more so in the coming "messianic" David.[49]

---

46 See Peter Plank, "Der byzantinische Begräbnisritus," in *Liturgie im Angesicht des Todes. 1: Judentum und Ostkirchen 1: Texte und Kommentare*, ed. H. Becker and H. Ühlein, PiLi 9 (St. Ottilien: EOS, 1997), 779–80, 782–83. It is possible that, like Ps 23, Ps 24 was originally not restricted to the burial of priests (Plank, 793). See also Elena Velkovska, "Funeral Rites according to Byzantine Liturgical Sources," *DOP* 55 (2001): 33, 37–38; Reiner Kaczynski, "Die Psalmodie bei der Begräbnisfeier," in *Liturgie und Dichtung*, 2:813, 824. In the Roman funeral liturgy, Ps 24 (23) was used at the funeral of children down to the 1950 *Collectio Rituum*, doubtless primarily because of v. 4 ("pure hands"/"pure heart"); see Kaczynski, 806–7, 829.

47 For the text, see *The Occasional Services*, vol. 3 of *The Great Book of Needs*, trans. St. Tikhon's Monastery (South Canaan: St. Tikhon's Monastery Press, 1999), 272; *Order for the Burial of a Priest*, ed. Orthodox Church in America (2017): https://www.oca.org/files/PDF/Music/Burial/burial-of-priest.pdf (retrieved 7/12/22), 237.

48 Braulik, "Christologisches Verständnis," 77; Braulik, "Rezeptionsästhetik, kanonische Inter-textualität und unsere Meditation des Psalters," in Braulik and Lohfink, *Liturgie und Bibel*, 524, 538.

49 Norbert Lohfink, "Was wird anders bei kanonischer Schriftauslegung? Beobachtungen am Beispiel von Psalm 6," in Lohfink, *Studien zur biblischen Theologie*. Stuttgarter biblische

This messianic rereading is continued in the New Testament, and conse-quently in the Christian liturgy, which, as our example of Psalm 24 has made clear several times, as a matter of course interprets the Psalms as speaking of Christ.

Balthasar Fischer (1912–2001), professor of liturgical studies in Trier and very active in the liturgical reform, followed in the footsteps of the Church Fathers by developing a Christian hermeneutics of the Psalms that sees the entire Psalter as "a prophetic book that is fulfilled in the Christ event."[50] He distinguishes three forms of the Christologization of the Psalms:

1. Among the so-called "Thou Psalms," in which God is addressed directly, he calls a psalm that Christ himself took up, or that is placed on his lips when he prays, *vox Christi ad Patrem* (voice of Christ to the Father). He calls this a "Christologization of the (human) 'below.'"[51] He gives the example of Psalm 41 (40), which Jesus quotes at the Last Supper (Jn 13:18), attesting that this psalm is fulfilled in him through Judas' betrayal.[52]

2. Other psalms in which Christ can be understood as the direct addressee are understood as *vox Ecclesiae ad Christum* (voice of the Church to Christ). Fischer points out that the Septuagint had already replaced the divine name YHWH with *Kyrios,* which became a title of Christ in the New Testament.[53] He calls this hermeneutics a "Chris-tologization of the (divine) 'above'"[54] and gives as his example the prayer of the dying Stephen (Acts 7:59; cf. Ps 31:6).[55]

Aufsatzbände 16. Altes Testament (Stuttgart: Katholisches Bibelwerk, 1993), 280.

50 Balthasar Fischer, "Die Psalmenfrömmigkeit der Martyrerkirche," in Fischer, *Psalmen als Stimme der Kirche,* 21. See Balthasar Fischer, "Christological Interpretation of the Psalms seen in the Mirror of the Liturgy," *QL* 71, no. 3 (1990): 227–35; Harald Buchinger, "Zur Hermeneu-tik liturgischer Psalmenverwendung. Methodologische Überlegungen im Schnittpunkt von Bibelwissenschaft, Patristik und Liturgiewissenschaft," *HID* 54, no. 3 (2000): 197.

51 Fischer, "Psalmenfrömmigkeit," 22.

52 See Fischer, 33. See, even more trenchantly, Ps 31:6, which is expanded on the lips of Jesus by the word "Father": "Father, into your hands I commend my spirit" (Lk 23:46), or Ps 22:2 "My God, my God, why have you abandoned me?" in Mk 15:34/Mt 27:46.

53 See Fischer, 22.

54 Fischer, 22.

55 Fischer, 34.

Both these principles, *vox Christi* and *vox ad Christum*, are explicitly present by the second century.[56] Augustine († 430) summed them up briefly in an analogous formulation as *Psalmus vox totius Christi, capitis et corporis* (The Psalm is the voice of the whole Christ, head and body).[57] We quote his vivid words:

> When we speak to God in prayer, the Son is not separated from the Father; when the Body of the Son prays, the head is not separated from the body. It is the one savior of his body, our Lord Jesus Christ, who prays for us, prays in us, and is prayed to by us. He prays for us as our priest. He prays in us as our head. He is prayed to by us as our God. Let us recognize therefore our voices in him and his voice in us.[58]

3. Psalms formulated only in the third person were often understood in the early Church as *vox de Christo* (voice about Christ), as the risen Lord himself taught the disciples on the way to Emmaus (cf. Lk 24:44).[59]

Fischer sums up: "The psalms speak to the early Church either about Christ or in him, or they hear Christ speaking in them."[60] This threefold hermeneutics goes back to the New Testament, and may therefore lay claim to validity down to the present day.

The varied use made of Psalm 24 has shown that the Liturgy knows not only a Christologization (as in points a to e), but also an ecclesialization (as in points f to i [and b]) as a basic hermeneutical pattern. For example, on All Saints, the central focus is on those who have gone up to "the mountain of the Lord," the heavenly Jerusalem, or who are still on the way up, that is to say, the pilgrim Church. In keeping with Augustine's dictum *psalmus vox totius Christi, capitis et corporis*, these two hermeneutical perspectives are theologically inseparable, and they are found together, as the example of Psalm 24 for the dedication of a church shows, when vv. 3–6 are understood with reference to those who enter and vv. 7–10 are understood with reference

---

56 See Fischer, "Christliches Psalmenverständnis im 2. Jahrhundert," in Fischer, *Psalmen als Stimme der Kirche*, 85-102.

57 Fischer, "Psalmenfrömmigkeit," 22, though without specifying the source. Cf., e.g., Augustine, *En. in ps.* 3.9–10 (CChr.SL 38:11,13). See Michael Fiedrowicz, *Psalmus vox totius Christi. Studien zu Augustins "Enarrationes in Psalmos"* (Freiburg/Br.: Herder, 1997), esp. 341-78, 424-26.

58 *Augustine, En. in ps.* 85.1 (CChr.SL 39:1176), quoted in *GILH*, 7.

59 See Fischer, "Psalmenfrömmigkeit," 22-23, 33-34.

60 Fischer, 23.

to Christ. Psalm 24 likewise shows (as in a [Mary] and h to j) that the psalms can be understood both individually and collectively (depending on the situation), especially since many psalms, as in the example we have chosen, employ both singular and plural formulations—and the individual is always a member of the body of Christ, the Church. These are basically different modes of role identification.[61]

Our example, Psalm 24, has also shown that the allocation of a psalm to a festal mystery or the occasion of a liturgical celebration can be due to a single verse that is frequently employed, literally or with slight variations, as an antiphon, and that functions as an interpretative key to the psalm as a whole. Precisely the variations are hermeneutically interesting, because they set accents and suggest one particular interpretation. In rare cases, they may even prescribe this interpretation.[62]

In addition to the content of the text, the function that a psalm has in liturgy also influences the way it is understood. The example of Psalm 24 has shown four ways of using psalms, including as *Responsorial Psalm in the Mass* or in the *Liturgy of the Hours*. We shall discuss this in separate sections below.

Psalm 24 is also *sung as an accompaniment*: at the consecration of a church, it interprets the entrance of the ministers and the faithful as the movement of the pilgrim people of God to the holy place, and also shows what a church is. On Palm Sunday, it links the historical event of Jesus' entrance to the procession that is carried out today. In both cases, the psalm offers an interpretation of the procession, indicating that it cannot be regarded merely as a change of location or as a form of participation by the people. On the contrary, the procession acquires a liturgical-theological dimension. *E contra*, in the concrete liturgical action, the psalm itself receives an interpretation and an actualization.

Something similar applies to *single verses* that are isolated from their context in the psalm and are recontextualized by accompanying a liturgical action. As in the *Attollite portas* rite of the Easter Vigil (and earlier on, in the consecration of a church), it is the psalm verse that gives the rite of knocking a comprehensible meaning. At the same time, the rite identifies the "ancient gates" with the church door and thereby interprets the psalm. There is thus a reciprocal interaction whereby word and action interpret each other.[63]

---

61 Cf. B.IX.34.

62 Cf., e.g., in the case of Psalm 24, the explicitly Mariological interpretation in the Common of Mary (above, under a).

63 Cf. A.V.18.

This is independent of whether, in terms of the genesis of liturgy, the action came first and was then (as in the casting of soil in the Byzantine funeral) additionally interpreted by means of a psalm verse, or whether initially only the text was spoken and was subsequently dramatized with a symbolic action (as one may suppose in the case of the *Attollite portas* rite). Thanks to its isolation, greater attention is paid to an individual affirmation in the psalm; and to some extent, the liturgical context gives it a new meaning that goes beyond the text of the psalm itself. In addition to an interpretative function of this kind, single psalm verses are also spoken in liturgy as small independent elements, e.g., Psalm 70 (69), verse 2: "God, come to my assistance ..." or Psalm 51 (50), verse:17: "Lord, open my lips ..." at the beginning of the Liturgy of the Hours.[64]

---

64 This opening is already found in the Rule of Benedict 9 and 17 (WEC 4:27, 30).

CHAPTER EIGHT

The Responsorial
Psalm in the Mass

The current liturgical documents call the Responsorial Psalm an "integral part of the Liturgy of the Word" (*GIRM* 61; *GILM* 19). It "has great liturgical and pastoral importance, since it fosters meditation on the word of God."[65] Nevertheless, the function of the Responsorial Psalm is not defined unambiguously.[66] A reflection on this point is important for a liturgical biblical hermeneutics that asks how Scripture—in this instance, the Responsorial Psalm—is used in the Liturgy, and above all, how it is understood there.

1. THE FUNCTION OF THE RESPONSORIAL PSALM

The preparatory Coetus XI for the postconciliar revision of the Mass lectionary envisioned four dimensions. The psalm was seen as: a response to the reading that had just been heard, as a meditative chant, as a reading from Scripture, and as a bracket around the two Testaments.[67] This is why the group avoided taking a single position regarding its purpose. The Responsorial Psalm was a novelty, because it was only after the liturgical reform of the Council that the psalm was related to the reading(s) on non-festal days.[68] While the bracketing function is not a matter of dispute and offered little

---

65 *GIRM*, 61.

66 See Dominik Daschner, "Meditation oder Antwort – Zur Funktion des Antwortpsalms," *HlD* 48, no. 2 (1994): 206; Rudolf Pacik, "Der Antwortpsalm," *LJ* 30, no. 1 (1980): 43-66.

67 See Nübold, *Perikopenordnung*, 323.

68 On the pre-conciliar praxis, see Josef Andreas Jungmann, *The Mass of the Roman Rite: Its Origins and Development (Missarum Sollemnia)*, trans. Francis Brunner, 2 vols. (New York: Benziger Brothers, 1951-55), 1:432-35. Moreover, the Psalms at the introit and the offertory,

scope for discussion, academic liturgical scholars have variously accentuated and evaluated the other functions attributed to the psalm. All agree that the Liturgy of the Word is a dialogical event between God and his people. The theology of liturgy sees the elementary three steps of the Liturgy of the Word as "*lectio – meditatio – oratio*,"[69] but this is suitable only up to a point in adequately characterizing the Responsorial Psalm.[70]

The interpretation of the psalm as a *meditation* on the reading follows this schema and can find support in *GIRM* 61 (quoted above). Above all, it corresponds to the anthropological constant well known from everyday communication, namely that it takes time to receive and reflect upon a word—especially if it is to encourage, to console, to exhort, and so on. The Responsorial Psalm thus allows what has been heard to resonate and to be understood, because it frequently takes up again aspects of the reading (sometimes word for word) and establishes a relationship between the reading and those present. It can also interpret what has been heard and enrich it.

Although the liturgical documents do not make this explicit, it can be demonstrated that the postconciliar liturgical reform was guided by the idea that the psalm is the community's *answer* to the Word of God it has just heard.[71] However, the term *psalmus responsorius* refers not primarily to its function as response, but to the responsorial singing/speaking of the refrain.[72] Dominik Daschner, who himself sees the psalm as an answer, maintains that it would be better to speak of a "reaction by the community,"[73] since the psalms themselves are often not a direct response of prayer. This more open formulation would correspond better to the various kinds of psalms, and this would provide a link to the meditative function.[74] One can object to these two evaluations by asking why no psalm appears after the second reading, and why in some cases the psalm was chosen, not in view of the first reading, but in anticipation of the Gospel or with reference to the season of the liturgical year.[75]

---

unlike the Psalm at Communion, were unrelated to the pericopes, as their ascending order itself shows (cf. the table in Jungmann, 331).

69 See Josef Andreas Jungmann, *Liturgy of the Word*, trans. H. E. Winstone (Collegeville, MN: Liturgical Press, 1966).

70 See Daschner, "Antwortpsalm," 153.

71 See Daschner, 200–214.

72 See Daschner, 134, 214.

73 Daschner, 216–17.

74 Both functions were often combined (see Daschner, 136–37).

75 See Nübold, *Perikopenordnung*, 325.

This leaves the third interpretation of the Responsorial Psalm as a *reading*—though, of course, a reading with a particular character. This was propagated especially by French liturgical scholarship[76] and seems to be gaining more and more adherents.[77] Although the poetical genre of the Responsorial Psalm demands singing, which is to be preferred to a mere recitation aloud,[78] it is only the manner of delivery that distinguishes it from the readings. The psalm itself remains a reading. The testimony of the Church Fathers is adduced as an argument. They unambiguously call the psalm a reading,[79] and it is well known that they frequently preached about it.

When we look at the genesis of the Responsorial Psalm, it is clear that only on feast days the gradual was chosen with a reference to the readings or because of a thematic link; otherwise, it was originally independent.[80] The fact that the Responsorial Psalm is to be sung from the ambo shows that it is a reading from Scripture.[81] It is not by chance that it is found in the lectionary and that the *GIRM* no longer mentions the singing by the entire congregation (which is scarcely feasible in praxis).[82] And so, it has the appearance

---

76 See Aimé-Georges Martimort, "Fonction de la Psalmodie dans la Liturgie de la Parole," in Becker and Kaczynski, *Liturgie und Dichtung* 2:837-56; see further bibliography in Daschner, "Antwortpsalm," 137 n. 16.

77 See Franz Karl Praßl, "Psallite sapienter. Gedanken zur Auswahl von Meßgesängen," in *Bewahren und Erneuern: Studien zu Meßliturgie* (FS Hans Bernhad Meyer), IThS 42, ed. R. Meßner (Innsbruck: Tyrolia, 1995), 255. He sees the Responsorial Psalm "not primarily as a meditative piece with contents related to the preceding reading, but rather as an integral component of the proclamation of Scripture—the poetical 'reading from the book of Psalms'"; Zerfaß, *Hermeneutik*, 175.

78 See *GILM*, 20-22; *GIRM*, 61.

79 See, e.g., Augustine, *Sermo* 165 (PL 38:902): "Apostolum audivimus, Psalmum audivimus, Evangelium audivimus: consonant *omnes divinae lectiones*, ut spem non in nobis, sed in Domino collocamus." (We have heard the Apostle, we have heard the Psalm, we have heard the Gospel: all the divine lessons are in harmony, so that we place our hope not in ourselves, but in the Lord.) See Michael Margoni-Kögler, *Die Perikopen im Gottesdienst bei Augustinus. Ein Beitrag zur Erforschung der liturgischen Schriftlesung in der frühen Kirche.* SÖAW.PH 810 (Vienna: Verlag der Österreichischen Akademie der Wissenschaft, 2018), 370-76.

80 On the development, see James McKinnon, "The Fourth-Century Origin of the Gradual," in McKinnon, *Temple, Church Fathers and Early Western Chant* 91-106; Michel Huglo, "Le Répons-Graduel de la Messe. Evolution de la forme. Permanence de la function," in *Chant grégorien et musique médiévale*, ed. M. Huglo, Variorum Collected Studies Series 814 (Aldershot: Ashgate, 2005), 53-73.

81 *GIRM*, 309 includes the Responsorial Psalm among the texts to be read at the ambo. *GILM*, 22, 33 envisages only the ambo, but *GIRM*, 20 specifies: "at the ambo or another suitable place."

82 This alternative was envisaged by *GILM*, 20.

of a word addressed to the congregation, not least because it often expands the content of the preceding reading. The understanding of the psalm as a reading underlines its character as proclamation, but this need not contradict its additional functions as meditation and as response.

Although these arguments are plausible, one must note that the concept of "reading" does not *per se* describe a function. In this context, it simply seeks to emphasize that here, as in the other readings, the Word of God is being read aloud, and that accordingly, the Psalm has no less dignity than the other readings.[83] Only this explains why it is an "integral part of the Liturgy of the Word." It is, however, easy to find examples of Responsorial Psalms that are addressed to the "you" of God and that in fact aim more at answer than at proclamation.

One can thus find arguments both for and against every understanding of the Responsorial Psalm. This shows that it cannot be brought into an unambiguous systematization; and even for the individual psalm, it can be difficult to tie it down to one particular function. The definition of a "primary function" of the Responsorial Psalm in the structure of the Liturgy of the Word is questionable because this is generated more in academic reflection than in the liturgical celebration itself. Rather, the various aspects complement one another, especially since the encounter with God in his Word cannot be enclosed within firm schemata and concepts. We have already seen that a reading can have various functions; and this is equally true of the psalms. The Responsorial Psalm can be seen, in terms of its recitation, as a sung reading with a refrain, but this does not determine its function (proclamation, meditation, answer in prayer or reaction). This is not a lack of system. It expresses, rather, the richness of the liturgical "modes of communication" of the Word of God. Thus, it was good that the liturgical documents avoided tying it down to one unambiguous function.

2. THE HERMENEUTICAL SIGNIFICANCE OF THE REFRAIN

There is unanimous agreement about the high significance that attaches to the refrain of the Responsorial Psalm, which allows the entire congregation to take part in the psalmody. The repetition and the melody imprint it on people's memory. This makes it a meditative element that promotes the interiorization of the Word of God.

---

83 See Zerfaß, *Hermeneutik*, 30 n. 98.

In the great majority of cases, the antiphon is taken from the Responsorial Psalm itself and highlights an important affirmation in the psalm,[84] but sometimes it varies slightly from the biblical text. The refrain often shows why this psalm was chosen and how it should be understood. This means that it plays an important role from a hermeneutical perspective, as we can see especially from the fact that different refrains to the same psalm focus on different aspects and thus highlight various themes and interpretations. Sometimes, the refrain is taken from the New Testament. On some feasts or Sundays in Advent, this antiphon suggests a Christological interpretation of the psalm. Only very rarely is this interpretation explicitly prescribed, as (for example) on the 2nd Sunday after Christmas, when the antiphon, "The Word was made flesh, and lived among us" (Jn 1:14), is taken from the Gospel of the day and explains how we are to understand the "Word" in the psalm verses "He [God the Father] sends out his word/Word to the earth" or "He makes his word/Word known to Jacob."

The refrain often underlines an important affirmation in the preceding reading. When repeated and meditated upon, it can help us to understand the text, so that the Scripture is explained by means of the Scripture. The refrain can also make us aware of an affirmation that is found both in the Reading and in the Gospel, thereby pointing ahead to the latter and helping us to grasp how the readings in the Liturgy of the Word belong together. In this way, it can unobtrusively make us aware of the dialogue and the unity of the two Testaments.[85]

When one looks at the Responsorial Psalms of the Sundays and feast days, one notes that the refrain is often formulated in the first person singular or plural or has personal formulations such as "The Lord is *my* light and *my* salvation."[86] This makes it easier for participants to join inwardly in the song. Sometimes, the "I" of a Psalm is expanded in the antiphon to a "we."[87] The faithful can thus identify with the speaker(s) of the psalm, but they can also make both the antiphon and the psalm from which it is taken their own.

The antiphon is frequently addressed to God and thus appears as the community's cry of prayer. The response can also be addressed directly to the one who prays, so that it becomes an exhortation to oneself as one sings

---

84 See Nübold, *Perikopenordnung*, 328. Two-thirds of the responses come from the part of the Psalm that is read aloud, while one-third consists of verses in the same Psalm that are not read aloud.

85 See B.VIII.30.

86 See, e.g., 3rd Sunday in Ordinary Time A.

87 See, e.g., Ash Wednesday: Ps 51 (50): "Have mercy on *me* ..." with the antiphon "Be merciful, O Lord, for *we* have sinned ..."

it (e.g., "If today you hear his voice, harden not your hearts").[88] When one repeats it, the refrain clearly takes on a greater intensity than if it were only heard read by another. Other exhortations such as "Give the Lord glory and honor"[89] are immediately put into action when one sings them. The context implies that the less frequent formulations in the third person, such as "Blessed are those who fear the Lord,"[90] can also be understood in reference to those who have assembled here and now for the celebration. Obviously, the refrain makes the congregation participants, not only on the formal level through singing, but also substantially through identifying with a role,[91] or through language that refers to the participants.

Since the psalm, reinforced by the refrain, is related both to the preceding reading (or to other scriptural texts) and to the congregation, it functions as a bridge between the biblical event and those celebrating here and now. The psalm thus makes an important contribution to the actualization of the Word of God. On Ash Wednesday (to take one example), the first reading proclaims the Lord's call to repentance (Jl 2:12-18), and then Psalm 51 shows that the community understands itself as the contemporary addressee of this call, accepts it, and answers it in prayer. It is easy to find other examples of the refrain taking up the reading and developing it, either through praise, thanksgiving, or petition, or else by itself becoming an affirmative confession of faith. The Responsorial Psalm thereby underscores a fundamental concern of the liturgical proclamation of Scripture, namely, that this should be and is a dialogue here and now between God and his people.[92]

---

88 See, e.g., 3rd Sunday in Lent A; 23rd Sunday in Ordinary Time A; 4th Sunday in Ordinary Time B; 27th Sunday in Ordinary Time C; and also on weekdays.

89 See, e.g., 29th Sunday in Ordinary Time A.

90 See, e.g., 33rd Sunday in Ordinary Time A.

91 See B.IX.34.

92 See B.VIII.28.2.

CHAPTER NINE

The Psalms in the Liturgy of the Hours

In the case of the Psalms, a liturgical hermeneutics must look particularly at the Liturgy of the Hours. Their use differs clearly from that of the Responsorial Psalm, since they were not chosen in dependence on a reading but are autonomous and form the prayer. Here we must ask how the Psalms in the Liturgy of the Hours are to be seen, and what hermeneutical guidance the Liturgy offers.

1. PSALMS AS PRAYER?

The *GILH* emphasizes the spiritual and poetical riches of the psalms. As the chapter title "The Psalms and their Close Relationship with Christian Prayer" (100-109) already indicates, the *GILH* tends to see the psalms as *prayer*, even if they do not have "the same quality of prayer that a prayer or collect composed by the Church may possess" (105), especially since they do not always speak directly to God. Because of such "difficulties,"[93] "aids" are suggested in order to understand the Psalms and "to turn them into Christian prayer" (110).

A look at the history of the Liturgy of the Hours supplies a broad horizon to this question.[94] In the cathedral office, the community sang fixed psalms

---

93 *GILH*, 105.

94 See Robert F. Taft, *The Liturgy of the Hours in East and West: The Origins of the Divine Office and its Meaning for Today*, 2nd ed. (Collegeville, MN: Liturgical Press, 1993); Reinhard Meßner, *Einführung in die Liturgiewissenschaft*, 2nd ed., UTB 2173 (Paderborn: Schöningh, 2009), 238-79; Angelus A. Häußling, *Tagzeitenliturgie in Geschichte und Gegenwart. Historische und theologische Studien*, ed. M. Löckener, 2nd ed., LQF 100 (Münster: Aschendorff, 2017) (with numerous individual aspects); Arturo Elberti, *La liturgia delle ore in Occidente. Storia e teologia*, Collana teologia liturgica (Rome: Ed. Dehoniane, 1998). On the Psalms, see

that were appropriate to the time of day and functioned as *prayer* to God. In the monastic office, on the other hand, the recitation was practiced *currente psalterio*, resulting in a sequence of psalms with very different genres and contents. It was not possible consciously to "pray" all the psalms. Rather, they were understood as a *reading*, on the basis of which the monk then formed his prayer, sometimes with silence and a psalm-oration, as his answer to the Word of God that was uttered in the psalm. The differentiation between these two acts could also be illustrated by the physical posture, for example, when the Egyptian monks sat during the psalm and then rose to pray.

Both of these are legitimate liturgical ways of using the Psalms. The subsequent coalescence of the cathedral and the monastic types[95] meant that they were no longer strictly separate—and for good reasons, since the Psalms themselves oscillate between reading and prayer. This is in accord both with the variety of the individual psalms and with what we said in the introduction to the present chapter about the anabatic and katabatic dimensions (the word of human beings and the Word of God) in the Psalms. Georg Braulik notes: "One ought consciously to keep open this alternative of a praying *out of* or *with* the psalms, on the one hand, and a praying *of* the psalms, on the other."[96]

A bridge between the two options may be hinted at already in Psalm 1:2, which Jerome († 420) translates as follows in the Vulgate: "in lege eius *meditabitur*." This also seems to have been the intention of the redaction of the Psalter and was described in the early Church as *ruminatio* ("rumination").[97] As *GILH* 104 puts it well: "Whoever sings the psalms properly, meditating as he passes from verse to verse, is always prepared to respond in his heart." The singing of the psalms can promote this attitude. This psalm-*meditatio*, grounded in the matter-of-factness with which the Psalms speak of God or to God, orients one inherently to standing in the presence of God and praising him. The Trinitarian doxology (*Gloria patri*), which has been added to the

---

Ambroos Verheul, "Les psaums dans la prière des heures hier et aujourd'hui," *QL* 71, no. 3/4 (1990): 261-95.

95 Already Benedict, who was oriented to the Liturgy of the Hours in the Roman basilica monasteries, adopted some cathedral elements, including fixed Psalms. Cf. *Regula Benedicti* 8-19, esp. 17-18 (WEC 4:27-31). In the Middle Ages, attention shifted from the Psalm as text to the singing of the Psalms as an act with a specific intention that was, however, often independent of the wording. See Paul Bradshaw, "From Word to Action: The Changing Role of Psalmody in Early Christianity," in *Like a Two-Edged Sword: The Word of God in Liturgy and History* (FS Canon Donald Gray), ed. M. R. Dudley (Norwich: Canterbury Press, 1995), 21-37.

96 Braulik, "Rezeptionsästhetik," 529 (italics original).

97 See Buchinger, "Hermeneutik," 219.

psalms since John Cassian († 430/35),[98] takes one explicitly into the dynamic of the praise of God and emphasizes this.[99] It is obvious that, precisely in the broad spectrum of their contents and their language, the Psalms complement and enrich "personal prayer." They help to form a bridge between Sacred Scripture and daily living.

2. ADDITIONAL REFLECTIONS ON THE HERMENEUTICS OF THE *GILH*

We shall now reflect on the hermeneutical aspects or instruments that the *GILH* mentions with regard to the Psalter and expand these. The *GILH* attaches great weight to the Christological interpretation of the Psalms. Although the one who prays should begin by "keeping to their literal meaning" (107), one must (*debet*) "pay attention to the full meaning of the psalms, especially that messianic understanding" (109), because one is praying the Psalms in the name of the Church. In terms of the literal meaning, each Psalm is preceded by the superscription from the Hebrew Bible.[100] Since "the psalms offer only a foretaste[101] of the fullness of time revealed in Christ" (101), an aid was added: "To promote prayer in the light of the new revelation, a phrase from the New Testament or Fathers is added as an invitation to pray in a Christian way" (111).[102]

This hermeneutical model of stages from the "literal" to the "full meaning" has been criticized. First of all, the fact of rereading within the Old Testament itself means that one cannot speak of one literal meaning in the singular; and the varied interpretations in the Church Fathers and in liturgy (as we have seen with Psalm 24) show that it is even less possible to speak of one single "full meaning."[103] The Christological interpretation of the Psalms is, of course, a proven hermeneutical instrument that is used in the Liturgy of the Hours especially in Holy Week, on feast days, or on Friday and on Sunday as the weekly Pascha. The *GILH* rightly says that the antiphons frequently

---

98 See John Cassian, *Institutis* 2.8 (SChr 109:72; WEC 3:166); Balthasar Fischer and Helmut Hucke, "Poetische Formen *[Psalmen]*," in Berger, *Gestalt des Gottesdienstes*, 182.

99 See *GILH*, 123.

100 See *GILH*, 107,111.

101 It is clear that the English text consciously avoids a literal translation of *umbra* as "shadow."

102 See André Rose, "Sous-Titres psalmiques de la 'Liturgia Horarum,'" in *Mens concordet voci [...]* (Paris: Desclée, 1983), 679-90.

103 See Buchinger, "Hermeneutik," 200, 204-07, 220-21.

offer a key to "the typological and festive interpreting" (113). But one cannot infer from this any basic obligatory rule (*GILH* 109: *debet* means "must") that the Psalms are to be interpreted in this way in principle. The problem lies in the exclusiveness of the Christological interpretation, which is in fact also contradicted by the testimony of the Church Fathers. The English translation tones down *debet* into "should," because unlike the *GILH*, the celebration of the Liturgy of the Hours leaves one free *not* to interpret a psalm on Friday as speaking of the suffering Christ.[104] The ability to grasp one and the same psalm in various ways is one aspect of the spiritual riches of the Liturgy of the Hours. Besides this, the psalms do not need to be turned into Christian prayer (*GILH* 110) through one specific Christological understanding, since they are a part of Sacred Scripture and are thus already a book of the Church.

The *GILH* also notes: "Whoever prays the psalms in the Liturgy of the Hours does not say them in his own name so much as in the name of the whole body of Christ" (108). The one who prays is thus summoned to transcend his or her own ego. This makes it possible also to pray psalms that do not suit one's momentary mood—because one is united to other members of the Church who are experiencing what the psalm expresses. And precisely this increases the breadth of the individual's prayer. Ultimately, this involves the hermeneutical mechanism of role identification, which remains a personal, conscious act of reception when one transcends one's own self.[105]

The antiphons can provide important help to understand a psalm because they underline something it says or give it a "special color" (*GILH* 113) appropriate to the liturgical year or to a specific occasion. If they are not taken from the Psalm itself, they can offer particularly interesting links to other passages in the Old and New Testaments, and this in turn makes manifest the unity of Scripture. *GILH* 112 also speaks of optional psalm collects that can contribute to the (Christian) understanding; it is, of course, also possible that such prayers have the restrictive effect of imposing one particular interpretation. They are not contained in the *Liturgia Horarum* but are found in the current American translation.

Another implicit hermeneutical statement is the expunging of the so-called imprecatory psalms—58 (57), 83 (82), 109 (108), and some verses in sixteen other psalms—"because of certain psychological difficulties" (*GILH* 131). The preparatory commission had argued for a replacement psalm and the inclusion of the imprecatory verses in parentheses, so that—especially when the people were present—one could have chosen to retain or omit

---

104 On freedom in the reception, see B.IX.33.1.

105 See B.IX.33.2.

them, but Pope Paul VI decided in 1968 to expunge them.[106] One can ask whether this decision, taken for pastoral reasons, was a better choice,[107] since these psalms or verses are problematic above all if they were to be understood directly as one's own prayer. For as we have seen, this is certainly not the only possible liturgical reception of the Psalms. Besides this, there may sometimes be situations in which people find their emotions expressed in such words and can thus let them flow into a prayer that brings healing.[108] The German Monastic Liturgy of the Hours has remained faithful to the Rule of Benedict (18,23) by retaining the entire Psalter and bracketing the imprecatory verses, in order to leave the decision to the communities themselves. The original reflections of the preparatory commission seem a sensible compromise between fidelity to the whole of Scripture and pastoral considerations. It would be prudent to assign the "imprecatory psalms" only to the Office of Readings (as in the Monastic Book of Hours) or to the little Hours, since these are prayed by persons with a greater familiarity with the Liturgy of the Hours.

This brings us to an even more important question about the distribution of the psalms, which likewise has hermeneutical implications, since the combination produces an intertextuality that likewise influences the interpretation of the individual psalms. One notices again and again how the juxtaposition of psalms with differing contents produces a certain stimulus in the Liturgy of the Hours as the various statements complement or develop or form a contrast to each other. The question here is: What criteria guide the combination of psalms? In principle, the liturgical tradition knows both the selection of individual psalms and the sequence that follows the Psalter. At the time of the postconciliar liturgical reform, exegesis focused primarily on the individual psalm and on the genres of the psalms, paying scarcely any attention to the context in the Psalter, and this is why the reform of the Liturgy of the Hours did the same. It began by assigning individual psalms to particular hours and days, then distributed psalms in keeping with their

---

106 See Huonder, *Psalmen*, 75, 97-102, 161, 186-90. The draft of *GILH* 131 contained the following sentence, later omitted: "One must, however, reject the opinion that any kind of doubt would exist with regard to their suitability for Christian prayer" (Huonder, 123). See Bugnini, *Reform of the Liturgy*, 508-11.

107 See Notker Füglister, "*Vom Mut zur ganzen Schrift. Zur vorgesehenen Eliminierung der sogenannten Fluchpsalmen aus dem neuen römischen Brevier,*" StZ 185 (1969): 186-200.

108 One of the arguments adduced by Dieter Böhler, "*Vom einsamen Murmeln des Gerechten zum Jubelchor der ganzen Schöpfung. Was es bedeutet, im Stundengebet nicht nur Psalmen, sondern den Psalter zu beten,*" Notitiae 45 (2008): 433, applies the early Christian Christological maxim to the imprecatory psalms: "*Quod non assumptum non redemptum.*"

genres (for example, a preference in Lauds for a psalm of lamentation and one of praise), and then filled the gaps with the remaining psalms, although here attention was paid to the canonical arrangement of the Psalter.[109]

This illustrates the influence of exegesis on liturgy. A critical reflection by liturgical scholarship must register an influence from exegetical currents and be aware that this will take different forms at different periods. Today, exegetes have given us a new insight into the redaction of the Psalter and into the unity of the Psalter as a canonical book,[110] and this has led to a greater understanding of the traditional distribution *currente psalterio* than was common in the period of the postconciliar reform of the Liturgy. This gives greater weight to the biblically based hermeneutics of the Psalter. The advantage here, once one's eyes have been opened to this approach, is that one can perceive the references within the Psalter that "lead on" from one psalm to the next.[111] The Rule of Benedict had already assigned fixed psalms to certain hours or days, and distributed the other psalms in their canonical order. It is certainly conceivable that different ways of using the Psalms— both a deliberate choice and the canonical sequence—and thereby different hermeneutics could be employed alongside each other in the Liturgy of the Hours.[112] This example illustrates how exegesis and liturgy have worked together and are related to each other.[113]

---

109 See, in addition to *GILH*, 126–35, especially Huonder, *Psalmen*, 58–104, 207–32, esp. 74, 227–32.

110 In the case of the Psalms, the canonical approach to exegesis not only looks at the individual Psalm, but locates it in the Psalter as a whole, or in the context of the whole of Scripture. See Erich Zenger, "Von der Psalmenexegese zur Psalterexegese," *BiKi* 56. No. 1 (2001): 8–15; Egbert Ballhorn, "Kontext wird Text. Die Psalmen in Forschungsgeschichte, in biblischer Zeit und in christliche Liturgie," *BiLi* 77, no. 3 (2004): 161–70.

111 See Lohfink, "Psalmengebet und Psalterredaktion," esp. 459; Böhler, "Im Stundengebet den Psalter beten," 431–34.

112 See Angelus A. Häußling, "Die Psalmen des Alten Testamentes in der Liturgie des Neuen Bundes," in Richter and Kranemann, *Christologie der Liturgie*, 101–02.

113 See C.39.

CHAPTER TEN

Hermeneutical Insights

In addition to the fundamental appreciation of the Psalms (in continuity with Judaism), of the expressive power of their poetry, their closeness to our lives, and so on, the many interpretative possibilities are surely the reason why they are so frequently employed in the Liturgy. As our example of Psalm 24 (23) has shown, the liturgical context or the occasion of the celebration functions as a hermeneutical lens.[114] It gives the psalm a certain color, so that usually one particular statement (sometimes a single verse) that has suggested the choice takes the central position.

The various uses depend on various hermeneutical approaches: a psalm can be understood in a literal and in a transposed sense. The redactions of the Psalter open a path to an interpretation in terms of David and Israel, and this path, continuing the New Testament interpretation, leads further in the Liturgy to Christ and the Church. A psalm can (but need not) be expounded Christologically as *vox de Christo* (voice about Christ), *vox Christi* (voice of Christ), or *vox ad Christum* (voice to Christ). This is an obvious interpretation above all on the feasts of Christ, but it is explicitly prescribed in the Roman liturgy only in rare instances.[115]

This section has drawn attention to the various ways of employing the Psalms. They can be chosen to accompany a liturgical action, whereby the psalm and the action interpret each other. Here, the entire psalm can be used, for example, as a processional chant, or else only single verses are taken from it. When they are detached and given a new context, they often acquire an additional meaning.[116]

Psalms are found more frequently as independent elements. The Responsorial Psalm in the Mass, as an "integral part of the Liturgy of the Word"[117] and as a sung reading, can take on various (complementary) functions:

---

114 See B.VII.23.

115 See B.IX.33.1.

116 See B.VII.23.1.

117 *GIRM*, 61; *GILM*, 19.

proclamation, meditation, and /or answer. This makes it clear that a general ascription of one function is impossible, because the Psalms (in a manner similar to the other readings) resist any strict systematization. This aspect must be borne in mind in reflection on a biblical hermeneutics. The refrain has a great hermeneutical importance for the understanding of the Psalm, and to some extent of the reading(s). It makes the congregation participants not only through the singing, but also through its formulation in the first person or through its relatedness in words or in contents to those present. The refrain, and to some extent the Responsorial Psalm as a whole, create a bridge between the Word of God that is proclaimed and those who are worshiping here and now. In this way, they take the dialogue between God and human beings to a deeper level.[118]

Another hermeneutics of the Psalms can be seen in the Liturgy of the Hours. The Psalms, as an independent element located between reading and prayer, serve the psalm-*meditatio* (cf. Ps 1:2) out of which the prayer grows— whether as a praying *of* the psalms themselves (if they present themselves directly as prayer) or as a praying *with* the psalms. In any case, the psalms that are recited promote personal prayer, because they bring the various situations of life into contact with God. Precisely the psalms, thanks to their specific linguistic character and their content, are capable of linking Scripture and daily life. Since the mood articulated in the psalms is not always one's own mood, they make it clear that the Liturgy of the Hours is always carried out in the name of the Church. They thus also display an ecclesial dimension of the hermeneutics of Scripture.[119]

Besides this, several passages in this section have made it clear that the mechanism of role identification, making the words of the Psalms one's own and speaking them either for others or in one's own person, is an important mode of the reception of Scripture.[120] We have also touched on the phenomenon of intertextuality[121] (between the Responsorial Psalm and the scriptural readings, or between the individual psalms in the Liturgy of the Hours).

When we pray with the Psalms, the Liturgy of the Hours shows how Scripture can become prayer. This is also the case with the prayers formulated by the Church, to which we turn in the next section.

---

118 See B.VIII.27.2.

119 See B.IX.33.2.

120 See B.IX.34.

121 See B.VII.23.

SECTION III

Prayers

The liturgical prayers are permeated by Sacred Scripture. Since they are "scriptural in their inspiration and their force" (*SC* 24), the present chapter will examine another form of the use of Scripture, which is not directly read as in the readings or psalms but shines through as a background foil that inspires the liturgical language of prayer. The way in which Scripture is used also shows how it is understood, and this in turn will illustrate further aspects of a liturgical hermeneutics of the Bible.

The structure of this section once again follows the conciliar article that speaks of "*preces et orationes*." Among the *preces*, the Eucharistic Prayers and the solemn prayers of the sacramental celebrations have a central position. Our example will be the prayers of episcopal ordination because the examination of the Roman and the Byzantine rites allows us to infer systematic conclusions and formal information with regard to the use of the Bible. A further reason is the breadth aimed at in part A, which results in part from discussing the various sacraments in order to establish a solid basis for systematic reflection. Chapter 12 looks at the various types of orations.[1]

---

1 No comparison with other rites is undertaken here. There are no comparable brief prayers in the Byzantine liturgy, and a comparison with the Milanese rite would not supply any new insights.

This section thus also covers a broad temporal spectrum. Our choice of the Roman prayer for the ordination of a bishop, which is taken from the *Apostolic Tradition*, means that our study is looking at a prayer text from the earliest period (the beginning of the third century); the newly formulated orations (such as the pericope orations of the Italian missal) clearly differ from this text. Within the same chapter, therefore, old and new texts will be combined, while paying attention to the differing age of liturgical texts. This is important for a liturgical hermeneutics of Scripture.

CHAPTER ELEVEN

Celebrations of the Sacraments
The Prayer for the Ordination of a Bishop

In accordance with Augustine's dictum, "*Accedit verbum ad elementum et fit sacramentum*,"[2] prayer is an essential aspect of the sacramental celebrations, alongside the sign or ritual. In a basic anamnetic-epicletic structure: recourse is first made to God's saving action in Scripture found in order to then formulate what we ask for in petition.

1. TODAY'S ORDINATION PRAYER IN THE ROMAN LITURGY (APOSTOLIC TRADITION)

The Old Roman prayer of episcopal ordination, as was already attested in the *Sacramentarium Veronense* (*Leonianum*) and later expanded by an Old Gallican insertion, was used for centuries,. The postconciliar liturgical reform replaced it by the even older ordination prayer in the *Apostolic Tradition*,[3] which contains in a concrete manner the tasks of the bishop as successor of the apostles. One important reason for this change was its (ecumenical) function as a bridge to the Ethiopians and the Maronites, who

---

2 Augustine, *Trac. in Ioh.* 80,3 (CChr.SL 36:529; WEC 3:26). "The word is added to the element and it becomes a sacrament."

3 *Apostolic Tradition* 3: FontC 1:216-20; WEC 1:200; Paul F. Bradshaw, *The Apostolic Tradition. A Commentary*, Hermeneia (Minneapolis: Fortress Press, 2002), 30-36. See Klemens Richter, "Zum Ritus der Bischofsordination in der 'Apostolischen Überlieferung' Hippolyts von Rom und davon abhängigen Schriften," ALw 17 (1975): 7–51; James F. Pugliesi, *Epistemological Principles and Roman Catholic Rites*, vol. 1 of *The Process of Admission to Ordained Ministry. A Comparative Study* (Collegeville, MN: Liturgical Press, 1996), 50-60, on the use of Scripture esp. 54-56; Paul F. Bradshaw, *Ordination Rites of the Ancient Churches of East and West* (New York: Pueblo, 1990), 46–47, 107–08; Paul F. Bradshaw, *Rites of Ordination. Their History and Theology* (Collegeville, MN: Liturgical Press, 2013), 58-63.

use the same prayer in an expanded form.[4] It is also valuable from a biblical perspective. We now present the text from the American Pontifical;[5] quotations and allusions are noted in parentheses.

a) Anaclesis

1. *God and Father of our Lord Jesus Christ,*
2. *Father of mercies and God of all consolation* (2 Cor 1:3),

b) Anamnesis

I:3 *who dwell on high and look on the lowly* (Ps 112:5–6 LXX),

4. *who know all things before they come to be* (see Dn 13:42);

II:5. and who laid down observances in your Church *through the word of your grace* (see Acts 20:32);

6. who from the beginning, foreordained a nation of the just, born of Abraham;

7. who established rulers and priests [principes et sacerdotes]

8. and did not leave your sanctuary without ministers,

9. and who, *from the foundation of the world,* were pleased to be glorified in *those you have chosen* (see Eph 1:4–6):

c) Epiclesis I: Sending of the Spirit (with anamnetic insertion)

10. Pour out now upon these chosen ones that *power* which is from you, the *Spirit of governance* (Ps 51:14; see Jn 15:26; Acts 1:8)

11. whom you gave to your beloved Son, Jesus Christ (see Mk 1:10 par.),

12. the Spirit whom he bestowed upon the holy Apostles (see Jn 20:22),

13. who established the Church in each place as your sanctuary

14. for the glory and unceasing praise of your name.

d) Epiclesis II: Petitions for Future Tasks

15. Grant, O Father, *knower of all hearts,* that these, your servants, *whom you have chosen* (see Acts 1:24; Is 42:1) for the office of Bishop

---

4 See Bernard Botte, "L'ordination de l'évêque," *MD* 98 (1969): 120; Bruno Kleinheyer, "Ordinationen und Beauftragungen," in *Sakramentliche Feiern II,* ed. B. Kleinheyer, GdK 8 (Regensburg: Pustet, 1984), 53 (see also Kleinheyer, 27–28).

5 *Rites of Ordination of a Bishop, of Priests, and of Deacons,* 2nd typical edition (Washington, D.C.: United States Conference of Catholic Bishops, 2003), 53–54.

16. may shepherd your holy flock (see Ez 34:11–16; Jn 21:15–17; Acts 20:28; 1 Pt 5:2–3).

17. *Serving you night and day* (1 Thes 2:9; Acts 20:31), may they fulfill before you without reproach the ministry of the High Priesthood;

18. so that, always gaining your favor,

19. they may offer up the gifts of your Holy Church.

20. Grant that, by the power of the *Spirit* of the High Priesthood, they may have the power to *forgive sins* according to your command (see Jn 20:23),

21. assign offices according to your decree,

22. and loose every bond (see Is 58:6 *LXX*) according to the power given by you to the Apostles (see Mt 16:19; 18:18).

23 May they please you by their *meekness* (2 Tim 2:25 *Gr.*; Jas 3:13) and *purity of heart* (Ps 51:12; Mt 5:8; 2 Tm 2:22),

24 presenting a fragrant offering to you (see Eph 5:2; Phil 4:18; 2 Cor 2:14–16; Gn 8:21; Ex 29:41)[6]

e) **Doxology**

25. through your Son Jesus Christ,

26. through whom glory and power and honor are yours

27. with the Holy Spirit in the holy Church,

28. now and for ever.

Instead of a detailed analysis of this prayer, let us look at striking points in the use of Scripture. Scripture leaves its mark upon the entire prayer. In the anamnesis, we notice first of all that the scriptural allusions are chosen with increasing concreteness to speak of the bishop. Initially, lines 3-4 speak briefly in a global manner of God's care and foreknowledge; the Old Testament passages cited here have no relation to the ordination. In 5-9, we then hear of God's choice of individuals from the descendants of Abraham to serve in the sanctuary down through the ages. The anamnetic insertion that follows the epiclesis links the bishop to the apostles, since he receives the same Spirit whom Christ gave to them. The bishop who receives ordination is thus always integrated into the Church and linked to it.

The anamnesis is not simply—as it might first appear — structured in an Old Testament part (3-9) and a New Testament part (11-14). The contents of the two Testaments are interwoven because although the starting point is the "nation of the just, born of Abraham," no clear boundary is drawn vis-à-vis

---

6 This expression occurs frequently in the Old Testament.

the New Testament. The conceptual pair "rulers and priests" (ἄρχοντες καὶ ἱερεῖς), which is often found in the *LXX*, can be interpreted as referring to Judah and the Levites,[7] or to the Christian office bearers. The text leaves it open whether it speaks of the bishop, who united both functions in his own person,[8] or of bishop and presbyter. The second possibility is suggested both by indications in the *Apostolic Tradition*[9] and by the fact that the threefold list of "leaders, priests, and levites," frequently found in the Books of Chronicles, Ezra, and Nehemiah,[10] was transposed to the threefold ministry. Another indicator that this anamnetic part does not refer only to the Old Testament is the following "now" (*et nunc*) of the epiclesis (10), because this implies a continuity "from the beginning" (6) down to the contemporary celebration of episcopal ordination. God's action in history embraces the Old and the New Testament, as well as the present day. While not in any way diminishing the newness of the Christ event, this also points to the continuity between Israel and the Church.

It is in the nature of things that Scripture marks the anamnetic part of the ordination prayer. But the epiclesis too is inspired by Scripture. The biblical foundation lends weight to the petition. Above all, the bishop's tasks are deduced in this way from Scripture, and the bishop is once more declared to be the successor of the Apostles. To him belongs in the first place the pastoral care, which is derived from the mission entrusted to Peter after Easter (16), and the priestly ministry as *summum sacerdotium*, which embraces indefatigable prayer, the celebration of the Eucharist, and the forgiveness of sins (17-20). The prayer then speaks of the ministries (ordination) and of the power of loosing (public penance in the Church?; 21-22). The ordination prayer has recourse three times to the commission or the authority of Jesus that has passed over to the Apostles and now belongs to the bishops. At the same time, Christ as model, as the one who is truly the Good Shepherd and high priest, shines through.

In these immediate references to Christ, the interlocking of anamnesis and epiclesis, which was already marked through the anamnetic insertion in the structure of the prayer as a whole, finds expression in individual verses too. In addition to the temporal link "now" (10), which we have

---

7 See Richter, "Bischofsordination," 25.

8 See Richter, 25. This interpretation is supported by Pierre-Marie Gy, "La théologie des prières anciennes pour l'ordination des évêques et des prêtres," *RSPhTh* 58 (1974): 602-3.

9 See August Jilek, *Initiationsfeier und Amt. Ein Beitrag zur Struktur und Theologie der Ämter und des Taufgottesdienstes in der frühen Kirche (Traditio Apostolica, Tertullian, Cyprian)*, EHS 23/130 (Frankfurt/M.: Lang, 1979), 13-14, 23-24.

10 See 1 Chr 23:2; 2 Chr 19:8; Ezr 1:5; 9:1; Neh 8:13; 9:38.

mentioned, there are literal citations from salvation history: "who *know all things* (4)/"*knower of all hearts*" (15); "*rulers* and *priests*" (7)/"Spirit of *governance*" (10) and "ministry of the *High Priesthood*" (17); "*those you have chosen* [in a general form] (9)/ "*whom you have chosen* for the office of Bishop" (15); "*bestowed upon the holy Apostles*" (13)/"*given by you to the Apostles*" (22). Behind these formal observations on the anamnetic-epicletic structure stands a central ecclesiological affirmation that sustains the presence of the episcopal ministry down through the ages: namely, that the Church continues, in the power of the Spirit, what Christ has established.

Let us now look at the passages cited above with their specific contexts within the Bible. It is important, when considering how Scripture is used, to determine how far the context from which the passages are taken also fits the new liturgical framework. In other words, is this context implicitly "cited along with the passage," or does this context rather tend to fade from view? In several cases, there is a logical relationship or continuity between the scriptural texts and the episcopal ordination. The references to the Gospels look back to the mission entrusted by Jesus, and thus present the bishop as the successor of the apostles (task of shepherding in Jn 20:15–17; power to loose in Mt 16:19, 18:18; gift of the Spirit with the authority to forgive sins in Jn 20:22–23). The Acts of the Apostles plays a not unimportant role, thereby linking the prayer to the early period of the Church: the reference to the election of Matthias to complete the number of the Twelve (Acts 1:15–26) unobtrusively introduces the collegiality of the apostles into the ordination prayer.[11] Paul's farewell speech to the elders in Miletus (Acts 20:17–38) is quoted twice. Here the bishops are directly mentioned as those appointed by the Holy Spirit to pasture God's Church as shepherds (Acts 20:28). Paul's admonitions to Timothy (23) who, according to tradition, was the bishop of Ephesus, are transposed to the bishop. The references to Scripture here are doubtless consciously chosen and are appropriate. The allusion to 1 Thes 2:9 (17: "Serving you night and day") is a further reference to the apostle Paul as model. Grammatically, this is to be understood as a coordinate to the ministry of shepherd and priest (and not only to the latter), although in the letter itself, Paul speaks only of his apostolic ministry and does not have any liturgical tasks in mind. Here, therefore, a scriptural passage is generalized or extended.

The expression "Spirit of governance" (*spiritus principalis*; *LXX*: πνεῦμα ἡγεμονικόν) from Psalm 51:14 plays a central role in the "epicletic core sentence" (10). Like the psalm, the prayer requests this Spirit from God (Ps 51:13),

---

11 See Richter, "Bischofsordination," 31.

but the context of the sinner who has repented and asks God for a constant spirit fades from view. There are other similar descriptions of the Holy Spirit in the epiclesis of the other two ordination prayers in the *Apostolic Tradition*. The "*spiritus gratiae et concilii presbyterii*" is besought for the priests, and the "*spiritus gratiae tuae et sollicitudinis*" for the deacons.[12] The prayer asks that the "*spiritus principalis*," whom the Father gave the Son (at his baptism in the Jordan) and whom the Son gave to the Apostles, may now be bestowed on the candidate for episcopal ordination. This too suggests that we should not place too much weight on the content of the psalm itself. What counts is rather the adjective, and the language with its biblical echoes. We find further information about the liturgical use of Scripture in a comparison with the Byzantine ordination prayer.

2. THE BYZANTINE PRAYERS FOR THE ORDINATION OF A BISHOP

In the Byzantine ordination liturgy ("cheirotonia"), two prayers are prescribed for each degree. During the episcopal ordination, the candidate kneels before the altar while the principal consecrator lays his hand on him during both prayers, and two other bishops spread out an open Gospel book over his head, with the text facing down, and likewise lay it on his head. In the translation,[13] the biblical quotations and allusions are printed in italics.

First Prayer

a) **Anaclesis**

1. Master, Lord our God [Δέσποτα Κύριε ὁ Θεὸς ἡμῶν],

b) **Anamnesis**

2. through Your illustrious Apostle Paul, you have established the order of ranks and degrees

3. for the service and divine celebration of your precious and most pure mysteries upon your holy altar:

---

12 *Apostolic Tradition* 7–8 (FontC 1:230, 236; WEC 1:202).

13 *The Order of Episcopal Naming, Presentation, Profession, Ordination, and Enthronement: A Supplement for the Divine Liturgy of Our Holy Fathers John Chrysostom and Basil the Great* (Pittsburgh: Byzantine Seminary Press, 2013), 17, 19. The prayers are also attested in the Euchologion Barberini gr. 336 (cf. *L'Eucologio Barberini gr. 336. Seconda edizione riveduta. Con traduzione in lingua italiana*, ed. and trans. S. Parenti and E. Velkovska, BEL.S 80 [Rome: CLV-Edizioni Liturgiche, 2000], 165–66, 333–34).

4. *first, apostles; second, prophets; and third, teachers* (1 Cor 12:28; see Eph 4:11).

c) Epiclesis

5. You, O Master of all, by the descent, power, and grace of your Holy Spirit,
6. strengthen this man whom you have chosen and made worthy of the yoke of the Gospel (see Mt 11:29–30) and of episcopal dignity
7. through the imposition of the hands of us bishops here present (see 1 Tm 4:14; 2 Tm 1:6).

d) Anamnetic Insertion

8. As you strengthened your holy *apostles and prophets*, as you *anointed kings*, as you *sanctified hierarchs,*
9. make his episcopacy blameless, adorn him with all honor, show him to be holy,
10. so that he may be worthy to ask for that which is for the salvation of the people and you hear him.

e) Doxology

11. For *holy is your name* and *glorified* is *your kingdom* (see Mt 6:9–10) of the Father, and of the Son, and of the Holy Spirit, now and ever and forever.

Second Prayer

a) Anaclesis

1. Lord, our God [Κύριε ὁ θεὸς ἡμῶν],

b) Anamnesis

2. because human nature is incapable of enduring your divine essence,
3. you, in your plan of salvation [οἰκονομία], *appointed* teachers for us,
4. *of like nature as ourselves, to stand before your altar to offer sacrifice and oblation for all your people* (see Heb 5:1–3).

c) Epiclesis

5. You, O Lord, make this man,
6. who has been shown to be *steward* of episcopal *grace* (see 1 Pt 4:10),
7. an *imitator* (see 1 Cor 11:1; 1 Thes 1:6) of you, the true *Shepherd* (see Jn 10), who *lay down your life for your sheep* (see Jn 10:11,15);

8. *a guide to the blind, a light to those in darkness, an instructor to the ignorant, a teacher to the young* (Rom 2:19–20), *a lamp to the world* (see Mt 5:14),

9. so that, having perfected the souls entrusted to him in this present life,

10. he may stand unashamed before your throne and receive the *great reward*

11. *which you have prepared* (see 1 Cor 2:9) for those who struggle for the preaching of your Gospel (see Mt 5:12; Lk 6:23; Phil 1:27).

d) Doxology

12. For yours are mercy and salvation, O our God, and we give glory to you, Father, Son, and Holy Spirit, now and ever and forever.

Let us now analyze the use of Scripture in these two prayers.[14] The first refers explicitly to the apostle Paul, through whom God has established the degrees and the ordering of the ministries, and then quotes literally 1 Cor 12:28 (see Eph 4:11), where apostles, prophets, and teachers are mentioned (2–4). Baumstark argues that this explicit quotation suggests that this prayer is more recent;[15] it was probably added to the second prayer at a later date (no later than the sixth century?).[16] The content of what is said is more important: the ordination prayer, echoing 1 Cor 12:4–31a, makes it clear that the initiative and the ordering come from God, who appoints apostles, prophets, and teachers, and distributes the various gifts of grace of the same Spirit for the good of the community. It is striking that the ordination prayer locates this "order of ranks" (2) in a more strongly liturgical context (3: "for the [...] divine celebration"), which is scarcely present in Paul.

This brief anamnetic part is followed by an epiclesis for the one chosen as bishop. This contains biblical language. It prays that he may be strengthened through the descent, the grace, and the power of the Holy Spirit (5). This sequence of three concepts has its origin in the intensifications common in Byzantine prayers; it is less likely to be meant to evoke specific biblical

---

14 See Paul De Clerck, "L'usage de l'Ecriture dans les prières d'ordination des liturgies byzantine, gallicane et romaine," in *Ordination et ministères*, ed. A. M. Triacca and A. Pistoia, BEL.S 85 (Rome: CLV-Edizioni Liturgiche, 1996), 108–9.

15 See De Cleck, 108; Anton Baumstark, *Liturgie comparée. Principes et méthodes pour l'étude historique des liturgies chrétiennes*, revised Bernard Botte, 3rd ed., Collection Irénikon (Chevetogne: Éditions de Chevetogne, 1953), 67.

16 See Bradshaw, *Ordination Rites*, 52; Bradshaw, *Rites of Ordination*, 93.

passages about (for example) the power of the Holy Spirit.[17] The same applies to the anamnetic insertion, which prays that the same strengthening may now take place as it took place in the past when God strengthened the apostles and prophets, anointed the kings, and sanctified the high priests (8). Although no one specific scriptural passage is in the background here, reference is made both to the New Testament (apostles) and the Old (kings and high priests). The prophets can be assigned to both Testaments, because Paul frequently mentioned apostles and prophets in one breath.[18] The bishop is basically presented in continuity with these groups of persons.

His tasks are described only in very general terms: the "yoke of the Gospel" (6) that he is found worthy to take upon himself refers to the task of proclamation, and recalls the "yoke" of Jesus, which is not oppressive (see Mt 11:29). It is only in the light of the logion of Jesus that the "yoke" is given a positive twist and becomes completely understandable. This applies likewise to the laying-on of the Gospel book, in the correlation between word and sign.[19] Alongside the apostolic task, the liturgical task is mentioned when the text speaks three times of the high priest and mentions in the introduction the service of the holy table (3, 6, 9).

The second (older) prayer, which is explicitly addressed to Christ (5), deepens and concretizes the first prayer. The anamnetic introduction speaks only of teachers whom Christ has appointed in his plan of salvation (3). But it is interesting that these teachers are described in greater detail with characteristics of the Jewish high priest in the Letter to the Hebrews (Heb 5:1–3). This is why the teacher is given the cultic task of presenting sacrifices and gifts for the people before the throne of God (3–4). There is, however, no reference to Christ as high priest, a term often used in the Letter to the Hebrews. The term "steward of episcopal grace" (6) is borrowed from 1 Peter 4:10, in such a way that, where the biblical text speaks of the "manifold grace" with which all the members of the community are to serve one another, this grace

---

17 The expression "power of the Spirit" is found, e.g., with regard to Jesus (Lk 4:14), the apostles (Acts 1:8), Paul (Rom 15:13, 19), or Timothy (2 Tm 1:14). It is possible that the words "descent," "power," and "grace" are a reminiscence of the Annunciation (Lk 1:35).

18 See, in addition to the ordination prayer (1 Cor 12:28; Eph 4:11), e.g., Eph 2:20; 3:5.

19 In the West, the Gospel book, interpreted as "yoke," was laid on the shoulders rather than on the head. The book held open over the head symbolizes the power of the Gospel that is to come upon the one chosen as bishop. See Bernard Botte, "Das Weihesakrament nach den Gebeten des Weiheritus," in Das apostolische Amt, ed. J. Guyot (Mainz: Matthias-Grünewald, 1961), 22; Kleinheyer, "Ordinationen," 29. The oldest manuscript (Barberini gr. 336, 8th century) does not have the "yoke"; the candidate for ordination takes the Gospel on himself. The laying-on of the Gospel book, in the manner described above, is in accordance with this (Gy, "Théologie des prières anciennes," 604, 611; Parenti and Velkovska, L'Eucologio, 165, 333).

is now called "high-priestly" and is related specifically only to the bishop. These cases exemplify how the context of a scriptural passage in the Bible itself is lost to view. The quotation from Rom 2:19–20 (8) is actually employed against the original meaning and the intention of the author, because Paul is speaking of Jews who "are confident" of being "a guide for the blind [see Mt 15:14] and a light for those in darkness, […] a trainer of the foolish and teacher of the simple"—but in reality are not so. The ordination prayer takes up this list literally and applies it in a positive twist to the bishop, so that it appears appropriate in the prayer. The use of Scripture is thus very carefree: it serves as a storehouse with usable verses that are isolated from their biblical context and situated in a new liturgical context. Paul De Clerck calls such a proceeding "typique de l'usage ancient de l'Ecriture," which is particularly marked by the oral culture, whereas today, thanks to the culture of writing, a different value is accorded to the con*text*.[20]

The content of the central petition deserves special attention: may the one who is chosen be an imitator/performer (μιμητής) of Christ the true Shepherd (7). Paul speaks several times of imitating: the Christians of his community are to be his imitators, just as he is an imitator of Christ.[21] This can be understood more deeply in terms of the theology of incarnation and of icons: the bishop is to be an icon of Christ (so to speak), one who makes visible the Christ who is invisibly present.[22] Naturally, this immediacy can apply only to his liturgical tasks. The metaphor of shepherd, where the laying down of his life (unlike the hired servant) is explicitly emphasized, likewise portrays the bishop as an imitator of Christ, just like the Apostle.

The ordination prayer also contains two allusions to the Sermon on the Mount: the list of tasks from Rom 2:19–20 is expanded by "a lamp in the world" (8; see Mt 5:14). Finally, the allusion in the final beatitude holds out the prospect of the "great reward" (10) for the "struggle" in preaching (see Mt 5:12). What the Sermon on the Mount postulates for all Christians is thus narrowed down to speak of the bishops.

---

20 De Clerck, "L'usage de l'Ecriture," 108.

21 See 1 Cor 11:1; 1 Thess 1:6.

22 See Michael Kunzler, "Darsteller des wahren Hirten (Μιμητὴς τοῦ ἀληθινοῦ Ποιμένος). Zugänge zum Wesen des Weiheamts am Beispiel der byzantinischen Bischofsweihe," in *Manifestatio Ecclesiae. Studien zu Pontifikale und bischöflicher Liturgie* (FS Reiner Kaczynski), ed. W. Haunerland, StPaLi 17 (Regensburg: Pustet, 2004), 27-33.

3. RESULT OF COMPARISONS

When we compare the ordination prayers of the Roman and the Byzantine liturgy, we see that they share the same basic anamnetic-epicletic structure of liturgical praying. In both cases, not only the anamnesis, but also the epiclesis has recourse to Scripture. The concepts of *"principes et sacerdotes"* in the anamnesis, and the mention of the "prophets" in the list of apostles – prophets – kings – and high priests, show that it is not possible to draw a clear boundary between the Old Testament and the New. For a biblical hermeneutics, this means that the intention here is not to evoke specific biblical passages; rather, Scripture as a whole is presupposed as background. The interpretative openness can be an indication that, with regard to God's plan of salvation (οἰκονομία), the two Testaments are perceived as a unity. It is nevertheless striking that the Byzantine prayers never quote the Old Testament (only kings and high priests are mentioned in the first prayer), while the prayer of the *Apostolic Tradition* not only has Old Testament quotations, but also establishes explicitly a relationship between the origins and the children of Abraham, via the Christ event, to the "here and now" of the celebration.

At the same time, quotations are employed that can be located more or less clearly; indeed, in the first Byzantine ordination prayer, the quotation is introduced as such. In most instances, passages are chosen that are thematically appropriate to the liturgical occasion because of their context in the Bible. Here, therefore, it is obvious that Scripture provided the substance of the ideas, so that a knowledgeable person who prays can and should hear the echo of the biblical background. To some extent, however, the context disappears from view; or, in the case of the second Byzantine ordination prayer, the quotation is in fact used against the original intention. This shows that the compilers of these liturgical texts did not have the deliberate intention of formulating prayers that would, as far as possible, be "in conformity" with the Bible. Rather, they had Scripture in their ears, so that it flowed *ex corde* into the prayers.

In both traditions, the bishop's tasks are derived from Scripture; the most important of these are described with the images of the shepherd and the high priest. In terms of biblical hermeneutics, the interesting point about the latter is that the Old Testament service in the Temple and the episcopal ministry are not merely typologically linked or compared. Rather, the functions of the Old Testament high priest are recognized in the tasks of the bishop.[23]

---

23 See Ernst Dassmann, "Die Bedeutung des Alten Testamentes für das Verständnis des kirchlichen Amtes in der frühpatristischen Theologie," in Dassmann, Ämter und Dienste in den frühchristlichen Gemeinden, Hereditas 8 (Bonn: Borengässer, 1994), 104.

With the exception of the concepts of shepherd and high priest, completely different passages are adduced in the two traditions. The ordination prayer of the *Apostolic Tradition* describes the bishop—united to the Church—as the successor of the Apostles, who receives the same Spirit and the same directives and powers as they did. It therefore makes more use of the corresponding passages in the Gospels and Acts. The Byzantine ordination prayers mostly transpose affirmations from the (Pauline) epistolary literature in a new context to the bishop. A striking element in the content of the second prayer is the description of the bishop as a μιμητής of the Good Shepherd. This binds him immediately to Christ (and not, as in the *Apostolic Tradition*, "only" to the apostles).

CHAPTER TWELVE

Orations

When we investigate the use of Sacred Scripture in the orations, and the underlying implications for a biblical hermeneutics, it is important to note the various "types" of orations. In what follows, we shall discuss "classic" collects, which derive from the Roman tradition, the orations for the feasts of saints, and the newly formulated alternative orations in the Italian missal, which are related to Scripture. We thus have an exemplary *tour d'horizon* through history down to the present day.

1. CLASSICAL COLLECTS OF
THE ROMAN TRADITION

In this chapter, we shall give priority to the collects because they are less dictated by their situation in the Mass than are the prayer over the offerings and the prayer after Communion, where their function within the celebration usually also determines their content. We take as our examples the collect of Pentecost Sunday and the collect of the 20th Sunday in Ordinary Time, to compare one oration related to the festal cycle and another that is not. Both are taken from the mid-seventh-century *Sacramentarium Gelasianum Vetus*:

On Pentecost
O God, who by the mystery of today's great feast
sanctify your whole Church
in every people and nation,
pour out, we pray, the gifts of the Holy Spirit
across the face of the earth
and, with the divine grace that was at work
when the Gospel was first proclaimed,

fill now once more the hearts of believers.
Through our Lord Jesus Christ.[24]

The Pentecost collect displays an interesting "liturgical" way of dealing with Scripture, which is found in other orations too. Only a few key words—the many peoples and nations, the pouring-out of the Spirit, the initial proclamation of the Gospel—allude directly to the pericope from Acts 2 that will subsequently be proclaimed, but we are immediately reminded of the entire narrative. Other biblical passages are subtly hinted at, such as the gifts of the Spirit (Is 11:2–3; Gal 5:22–23), the extension to the Gentiles (Acts 10:35), or the pouring-out of the love of God into human hearts, which is brought about by the Spirit (Rom 5:5). Above all, this oration displays one characteristic of the liturgical understanding of Scripture, namely, the uniting of the various temporal levels in the interlocking of the memory of salvation and petition: May God do today ("now once more") for the assembled faithful what he did on the first Pentecost feast. It is taken for granted that one may link in one single sentence God's activity today ("who by the mystery of today's great feast sanctify your whole Church") with the story of Pentecost ("in every people and nation"). Here, we have not only the remembrance of the Pentecost event in the past. It is proclaimed as something effective today and is placed in relation to the community that celebrates the feast.

The collects in Ordinary Time in *MRom* 1970/2002, unlike those of the festal cycles, are freer in their contents and tend to be kept general. This can be explained by their function as "collects," that is to say, as prayers that "collect together" the silent prayer that precedes them. Their highly theocentric character is striking: often, Christ is mentioned only in the concluding doxology.[25] In the context of the present study, it is important that they are less "in conformity with Scripture" in the literal sense, because they scarcely ever have recourse to one particular biblical passage. The observation of the rules of the *cursus* means, of course, that lengthier direct quotations are not to be expected.[26] Although individual key words frequently display similarities to biblical affirmations, their perception depends on the individual's knowledge

---

24 *Missal*, 453. Latin: *Missale Romanum ex decreto sacrosancti Oecumenici Concilii Vaticani II instauratum auctoritate Paul PP. VI promulgatum Ioannis Pauli PP. II cura recognitum. Editio typica tertia* (Vatican City: Typis Vaticanis, 2002), 445 = *Liber sacramentorum romanae aecclesiae ordinis anni circuli [...]. Sacramentarium Gelasianum*, ed. L. C. Mohlbert, RED.F 4, 3rd ed. (Rome: Herder, 1981) [= GeV], 100 n. 638.

25 See Irmgard Pahl, "Die Stellung Christi in den Präsidialgebeten der Eucharistiefeier," in Meßner, *Bewahren und Erneuern*, 100–1.

26 Jungmann, *Missarum Sollemnia*, 1:377–78.

of the Bible, since the biblical references do not impose themselves on the hearer. An examination of the collects shows that their authors were clearly not aiming for closeness to the Bible as a quality feature. Sometimes, however, biblical allusions are clarified in the translations, as in the collect below.

On the 20th Sunday of Ordinary Time
O God,
who have prepared for those who love you
good things which no eye can see (1 Cor 2:9 [*bona invisibilia*
    praeparasti]),
fill our hearts, we pray, with the warmth of your love,
so that, loving you in all things and above all things,
we may attain your promises,
which surpass every human desire.
Through our Lord Jesus Christ.[27]

2. ORATIONS COMMEMORATING THE SAINTS

Orations commemorating the saints have a different character, because they are inspired by the life of the saint. Obviously enough, the orations for biblical saints borrow from Scripture, since its narrative directly supplies hagiographical material. Nevertheless, it is worth taking a closer look at the feast of the apostle Matthew (September 21) as an example. The collect refers to his calling (Mt 9:9–13, Gospel of the feast) and asks that we, like Matthew, may follow Christ firmly:

O God, who with untold mercy[28]
were pleased to choose as an Apostle
Saint Matthew, the tax collector,
grant that, sustained by his example and intercession,
we may merit to hold firm in following you.
Through our Lord Jesus Christ.[29]

---

27 *Missal*, 480; Latin: *MRom 2002*, 470; GeV 176 n. 1178.

28 The prayer emphasizes God's mercy, probably with recourse to Bede the Venerable (672-735), *Homiliarum Evangelii Libri* I.21 (CChr.SL 122:149): "*miserando atque eligendo.*"

29 *Missal*, 953.

The prayer after Communion is marked even more clearly by a transposition from the saint to the assembled community:

> Sharing in that saving joy, O Lord,
> with which Saint Matthew welcomed
> the Savior as a guest in his home, we pray:
> grant that we may always be renewed
> by the food we receive from Christ,
> who came to call not the just, but sinners to salvation.[30]

This not only takes up once more the Gospel that has been proclaimed; it is also an example of the "liturgical exposition of Scripture" that allows the scriptural text anamnetically to become an event in the celebration of the Eucharist here and now. It also illustrates the unity of Word and sacrament.[31] This liturgical interpretation is, of course, not the only one possible, especially given that it selects only individual aspects; but the fact it is included in a liturgical text means that it is backed by an authority of the Church's magisterium.

The post-biblical saints form a much larger group. I have shown how the readings for their feasts establish in various ways relationships between scriptural pericopes and the saints' lives.[32] An analogous procedure can be seen in some orations on saints' days. Our example is the collect for Saint Anthony Mary Zaccaria (1502–39; feast day July 5), because it contains an explicit reference to the biblical-Pauline basis:

> Grant, O Lord, that in the spirit of the Apostle Paul
> we may pursue the surpassing knowledge of Jesus Christ
>   (see Eph 3:19),
> for, having learned it,
> Saint Anthony Zaccaria
> constantly preached your saving word (see Acts 13:26) in the Church.
> Through our Lord Jesus Christ.[33]

There is a subtle reference here to Paul's sermon in the synagogue at Antioch. We find a biblical-biographical character of the orations for saints both in the

---

30 *Missal*, 953.
31 See B.VIII.29.2.
32 See A.I.3.3.
33 *Missal*, 899.

tradition and in the postconciliar reform of the Latin missal. For example, the collect for Saint Agnes (January 21) from the eighth-century Gelasian Gellone sacramentary already anticipates the reading (1 Cor 1:26–31): "Almighty ever-living God, who choose what is weak in the world to confound the strong."[34] The collect for Saint Matthew, described above, comes from the 1738 *Missale Parisiense*.[35] The collect for Saint Anthony Mary Zaccaria, whose memorial was adopted by the *Missale Romanum* in 1897, was probably composed for that occasion.[36] Orations newly formulated in Latin, such as for Saint Sebastian (January 20),[37] also employ clear echoes of Scripture in the allusions to the life of the saint and in the petition to which this leads: "Grant us, we pray, O Lord, *a spirit of fortitude* [see Is 11:2], so that, taught by the glorious example of your martyr saint Sebastian, we may learn to obey you rather than men [see Acts 5:29]."[38]

On the basis of these individual examples, we can note, with regard to the use of the Bible (although this does not apply to every oration, and other phenomena occur), that the orations often transpose biblical motifs to the saints, thereby making these motifs vivid and relevant. The structure of the oration (e.g., "God, who ...") makes it clear that the central reality is not the exemplary personal "lifetime achievement" of a saint, but always God's salvific action (in and through the saint). The epiclesis, linked to the anamnesis, makes clear the wish that this salvific action may also be effective today. In the saint, therefore, the action of God, to which Scripture bears witness, emerges once again in the perspective for the present day. This is why a biblical text suited to the saint often imprints its mark on the oration, creating an inherent bond between Scripture, the saint who is celebrated, and the assembled community. Many orations for saints thus draw our attention to the anamnetic character of the liturgical use of Scripture.[39]

---

34 *Missal*, 809; on the sources of the orations of the *MRom* 1952, see Placide Bruylants, *Les oraisons du Missel Romain. Texte et histoire*. Études liturgiques 1, 2 vols. (Louvain: Centre de Documentation et d'Information Liturgiques, 1952), 1:76; 2:223. On the sources for the orations newly included in the *MRom* 1970, see Antoine Dumas, "Les sources du nouveau missel romain," *Notitiae* 7, no. 60–63, 65 (1971): 37–42, 74–77, 94–95, 134–36, 276.

35 Dumas, 276.

36 Bruylants, *Oraisons du Missel Romain*, 1:115.

37 Dumas, "Sources," 41.

38 *Missal*, 808.

39 See B.VIII.27.

3. OPTIONAL ORATIONS REFERRING TO SCRIPTURE IN THE ITALIAN MISSAL (2ND ED. 1983; 3RD ED. 2020)

In the two types of orations studied above, the degree of closeness to Scripture, and especially the relation to the scriptural readings of the Mass, varied. Outside the festal cycles, the classical collect has no reference whatsoever to the following scriptural readings, and this is easily explained by its function in the history of liturgy. When the collect was introduced into the Roman Mass between 430 and 450, it was the conclusion of the entrance, so that it looked back rather than forward. Similarly, the prayer over the offerings was the conclusion of the offertory, and the prayer after Communion was the conclusion of the communion part.[40] In the collects of the festal cycles and of the feasts of saints (especially the biblical saints), on the other hand, we see an (occasional) agreement between prayer and reading, which occurs "naturally" (so to speak). There is a different understanding in those orations that are explicitly tied to Scripture. The classic example here are the orations after the Scripture readings of the Easter Vigil, which present a bridge between the Old Testament text, the Christ event, and (in part) the celebration of initiation. In terms of biblical hermeneutics, they thereby express the anamnetic character of the proclamation of Scripture.[41]

We shall look here at the newly formulated optional orations in the vernacular languages. Our example is the Italian missal. The pericope orations were newly formulated for the second edition (1983) and made available in a detailed appendix; this was shortened for the third edition (2020).[42] Alternative collects are provided for all Sundays and solemnities in the three Years of readings; out of "respect for the living inheritance,"[43] no alternatives are offered for the more important solemnities. These are not simple "looks ahead" that anticipate the content of the proclamation. Their intention is to prepare the congregation for what will be read and to make them sensitive to what they will hear. They can also be used as the conclusion of the intercessions.[44] In addition to the Gospel, they take up one reading (or sometimes even both), creating out of these elements a self-contained and

---

40 Jungmann, *Missarum Sollemnia*, 1:359-60.

41 See Zerfaß, *Hermeneutik*, 15-29; Anthony Ward, "The Orations after the Readings at the Easter Vigil in the 2000 'Missale Romanum.'" *EL* 123, no. 4 (2009): 460-507.

42 See *Messale Romano riformato a norma dei decreti del Concilio Vaticano II e promulgato da Papa Paolo VI e riveduto da Papa Giovanni Paolo II*. 3rd ed. (Rome: Fondazione di Religione Santi Francesco d'Assisi e Caterina da Siena, 2020), 1003-54 [2nd ed. 1983: 962-1016].

43 *Messale Romano*, VII (Presentazione no. 4).

44 *Messalo Romano*, VIII.

coherent prayer text. Our example is the 24th Sunday in Year B, with a literal English translation:

1	O Padre, che conforti i poveri e i sofferenti,	O Father, who comfort the poor and the suffering,
2	e tendi l'orecchio ai giusti che ti invocano,	and turn your ear to the righteous who call upon you.
3	assisti la tua Chiesa che annuncia il Vangelo della croce,	Help your Church which announces the Gospel of the cross,
4	perché creda con il cuore,	so that it may believe with the heart
5	e confessi con le opere che Gesù è il Messia.	and confess with works that Jesus is the Messiah.
6	Egli è Dio, e vive e regna con te,	He is God, and lives and reigns with you
7	nell'unità dello Spirito Santo,	in the unity of the Holy Spirit,
8	per tutti i secoli dei secoli.[45]	through all the ages.

When the oration states that the Father strengthens the poor and the suffering, and hears the righteous who call on him (1-2), this refers, without a literal echo, to the first reading (Is 50:5–9a) and the Responsorial Psalm that follows (Ps 116:1–6, 8–9). The collect then weaves in the theme of the second reading (Jas 2:14–18), the unity between faith and works (4-5). The oration expresses this unity, which James emphasizes, in linguistic terms by means of a parallelism: "believe *with the heart*" (an expansion taken literally from Rom 10:10) and "confess with works." The core affirmation of the Gospel (Mk 8:27–35), Peter's messianic confession, is then very skillfully added as that which is to be believed and confessed, namely "that Jesus is the Messiah."

The successful linguistic formulation in contemporary Italian in these collects is striking, as is the richness of their contents, which is due to the references to the scriptural readings (and the prayers in the second edition were even more elaborate). They are a genuine enrichment of the liturgical prayer. For a biblical hermeneutics, it is interesting to note that even readings that were not chosen for reasons of consonance, namely, the second reading and the Gospel in Ordinary Time, are skillfully joined together. In some cases, the collect unites all three readings. These alternative collects thus make clear the unity of the proclamation of Scripture on one and the same Sunday, and indeed the unity of Scripture itself. Doubtless, not all the references will in fact be perceived as such in the celebration of the Mass,

---

45 *Messale Romano*, 1041.

especially when the collect is prayed before the readings. But this is a sign of their quality, not a defect. "A good text is understandable in the sense that one always understands something, but never exhausts its meaning. A shallow text is read once and has nothing more to say."[46] We should also bear in mind that in Italy the faithful can usually read along the texts of the Liturgy of the Word on leaflets ("La Domenica").[47] There both the general Sunday collect and the alternative pericope collect is printed.

4. ICEL COLLECTS

The International Committee on English in the Liturgy (ICEL) had prepared Scripture-related collects from 1982 to 1998 and published them in 1999.[48] Even though they were not included in the Missal,[49] but only in the Canadian Book for Sunday Celebrations of the Word[50] (the same was done in Germany[51]), the ICEL collects should at least be mentioned here. On the same 24th Sunday in Year B, the prayer takes up the two main aspects of the Gospel reading and focuses both on proclaiming Christ and following him in our daily lives ("works", "taking up the cross"):

> Make us one, O God,
> in acknowledging Jesus the Christ.
> As we proclaim him by our words,
> let us follow him in our works;
> give us strength to take up the cross
> and courage to lose our lives for his sake.

---

46 Dieter Böhler, "Anmerkungen eines Exegeten zur Instructio quinta 'Liturgiam authenticam'," *LJ* 54, no. 4 (2004): 214.

47 This is a well-established custom, but it deprives the proclamation of Scripture of a part of its ritual form. Listening to the Word of God – faith comes from hearing (see Rom 10:17) – thus becomes reading for oneself.

48 International Committee on English in the Liturgy, *Opening Prayers. Scripture-related Collects for Years A, B and C from the Sacramentary. The ICEL Collects* (Norwich: Canterbury Press, 1999). See Peter John Scagnelli, *Creativity within Continuity. The ICEL Scriptural Collects* (ProQuest Dissertations Publishing, 2003).

49 See Keith F. Pecklers, *The Genius of the Roman Rite. On the Reception and Implementation of the New Missal* (Collegeville, MN: Liturgical Press, 2009), 56.

50 See *Sunday Celebration of the Word and Hours. Approved by the National Liturgy Office for Use in Canada* (Ottawa, Ontario: Publications Service, Canadian Conference of Catholic Bishops, 1995), 46–198.

51 On German and French pericope orations, Benini, *Liturgische Bibelhermeneutik*, 156-166.

We ask this through our Lord Jesus Christ, your Son,
who lives and reigns with you in the unity of the Holy Spirit,
God for ever and ever.[52]

---

52 ICEL, *Opening Prayers*, 102.

CHAPTER THIRTEEN

Hermeneutical Insights

W e need not recapitulate all the details here. We have noted the fundamental fact that the prayers of the Liturgy are formed to a high degree by Sacred Scripture. What *SC* 24 formulates in general terms becomes visible in the examples of the episcopal ordination and the various types of orations. The exceptions here are the Latin collects for Ordinary Time.

With regard to the construction of these prayers, the anamnetic-epicletic structure that is a characteristic of liturgical prayer has become clear. Scripture can provide inspiration for both of these parts, which are often interwoven. The quotations and the even more frequent allusions serve not only to shape a prayer in conformity to the Bible on an external level, but also, and primarily, to communicate a basic biblical and biblical-hermeneutical message: namely, we request now, for the present day, what is established in Scripture. Signal words such as "now" (prayer of episcopal ordination in the *Apostolic Tradition*) or "now once more" (collect of Pentecost) are one indicator of this anamnetic use of Scripture. The orations for the saints' days likewise have a biblical-biographical character that frequently establishes a connection between the Scripture, the saint, and today's faithful. With regard to the temporal sequence and the unity of the Testaments, the prayers for the ordination of a bishop (especially in the *Apostolic Tradition*) display the following interleaving: "Old Testament— New Testament—today."

The comparison between the traditions has shown, in the case of episcopal ordination, that in addition to shared basic ideas, very different biblical passages are drawn upon for one and the same celebration. The *Apostolic Tradition* draws most heavily on the Gospels and Acts, while the Byzantine prayers rely more on Paul. For a liturgical hermeneutics of the Bible, this means that in liturgy a choice is always made from the "pool" of Sacred Scripture, one which thereby posits a theological accentuation.

In the various modes of quotation/allusion, we have seen that biblical passages can be used in liturgical prayer with, without, and even against their context in the Bible itself. The last of these is exceptional (probably in older prayers). It is clear that it was natural, in a more strongly oral culture, for the passages to be quoted from memory, whereas today more attention is paid to their context.

Baumstark's axiom for the history of the Liturgy stated that the more recent prayers refer to Scripture more through literal quotations, while the oldest prayers display a more free approach in this regard. This applies by analogy all the more strongly to the modern period, since a conscious conformity to the Bible appears above all in the newly formulated alternative orations. In particular, the pericope orations display prayer with and on the basis of Scripture (backed by the Church's magisterium) and make it clear that Bible and Liturgy together become a school of prayer. It is out of Scripture that the prayer of the Church is to be formed. And this means *e contra* that the Scripture is heard in the attitude of prayer.[53] At the same time, the pericope orations show vividly that prayer is always a response to the revelation of God that has taken place. They point in this way to the dialogical character of the Liturgy.[54]

Our examples have shown that the Liturgy functions as an interpreter of Scripture when prayers and orations undertake a "liturgical interpretation of Scripture." They take individual aspects of the pericopes, emphasize them, transpose them into today and apply them to the community. The sacramental re-reading of the Gospel in the prayer after communion on Saint Matthew's feast, which pointed out that Word and sacrament belong together, was interesting in this regard. An interpretation of Scripture through the Liturgy is found not only in the prayers but also in the songs, which we shall discuss in the next section.

---

53 See B.VI.21.
54 See B.VIII.28.2.

SECTION IV

Songs

In accord with *SC* 24, we shall now investigate the songs from the hermeneutical perspective of their use of the Bible. We shall look in particular at the *texts* in their specific liturgical function. For the sake of concision, we shall not look at the church-musical aspect, although the melody can have an effect on the understanding of the texts. This section looks at the broad field of songs in two chapters: the Liturgy of the Hours (14) and the celebration of the Mass (15). Our examples in the first chapter, taken from the vast treasure of the tradition, are the hymns that celebrate the Cross in the Roman and the Byzantine liturgy, since these: thematize an important aspect of the faith, are sung in a prominent position in the liturgical year (Holy Week and the Exaltation of the Cross), and were written in both traditions by celebrated authors. In the second chapter, our examples are the Communion antiphons, because they accompany a central rite of the Eucharist and have a clearly defined function. Since they partly take up the Gospel again, they have a particular significance for a *liturgical* hermeneutics of the Bible.

CHAPTER FOURTEEN

Hymns about the Cross of Christ in the Liturgy of the Hours

1. VENANTIUS FORTUNATUS' HYMNS ABOUT THE CROSS

Venantius Fortunatus (born 530/540 near Treviso; † after 600 in Poitiers) is without doubt the most important representative of the Western hymns about the Cross. As the poet at the royal court in Poitiers, he wrote six poems on the occasion of the translation of a relic of the Cross ca. 569.[1] Two of these have maintained their position as hymns in the Liturgy down to the present day: *Pange lingua* and *Vexilla regis*.

1 See Louis van Tongeren, *Exaltation of the Cross. Toward the Origins of the Feast of the Cross and the Meaning of the Cross in Early Medieval Liturgy*, LC 11 (Leuven: Peeters, 2000), 236-48; Joseph Szövérffy, "Venantius Fortunatus and the Earliest Hymns of the Holy Cross," in: Joseph Szövérffy, *Hymns of the Holy Cross. An Annotated Edition with Introduction*, Medieval Classics 7 (Brookline: Classical Folia Editions, 1976), 7-20. The author has prepared the commentary on these hymns for the ICEL commentary on the newly translated hymns of the Liturgy of the Hours.

14.1.1. The Texts and Their Use in the Liturgy

Pange, lingua[2]

1	*Pange, lingua, gloriosi* *prœlium certaminis,* *et super crucis tropœo* *dic triumphum[3] nobilem,* *qualiter redemptor orbis* *immolatus vicerit.*	Sing, my tongue, in exultation Of our banner and device! Make a solemn proclamation Of a triumph and its price: How the Savior of creation Conquered by his sacrifice!
2	*De parentis protoplasti* *fraude factor condolens,* *quando pomi noxialis* *morte morsu corruit,[4]* *ipse lignum tunc notavit,* *damna ligni ut solveret.*	For, when Adam first offended, Eating that forbidden fruit, Not all hopes of glory ended With the serpent at the root: Broken nature would be mended By a second tree and shoot.
3	*Hoc opus nostrœ salutis* *ordo depoposcerat,* *multiformis perditoris* *arte ut artem falleret,* *et medelam ferret inde,* *hostis unde lœserat.*	Thus the tempter was outwitted By a wisdom deeper still: Remedy and ailment fitted, Means to cure and means to kill; That the world might be acquitted, Christ would do his Father's will.
4	*Quando venit ergo sacri* *plenitudo temporis,* *missus est ab arce Patris[5]* *natus, orbis conditor,* *atque ventre virginali* *carne factus prodiit.[6]*	So the Father, out of pity For our self-inflicted doom, Sent him from the heavenly city When the holy time had come: He, the Son and the Almighty, Took our flesh in Mary's womb.

Table continued on next page.

2 Latin text: *Liturgia Horarum iuxta ritum Romanum. Editio typica altera. Officium Divinum ex Decreto Sacrosancti Oecumenici Concilii Vaticani II insturatum auctoritate Pauli PP. VI promulgatum*, 4 vols. (Vatican City: Libreria Editrice Vatiana, 2000), 2:330-32; *AHMA* 50:71; *Missale Romanum* 2002, 327–29. The fifth stanza is missing in the *Liturgia Horarum*. See *Hymni ad usum in Liturgia Horarum. Redacti a Marco Benini cum praefatione episcopi Eystettensis Dr. Gregorii Maria Hanke OSB*, ed. Bischöfliches Seminar Eichstätt, 2nd ed. (Eichstätt: Bischöfliches Seminar, 2007), 109-11. The text printed here keeps to the original; the doxology comes from the *Liturgia Horarum*. Translation: *Missal*, 333–36 (ICEL has prepared a literal translation for the Commentary on the ICEL Hymnal).

3 See Col 2:14–15.

4 See Gn 3:6.

5 See Gal 4:4.

6 See Jn 1:14.

5	*Vagit infans inter arta* *conditus præsepia;* *membra pannis involuta* *virgo mater alligat,* *et pedes manusque, crura* *stricta pingit fascia.*	Hear a tiny baby crying, Founder of the seas and strands; See his virgin Mother tying Cloth around his feet and hands; Find him in a manger lying Tightly wrapped in swaddling- bands!
6	*Lustra sex qui iam peracta* *tempus implens corporis,* *se volente, natus ad hoc,* *passioni deditus,* *agnus in crucis levatur* *immolandus stipite.*[7]	So he came, the long-expected, Not in glory, not to reign; Only born to be rejected, Choosing hunger, toil and pain, Till the scaffold was erected And the Paschal Lamb was slain.
7	*Hic*[8] *acetum, fel, arundo,* *sputa, clavi, lancea:* *mite corpus perforatur,* *sanguis, unda profluit;*[9] *terra, pontus, astra, mundus,* *quo lavantur flumine!*	No disgrace was too abhorrent: Nailed and mocked and parched he died; Blood and water, double warrant, Issue from his wounded side, Washing in a mighty torrent Earth and stars and oceantide.
8	*Crux fidelis, inter omnes* *arbor una nobilis!* *Nulla talem silva profert,* *flore, fronde, germine.* *Dulce lignum, dulce*[10] *clavo* *dulce pondus sustinens!*	Faithful Cross the Saints rely on, Noble tree beyond compare! Never was there such a scion, Never leaf or flower so rare. Sweet the timber, sweet the iron, Sweet the burden that they bear!
9	*Flecte ramos, arbor alta,* *tensa laxa viscera,* *et rigor lentescat ille* *quem dedit nativitas,* *ut superni membra regis*[11] *mite*[12] *tendas stipite.*	Lofty timber, smooth your roughness, Flex your boughs for blossoming; Let your fibers lose their toughness, Gently let your tendrils cling; Lay aside your native gruffness, Clasp the body of your King!

7 See Jn 1:29; Rev 5:12; Is 53:7; Christ as Passover lamb (Ex 12:3–14; Jn 19:4; 1 Cor 5:7). These biblical passages are echoed in v.10:3 also.

8 The *Liturgia Horarum* alters this to "En" ("Behold").

9 See Jn 19:34.

10 "Dulce" is ablative here (classical Latin: "dulci"). The Liturgia Horarum alters it to "dulci."

11 See Mk 15:2, 9, 12, 18 par.; see also Mt 2:2; Jn 1:49; 12:13.

12 Like "dulce" above, "mite" is ablative and belongs to "stipites." The *Liturgia Horarum* alters it to "miti."

10	*Sola digna tu fuisti* *ferre pretium sæculi,*[13] *atque portum præparare* *nauta mundo naufrago,* *quem sacer cruor perunxit,* *fusus Agni corpore.*	Noblest tree of all created, Richly jeweled and embossed: Post by Lamb's blood consecrated; Spar that saves the tempest-tossed; Scaffold-beam which, elevated, Carries what the world has cost!
11	*Æqua Patri Filioque,* *inclito Paraclito,* *sempiterna sit beatæ* *Trinitati gloria,* *cuius alma nos redemit* *atque servat gratia. Amen.*	Wisdom, power, and adoration To the blessed Trinity For redemption and salvation Through the Paschal Mystery, Now, in every generation, And for all eternity. Amen.

It is an open question whether this hymn was immediately taken into the Liturgy, via the procession that welcomed the relic (for example, in Poitiers), but this is certainly possible. The liturgical use of this hymn in the Liturgy of the Hours (Passiontide) and at the Veneration of the Cross on Good Friday is attested from the ninth century.[14] The hymn is found in the *Liturgia Horarum* in Holy Week in two parts, at the Office of Readings and at Morning Prayer, without the fifth stanza.[15] It can also be sung at the Veneration of the Cross on Good Friday.[16]

Vexilla regis[17]

1	*Vexilla regis prodeunt,* *fulget crucis mysterium,* *quo carne carnis conditor* *suspensus est patibulo.*	The banners of the King go forth, the gleaming mystery of the Cross, by which the Maker of all flesh was yoked in flesh upon the wood;

Table continued on next page.

13 See 1 Cor 6:20; 7:23; 1 Pt 1:18–19.

14 On the oldest manuscripts, see *AHMA* 50:71–72.

15 See *Liturgia Horarum*, 2:330-32.

16 See *Missal*, 333-36.

17 See *Liturgia Horarum*, 2:329–30 (without stanzas 2, 4, and 7 here marked with *); Benini, *Hymni*, 107–08; *AHMA* 50:74. ICEL Translation approved for the future edition of the Liturgy of the Hours: *The Divine Office Hymnal*, ed. United States Conference of Catholic Bishop (Chicago: Gia Publications, 2023), no. 97. Stanzas 2, 4, and 7 are taken from: *The Psalter or Seven ordinary Hours of Prayer according to the use of the illustrious and excellent Church of Sarum [...]* (London: Masters, 1852), 345–46.

2	*Confixa clavis viscera tendens manus, vestigia, redemptionis gratia hic immolata est hostia.[18]	*Behold! The nails with anguish fierce, His outstretched arms and vitals pierce: Here our redemption to obtain, The Mighty Sacrifice is slain.
3	Quo, vulneratus insuper mucrone diro lanceæ, ut nos lavaret crimine, manavit unda et sanguine.[19]	Where, wounded as he hung on high by ruthless blade of sharpened spear, there flowed forth water mixed with blood, to wash us clean from every sin.
4	*Impleta sunt quae concinit David fideli carmine, dicendo nationibus: regnavit a ligno Deus.[20]	*Fulfilled is all that David told In true prophetic song, of old: Unto the nations, lo! saith he, Our God hath reignèd from the Tree.
5	Arbor decora et fulgida, ornata regis purpura,[21] electa digno stipite tam sancta membra tangere!	O noble tree with blood adorned, the splendid purple of the King, wood chosen from a worthy stock to touch and bear such holy limbs.
6	Beata, cuius brachiis pretium pependit sæculi,[22] statera facta est corporis prædamque tulit tartari.	O blessed tree whose branches bore the price and ransom of the world! Like scales it weighed the body's worth and bore away the spoils of hell.
7	*Fundis aroma cortice, vincis sapore nectare, iucunda fructu fertili plaudis triumpho nobili.	*With fragrance dropping from each bough Sweeter than sweetest nectar thou; Decked with the fruit of peace and praise, And glorious with Triumphal lays.
8	Salve, ara, salve, victima, de passionis gloria, qua vita mortem pertulit et morte vitam reddidit!	Hail altar, victim, sacrifice, for glory gained through grief and death, by which our Life endured to die and through his death restored our life.
9	+O crux, ave, spes unica! Hoc passionis tempore piis adauge gratiam reisque dele crimina.	O Cross, all hail, our only hope, in this most holy Passiontide, increase the grace of loving hearts and rid the guilty of their sin.

18 See Eph 5:2 (Christ's laying down of his life on the cross as "hostia").

19 See Jn 19:34.

20 See Ps 96:10 (Vetus Latina).

21 See Mk 15:17; Jn 19:2–3.

22 See 1 Cor 6:20; 7:23; 1 Pt 1:18–19.

| 10 | +*Te fons salutis, Trinitas,*
 collaudet omnis spiritus;
 quos per crucis mysterium
 salvas, fove per sæcula. Amen. | O Triune God, let all sing praise <br> to you, the font of saving grace;
 sustain for ever those you save <br> by wondrous mystery of the Cross. Amen. |

Originally, the hymn had only the first eight stanzas. In accord with the medieval mentality, a stanza with an explicit petition for the forgiveness of sins and the customary doxology were added. In the *Liturgia Horarum*, the hymn is prescribed for Vespers in Holy Week (apart from Holy Thursday) and on the Feast of the Exaltation of the Cross (September 14), once again omitting stanzas 2, 4, and 7.

1.2. The Biblical-Theological Motifs and Their Hermeneutical Significance

Instead of analyzing each hymn individually, we shall investigate the biblical-theological motifs of the two hymns and their relevance to a liturgical hermeneutics of the Bible. The points of view that emerge are numbered in square brackets, so that we can come back to them in the concluding comparison with the Byzantine hymns about the Cross. This comparison will not be carried out primarily on the textual level, but will begin with the underlying theological and hermeneutical aspects. The examples will show how two distinct liturgical traditions take up the same theme in liturgical songs and thereby interpret the Scriptures.

The Unity of the Testaments and Their Christological Interpretation

[1] Venantius gives the *Pange, lingua* (hereafter: *PL*) its structure by employing the great contexts of *salvation history*: the fall in paradise (stanza 2-3); the incarnation (4-5); the crucifixion of Christ for the redemption of humankind (6-10). The restriction to these three central aspects supports a clear line of thought and may reflect a theological development that valued these aspects above all as soteriologically significant. Venantius speaks explicitly of the "*ordo*" (3:1) that demanded the work of redemption. He thus links together the primal sin and death with salvation on the cross. It is obvious that the Pauline theology of the parallel between Adam and Christ lies in the background.[23]

---

23 See Rom 5:12–21; 1 Cor 15:22–23, 45–49.

[2] *Typology* is very important in the hymn. Venantius employs poetical metaphors to transpose onto a material level what Paul affirms by speaking about the persons: the wood (2:5) of the tree in paradise and of the Cross, which has become the new "tree of life" (Gn 2:9; stanzas 8-10). Venantius stands here wholly within the tradition of patristic exegesis.[24] Although the tree in paradise is not mentioned explicitly in the *Vexilla regis* (hereafter: *VR*), the metaphor of the Cross as tree of life is equally easy to grasp (*VR* 5-7), especially because all the trees of paradise are called *lignum* (not *arbor*) in the Vulgate. The materiality doubtless refers indirectly to the relic of the Cross, thereby giving the theme a high measure of vividness. Another typological exegesis is included in the hymns through the pair "Lamb – Christ" (*PL* 6:5; 10:6; *VR* 2:4). This links the preservation from the destroyer (see Ex 12:13), and the exodus as God's liberating deed *par excellence* in the Old Covenant, with the event of redemption on the Cross, an idea that goes back to Paul: "Our paschal lamb, Christ, has been sacrificed" (1 Cor 5:7). Besides this, the mention of the sacrificed lamb evokes Is 53:7 in a Christological interpretation.

The quotation from Ps 96(95):10 in *VR* 4:3-4 is particularly interesting. It comes, not from the Vulgate, but from a Christian interpolation found already in Justin (ca. 100-165), which added "*a ligno*" to "*Dominus regnavit*" and thus made it possible to interpret the psalm as speaking of Christ on the Cross.[25]

With regard to biblical hermeneutics, these observations display the unity in principle of the two Testaments, which is taken for granted in the hymns. Typological interpretations of this unity can be understood only on the basis of Christ. For Venantius (and for Christian liturgy), Christ and his saving work—that is, his paschal mystery— are the starting point of the interpretation.

---

24 See, e.g., Ambrose, *In Ps* 35.3 (CSEL 64:51): "*paradisum nobis crux reddidit Christi; hoc est lignum, quod Adae dominus demonstrauit.*" See Gerardus Quirinus Reijners, *The Terminology of the Holy Cross in Early Christian Literature As Based Upon Old Testament Typology* (Nijmegen: Dekker & van de Vegt, 1965).

25 See Jean Marc Prieur, "'Le Seigneur a régné depuis le bois.' L'adjonction chrétienne au Psaume 95,10 et son interprétation." In *Rois et reines de la Bible au miroir des Pères*, Cahiers de Biblia patristica 6 (Strasbourg: Univ. Marc Bloch, 1999), 127-40; Giorgio Otranto, *Esegesi biblica e storia in Giustino (Dial. 63-84)*, QVetChr 14 (Bari: Istituto di Letteratura Cristiana Antica, 1979).

A Theological Interpretation of the Biblical Text
with Poetic Means for Those Who Pray

[3] Venantius' hymns do not recount anew the Passion narrative, but instead *employ their poetical-metaphorical presentation to promote a theological interpretation*. A summary of the Passion account is found only in *PL* 7, in a few key words: vinegar, gall, reed, spitting, nails, lance—one single verse makes the whole account present. Only the scene of the piercing with the lance is presented in any detail (*PL* 7:3–6; *VR* 3). The theological interpretation is more important for Venantius. He interprets the Cross in *PL* fundamentally as a *tropæum* (1:2), as the trophy of redemption.

The first stanza is an overture that anticipates the central basic idea, namely, that the redeemer of the world is sacrificed on the Cross and triumphs victoriously. Venantius could claim a biblical fundamental here: "He [God] obliterated the bond against us, with its legal claims, which was opposed to us, nailing it to the *cross*; despoiling the principalities and the powers, he made a public spectacle of them, leading them away *in triumph* by it" (Col 2:14–15). Venantius further elaborates Colossians' interpretation of what happened on the Cross. Roman soldiers gave the name *tropæum* to a wooden stake that they drove into the earth at the place where the enemy was put to flight, and on which they hung up the weapons and shields they had captured, as a sign of victory.[26] This was therefore a highly suitable metaphor to express Christ's victory over sin and death, and patristic authors had already meditated extensively on it.[27] The same understanding had found an expression in art, in the cross adorned with gems.[28] A procession with the relic of the Cross (as in Poitiers) exhibited the triumphal procession of the Cross (with banners; *VR* 1:1), just like those of Roman emperors in the past, and the royal titles of Christ (*VR* 1:1; 5:2; *PL* 9:5) are appropriate here.

The most important image for the Cross in Venantius is, of course, the Tree of Life (*PL* 8–10; *VR* 6–7), which has no parallel among all the trees and bears rich fruit, because Christ has brought salvation once and for all on the tree of the cross. Venantius skillfully brings two biblical metaphors together: Christ, as "ransom of the world" (*PL* 10:2),[29] becomes the fruit on the tree of life. He goes beyond Scripture when he speaks of the cross as scales (on which the ransom is paid; *VR* 6:3) or of the sweetness of the tree, the nails,

---

26 See Stefan Heid, "Kreuz," *RAC* 21 (2006): 1099–148, as sign of victory, Heid, 1118–21.

27 See Jean-Marc Prieur, *Das Kreuz in der christlichen Literatur der Antike*, TC 14 (Berne: Lang, 2006).

28 E.g., on the triumphal arch in Santa Maria Maggiore in Rome (5th century).

29 Mt 20:28; Mk 10:45 ("red-emptio"); 1 Cor 6:20; 7:23, and 1 Pt 1:18–19.

and the burden/fruit (*PL* 8:5–6; *VR* 7:1–4). All these images place the accent on redemption as the result of Jesus' laying down of his life on the cross; it is only this that allows us to understand the images. The cruelty of the cross disappears from sight. Venantius also employs the metaphor of the ship, which was common in patristic writing (*PL* 10).[30] Indeed, the Cross is personified as sailor or helmsman, who is anointed with the blood of the Lamb[31] and prepares the longed-for harbor for the shipwrecked world.

Venantius also employs a cultic terminology. The Cross becomes the altar on which the Lamb of God is sacrificed as *hostia/victima* (*VR* 2:4; 8:1; *PL* 6:5) and wins the victory at once (*PL* 1:6: "*immolatus vicerit*"). In other words, through his death, he restores life for all (*VR* 8:3–4). This alludes to the paschal mystery (*VR* 8:2: "*passionis gloria*"), and the mention of the altar may possibly likewise hint at the Eucharist as the celebration of his death and Resurrection. Other theological motifs that are briefly touched upon in the hymns are the theory of the devil's outwitting (*PL* 3:4: "*arte ut artem falleret*") or the redeeming of the deceased from the realm of death (*VR* 6:4: "*prædam tulit tartari*").

[4] In its theological interpretation, the hymn accentuates *the significance of the passion for those at prayer here and now*. It is interesting that the only element from the passion narrative that Venantius elaborates in greater detail in the two hymns is the piercing with the lance: water and blood flow for the cleansing of the entire cosmos (*PL* 7:5) and for "us" for the forgiveness of sins (*VR* 3:3). This is the only passage formulated in the first person. It is clear that the "we" (as in numerous other classic hymns, unlike modern subjectivisms) is very consciously employed in order to underline the relationship between the event of the Cross and the persons who pray. At the same time, the vivid images and the direct address of the cross (*PL* 8–10; *VR* 5–9) place those who sing the hymn in an immediate, emotional relationship to the event of redemption, and make them anamnetically contemporaries of salvation.

Praise clearly dominates in both hymns. It is the appropriate response of thanksgiving to Christ's laying down of his life on the cross. Neither hymn contains any petitions; only the stanza added subsequently to *VR* (9) contains a request for an increase of grace and the forgiveness of sins.

With regard to the liturgical hermeneutics of the Bible, we can note in general terms that when hymns take up biblical themes—as is frequently

---

30 See Hugo Rahner, *Symbole der Kirche. Die Ekklesiologie der Väter* (Salzburg: Müller, 1964), 239–564, on Venantius Rahner, 344, 352–53, (390.393–94), 556.

31 This is surely an allusion to the messianic-kingly dignity of Christ.

done by the festal hymns (and others)[32] that are used today—they always undertake a selection, and thereby an accentuation. They aim, not at a retelling of the story, but at a poetical condensation that can also develop biblical ideas further. Through their use of metaphors, they often undertake an easily memorized interpretation of the scriptural passages and establish a relationship between these texts and the persons at prayer. Here, the question arises whether the metaphors they employ and their affirmations are still understood today—for example, the Roman trophies or the banner of the king. This was taken for granted by Venantius and helped him to make clear the biblical message and to translate it into his own historical period, but it has become somewhat foreign today. This touches on fundamental hermeneutical questions about reception,[33] which, of course, are also raised by the Psalms and by the biblical texts in general, which have a background and a milieu different from today's world.

2. BYZANTINE POETICAL COMPOSITIONS ABOUT THE CROSS

In the case of the West, we have chosen two hymns about the cross by Venantius. For the East, we shall also choose two prominent poetical texts on the same subject: a kontakion by Romanos Melodos and a canon by Cosmas of Jerusalem. Although we cannot print these lengthy texts here, we shall look at their liturgical function and use and at the biblical-theological motifs they contain.

2.1. The Kontakion of Romanos Melodos on the Victory of the Cross (Veneration of the Cross in Great Lent)

The Kontakion's Genre and Liturgical Use

A kontakion consists of a large number of stanzas with the same metrical construction, the so-called "*oikoi*" ("houses"), all of which close with the same refrain. The last oikos is a concluding prayer. The kontakion is introduced with a prooemium (sometimes two or three) that has the same refrain, but a different meter. Thanks to his poetical quality and originality and to the large number of his compositions, Romanos Melodos (born

---

32 Numerous references to Scripture are found also in the hymns in Ordinary Time, e.g., in Vespers of the first weekly cycle with their references to God's work of creation.

33 See B.IX.33.2.

ca. 485 in Emesa [today's Homs in Syria], † before 562 in Constantinople) is regarded as the kontakion poet *par excellence*. Romanos wrote kontakia for all the feasts of the liturgical year, on Old Testament narratives, on numerous Gospel pericopes, on saints or the consecration of churches, on penance, and more. The preferred length is 18 *oikoi*, and usually not more than 24.[34]

In the context of the present study, their liturgical use is particularly interesting. In Romanos's own time, his kontakia were read during the Eucharist after the Gospel, that is to say, as a rhymed sermon.[35] The many dialogues in direct speech and the description of the emotions of the *dramatis personae* make the kontakia come alive, and their refrain involves the hearers. Romanos used signal words such as "today" and "now" in order to bring into the present the feast day or the pericope that has been read.[36] While adding many imaginative details, he remained faithful to the Bible.[37] The place where they were declaimed corresponded to this exegetical-catechetical function. In big churches, the soloists probably stood on the ambo, while the choir had their place beneath it and sang the refrain (together with the people).[38]

The kontakia had an additional place in the Liturgy at the time of their composition: they were sung as an Office ("asmatikos") at the Vigil or at the Orthros of great feasts, and on the Sundays and Wednesdays of Great Lent and of Eastertide, probably at the end of the Pannychis.[39] As Romanos himself indicates,[40] their place was after the readings, the last of which was the Gospel that served as the starting point for the kontakion.[41] But as early

---

34 See *Romanos Melodos. Die Hymnen*, ed. and trans. by J. Koder, 2 vols., Bibliothek der griechischen Literatur 62, 64 (Stuttgart: Hiersemann, 2005–06).

35 See Hughes Oliphant Old, *The medieval Church*, vol. 3 of *The Reading and Preaching of the Scriptures in the Worship of the Christian Church* (Grand Rapids, MI: Eerdmans, 1999), 7–20 (esp. 16–20: The Kontakion as Homiletical Poetry). Koder, *Hymnen* 1:21–22, 35.

36 Koder, *Hymnen* 1:21–22, 41–42.

37 Koder, 1:45.

38 See Herbert Hunger, "Romanos Melodos. Überlegungen zum Ort und zur Art des Vortrags seiner Hymnen. Mit anschließender kurzer Strukturanalyse eines Kontakions (O. 19. SC 35, Maria unter dem Kreuz)," *ByZ* 92, no. 1 (1999): 1–9.

39 Koder, *Hymnen* 1:21.

40 See *Kontakia of Romanos, Byzantine Melodist. 1: On the Person of Christ*, ed. M. Carpenter (Columbia: University of Missouri Press, 1970), 111: "After a Psalm was sung, we were gladdened by a well-ordered reading of Scriptures. Again we sang hymns to Christ" [Hymn on the man possessed with devils, oikos 1].

41 See Alexander Lingas, "The Liturgical Place of the Kontakion in Constantinople." In *Liturgy, Architecture and Art of the Byzantine World: Papers of the XVIII International Byzantine Congress (Moscow, 8-15 August 1991) and Other Essays Dedicated to the Memory of Fr. John Meyendorff*, ed. C. C. Akentiev, Byzantinorossica 1 (St. Petersburg: Byzantinorossica, 1995), 50–57, esp. 53.

as the mid-seventh century, and especially after the end of the Iconoclastic Controversy (843), the kontakion, which had its primary place in the community liturgy, was increasingly supplanted by the canon, a genre with a monastic character.[42] Today, only the (first) prooemium and the first oikos are inserted after the sixth Ode in the Orthros. In this reduced form, it is scarcely any longer possible for the kontakion to be perceived as a specific genre. It has lost most of its function as a catechesis that expounds the Scripture for the community.

The Kontakion about the Victory of the Cross and Its Biblical-Theological Motifs

This kontakion was probably originally composed for Good Friday. Today, the first prooemium and the first oikos are sung after the sixth Ode in the Orthros on the Sunday of the Veneration of the Cross (3rd Sunday in Great Lent) and on the following Wednesday; only the first prooemium on the Friday of that week.[43]

No longer does the fiery sword guard the gate of Eden
For the wood of the cross—marvelous fetter—suddenly assaulted it.
The sting of death and the wrangling of Hades were nailed to it;
But Thou, Savior, hast appeared, crying to those in Hades: "Enter
Again into Paradise."

Pilate fixed three crosses on Golgotha,
Two for the robbers, and one for the Giver of life.
When Hades saw Him, he said to those below:
"O my priests and forces, who has fixed the nail in my heart?
A wooden spear has pierced me suddenly and I am torn apart.

I am in pain—internal pain, I have a bellyache;
My senses make my spirit quiver,
And I am forced to vomit forth
Adam and those descended from Adam, given to me by a tree.
The tree leads them back
Again into Paradise."[44]

---

42 Lingas, 56–57.

43 *Anthologhion* 2:712–13, 740, 757.

44 Carpenter, *Kontakia of Romanos*, 1:230. Greek text with French translation: *Romanos le Mélode. Hymnes. Introduction, texte critique, traduction et notes*, ed. and trans. J. Grosdidier de Matons. 5 vols. SChr 99, 110, 114, 128, 283 (Paris: Éd. du Cerf, 1964-81), 4:263-311.

Even in this abbreviated form, we find a basic idea similar to that in Venantius, namely, that the wood of the Cross has reopened the paradise that was shut so that the deceased are taken up out of Hades "again into Paradise" (refrain).

We shall look at the use of biblical-theological motifs in the kontakion as a whole, which is constructed as follows. Through the raising up of the Cross of Christ, Hades feels "a wooden spear" piercing his entrails. He recognizes that his end has come (oikos 1), while the serpent (the devil) still believes that he has won the victory through the wood of the Cross, which he himself has set up (2). This leads to a dialogue between the two of them (1-9). But when the devil hears Christ promising paradise to the Good Thief and sees blood and water pouring forth (10-11), he joins Hades in lamenting his defeat and his damnation, especially since Christ forgives only those who do not know what they are doing (12-16). Hades and the devil take the decision not to kill anyone in future (17). The concluding prayer praises the wood of the Cross (18).

Although the kontakion differs from Venantius' hymns through the dialogue between the devil and Hades and its broad narrative form, the two poets agree in the fundamental salvation-historical perspective [1] and in the use of typology [2], which is further elaborated in Romanos as a result of the much greater quantity of text. He names additional anticipatory images of the Cross: the wood with which Elisha lifted the ax from the Jordan;[45] Moses' staff, which led the people out of Egypt;[46] Noah's ark, which brought rescue;[47] the wood with which Moses made the bitter water sweet in Marah;[48] Solomon's ship, in comparison to which the Cross brought the much greater wealth of the redemption.[49] Romanos uses other metaphorical expressions for the Cross [3]: it is a piece of wood that, as with Elisha's ax, now lifts up Adam on high;[50] it is Christ's throne and judgment seat,[51] and a seal for the race of Adam.[52] Romanos, employing the distinct style of the kontakia, differs from Venantius in going back several times in a narrative form to the Passion. His narrative, however, is not simply chronological,

---

45 See Oikos 3; 2 Kgs 6:1-7.

46 See Oikos 5 and 13; Ex 4:1-4; 14:16.

47 See Oikos 13; Gn 8.

48 See Oikos 15; Ex 15:23-25.

49 See Oikos 18; 1 Kgs 10:22 *LXX*.

50 See Oikos 3; 2 Kgs 6:5-7.

51 See Oikos 9.

52 See Oikos 17.

but is formulated from the perspective of Hades and the devil.[53] In general terms, Romanos displays a striking closeness to Scripture, which serves as the primary source for all his kontakia. His typological interpretations, taken from the patristic tradition,[54] show the close union between the Old and the New Testament. At the same time, Romanos often notes a progression in the realization of salvation, and thereby a higher value of the New Testament antitype in relation to the Old Testament type.[55]

2.2. The Canon of Cosmas of Jerusalem for the Feast of the Exaltation of the Cross

The Canon Genre and Its Use in the Liturgy

The canon[56] has its liturgical place in the Orthros. In imitation of the Easter Vigil with the biblical odes (known in the West as "*cantica*"), biblical songs were also introduced into the Orthros in Jerusalem. The starting point was probably the song of the three young men in Daniel 3. The nine (earlier fourteen) biblical odes[57] were furnished with ode troparia that took up the theme of the scriptural passages and interpreted them with regard to Christ or a festal mystery, so that from the 6th/7th century, a poetical nine-ode-canon developed. The second biblical ode (Dt 32) was omitted on great feasts because of its penitential character, although it continued to be included in the numbering. Gradually, the poetical odes supplanted the biblical odes; only the Magnificat was retained. The individual odes are in part a very ample adaptation of the biblical odes (which are no longer sung) in view of a specific content of the feast. This also makes them an interpretation of

---

53 He mentions explicitly the Good Thief (Oikos 5 and 9; Lk 23:40–43), the darkening of the sun, the tearing in two of the Temple veil, the trembling of the earth and the resurrection of the dead from the tombs (Oikos 7; Mt 27:45–52), and the blood and water from the wound in Jesus' side (Oikos 11: Jn 19:34).

54 José Grosdider de Matons, *Romanos le Mélode et les origines de la poésie religieuse à Byzance*, Beauchesne religions (Paris: Beauchesne, 1977), 258-60 gives a list of 43 such typologies.

55 See in the Hymn on the victory of the cross: "*Beyond the wand which brought the people out of Egypt, this wood has been active, for it leads Adam again into paradise*" (Oikos 5; Carpenter, Kontakia 1:232). "Antithetical images" are also employed (Oikos 8 [Carpenter, 1:233]: the "crosses" (trees) of Haman, Sisera, and of Joshua the son of Nun did not terrify Hades—but the Cross of Christ did so; Est 7:10; Jgs 4:21; Jos 10:26–27).

56 See Oleksandr Petrynko, *Der jambische Weihnachtskanon des Johannes von Damaskus. Einleitung, Text, Übersetzung, Kommentar.* JThF 15 (Münster: Aschendorff, 2010), 21-50.

57 1) Ex 15:1–19; 2) Dt 32:1–43; 3) 1 Sm 2:1–10; 4) Hb 3:2–19; 5) Is 26:9–20; 6) Jon 2:3–10; 7a) Dn 3:26–45; 7b) Dn 3:52–56; 8) Dn 3:57–88; 9a) Lk 1:46–55; 9b) Lk 1:68–79.

the biblical odes in the light of the New Testament, a fact that is relevant to a liturgical hermeneutics of Scripture; but the troparia sometimes have no connection to the biblical odes. The most important authors of canons were Andrew of Crete († 740), John Damascene († before 754), and Cosmas of Jerusalem (or of Maiuma, probably the adoptive son of John Damascene; † after 750). Cosmas is the author of the canon for the feast of the "Universal Exaltation of the Precious and Life-giving Cross" (September 14).

The Canon for the Exaltation of the Cross[58] and Its Biblical-Theological Motifs

We shall not examine the lengthy text in detail but emphasize once again the biblical-theological motifs. Typology plays an important role, as the following overview shows:

Ode	Biblical Anticipatory Images of the Cross and the Passion
1	Staff with which Moses divided the sea (Ex 14:6, with the addition that Moses sketched a sign of the cross with the staff)
	The uplifted arms of Moses that led to victory (Ex 17:8–16)—anticipatory image of the Passion of Christ, with his arms spread out on the cross
	Bronze serpent that Moses set up as a remedy against the destroyer (Nm 21:4–9; Jn 3:14)
3	Staff of Aaron, which blossomed and pointed to the priestly ministry (Nm 17:23)—blossoming of the tree of the Cross for the formerly infertile Church
	Staff with which Moses brought forth water from the rock (Ex 17:1–7)—water from the wound in Christ's side (Jn 19:34)
4	Moses makes the bitter water of Marah sweet with a piece of wood (Ex 15:23–25)
	Elisha lifts the lost ax from the Jordan with a piece of wood (2 Kgs 6:1–7)
	The cruciform arrangement of the camp of the Israelites, in the midst of which the tent of revelation stood (Nm 2)

---

58 Greek text: Ἀνθολόγιον τοῦ ὅλου ἐνιαυτοῦ περιέχον καθημερινὴν Ἀκολουθίαν ἐκ τοῦ Ὡρολογίου, τῆς Παρακλητικῆς καὶ τῶν Μηναίων (ἀπὸ τῆς Α΄ Σεπτεμβρίου μέχρι τῆς ἀρχῆς τοῦ Τριῳδίου). Rome 1967, 1:665-72; Italian translation: *Anthologhion* 1:619-25; German translation: Benini, *Liturgische Bibelhermeneutik*, 194–97.

5	Cross as the tree on which the devil, who had once seduced by means of a tree, was decoyed, and brought low
	The cherub that guarded Eden with a fiery sword (Gn 3:24) shrank back in fear before the Cross and made way for Christ.—The powers under the earth also trembled and bent their knee before Christ (Phil 2:10)
6	Jonah placed his hands in the form of a cross, as an anticipatory image of the Cross of Christ (this is not related in the Bible; there may possibly be a conflation with Gn 48:13 as in the following troparia). Through his coming forth from the fish on the third day he points to the Resurrection (Jon 2:1, 11; Mt 12:40 par.)
	Jacob crossed his hands when he blessed Ephraim and Manasseh (Gn 48:13) as an anticipatory image of the Cross
7	Tree in paradise (Gn 3)
	Israel (Jacob) embraces the staff of Joseph (Gn 47:31 LXX) in order to point to the glorious Cross
8	Praise of the Cross without typological references
9	Mary as the paradise that brought forth Christ, who in turn planted the tree of life that is the Cross
	The sourness of the tree in paradise (because of guilt) was once again made sweet like the water of Marah (Ex 15:23–25)

The typological exposition [2] of Old Testament passages dominates the canon. One point of emphasis is the exodus event. In some passages, such as Jacob's blessing or Elisha's lifting of the ax, the relationship to the Cross is achieved only via key-word associations (the crossing of the patriarch's arms, or the "wood") that do not display any inherent theological connection. This means that the biblical-theological quality of the typologies employed by Cosmas is quite varied. The poetry occasionally adds to the biblical text in order to make the transition to the theme of the Cross (Moses' sign of the cross [ode 1] or Jonah's crossed hands [ode 6]). It is interesting to note that, unlike the poems about the Cross discussed above, New Testament references and the Passion narrative play only a subordinate role [3]. The original biblical *cantica* have had scarcely any influence on this canon. Only the Song of Moses (Ex 15:1–19) is echoed, when the events of the wandering in the wilderness are celebrated as anticipatory images of Christ's paschal mystery. In odes 6 to 9, only the *hirmos* refers back to the biblical *cantica*, and only 6 and 9 have a thematic reference to the Cross.

CHAPTER FIFTEEN

The Communion Antiphons of the Roman Mass

As with the other genres, we must likewise make a selection from the chants of the Mass. In the hymns, we investigated "independent" *action-songs.* In order to do justice to the breadth at which we aim in part A of this study, we shall now look at *accompaniment-songs,* which have a different function. As I mentioned in the introduction to this section, the Communion antiphons are particularly suited to the question of a *liturgical* hermeneutics of the Bible, not only because they are assigned to a central rite of the eucharistic celebration, but also because they quite frequently take up the Gospel again and establish a fundamental relationship between Scripture and Eucharist.

A brief historical survey is helpful, especially since the Communion antiphons are among the oldest chants in the Mass.[59] There are clear indications from the fourth century that the Psalms were used during Communion. For example, Cyril († 387) or John of Jerusalem († 416),[60] Jerome,[61]

---

59 See Jungmann, *Missarum Sollemnia,* 2:391-400; Augustinus Hollaardt, "Sens, contenu et formes du chant de communion," *QL* 78, no. 1 (1997): 5-15; Guido Fuchs, "Theologie der Eucharistie im Spiegel eucharistischer Gesänge," *ALw* 31, no. 3 (1989): esp. 317-21; Peter Browe, "Mittelalterliche Kommunionriten," *JLw* 15 (1941): 57-61.

60 See Cyril, *Myst. Cat.* 5.20 (FontC 7:162; WEC 2:337).

61 See Jerome, *In Isaiam Commentarius* 2.5.20 (CChrSL 73:77).

Augustine,[62] and Cassidorus († after 580)[63] all attest the classic Communion verse, Psalm 34:9, "Taste and see how good the Lord is." When the *Apostolic Constitutions* describe Communion, they state explicitly that Psalm 34 was sung.[64] John Chrysostom in Antioch attests Psalm 145, from which the communicants sang: "The eyes of all are waiting for you, and you give them food at the proper time" (v. 15).[65] Originally, the people probably took part in the singing at Communion by joining in the refrain, but from the early Middle Ages onward, a schola took over the Communion chant completely,[66] so that the texts increased in number and their melodies in complexity. Fewer of the laity received Communion, and this meant that, from the tenth century onward, the psalm was reduced to the antiphon, with an increasingly elaborate melody. This often referred to the liturgical year, interpreting the psalms as *vox Christi, de Christo*, or *ad Christum*[67] (a very similar process can be observed in the case of the *koinonikon* in the Byzantine liturgy).[68] After Pentecost, the antiphons were taken from the Psalter in ascending sequence.[69] In the same period, the psalms lose their central position, so that roughly one-half of the Communion antiphons of the so-called Gregorian repertoire are taken from the psalms, and the other half from the New Testament,

62 Augustine interprets v. 6 (*"accedite ad eum et illuminamini"*) as the act of going forward to receive Communion, and he describes the effect of Communion as enlightenment. V. 9 is also related to Communion (*Enarratio in Ps* 33.10,12). See Henri Leclercq, "Communion (rite et antienne de la)," *DACL* 3 (1914): 2433; Fuchs, "Theologie der Eucharistie," 317 with n. 29, is more critical; see also Robert F. Taft, *The Precommunion Rites*, vol. 5 of *A History of the Liturgy of St. John Chrysostom*, OCA 261 (Rome: Pontificium Institutum Studiorum Orientalium, 2000), 277.

63 See Cassiodorus, *Expositio in Ps.* 33.6,9,12 (CChr.SL 97:293).

64 See *Apostolic Constitutions* 8.13.16 (SChr 336:211; WEC 2:263); Taft, *Precommunion Rites*, 275–76.

65 See Chrysostom, *Expositio in Ps.* 144 (PG 55:464; WEC 2:175); Taft, *Precommunion Rites*, 274–75.

66 The oldest testimony to this is *Ordo Romanus I*:117.122. See Michel Andrieu, *Les Ordines Romani du haut Moyen Âge*, vol. 2, SSL 23 (Louvain: Spicilegium Sacrum Lovaniense, 1948), 105, 107; James McKinnon, *The Advent Project. The Later-Seventh-Century Creation of the Roman Mass Proper* (Berkeley, CA: University of California Press, 2000), 326–55.

67 See A.II.7.2.

68 Taft, *Precommunion Rites*, 261–318; Thomas H. Schattauer, "The *Koinonicon* of the Byzantine Liturgy: An Historical Study," *OCP* 49 (1983): 91–129; Gerasimos Koutsouras, "*Koinonikon*. The Hymnological Context of Holy Communion," *Phronema* 21 (2006): 61–82. See in general André Rose, "Le chant de communion en divers rites chrétiens," in *Liturgie et charité fraternelle*, ed. M. Triacca and A. Pistoia, BEL.S. 101 (Rome: C.L.V.-Edizioni Liturgiche, 1999), 19–30.

69 Hollaardt, "Chant de communion," 9.

preferentially from the Gospel of the day. Finally, the Communion antiphon was integrated into the missal. From the thirteenth century onward, it was called simply "*communio*," and then "*postcommunio*," because it was sung or prayed only after the communion (of the priest).[70]

Let us now see how today's Communion antiphons were selected and examine the hermeneutical consequences of this choice. For the Sundays in Ordinary Time, one Communion antiphon from the Old Testament and one from the New are provided. The former is mostly taken from the psalms, in such a way that a Christological or specifically eucharistic interpretation is suggested (key words such as "food," "table," "altar," etc.). It can also be a general summons to praise God (which can also be understood as directed to Christ). The New Testament Communion antiphon is almost always taken from the Gospels. Usually, it is a logion of Jesus. These antiphons are formulated with striking frequency in the first person—in other words, they appear as *ipsissima verba Christi*.[71] In terms of biblical hermeneutics, this involves a skillful form of actualization or anamnesis: the Christ who is present in the Eucharist addresses this logion directly to the assembly. This becomes all the clearer when (as is often the case, at least in German-speaking regions) the Communion antiphon is recited by the priest when he shows the congregation the Body of Christ ("Behold the Lamb of God ..."). The three-year cycle means that there is no consciously intended harmony between the Communion antiphon and the readings, although there are occasional agreements with the Gospel.[72]

On the Sundays and feast days of the Easter cycle, the Communion antiphon usually takes up the Gospel again. On the 1st and 2nd Sundays in Lent, and on Palm Sunday (temptation, transfiguration, and passion according to the synoptic Gospels), a Communion antiphon from the Matthean pericope is prescribed. The words of Jesus to the Samaritan woman (Jn 4:13–14) are used on the 3rd Sunday, when this pericope is read. On the 4th and 5th Sundays, three verses are given in accordance with the Gospel.[73] A similar reference can be seen on Sundays 2 to 7 in the Easter season and on the

---

70 Jungmann, *Missarum Sollemnia*, 2:396–97.

71 This is the case on the following Sundays in Ordinary Time: 1, 3, 8–9, 12, 14–15, 16 (Rev 3:20), 18–21, 23, 25, 31, 33–34. On the 11th and 13th Sundays in Ordinary Time, the communion antiphons are taken from the high-priestly prayer (Jn 17:11 and 17:20–21), and are thus addressed to the Father. We find a logion of Jesus without the first-person formulation on Sundays 4–6, 17, 22, 29. The Communion antiphon is taken from the epistolary literature on Sundays 2, 10, (16), 24, 26–28, 30.

72 Links are present, e.g., on Sundays 3–4 A, Sundays 18–20 B, and Sunday 29 B.

73 Except on the 4th Sunday B.

Ascension and Pentecost (Vigil Mass). Taking up the Gospel again in this way, as often happens on the weekdays in Lent, is more than the repetition of a core statement. What was proclaimed in the Liturgy of the Word can now be recalled to mind and can be deepened in a personal manner in Communion. Above all, this is formally an expression of the unity between the Liturgy of the Word and the eucharistic celebration; substantially, it is also an expression of the theological link between Christ in the Word and Christ in the sacrament.[74]

The link between the two main parts of the Mass also finds expression through occasional references in the Communion antiphon to the reading. On Holy Thursday and Pentecost Sunday, this is due first and foremost to the important readings (the oldest tradition about the Last Supper in 1 Corinthians 11; the sending of the Spirit in Acts 2), which are taken anamnetically into the present day. This can also be observed on some weekdays in Lent.[75]

The Communion antiphons of the Christmas cycle are also hermeneutically interesting, since they are often taken from the Old Testament. On the 1st Sunday in Advent, the antiphon comes from the messianic Psalm 85; on the 2nd Sunday, from the first reading (C; Bar 5:5; 4:36); on the 3rd Sunday, from the reading from Isaiah (A; Is 35:4); and on the 4th Sunday, Is 7:14, which is quoted in Mt 1:23 (reading and Gospel A). Although a literal quotation from the first reading is found only in certain reading years (and does not occur on the weekdays), the important point here is the basic affirmation that a Communion antiphon from the Old Testament makes in Advent: namely, the Liturgy confesses that what the prophets (or the psalms, understood as prophetic texts) announced is fulfilled in Christ, who is present in the Eucharist. The liturgy thus indicates that the fulfillment of the promise is to be understood in a double sense: both in the Son of God who became a human being in history and in the Lord who is sacramentally present. The prophecy is thus fulfilled in the "today" of the Liturgy.[76] The same applies to the Old Testament Communion antiphons at Christmas (Christmas Eve and the dawn and morning Masses) and on the feast of the Holy Family.

On the weekdays in Advent from December 17 onward, the Communion antiphon is mostly taken from the Gospel that has been proclaimed[77] in order to signal that the promised Messiah is the same one who is received

---

74 See B.VIII.29.

75 See Friday of week 1; Thursday (and Friday) of week 2; Thursday of week 3; Tuesday, Thursday, and Saturday of week 4; and perhaps Wednesday of week 5.

76 See B.VIII.30.

77 The exceptions are December 17 and 23.

in Communion. In Christmastide, a eucharistic interpretation of the day's Gospel is sometimes found in the Communion antiphons, so that the Eucharist appears as a continuation of the Incarnation. For example, when the antiphon "To all who would accept him, he gave the power to become children of God" (Jn 1:12) is sung on the 2nd Sunday after Christmas, the "accepting/receiving" is made literally concrete in the reception of Communion.[78] Similarly, the Communion antiphon on the Epiphany, "We have seen his star in the East, and have come with gifts to adore the Lord" (Mt 2:2), posits an identification of those who come to Communion ("we") with the Magi. The temporal levels are consciously brought into relation to each other, and the prostration of the Magi before Jesus becomes the image of the adoration that takes place in the Eucharist and has a continuing effect on life.

This brings us to the phenomenon of the role identification that is realized in various ways (depending on the original speaker and addressee) in the Communion antiphons, independently of the period in the liturgical year.[79] The Communion antiphon can be the word of Christ to the community, as we have said; it can also be a word of prayer to Christ in praise or confession. In either case, it can be a kind of "brief dialogue" between Christ (in the Eucharist) and the community, a dialogue that can be continued in song or in silence. Those who receive Communion thus receive a specific impulse, sometimes harking back to the Liturgy of the Word, that can echo in them. This can be spiritually helpful because the attention in the Eucharist, which always embraces Christ in his totality, is directed to a more concrete aspect.

In the case of the Communion antiphons (as we have already seen with the pericope orations),[80] it is useful to look more closely at the third edition of the Italian missal (2020). It continues the praxis of the second edition by introducing one or more alternative Communion antiphons for the Sundays and feast days, as well as for the weekdays in the festal cycles.[81] These are taken from the Gospel of the day, where this had not already been the case in the *MRom* 2002. In addition to the Communion antiphon(s) taken over from the *MRom*, a Sunday Mass formula usually contains three additional antiphons for years A, B, and C. The frequent choice of logia of Jesus in direct speech, which we have seen in the *Roman Missal* on the Sundays in

---

78 *Missal*, 814. In the Latin (and in other translations), the verb is "*receperunt*," suggesting the reception in Communion.

79 See B.IX.34.

80 See A.III.12.3.

81 The Communion antiphons related to the Gospels are inserted in the section of the missal where the orations for the weekdays in Advent, Christmas season, and Easter season are printed (see *Messale Romano,* 1055-99; 2nd ed.: 929-61).

Ordinary Time, is striking here too. The primary intention in the expansion of the number of Communion antiphons is not to increase the consonance of a Mass formula, but to underline the unity of Word and Eucharist, and to make possible a eucharistic rereading of the Gospel.

CHAPTER SIXTEEN

Hermeneutical Insights

We have seen that Scripture is the fundamental source on which liturgical chant draws in history and in the present day. The hymns about the Cross in both the Latin and the Byzantine traditions clearly show typology[82] as an important hermeneutical instrument, with its strengths and weaknesses. It can offer a salvation-historical panorama that binds together theologically central events in God's salvific action (e.g., the Fall and the Redemption). The typological references in the hymns showed that their authors took for granted both the unity of the two Testaments and their interpretation on the basis of Christ—an understanding that the Liturgy too shares, since they have had their place in the Church's worship for centuries.

The typological references are often comprehensible only on the basis of Christ, or in the light of the New Testament, because they go beyond the original meaning in the Old Testament. Their liturgical use shows that an interpretation of this kind is regarded as legitimate and meaningful. This is made clear by the Old Testament communion antiphons, which find their fulfillment in Christ present in the Eucharist, and hence in the "today" of the Liturgy.[83] Nevertheless, certain weaknesses also came to light, because some typological interpretations appear arbitrary from our contemporary perspective, when the hermeneutical "bridge" is merely an association between key words instead of a substantially justified reference. On this point, however, one should bear in mind the poetical genre. A further difficulty arises when the poetry is based on an interpolated text or undertakes additions to the biblical text in order to make an interpretation plausible. Despite this, however, it must be accepted that the fundamental affirmation that was intended remained correct.

82 See B.VIII.30.1.

83 See B.VIII.30.2.

At the same time, we have seen that chants usually do not intend to offer an informative retelling of a biblical text. Rather, they select texts that suit the feast or the occasion, and their primary intention is to offer an interpretation of this, often in relation to those who have assembled for liturgy and who sing the chant. The metaphors play a central role in poetical texts. They make it possible in the songs to create an imaginative-poetical and musical access to Scripture and to its theological message that goes deeper than the spoken word on its own.[84] Since liturgical songs are often traditional material from earlier centuries, a liturgical hermeneutics of the Bible must ask whether the employed biblical and post-biblical images and modes of understanding remain comprehensible, or else how one could make them accessible today.[85]

The Communion antiphons too bring hermeneutical mechanisms of the Liturgy to light. Since many Communion antiphons in the missal are direct quotations from Jesus, and are often formulated in the first person, they appear in connection with Communion as words that the Lord himself addresses to his community, words that are meant to echo further in an internal dialogue, perhaps with the support of music. This is a skillful way of actualizing words from Scripture.[86] If these words are in harmony with the day's Gospel, they emphasize, through a sacramental rereading, both the unity between the Liturgy of the Word and the Eucharist, and the relationship between Christ's two modes of presence in Word and sacrament.[87] We have also noticed once again here the use of role identification as a means of reception.[88]

All the examples in this section show that the function of a song in its liturgical setting says something important about the text itself. A processional chant at Communion is subject to other conditions than a hymn at the beginning of an Office in the Liturgy of the Hours; and the same text has yet another effect at the Veneration of the Cross on Good Friday. However, the original function of a historical song must not be forgotten, as we could note in the case of the *kontakia*, which, as a sung sermon, have a function and a manner of delivery that are clearly different from the hymns in the Western Liturgy of the Hours. A liturgical hermeneutics of Scripture must always bear in mind the environment in which a biblical text, or one

---

84 See B.VI.21.

85 See B.IX.33.2.

86 See B.VIII.27.2 and B.VIII.28.2.1.

87 See B.VIII.29.2.

88 See B.IX.34.

inspired by Scripture, is used.[89] Besides this, the closeness to Scripture of an accompanying song means that it is making a biblical interpretation of the liturgical action. For example, the Communion antiphon on the Epiphany links the act of going forward to the altar with the path taken by the Magi and presents their adoration as the spiritual attitude appropriate to Communion. The biblical interpretation of the rites will be studied in the next section on actions and signs that acquire their meaning and significance from Scripture.

---

[89] See B.VII.23.

SECTION V

Actions and Signs

This section shows a different way of using Scripture than those studied up to this point. According to *SC* 24, actions and signs also receive their meaning from Sacred Scripture. Our selection from the dramatic liturgy of the Church year is the Washing of the Feet on Holy Thursday (in the Roman and Byzantine rites), and from the Liturgy of the sacraments, the Clothing with the White Baptismal Garment. The former is a Gospel narrative, and the latter the ritual realization of a biblical metaphor.[1]

1 Other examples, such as the procession on the Presentation of the Lord ("Candlemas") and the Ephphetha rite, are discussed by Benini, *Liturgische Bibelhermeneutik*, 225-39. See also Marco Benini, "Liturgical Actions: Anamnesis and/or Mimesis of Sacred Scripture? Exemplified by the Rite of Footwashing (Holy Thursday) and Ephphetha (Baptismal Liturgy)," *Worship* 95, no. 1 (2021): 34-50.

CHAPTER SEVENTEEN

The Washing
of Feet on Holy Thursday

While the rite of Washing the Feet obviously goes back to Jesus' example at the Last Supper (John 13), the exact origins of its use on Holy Thursday are obscure. It probably came into existence at the close of the fifth century in Jerusalem and was spread from there by monks[2] in East and West.[3]

1. THE WASHING OF THE FEET IN THE ROMAN RITE[4]

There were two basic forms of the Washing of the Feet, as (for example) the Rule of Benedict shows: washing the feet of the brethren[5] (*mandatum fratrum*) and those of the poor or of guests[6] (*mandatum pauperum*). The *Rule of the Master* also knows a solemn washing of the feet on Holy Thursday.[7]

---

2 See Thomas Schäfer, *Die Fußwaschung im monastischen Brauchtum und in der lateinischen Liturgie. Liturgiegeschichtliche Untersuchung*, TAB I. Abt. 47 (Beuron: Beuroner Kunstverlag, 1956).

3 See Pier Franco Beatrice, *La lavanda dei piedi. Contributo alla storia delle antiche liturgie cristiane*, BEL.S 38 (Rome: Ed. Liturgiche, 1983), 197–210, esp. 200–1, 204, 208; Bernhard Kötting, "Fußwaschung," *RAC* 8 (1972): 743–77.

4 Schäfer, *Fußwaschung*, 89–99; Winfried Haunerland, "Die Fußwaschung am Gründonnerstag—Evangelienspiel oder Nachfolgehandlung?," *LJ* 48, no. 2 (1998): 79–95; Hermanus A. P. Schmidt, *Hebdomada sancta. 2: Fontes historici, commentarius historicus* (Rome: Herder, 1957), 763–76; Peter Jeffery, *A New Commandment. Toward a Renewed Rite for the Washing of Feet* (Collegeville, MN: Liturgical Press, 1992).

5 See *Regula Benedicti* 35.9.

6 See *Regula Benedicti* 53.13-15. The washing of the feet was regarded already in biblical times as a sign of hospitality (see Gn 18:4; 1 Sm 25:41; 1 Tm 5:10).

7 See *Regula Magistri* 30.2-7 and, on Holy Thursday, *Regula Magistri* 53.42-46 (WEC 4:22).

This was made obligatory for all the cathedral churches in Spain and southern Gaul at the 17th Council of Toledo in 694.[8]

In Rome,[9] the pope and the clergy washed the feet of their servants by the seventh century, but without any liturgical form. From the twelfth century onward, the pope washed the feet of twelve subdeacons and thirteen poor persons during Vespers on Holy Thursday. The thirteenth person was meant to represent Christ, who identified himself with the "least of his brothers" (see Mt 25:40). The two washings of the feet were combined around the mid-fifteenth century, so that the *mandatum* was now performed either on the canons or on the poor. The *Caeremoniale Episcoporum* of 1600 refers to the various customs. It also speaks of thirteen canons and gives preference to the Washing of the Feet of thirteen poor persons, as a sign of greater humility. The number thirteen shows clearly that the intention was not an exact staging of the Gospel narrative.[10] The *MRom* of 1570 explains in the rubrics only a washing of the feet of the clergy (without giving a number).[11]

The Holy Week reform of 1955 introduced the Washing of the Feet as an option following the homily in the Mass of the Last Supper and allowed its celebration in parishes for the first time.[12] The development of the rubrics is particularly interesting. In 1955, they spoke of "twelve selected men," but the number twelve was omitted from the postconciliar Roman Missal (1970), which now spoke only of "men."[13] In the USA, the Bishops' Committee on the Liturgy allowed the washing of women's feet in 1987.[14] Pope Francis had the rubric altered in 2016 to "Those who are chosen from amongst the people of God."[15] The selection, which leaves open the number and the gender of

8 See Schäfer, *Fußwaschung*, 71; Beatrice, *Lavanda*, 205–6.

9 See Benini, "Liturgical Actions," 36-38 with bibliography.

10 See Peter Jeffery, "Mandatum Novum Do Vobis. Toward a Renewal of the Holy Thursday Footwashing Rite," *Worship* 64, no. 2 (1990): at 133 notes: "The footwashing ceremony itself never developed into a liturgical drama during the Middle Ages."

11 See *MRom 1570,* 239 (n. 1193).

12 See *Ordo Hebdomadae Sanctae instauratus. Editio typica* (Vatican City: Typis Polyglottis Vaticanis, 1956), 79-81; Annibale Bugnini and Carlo Braga, eds., *Ordo Hebdomadae Sanctae instauratus. Commentarium [...],* BEL.H 25 (Rome: Edizioni Liturgiche, 1956), 73-75, 89-93, esp. 75.

13 See *MRom 1970,* 244.

14 See Bishops' Committee on the Liturgy, "Newsletter 23, February 1987," in *Thirty-Five Years of the BCL Newsletters 1965-2000* (Washington, D.C.: United States Conference of Catholic Bishops, 2004), 1043–44.

15 Congregation for Divine Worship and the Discipline of the Sacraments, Decree *In Missa in Cena Domini,* January 6, 2016. (http://www.vatican.va/roman_curia/congregations/

persons, is meant to "represent the variety and the unity of each part of the people of God."[16] This once again emphasizes more strongly that the aim is not an accurate staging of the details in the Gospel.

Nevertheless, the washing of feet *per se* links the rite clearly to the biblical account, precisely because one scarcely ever washes the feet of another person today. Besides this, as is customary in the Liturgy, the priest takes on the representation of Christ. There are other mimetic elements too, such as the laying aside of the chasuble[17] or the putting on of a linen apron, which is envisaged only in the Ceremonial for Bishops (see Jn 13:4; this was always prescribed in 1955),[18] although such elements are considerably restrained, in comparison to some Eastern rites of the washing of feet, as we shall see below.

The intensity of the mimesis diminished between 1955 and 2016 thanks to the alterations of the rubrics.[19] But it is not the mimesis that makes the rite congruent with the Bible. This occurs only when it makes Jesus' intention plain, as the 2016 commentary of the Congregation of Divine Worship accompanying the decree about the Washing of the Feet explicitly states: "The significance does not now relate so much to the exterior imitation of what Jesus has done, but rather as to the meaning of what he has accomplished which has a universal importance, namely the giving of himself 'to the end' for the salvation of the human race, his charity which embraces all people and which makes all people brothers and sisters by following his example."[20] This formulation shows that the rite also has an anamnetic dimension, because its "significance," Jesus' gift of himself for the salvation that embraces everyone, is now made present in a special way in those who take part in this rite. The footwashing of the various representatives of the

---

ccdds/documents/rc_con_ccdds_doc_20160106_decreto-lavanda-piedi_en.html [retrieved 05/21/2021]).

16 *In Missa in Cena Domini*, January 6, 2016.

17 *Missal*, 300 adds the words "if necessary."

18 See *Ceremonial of Bishops. Revised by Decree of the Second Vatican Council and Published by the Authority of Pope John Paul II* (Collegeville, MN: Liturgical Press, 1989), 89 (n. 301). It also states that if the bishop is wearing the dalmatic, he does not remove it—obviously a sign of the diaconal ministry.

19 It is also noticeable in the papal liturgy that John Paul II washed the feet of twelve priests, so that the imitation of Jesus, who washed his disciples' feet, was somewhat stronger than with Benedict XVI, who washed the feet of twelve laymen.

20 https://www.vatican.va/roman_curia/congregations/ccdds/documents/rc_con_ccdds_doc_20160106_commento-decreto-lavanda-piedi_en.html (retrieved 05/21/2021).

people of God makes clear that Christ's love is for everyone. The anamnesis makes use here of the ritual mimesis.[21]

The rite of the Washing of the Feet also contains the important commission by Jesus to do this in daily living (see Jn 13:15). As is customary, the accompanying chants interpret the liturgical action. Most of the antiphons emphasize above all Jesus' commission. The chants also help all those taking part in the Mass of the Last Supper to make their own what they themselves experience or see. Each one can perceive the commission of the Lord as addressed them and can identify with the disciples. This is why (at least intentionally) there are no passive "spectators": the commission is already carried out in the rite, which is an act of imitation. The rite is the response to Jesus' commission, which has been heard in the Gospel reading (and perhaps expounded in the homily). This begins in the form of a sign in liturgy, and it should find its continuation in daily living.

2. THE WASHING OF THE FEET IN THE BYZANTINE RITE

The Byzantine Washing of the Feet[22] displays some differences that are of hermeneutical interest. The rite takes place only in the cathedrals and monastic churches at the end of the Liturgy of Saint Basil. The ministers go into the narthex to the accompaniment of Psalm 51 (50). After chants comes the customary litany for peace, expanded with two specific prayers for the blessing of the water and for the forgiveness of sins, and two prayers by the celebrant. The proclamation of the Gospel is in two parts: during the proclamation of John 13:3–12a, the superior washes the feet of twelve members of the community. He then himself proclaims the following section, John 13:12b–17, in which Jesus explains the sign. After a third prayer by the priest, the community returns into the nave, and the Divine Liturgy concludes.

Two elements are particularly noteworthy in comparison to the Western tradition. First, we note that the mimesis is very prominent, as we see already in the parallelization of the proclamation of the Gospel and its simultaneous scenic presentation—something otherwise unusual in the Liturgy. At

---

21 Benini, "Liturgical Actions."

22 The following sequence keeps to the Εὐχολόγιον τὸ μέγα (Athens: Παπαδημητρίου, 1992), 361-67; *Triode de carême*, trans. D. Guillaume, 3rd ed. (Parma: Diaconie apostolique, 1997), 509-12. See André Lossky, "Lavement des pieds et charité fraternelle: L'exemple du rite byzantin," in Triacca and Pistoia, *Liturgie et charité fraternelle*, 87-96; historical: André Lossky, "La cérémonie du lavement des pieds. Un essai d'étude comparée," in *Acts of the International Congress Comparative Liturgy Fifty Years after Anton Baumstark (1872-1948) […]*, ed. R. F. Taft and G. Winkler, OCA 265 (Rome: Pontificio istituto orientale, 2001), 809-32.

the corresponding passages in the Gospel, the superior removes his vestment, girds himself with a linen cloth, pours water into the bowl, etc. At each one who has the role of an apostle, v. 5 ("He began to wash the disciples' feet") is repeated. The role of the apostle Peter is deliberately assigned to the one highest in rank, or to the bursar, and it has sometimes (especially from the twelfth century onward) been given additional emphasis through a dialogue between the one with the role of Christ and the one with Peter's role. Although this praxis did not become universal, and was not included in the Euchologion to Mega, the 1997 edition of the *Triodion* notes that, where it is customary, the washing of the feet can be carried out in this dialogue form;[23] and this is what the Russian Orthodox patriarch does today. Independently of the dialog, the rite is a clear dramatization of the text that is heard simultaneously. After the superior has resumed his vestment, he proclaims the second part of the Gospel, in which Christ speaks. The division of the Gospel in two thus means that the pointedly emphasized commission to imitate what Jesus has done is heard only after the ritual Washing of the Feet, which (unlike in the Roman rite) is understood, not yet as an act of discipleship, but exclusively as a scenic representation. This understanding is also supported by the prayers, the first of which precedes the Gospel as a petition for those "who will *imitate* [μιμουμένους] the glorious example of this condescension."[24]

A second important difference is the aspect of the forgiveness of sins, which permeates the *akolouthia* with reference to John 13:10–11. On the way to the narthex, the place of the penitents, the penitential Psalm 51 (50) is sung. Vv. 4 and 9 help to spiritualize the Washing of the Feet, in the sense of a washing away of guilt.[25] The chants and prayers likewise contain elements that thematize the purification and sanctification of souls.

A comparison with the Roman tradition shows that the Byzantine tradition has features in common, such as the humility of Christ and the commission to love one's neighbor. But it also posits other accents that come from the more Platonic understanding of worship and from spiritual motifs (e.g., human sinfulness in the presence of the merciful God). This is why the same text is ritualized, and hence also interpreted, in two different ways. For a liturgical hermeneutics of the Bible, this example shows that the theological-spiritual backgrounds also make their contribution.

---

23 See *Triode*, 511.

24 See Εὐχολόγιον τὸ μέγα, 363.

25 Lossky, "Lavement," 90.

The Byzantine tradition also knows a washing of the feet of the poor, but as in the West, this was not at the center of a liturgical celebration. It was performed at the imperial court in Constantinople.[26]

---

26 Lossky, "Lavement," 96; Lossky, "Cérémonie," 829; Beatrice, *Lavanda*, 205.

CHAPTER EIGHTEEN

The Clothing with
the White Baptismal Garment

The baptismal garment is widely attested in the mystagogical catecheses and other sources from the fourth century in the East (Cyril/John of Jerusalem, John Chrysostom, Theodore of Mopsuestia [† 428/429], and others) and in the West (Zeno of Verona [† 371/372], Ambrose, Augustine, and others).[27] The newly-baptized often wore the white garment for an entire week; this was reflected in the name of the Sunday after Easter as "Dominica in Albis" ("Sunday in white garments").[28] It is easy to envision the development. Logically enough, the newly-baptized, who had taken off their clothes for the bath in water, had to put something on afterward. A new—and probably white—garment expressed the fact that, with baptism, they had begun a new life. Later, this was also "officially" handed over to them. It is thought that the origin of such a baptismal garment may be as early as the mid-third century.[29] This is a clear example of an action that was initially a matter of practical necessity and was later given a theological interpretation (as in the catechesis) and ritualized.[30]

In the context of this ritualization, an obvious move was then to accompany the handing over of the garment with an interpretative word. The formula from the Old Gallican *Missale Gothicum* was: "*Accipe vestem candidam,*

---

27 See Ante Crnčević, *Induere Christum. Rito e linguaggio simbolico-teologico della vestizione battesimale*, BEL.S 108 (Rome: CLV-Edizioni Liturgiche, 2000), 183–310; Johannes Quasten, "The Garment of Immortality. A Study of the 'Accipe vestem candidam,'" in *Miscellanea Lercaro* I, 391–401.

28 The German Missal still contains the name "Weißer Sonntag," i.e. "White Sunday."

29 Crnčević, *Induere Christum*, 323, 326.

30 Crnčević, 321–38, esp. 323–27.

quam immaculatam perferas ante tribunal domini nostri Iesu Christi"[31] ("Accept this white garment, and bring it unstained before the tribunal of our Lord Jesus Christ," subsequently expanded). It became established and is still used in adult baptism today.[32] A different formula is employed in the postconciliar celebration of infant baptism: "N., you have become a new creation and have clothed yourself in Christ. May this white garment be a sign to you of your Christian dignity. With your family and friends to help you by word and example, bring it unstained into eternal life."[33]

The baptismal garment has several meanings which are made clear through the scriptural references. First, the color itself has a moral-ethical meaning, especially in the initiation of adults, because white symbolizes purity and the forgiveness of sins.[34] The act of receiving the garment underlines that this forgiveness is a gift of God. The accompanying word recalls Romans 13:14, a passage in which Paul formulates ethical directives for Christian living. The white baptismal garment implicitly presents these directives: the garment is clean and must be preserved free from soil, and the same is true of our conduct of life (the accompanying word contains the imperative "bring that dignity unstained into eternal life").

Scripture supplies an important Christological interpretation: "For all of you who were baptized into Christ have clothed yourselves in Christ" (Gal 3:27). This biblical reference allows the motif of being a child of God through faith (3:26), of being "in Christ" and belonging to him (3:28–29) to resonate. The new garment is a sign of the dignity of the baptized, who have become "a new creation"[35] because they have died and risen to life with Christ (see Rom 6:1–11). The baptismal garment thus makes visible to the senses the new invisible spiritual reality of unity with the risen Lord.

The garment also points to the ecclesiological significance of Baptism (Gal 3:26–28), especially in celebrations with several newly-baptized, all of whom—independently of sex, status, origins, etc.—receive the same garment:

---

31 *Missale Gothicum (Vat. Reg. Lat. 317)*, ed. L. C. Mohlberg, RED.F 5 (Rome: Herder, 1961), 68 n. 263; see Crnčević, *Induere Christum*, 357, 552–55.

32 See *Ordo initiationis Christianae adultorum. Rituale Romanum ex decreto sacrosancti oecumenici concilii Vaticani II instauratum auctoritate Pauli pp. VI promulgatum. Editio typica* (Vatican City: Typis Polyglottis Vaticanis, 1972), 85–86.

33 *The Order of Baptism of Children, English translation according to the Second Typical Edition, for use in the dioceses of the United States of America [...]* (Washington, D.C.: United States Conference of Catholic Bishops, 2020), 69, 86, 102, 109.

34 See Rev 3:4.

35 2 Cor 5:7; Gal 6:15.

"There is neither Jew nor Greek, there is neither slave nor free person, there is not male and female; for you are all one in Christ Jesus" (3:28).

The eschatological significance of the baptismal garment is clearer since it points to the innumerable throng of the redeemed who stand before God "in white garments" (Rev 7:9–17; 19:8, 14). As the accompanying word reminds us, baptism already gives us a share in this.

These observations and interpretations are also relevant to a biblical hermeneutics. The baptismal garment makes clear in an exemplary way that theological metaphors (Paul: putting on Christ as a garment; Revelation: a white garment) are translated in the Liturgy into symbol and ritual. Several scriptural passages find expression here in one single, polyvalent sign. This means that, while the liturgical translation intensifies the affirmations of Scripture, they are at the same time also stripped down, because it is not possible for all the aspects of a text to be represented in the same way in the sign and in the words that interpret it. On the one hand, it is only the accompanying words, which point to Scripture, that allow the sign to become completely comprehensible. This means that Scripture has a kind of "prerogative of interpretation" vis-à-vis the liturgical signs. On the other hand, however, affirmations of Scripture (and thus, above all, the spiritual reality) do not only *find utterance* by means of the translation into ritual. This translation also makes it possible to *experience* this with the senses. By bringing Scripture to our experience, the Liturgy underscores the performative character of the Word of God.

CHAPTER NINETEEN

Hermeneutical Insights

L iturgical actions often depict the action of Jesus with more or less strongly mimetic elements. This gives such acts of worship a special vividness that allows the sign to work more strongly than would the word on its own. Just as the preaching of the Gospel is more than imparting historical information, these rites are more than a catechetical illustration. Since the mimesis cannot be strictly separated from the anamnesis, the liturgical actions support the re-presentation of what Jesus did to the participants. The ritually staged Scripture —one could speak here of a ritual quotation[36]—becomes performative in the celebration.[37] In the liturgical celebration, the Church continues what Christ did on earth.[38]

Sometimes, the liturgical action (such as the Washing of the Feet in the Roman rite) already appears as a response to the Word of God, as an act of discipleship that begins in the Liturgy and ought to find its continuation in life. In this way, the rite anticipates what is to take place in daily life. It is, of course, always the case that only individual aspects are taken into the rite. Sometimes, as in the Clothing with the Baptismal Garment, several scriptural passages serve as points of reference. The white garment shows that liturgical signs can also translate passages outside the Gospels into a ritual form. These two examples touch on the anamnetic function of the use of Scripture, which is thus marked out as a significant element in a liturgical hermeneutics of the Bible.

Reflection on the history of liturgy shows that frequently, liturgical signs and actions have acquired an interpretative accompanying formula only at a later stage; this formula was often borrowed from Scripture. This is, by the way, completely in accord with Anton Baumstark's observations about the

---

36 See B.VIII.27.2.

37 See B.VIII.28.3.

38 See B.VIII.26 and B.VIII.27.

verbalization of liturgical actions.[39] Our discussion of the rites of the baptismal liturgy has shown that postconciliar liturgical reform—in accordance with *SC* 24— has given word and sign a stronger orientation to the Bible.

---

39 See Robert F. Taft, "Anton Baumstark's Comparative Liturgy Revisited," in *Comparative Liturgy Fifty Years after Anton Baumstark (1872-1948). Acts of the International Congress. Rome, 25-29 September 1998*, ed. R. F. Taft and G. Winkler, OCA 265 (Rome: Pontificio istituto orientale, 2001), 191-232, esp. 200, 209-10; see also Fritz West, *The Comparative Liturgy of Anton Baumstark*, Joint Liturgical Studies 31 (Bramcote: Grove Books, 1995); Fritz West, "A Reader's Guide to the Methodological Writings of Anton Baumstark," *Worship* 88, no. 3 (2014): 194-217.

PART B

Systematic Overview: Dimensions of a Liturgical Hermeneutics of Sacred Scripture

W hen one brings together the individual stones in a mosaic, they form a picture. Nevertheless, a certain distance is necessary if one is not only to grasp the colors or preciousness of the individual stones, but get an overview of the picture that is more than the sum of its single components.

This is why the more strongly observational and descriptive part of this book is now followed by a systematic overview. The first insights gained from Part A have been the biblical influence on liturgy as a whole, and the eminent role that Scripture plays in liturgy. We have also made some observations with regard to its hermeneutics, which is generated by the celebration of the Liturgy. This will now be developed and studied on a deeper level.

Part B has the following structure: The first section illustrates the various approaches to Scripture that the celebration of the Liturgy opens up, thereby offering paths to understanding the Bible. The second section underlines how the liturgical context is a central hermeneutical key to Scripture. Here, we shall look at the intertextual references to the entire context of the celebration and to the texts of the other readings, which have a significant influence on the understanding of a pericope. The immediate liturgical context, that is the ritual framework surrounding the readings, is also hermeneutically important for the proclamation of the Word.

The third chapter, "Theological Aspects of the Liturgical Hermeneutics of Scripture," is the most important in terms of content. Here we shall look at the various functions of Scripture in the Liturgy, the fundamental anamnetic dimension of the Word of God, its sacramentality, and the relationship between Word and sacrament. We shall also present Christological and pneumatological reflections.

Finally, the fourth section takes up the reception of Scripture, which can be understood as an act of *participatio actuosa.* Its numerous patterns of interpretation and identification encompass both cognitive and spiritual components.

Approaches to Scripture through the Celebration of the Liturgy

CHAPTER TWENTY

Various Approaches
to the Liturgy in Detail

For believers, the Liturgy is the most frequent path to the Word of God. Accordingly, we shall investigate which specific approaches the celebration of the Liturgy generates.

1. APPROACH VIA THE LITURGICAL YEAR

The first mode of liturgical approach to Scripture is the liturgical year. First, the sequence of the Gospel readings in the festal cycles makes possible to imitate the life of Jesus, to some extent. In the heart of the liturgical year, the paschal Triduum—the laying down of his life, his dying, and his rising—is celebrated as the central element. The forty days of Lent, as a journey toward Easter, become a way to accompany Christ on the path to his dying and rising.[1] A clear parallel to the life of Jesus is also found on the Second Sunday of Easter, with the encounter between the risen Lord and Thomas on the eighth day. The Ascension and Pentecost on the fortieth and fiftieth days adopt the biblical chronology. We find something similar in the context of Christmas, with the circumcision on the eighth day (January 1) and the Presentation in the Temple on the fortieth day (February 2), or with the Annunciation of the Lord on March 25, nine months before Christmas, and the birth of John the Baptist on June 24, six months before Christmas. In Ordinary Time, a chronological relationship can be seen only immediately after the Baptism of the Lord, when the beginning of Jesus' public ministry is proclaimed in the Gospels.

1 See A.I.3.2.4.

Although tendencies to imitate are contained in the celebration of the liturgical year, the Liturgy does not aim at a "sequel" to the life of Jesus. Rather, the participant in the Liturgy over the course of the year lives with the proclaimed Scripture and receives thereby a personal share in the life of Christ. *Verbum Domini* 52 speaks of "the sage pedagogy of the Church, which proclaims and listens to Sacred Scripture following the rhythm of the liturgical year."[2] "Pedagogy" here means more than the simple communication of knowledge regarding the most important pericopes and the mysteries of the faith expressed in them. With recourse to *SC* 102, *Verbum Domini* emphasizes that the celebration makes present what is proclaimed, so that the believers encounter it and receive salvation. Thus, the anamnetic character of the proclamation of Scripture comes into effect.

Over the course of the liturgical year, particular emphasis is laid on individual books or specific kinds of texts.[3] For example, messianic texts (especially from the prophet Isaiah) are read in the Mass and the Office of Readings every Advent. This, of course, gives prominence to the understanding of the prophets primarily as those who announced the coming of the Messiah; other prophetic tasks move into the background. This means that the prevailing atmosphere of this period in the liturgical year—similarly when the fourth Servant Song (Is 52:13–53:12) is read on Good Friday—opens up a specific access to the prophets, though it undoubtedly does not cover the entire spectrum of prophecy. The continuous reading of the Acts of the Apostles in the Easter season up to Pentecost, common to both East and West, attests that the source of the Church's life from the very beginning has been the Paschal Mystery of Christ and the power of the Spirit; it also portrays life in the earliest Church. An ascending structure of the Johannine signs can be observed on the Sundays of Lent in year A.[4] The continuous reading of 1 John in the Christmas season entails a special perspective that opens up a perfectly fitting access to this text. In the Milanese order of readings, access to the most important figures of the Old Testament is opened up in the period after Pentecost.[5]

For the Psalms, different liturgical periods bring varying verses to the foreground, giving a specific color to the text as a whole and to what it affirms. In addition, the prayers, chants, and specific rites communicate an

2 *VD* 52.

3 See references in A.I.3.3.

4 See A.I.3.2.3.

5 See A.I.3.2.

access to the contents of Scripture which corresponds to the periods of the liturgical year.[6]

2. SITUATIONAL ACCESS

In the occasional services like funerals, or at the celebrations of the sacraments, the Liturgy communicates a situational access to Scripture, taking the concrete existential situation as its starting point and linking this to the testimony to God's loving care. Persons experiencing emotional situations are often more open for an interpretation on the basis of faith, and hence for the Word of God. A suitable choice of readings not only corresponds to the individual form of such celebrations (which is frequently desired); it can also increase interest in the scriptural readings and in their message. As we have seen in detail in Part A regarding the Anointing of the Sick,[7] identification with the scriptural personages constitutes an important bridge between God's salvific action and the world in which the participants live today. In principle, therefore, the situational access via the Liturgy brings out the special relationship of Scripture to people's lives.

In the Liturgy of the Hours, the approach of the *veritas horarum*, celebrating prayers at the appropriate time of day, can lead to a certain objective agreement between the situation of the celebrating community and a text of Scripture. For example, when a morning psalm is sung at Lauds, the beginning of the day, which all participants experience, and it correlates with the biblical text that is read. Beside this, there is frequently a subjective concurrence between the individual and an emotion depicted in the Psalm, or an idea that is expressed in a scriptural reading. In this way, those who pray can rediscover their own life between the lines of the breviary and bring this life before God.

3. ACCESS VIA REPETITION AND FAMILIARITY

Rite and liturgy live by repetition. Certain parts of Scripture recur again and again in the liturgical celebration and imprint themselves on one's mind. They can have a profound influence on people and bring about an intimate familiarity with the Word of God. Over time, scriptural texts join together with other scriptural or liturgical texts, so that a network of relationships

---

6 See A.II.7.1; A.IV.14; A.V.17.

7 See A.I.4.1.

develops. These allow one to perceive ever new allusions and references—or indeed, create these allusions and references. This network promotes the interiorization of the Word of God and opens up a deeper access to Scripture.

The example of the Responsorial Psalm has shown that the refrain makes an impact precisely through repetition, while often at the same time interpreting the psalm and/or bringing it into a relationship with the hearers.[8] This applies by analogy to Scripture in the Liturgy. Thus, chants and hymns can help to interpret or understand a passage in the Bible,[9] and this can also be the case with the orations (especially the pericope orations).[10]

Liturgy, however, is more than text. Liturgy is a living celebration, and this means that it lives especially from the relation to life discussed under point 20.2 above, and from the ensemble of religious experiences. A text will be understood differently in the changing existential situations, and various aspects will move into the foreground. And this is why it is only the repetition of the scriptural texts that reveals the richness of their content. Liturgy gradually opens up this content and allows it to bear fruit.

4. POETICAL AND MUSICAL ACCESS

The Liturgy opens up a further access to Scripture—and through it, to God—by means of poetry and singing. Already within the Bible, the Psalms display the power of poetical discourse, which puts our life into words before God ("theo-poetry").[11] Liturgical singing can help us to join consciously in the prayer of the Psalms.

The hymns too,[12] which are permeated by Scripture, have their share in this process. In particular, their poetical-metaphorical language permits an imaginative access that is capable of addressing people more deeply (e.g., "Faithful Cross, above all other"). At the same time, a hymn expresses in a memorable way the theological message of the scriptural passages it takes up, and transposes these in compact words onto those who pray. In comparison to the Byzantine hymnography, which has more strongly narrative features, Latin hymns often prefer a theological interpretation of the biblical texts to

---

8 See A.II.8.

9 An example is the interpretation of the Cross in the hymns previously discussed (see A.IV.14.), or the interpretation of the gifts of the Magi in Prudentius' hymn (see *Liturgy of the Hours*, 1:277).

10 See A.III.12.

11 See A.II. (Introduction).

12 See A.IV.14.

which they refer, rather than a detailed retelling. We should emphasize the quality of the texts used in liturgy, since less successful poetical compositions were either received only locally, or else were expunged in the course of history. Singing, which customarily intensifies attention to the content of the words, is (originally) a constitutive element of the hymn.[13]

We should also mention here the Prefaces[14] and the chants of the Ordinary of the Mass, which likewise display a biblical vocabulary, and above all the vernacular hymns, which often draw on Scripture. Congregational singing and melody help to make an impact more easily than biblical texts that are "only" heard or read.

5. RITUAL AND VISUAL ACCESS

Through the translation of Scripture into signs and actions, the Liturgy also opens up a ritual access that makes the Bible vivid and allows it to be experienced directly. This promotes a holistic *participation* in the biblical event of salvation.

In addition, art in the church building, pictures, statues, stained glass windows, or similar things often depict biblical scenes, which they communicate in their own specific way. The visual access plays an important role in popular piety.

6. BIOGRAPHICAL ACCESS BY MEANS OF THE SAINTS

The Liturgy also opens up a biographical access to Scripture via the commemoration of the saints.[15] Since the pericopes of feast days are often illustrated by the life of the saint, the *vita* of a saint makes the pericope comprehensible, or literally "fills it with life."

Moreover, it frequently happens that a saint's life can also offer an interpretation of aspects of the continuous reading on a weekday. Even when, at first sight, there appears to be no direct connection, and the pericope would not lead our thoughts to this particular saint, the example of his or her life

---

13 See Augustine, *Enarrationes in psalmos* 72.1: "*Si* [...] *non cantetur, non est hymnus.*" which means "If it is not sung, it is not a hymn." (CChr.SL 39:986; WEC 3:29).

14 See, with the biblical references in each instance, *The Prefaces of the Roman Missal. A Source Compendium with Concordance and Indices*, ed. A. Ward and C. Johnson (Rome: Tipografia Poliglotta Vaticana, 1989).

15 See A.I.3.3.

can contribute an impulse to the reading. The saints are "official ecclesiastical" interpreters (so to speak) who illustrate the principle that Scripture can be read, understood, and above all, lived on the basis of the faith and the community of the Church.

CHAPTER 21

Access from the Celebration of Faith

Behind the access routes mentioned above, there stands a fundamental perspective: namely, since liturgy is the celebration and articulation of the Church's faith, Scripture is also received in the Liturgy from the perspective of faith. That is, it is understood as the Word of God, as "Sacred Scripture."

This is appropriate in view of the genesis of Scripture, which itself is a testimony, shaped over time, to the experience of faith that human beings have had with the God who reveals himself in history. The biblical authors themselves wrote the scriptural texts on the basis of their faith. Since one basic hermeneutical principle demands that a text should be understood in the spirit in which it is written,[16] an access on the basis of faith, such as is practiced in the Liturgy, is appropriate and in accord with Scripture. Abbot Ildefons Herwegen (1874-1946) of Maria Laach wrote that the Liturgy

> "displays to us Sacred Scripture and gives it to us directly from the inside. It brings us into the center of its own genesis, immerses us in the source of inspiration, so that it is no longer from the outside with our own disposition (like any reader, even one who lacks faith) that we approach Sacred Scripture, but in an immediate bond of life with the divine Inspirer."[17]

As these words show, the historically oriented idea of the genesis of Scripture must be complemented by the theological aspect that the Liturgy aims at a "bond of life" with the living God. The dimension of "celebration" itself makes it clear that the Liturgy is not concerned primarily with the reading or the intellectual study of a text. Rather, the text is the medium of an encounter with God here and now. His Word is thus not only testimony

16 See *DV* 12.

17 Ildefons Herwegen, "Die Heilige Schrift in der Liturgie der Kirche," *LiZs* 3, no. 1 (1930/31): 17.

to the past; it is also a Word that goes forth today, a Word addressed to the human being who is to receive it in faith, a Word to which one must make a response in prayer and in one's life.[18] The participant in liturgy encounters Scripture (in its various liturgical uses) with the attitude of one who prays and believes

This can be illustrated by the axiom of Prosper of Aquitaine († 455), *legem credendi lex statuat supplicandi* (*DH* 246: the law of praying establishes the law of believing), which was reduced to the brief formula *lex orandi, lex credendi,* when this axiom is applied to the context of Scripture in the Liturgy. The direction envisaged by Prosper is unambiguous: the Liturgy (*lex orandi*) shows and influences the content and the manner of believing (*lex credendi*). Scripture can be integrated into the sequence *lex orandi, lex credendi* in the sense of a *lex audiendi*.[19] Prayer (*lex orandi*) and faith (*lex credendi*) determine the way in which Scripture is heard or received in the Liturgy.

For a liturgical hermeneutics of the Bible, this means that Scripture is understood in the manner that is proper to the Liturgy. In other words, the access to the Bible consists in the celebration of the faith. Regarding the prayers that are influenced by Scripture, and especially to the pericope orations that we have examined,[20] the Liturgy itself shows how it receives Scripture into the *lex orandi,* or how it leads to Scripture on the basis of the *lex orandi.* The context of worship means that an access on the basis of faith is presupposed. But it also means that this same access is supported, because it is from the hearing of the Word that faith arises (see Rom 10:17), and faith is articulated and strengthened in the Liturgy in the modes of prayer and celebration.

With regard to a biblical hermeneutics, *Verbum Domini* gives particular emphasis to the role of an access from faith, referring here to the Liturgy: "A faith-filled understanding of Sacred Scripture must always refer back to the Liturgy, in which the word of God is celebrated as a timely and living word."[21] Benedict XVI insists that believers must be taught "to savor the deep meaning of the word of God which unfolds each year in the Liturgy, revealing the fundamental mysteries of our faith. This is in turn the basis for a correct

---

18 For greater detail on this point, see B.VIII.28.2.

19 In a similar manner, the *lex agendi* too was attached to the axiom. See Kevin W. Irwin, *Context and Text. A Method for Liturgical Theology. Revised Edition* (Collegeville, MN: Liturgical Press, 2018), passim, here esp. 8–11, 46–47, 51–56, 63–64, 621–25.

20 See A.IV.15 and 15.3. The Psalm orations would be another example here.

21 *VD* 52.

approach to Sacred Scripture."[22] In other words, one who chooses the Liturgy as an access path to Scripture, or who understands the Liturgy in the same way that the Church does in the celebration of liturgy, is "on the right track."

The text certainly does not intend to affirm that the Liturgy is the only correct access route to Scripture; after all, Joseph Ratzinger / Benedict XVI himself had recourse to selected insights of historical-critical exegesis, and he underlined its merits.[23] These insights can also be used in preparing a homily, to acquire a better understanding of the texts; in this way, they flow into the Liturgy.[24] In view of the line of argument in this article, Benedict XVI doubtless understands "a correct approach" as an access route from the faith that sees the Word of God as a "timely and living word." One reason for the particular emphasis he places on the Liturgy is that for Benedict, in principle, "authentic biblical hermeneutics can only be had within the faith of the Church,"[25] and that, with regard to Scripture, the Liturgy already of its very nature bears within itself the two contexts—Church and faith. *Verbum Domini* 52 thus declares that the access route from the faith that is celebrated in the Liturgy is a fundamental criterion for every way of approaching Scripture. This indirectly underscores the significance of a biblical hermeneutics that grows out of the celebration of the Liturgy.

---

22 *VD* 52.

23 See Joseph Ratzinger / Benedict XVI, *Jesus of Nazareth*. 1: *From the Baptism in the Jordan to the Transfiguration*, trans. A. Walker (New York: Doubleday, 2007), xii–xx.

24 See *Homiletic Directory*, 29.

25 *VD* 29. See also Rudolf Voderholzer, "Zum Verständnis von 'traditio/paradosis' in der Frühen Kirche. Unter besonderer Berücksichtigung der 'Regula fidei'," in Voderholzer, *Offenbarung. Tradition und Schriftauslegung. Bausteine zu einer christlichen Bibelhermeneutik* (Regensburg: Pustet, 2013), 105–18, esp. 114, 117–18; Ludger Schwienhorst-Schönberger, "Wiederentdeckung des geistigen Schriftverständnisses. Zur Bedeutung der Kirchenväterhermeneutik," *ThGl* 101, no. 3 (2011): 414–15.

CHAPTER 22

Hermeneutical Insights

The liturgical approach to Scripture does more than communicate knowledge (although this also happens *en passant*). Rather, it has a basic theological orientation. As the celebration of faith, the Liturgy wishes, by means of Scripture, to open up access to God himself. This is in accord with Jesus' answer to Jude Thaddaeus when he asks why Christ will reveal himself only to the disciples, rather than to the world: "Whoever loves me will keep my word, and my Father will love him, and we will come to him and make our dwelling with him" (Jn 14:23).

The revelation of God, or the encounter with Christ, can occur only with human beings who have a personal relationship and hold fast to his word. The Liturgy, which is permeated in various ways by the Word of God and articulates the relationship of faith, is a form of this "holding fast in love to the word of Christ." This then opens up a dwelling (μονή), God's "habitat," in the human being. Thus, Scripture functions in the Liturgy as the medium of the encounter with God that takes place here and now.

Liturgical Context as a Hermeneutical Key

One central factor in the interpretation of a text is the context in which it stands. Every liturgical celebration supplies a context of this kind, thereby both offering a hermeneutical key and functioning as an interpreter of Scripture.[1]

---

1 See Triacca and Pistoia, *Liturgie, interprète de l'écriture.*

CHAPTER 23

Intertextuality

The concept of intertextuality is borrowed from literary studies.[2] There, it designates the "text-text relationship" whereby one text enters into dialogue with others revealing the polyvalence of the texts. In liturgy too, it is possible to experience how texts interpret each other, allowing a text to appear in a new light, or drawing our attention to one particular key word, and so on. This is what is meant by intertextuality in the narrower sense of the term, but the Liturgy is not based only on texts, since the context in a wider sense embraces the liturgical season in the Church, the situation of a celebration, ritual actions, etc.[3]

1. INTERPRETATION THROUGH THE ENTIRE LITURGICAL CONTEXT OF A CELEBRATION

Interpretation through other liturgical texts

First of all, intertextual relationships between proclaimed scriptural texts and other liturgical texts can contribute to the interpretation. It is clear, for example, that the Prefaces from the 3rd to the 5th Sunday in Lent interpret the Gospels of year A in relation to the preparation for Baptism or the renewal of the baptismal promises. Likewise, when they are heard, many

---

2 See Oliver Scheiding, "Intertextualität," in *Gedächtniskonzepte der Literaturwissenschaft. Theoretische Grundlegung und Anwendungsperspektiven*, ed. A. Erll and A. Nünning, Media and Cultural Memory 2 (Berlin: De Gruyter, 2005), 53-72.

3 The Latin *textum* originally means "something woven together," and thus is wider than our modern understanding of "text."

orations, especially the psalm and the pericope orations,[4] can subtly draw attention to specific aspects of the scriptural readings; or else, they take these aspects up anew and thus offer a "liturgical exegesis of Scripture." The most prominent examples are the orations after the readings at the Easter Vigil.[5]

The Homiletic Directory explicitly emphasizes that the homily can also refer to the liturgical prayers, "because the prayers provide a useful hermeneutic for the preacher's *interpretation* of the biblical texts."[6] Since the liturgical texts are determined by the Church's magisterium, they possess a certain normativity for the interpretation of Scripture, without however prescribing this. Similarly, the selected patristic texts in the Office of Readings often take up the immediately preceding biblical reading, so that they provide "an authentic interpretation of the word of God, so that 'prophetic and apostolic interpretation may be guided in a Catholic and ecclesial way.'"[7]

Interpretation through the occasion of the celebration

Independent of individual texts, the occasion of the liturgical celebration also functions as an interpretation. For example, the Zacchaeus pericope can sound very different, depending on the context. On the 31st Sunday in year C, the text stands in the foreground without any specific side-reference. But in the context of the dedication of a church, Jesus' words, "Today salvation has come to this house" (Lk 19:9), are transposed to the church building, which thus appears as the house of the presence of Christ and the place of salvation for human beings. In the Byzantine liturgy, the Zacchaeus pericope serves as one of the seven Gospel readings at the Anointing of the Sick. Clearly, the focus is on the salvation that is promised individually for the sick person, who can identify with Zacchaeus.[8] When this pericope is proclaimed in Milan on the last Sunday before Lent, the Sunday of Divine Clemency, it is the aspect of Zacchaeus as a sinner that stands in the foreground: he experiences salvation in the form of forgiveness, and repents.[9] Naturally,

---

4 See A.III.12.3 and A.III.12.4. Outside feast days, the coordination of oration texts with the readings is a recent phenomenon.

5 On the Easter Vigil, see Zerfaß, *Hermeneutik*, 15–29; Ward, "Orations after the Readings at the Easter Vigil."

6 *Homiletic Directory*, 11; italics added. See also *Homiletic Directory*, 15: "Clearly, this means that the liturgical setting is an essential key to interpreting the biblical passages proclaimed in a celebration."

7 *GILH*, 163 (with a quotation from Vincent of Lérins).

8 See A.I.4.1.

9 See A.I.3.2.3.

the common element in the varying interpretations is that the salvation described in the text is promised in the "today" (Lk 19:5, 9) of the liturgical celebration. Accordingly, precisely in their difference, they show that anamnesis is an essential characteristic of the liturgical use of Scripture.[10]

The example of the dedication of a church displays the same phenomenon in the case of the Psalms (in the ecclesiological interpretation of Psalm 24),[11] the prayers, and the chants. For example, the image of the living stones is applied unambiguously in 1 Peter 2:5 to the believers, but the church building too resonates in the collect that employs this image.[12] With poetical skill, the hymn *Urbs Ierusalem beata* establishes a relationship between the heavenly Jerusalem (Rev 21) and the Church on earth.[13]

Interpretation through the liturgical year

The Church year can not only prompt a selection that suits the specific season (e.g., Luke 2 at Christmas), but can also underscore what is said in the Gospel. Thus, the farewell discourses of Jesus and the so-called high-priestly prayer are read from the 5th to the 7th Sunday in Eastertide. Since their place in the Johannine narrative is after the Last Supper, they fit this period—not chronologically, but undoubtedly in terms of their theme and their theology. The context of the Easter season makes it clear that the realization of these words of Jesus will be made possible only thanks to his Resurrection and to his abiding presence with his disciples.[14] We have already pointed out that the pericopes of the Samaritan woman and of the man born blind are read before Easter in the Roman and Milanese rites, and after Easter in the Byzantine rite. But in both cases, they are interpreted on the basis of the liturgical year, i.e., as pointing to Easter and to incorporation into the Paschal Mystery (in the West) or as the unfolding of this same mystery (in the East).[15] We have also mentioned the interpretation of the Psalms on the basis of the liturgical

---

10 On this, see B.VIII.27.

11 See A.II.7.1.

12 See *Missal*, 1036.

13 See *Liturgia Horarum* 1:1051–52.

14 As an example, let us take the 5th Sunday C: the newness of the "new commandment" (see John 13:34) lies, not in the sublimity of the ethical demand, but in the "new foundation of being that is given to us. The newness can come only from the gift of being-*with* and being-*in* Christ": Joseph Ratzinger / Benedict XVI, *Jesus of Nazareth. 2: From the Entrance Into Jerusalem To The Resurrection* (San Francisco: Ignatius Press, 2011), 64.

15 See A.I.3.2.4.

year.[16] Many prayers and songs give color to related biblical texts depending on the liturgical year. For example, in Venantius' hymns about the Cross, the tree of paradise points typologically to the Cross.[17]

Interpretation through the liturgical setting

Part A drew attention to the importance of the liturgical setting for the interpretation. The various functions and principles of the selection of the readings in the Mass, the celebrations of the sacraments, and the Liturgy of the Hours as short readings or in the Office of Readings, show how much the external framework itself determines the hermeneutic.[18] One can observe something similar with the Psalms. When a psalm functions as the chant accompanying a procession,[19] and even when only one single verse is spoken or sung as a Communion antiphon,[20] the action and the text interpret each other. First, the Scripture interprets the action, but the liturgical setting also necessarily has repercussions on the understanding of the biblical words. For instance (as our example of the Feast of Saint Matthew has shown),[21] when the prayer after Communion or the Communion antiphon[22] refers back to the Gospel, it is interpreted as a eucharistic rereading with a view to the communicants. The liturgical use often interprets a passage that remains open in the text itself, or the liturgical context selects one of many interpretative possibilities. For example, the praise and the invocation of God over the water at Baptism have recourse to Gn 1:2 and clearly interpret the Spirit hovering over the water—where the interpretations range from a chaotic storm to the Holy Spirit—as the Spirit of God.

Interpretation via theological-spiritual backgrounds

In our comparison of the Roman and the Byzantine traditions, we noted that different theological-spiritual accents led to a different selection (e.g., in

---

16 See A.II.7.

17 See A.IV.14.1.

18 See A.I.

19 See A.II.7. (e.g., Psalm 24 on Palm Sunday or at the dedication of a church).

20 See A.IV.15 and A.IV.16.

21 See A.III.12.2.

22 See A.IV.15 and, in general, A.IV.16.

the Lenten readings)[23] and to a differing ritual translation of the scriptural texts (e.g., at the Washing of the Feet).[24]

Considering the variety of interpretations from a methodological perspective, two mechanisms are hermeneutically significant: the isolation from a literary context in the Bible (although this context is never abolished, even if participants may certainly be less conscious of it), and a new contextualization with other biblical and liturgical texts. These make possible a multiplicity of meanings because the link to the new context can bring in additional aspects. This discussion clearly shows the *potentiality of the Word of God*. It is only gradually, in the various contexts, that different aspects of the potential for meaning that is stored up in the Word of God become visible. This potential can go beyond the original meaning of the individual text, while however remaining in accord with its "potentiality of meaning."[25] In an exceptional case a quotation is introduced into a new context *against* its original context.[26] This procedure of isolation and new contextualization may appear ambivalent, at least to our modern way of understanding, even if the new line of thought remains meaningful. However, the criterion laid down by the Church for the formulation of liturgical prayers was not a regulation about the quotation and combination of texts, but rather agreement with the faith, in order that the combination of decontextualized scriptural passages would not generate affirmations that contradict the doctrine of the faith.

2. INTERPRETATION THROUGH THE ORDER OF READINGS (CORRELATION WITH OTHER SCRIPTURAL TEXTS)

Every order of readings is itself already an interpretation. This begins with the division of the text into pericopes, since this means extracting it from its immediate context in the biblical book. Sometimes, this produces variations in meaning. For example, Mark closes his account of the healing of Bartimaeus (Mk 10:46–52) by saying that he followed Jesus on his way. This means that he followed Jesus immediately on his entry into Jerusalem (Mk 11:1–11)—in other words, to his Death and Resurrection. But this cannot be seen in the way this text is used on the 30th Sunday B. This phenomenon

---

23 See A.I.3.2.4.

24 See A.V.17.

25 Pontifical Biblical Commission, *The Jewish people and their sacred scriptures in the Christian Bible* (Vatican City: Libreria Editrice Vaticana, 2002), no. 64 and Preface. This concept is employed here in connection with the Christian interpretation of the Old Testament.

26 See A.III.11.2. (the second Byzantine prayer at episcopal ordination).

applies even more so to Old Testament texts, which are kept as short as possible in the Roman order of readings for Sundays.

A more important factor is the correlation with other scriptural texts, given that, in the OLM, the proclamation of the Word consists of three readings on Sundays and two on weekdays, with the Responsorial Psalm and the acclamation before the Gospel.[27] The *GILM* emphasizes the importance of the order of readings for the understanding of the texts:

> The first requirement for one who is to preside over the celebration is a thorough knowledge of the structure of the Order of Readings so that he will know how to inspire good effects in the hearts of the faithful. Through study and prayer he must also develop a full understanding of the coordination and connection of the various texts in the Liturgy of the Word, so that the Order of Readings will become the source of a sound understanding of the mystery of Christ and his saving work.[28]

In keeping with the Augustinian principle: *scripturam per scripturam intellegi*,[29] it is in fact often possible to combine texts in such a way that they shed light on each other. If the Gospel uses or at least alludes to a quotation from the Old Testament, its context too is heard via the reading.[30] For example, the order of readings on December 19 has the announcement of the birth of the Baptist (Lk 1:5–25) preceded by a text on which Luke has worked, the announcement of the birth of Samson (Jgs 13:2–7, 24–25a). Background information needed to understand the Gospel is sometimes given in the reading.[31] Here, therefore, intrabiblical relationships, which both historical-critical and canonical exegesis[32] point out, are taken up and made transparent in the Liturgy in order to facilitate better understanding of the Gospel. The order of readings is also meant, through the intertextuality with other readings, to help make "difficult texts" more comprehensible.[33] As we have

---

27 Intertextual relationships can, of course, arise even when the texts are not chosen to correlate with one another (for example, when there are two continuous readings on the weekdays in Ordinary Time).

28 *GILM*, 39.

29 Fiedrowicz, *Psalmus vox totius Christi*, 138–42. ("Understanding Scripture by Scripture.")

30 See *GILM*, 67.

31 See, e.g., the 6th Sunday in Ordinary Time B. It is only the regulation that lepers must shout: "Unclean, unclean!" and remain outside the camp (Lv 13:45–46) that makes clear that something remarkable happens when Jesus actually touches the leper (Mk 1:40–45).

32 On this, see also C.39.

33 *GILM*, 86.

shown, the Responsorial Psalm too can be an aid to understanding, since it looks back to the preceding reading and has a bracketing function between the Old Testament and the New; it can also accentuate, which is itself an interpretation.[34] These observations are, of course, theologically relevant. The order of readings thereby clearly provides not only the aid to understanding and interpretation, but also, and primarily, underscores the unity of the two Testaments of the one Bible.[35]

The combination of scriptural texts can also expose the hidden potentials of meaning which would lie undiscovered if one were to look only at an individual text. This "surplus value" applies not only to prophetic passages that are understood Christologically, nor only to Psalms. An additional interpretation, or a (spiritual) transposition to the hearers, can also take place subtly through the acclamation before the Gospel. For example, the healing of a blind man is introduced with words from Ephesians 1:17–18: "May the Father of our Lord Jesus Christ *enlighten the eyes of our hearts,* that we may know what is the hope that belongs to his call."[36] In this case, a new aspect is brought in through the Liturgy.

There is, of course, also a danger in a deliberate combination of pericopes, namely, that they will be heard exclusively in the manner envisaged by those who conceived the order of readings. This could suggest a certain "mainstream" interpretation, while other (perhaps more important) aspects of the texts would go unnoticed. This phenomenon is obvious when one compares one and the same pericope in the Roman and in the Milanese lectionaries. Our example is the Gospel of the narrow gate (Lk 13:22–30), which is read in the Roman order on the 21st Sunday in Ordinary Time C, and in the Milanese order on the 5th Sunday after Pentecost C. Although the time in the liturgical year is comparable, the selection is taken in opposite directions.[37] In Milan, Abraham is in the foreground, in the course of the exemplary *tour d'horizon* of the Old Testament figures (Abraham's intercession for Sodom in Genesis 18:1–2a, 16–33; the faith of Abraham the founding father in Romans 4:16–25), so that the special focus in the Gospel lies on v. 28: "... when you see Abraham, Isaac, and Jacob and all the prophets in the kingdom of God and you yourselves cast out." In the Roman order, Isaiah 66:18–21 (the gathering of the brethren from all the peoples on Zion) is placed alongside v. 29

---

34 See A.II.8.

35 See *GILM*, 106; B.VIII.30.

36 This example is taken from Wednesday of the 6th week in Ordinary Time (Gospel: Mk 8:22–26).

37 See A.I.3.1.2.

("And people will come from the east and the west and from the north and the south and will recline at table in the kingdom of God"). The mention of Abraham plays a subordinate role here, whereas in Milan, Abraham was the very reason for the choice of this particular Gospel.

CHAPTER 24

The Ritual Form of the Proclamation of the Word

The immediate context in which a scriptural text is proclaimed is important for a liturgical hermeneutics of the Bible. The ritual framework does not interpret a specific content of the pericope (B.VII.23.). Instead, it makes the fundamental declaration that the text proclaimed is not simply a human communication, but the Word of God addressed to the assembled community. We become all the more conscious of this fundamental insight of liturgical theology, which is emphasized architecturally by the ambo as the place of proclamation of the Word,[38] when we compare selected Christian rites from West and East. This is in accord with the methodological approach of this present study, inspired by SC 24, where the Eastern and Western traditions are mentioned explicitly. A brief look at the synagogue liturgy will show that the ritual staging in Jewish worship likewise emphasizes that the reading from the Torah is an event of revelation here and now.

1. THE PROCLAMATION OF THE WORD IN THE MASS OF VARIOUS CHRISTIAN RITES[39]

1.1. Reading(s) Other than the Gospel

The Reader and the Number of Readings

It goes without saying that the reader/lector has an important task in the Liturgy of the Word. The description of the Mass in the *Apology* of Justin Martyr (ca. 150) already has an explicit mention of the reader.[40] In the

---

38 See Benini, "Ambo."

39 For more detail, see Benini, *Bibelhermeneutik*, 287–314.

40 See Justin, *Apology* 1.67.4 (FontC 91:198–99; WEC 1:68).

Apostolic Tradition, the bishop appoints laymen as readers by placing the book in their hands.[41] However, medieval developments, including the retention of Latin as the liturgical language, meant that the ministry of reader became a stage men passed through on the way to the priesthood; it was ultimately integrated into what was called the minor orders. At Vatican II, SC 29 affirmed that lectors "exercise a genuinely liturgical function." And in 2021, with the Motu proprio *Spiritus Domini,* Pope Francis has opened the official commissioning as an Instituted Lector to women.

Like the Alexandrian liturgical family, the Roman liturgy does not know any blessing at the reading in the celebration of Mass. The other rites, however, highlight the official function of this ministry by means of a blessing before the reading. This, and the number of readings, can be seen clearly in the following table.

Liturgy	OT	NT (+ Gospel)	Blessing on Reader
Roman	1	1	– (exception: Congo/Zaire)
Milanese[42]	1	1	+
Syro-Malabar[43]	2	1	+
Armenian[44]	1	1	–
Syro-Malankara[45]	–	2	+

Table continued on next page.

41 See *Apostolic Tradition* 11 (FontC 1:243; WEC 1:203). The lector is explicitly distinguished from those who are ordained through the laying on of hands.

42 See *Messale Ambrosiano secondo il rito della Santa Chiesa di Milano. Riformato a norma dei decreti del Concilio Vaticano II. Promulgato dal Signor Cardinale Giovanni Colombo,* 2nd ed. (Milan: Centro Ambrosiano di Documentazione e Studi Religiosi, 1986).

43 See *The Order of the Syro-Malabar Qurbana,* ed., Commission for Liturgy, Major Archiepiscopal Curia Mount St. Thomas (Kochi: Don Bosco IGACT), 28–34; Paul Pallah, ed., *La liturgia eucaristica della Chiesa siro-malabarese,* RivLi / Quaderni 3/1 (Padua: Messaggero, 2000); Cyrus Velamparampil, *The Celebration of the Liturgy of the Word in the Syro-Malabar Qurbana. A Biblico-Theological Analysis,* Oriental Institute Publications 194 (Kottayam: Oriental Institution of Religious Studies, 1997), esp. 121–294; Pauly Kannookadan, *The East Syrian Lectionary. An Historico-Liturgical Study* (Rome: Mar Thoma Yogam, 1991).

44 See Daniel Findikyan, ed., *The Divine Liturgy of the Armenian Church. With Modern Armenian and English Translations, Transliteration, Musical Notation, Introductions and Notes* (New York: St. Vartan Press, 2000), 17.

45 See Johannes Madey and George Vavanikunnel, eds., *Qurbana oder die Eucharistiefeier der Thomaschristen Indiens* (Paderborn: Sandesanilayam, 1968).

Byzantine[46]	–	1	(+)
Maronite[47]	–	1	+
Coptic[48]	–	3 (+ reading for saint)	–
Ethiopic[49]	–	3	–

In the Ambrosian liturgy, the reader stands at the ambo and bows to the presider before he proclaims the reading, asking: "Bless me, Father." The presider replies audibly, before the Old or New Testament reading: "May the prophetic/apostolic reading + enlighten us and profit us for salvation."[50] The reader makes the Sign of the Cross; this blessing at the reading, however, is a prayer for all those present. As an alternative, the priest can pronounce an explicit blessing on the one who reads: "Read + in the name of the Lord."[51] The Missal for the dioceses of the Democratic Republic of the Congo (formerly Zaire), which adapts the Roman rite to the customs and the mentality of people in central Africa (inculturation), also has a blessing at the reading.[52]

Among the Antiochene liturgies, an elaborate blessing at the reading is found in the Syro-Malabar rite. Before the two Old Testament readings, the presider says to the reader: "May the Lord, who enlightens us through His teaching, be glorified. May His grace always be upon You + and your listeners," or in the brief form: "May God + bless you."[53] Before a reading from Paul, the blessing formula is: "May Christ enlighten you with His teachings. In His great mercy, may He make You a true mirror for those who hear from your

---

46 See Galadza, *Divine Liturgy.*

47 See *Book of Offering according to the Rite of the Antiochene Syriac Maronite Church: According to the Bkerke 2005 Edition. Approved by the Maronite Bishops of the English-Speaking Eparchies of Australia, Canada and the United States of America and Promulgated by the Maronite Patriarch* (no place given, 2012).

48 See Peter D. Day, *Eastern Christian Liturgies: The Armenian, Coptic, Ethiopian and Syrian Rites: Eucharistic Rites with Introductory Notes and Rubrical Instructions* (Shannon: Irish University Press, 1972), 73-103.

49 Day, 113-52.

50 *Messale Ambrosiano*, 1, (15).

51 *Messale Ambrosiano*, 1, (15).

52 Chris Nwaka Egbulem, *The "Rite Zaïrois" in the Context of Liturgical Inculturation in Middle-Belt Africa Since the Second Vatican Council* (Washington, DC: ProQuest Dissertations Publishing, 1989), 362-63.

53 See *Syro-Malabar Qurbana*, 28. In the Maronite rite too, the blessing is pronounced upon both reader and hearers (*Book of Offering*, 16).

lips the words of His teaching," or: "May Christ + bless you."[54] As in Milan, here too there is a differentiation between the Old Testament reading ("God/ Lord") and the New Testament reading ("Christ"), and the blessing in the more detailed form extends to both the reader and those present.

The blessing at the reading in the Byzantine rite is much shorter. Usually, the reader, with the lectionary in his hands, goes during the immediately preceding *prokimenon* to the priest and receives in silence the gesture of blessing without accompanying words. At the close, the words "Peace be to you who read aloud!" are addressed to him.

With regard to a liturgical hermeneutics of the Bible, this blessing is a ritual that emphasizes the importance of the act of proclamation, and hence of the Word that is proclaimed. At the same time, the blessing makes it clear that the reader is delivering the reading in the name of the Church or "in the name of the Lord" (Milan). In the elaborate blessings, which also include the hearers, the spiritual and performative dimension of the Word of God is also expressed. The Word may enlighten and make us wise, profit us for salvation, and pour down the mercy of God on both the reader and the hearers.

The Immediate Framework of the Reading

In almost all the rites,[55] the introductory formula contains the information about the book from which the reading is taken, thereby also mentioning the human author (e.g., Paul). The double authorship of Scripture as God's Word in the human word is expressed in the Roman and Milanese rites through the concluding formula *Verbum Domini*. Not merely venerable human words are read: in these words, God himself speaks. Similarly, the response *Deo gratias* is meant to express this awareness and to show that the assembly "has listened to [the word of God] in faith and gratitude."[56] The response of the community in the Zaire rite makes the same affirmation: "We accept it."[57] The response in the Syro-Malabar rite is: "Praise be to the Lord, our God" after the reading from the prophets, and "Praise be to Christ, our Lord" after the reading from Paul.[58]

---

54 See *Syro-Malabar Qurbana*, 31.

55 An exception is the Armenian rite, which does not mention the Book; see Jean Michel Hanssens, *Institutiones liturgicae de ritibus orientalibus*, 4 vols. (Rome: Pontificae Universitatis Gregorianae, 1930-32), 3:178.

56 *GILM*, 18; *PLA*, 27.

57 Egbulem, *Rite Zaïrois*, 363.

58 See *Syro-Malabar Qurbana*, 28, 31. There is no similar concluding formula to the reading from the Torah; accordingly, the two Old Testament readings appear ritually as a unity. See also Velamparampil, *Word in the Syro-Malabar Qurbana*, 128-35.

In the Syro-Malankara rite, a performative aspect is added to the doxological element in the response to the reading: "Praise to the Lord of the apostles, and mercy for us in eternity."[59] Some liturgies also have preparatory songs and prayers. In the Syro-Malankara rite, for example, the people sing a short hymn before each reading. Its final stanza aims particularly to promote readiness to hear and believe: "Chosen apostles, sent by God into the world, preached the Gospel of the Son among the peoples and proclaimed the kingdom of heaven to the ends of the earth. And they said: Blessed are those who believe."[60] During this hymn, the priest prays silently, in preparation for the three following readings, that those present may be able to keep the commandments of the Lord (Gospel), of the apostles (first reading), and of Paul (second reading).[61]

The formulas, prayers, and songs we have seen up to this point speak of the message itself. In the considerably longer prayers and songs of the Alexandrian liturgical family, the apostles as persons move more strongly into the foreground, when the request is made before the reading for the blessing of Paul, Peter, and others. For example, the introductory prayer before the reading in the Coptic liturgy asks: "The Acts of the Apostles; may their blessing be with us."[62] This embeds the proclamation in an immediate context of prayer that is meant to prepare the community to hear the Word of God. At the same time, the prayers also display a performative effect of the Word of God, because through the proclamation (independently of the individual content of the pericopes) the blessing of God (and of the apostles) comes down upon the hearers.

1.2. The Proclamation of the Gospel

The Proclaimer and the Blessing at the Gospel

In the Roman, Milanese, Byzantine, and Armenian liturgies, in which a deacon proclaims the Gospel, he asks the presider for a blessing on the reading. The assignment to the deacon probably grew out of his close relationship to the bishop.[63] Today's Western formula, "May the Lord be in your heart and

---

59 Madey and Vavanikunnel, *Qurbana*, 144.

60 Madey and Vavanikunnel, 143.

61 See Madey and Vavanikunnel, 143.

62 Day, *Eastern Liturgies*, 81.

63 According to *Apostolic Tradition* 8, the deacon is ordained "to serve the bishop" (FontC 1:233; WEC 1:202). See Radek Tichý, *Proclamation de l'Évangile dans la messe en occident. Ritualité, histoire, comparaison, théologie*, StA 168 (Rome: Pontificio Ateneo S. Anselmo, 2016),

on your lips …,"[64] subtly points to the presence of Christ in the proclamation. In the Roman rite, the priest blesses in a low voice at his place, while in Milan, the deacon is already at the ambo, so that the blessing at the reading is spoken audibly.[65] The Byzantine formula underlines the performative power of the Gospel: "May God, through the intercession of the holy, glorious, all-praiseworthy apostle and evangelist [Name], + grant that you proclaim the Good News with great power for the fulfillment of the Gospel of his beloved Son, our Lord Jesus Christ."[66] In the Maronite, Syro-Malankara, and Syro-Malabar liturgies, the priest himself proclaims the Gospel.[67]

Gospel Acclamation / Trisagion and Gospel Procession

In the Western and Antiochene liturgical families, the singing of the Alleluia precedes the proclamation of the Gospel. All rise as a sign of reverence and attentiveness. Since "Alleluia" occurs only once in the New Testament, in the context of the wedding feast of the Lamb in Revelation 19 (esp. v. 6), the procession hints at the eschatological reign of Christ, whose coming is staged proleptically in the proclamation of the Gospel.[68]

Just as in antiquity, a ruler was greeted solemnly with lights and incense on his arrival at a city,[69] so too the Gospel represents the exalted Christ, who comes forth from his heavenly sanctuary (staged by means of the altar) and accompanied by the liturgical ministers, himself speaks in the proclamation. Candles and incense, which were marks of honor in classical antiquity for the

---

31–41; Jungmann, *Missarum Sollemnia*, 1:443. Originally, the Gospel was read by a reader, but it was reserved to the deacon from the fourth century onward (see Otto Michel, "Evangelium," *RAC* 6 [1966]: 1149–50).

64 *Missal*, 523.

65 See Tichý, *Proclamation*, 126–43.

66 Galadza, *Divine Liturgy*, 126. On the gradual development of this formula, see Mateos and Hawkes-Teeples, *Liturgy of the Word*, 228–33.

67 See *Book of Offering*, 17; Madey and Vavanikunnel, *Qurbana*, 145; Velamparampil, *Word in the Syro-Malabar Qurbana*, 127.

68 Zerfaß, *Hermeneutik*, 197–98, with reference to Reinhard Meßner, "Der Wortgottesdienst der Messe als rituell inszenierte Christusanamnese," *HlD* 66, no. 3 (2012): 81.

69 On light and incense in the Roman and Byzantine imperial cult, see Andreas Alföldi, *Die monarchische Repräsentation im römischen Kaiserreiche: Mit einem Register von Elisabeth Alföldi-Rosenbaum* (Darmstadt: Wissenschaftliche Buchgesellschaft, 1970), 111–18, on the Gospel procession Alföldi, 115; Otto Treitinger, *Die oströmische Kaiser- und Reichsidee nach ihrer Gestaltung im höfischen Zeremoniell,* 2nd ed. (Darmstadt: Wissenschaftliche Buchgesellschaft, 1956 [reprint from 1938]), 67–71, on the Gospel procession Treitinger, 69; Nikolaus Gussone, "Der Codex auf dem Thron. Zur Ehrung des Evangelienbuches in Liturgie und Zeremoniell," in Neuheuser, *Wort und Buch*, 195-98, 228.

ruler or for high dignitaries, are employed in the Liturgy—in all the rites—
for the proclamation of the Gospel.[70] For a biblical hermeneutics, this means
that the presence of the risen Christ in his Word is staged ritually through
the procession and the Alleluia. The link to Revelation 19 also contributes an
eschatological accent by pointing to the eternal reign of Christ.[71]

In the Syro-Malankara liturgy, the Alleluia frames the cry of homage:
"Offer him the sacrifice of praise, bring pure sacrifices and enter the courts
of the Lord. Worship the Lord before his altar"[72] (see Ps 96:8; Ps 29:1–2). The
Syro-Malabar liturgy links the Alleluia to Psalm 45:2, so that the presider
says, with reference to the Gospel that he will then proclaim, "My heart is
stirred by a noble theme."[73] In both liturgies, verses from royal psalms are
interwoven in the Alleluia. The accord among the various rites makes clear
the extent to which the Gospel processions are ritual dramatizations of the
coming of the heavenly king. In the most solemn Syro-Malabar form (the
raza), the procession is preceded by yet another veneration of the Gospel
in the form of further songs, which both emphasize what the Gospel brings
about (it heals body and soul; frees from guilt; is a life-giving spiritual treasure) and summon the believers to hear and receive the message. After stating that Christ sent the apostles out to preach, the hymn concludes: "And
now Saint N. explains what he saw and heard; and therefore, whoever has
ears to hear, let him hear."[74]

Liturgical fans with small bells are sometimes carried, especially to
intensify the solemnity (in some pontifical Masses). Such a fan (*rhipidion*)
is a metal plate engraved with the image of a seraph and fastened to a staff, so
that the adoration of the angels is depicted in the Liturgy. The fans are carried
at processions, usually in pairs, and they are waved in the Syro-Malankara
rite during the central parts of the Qurbana (eucharistic liturgy), in order to
highlight visually and acoustically the significance of these parts.[75] The fans
strengthen the staging of the Gospel procession as the coming of Christ. This

---

70 Already Jerome, *Contra Vigilantium* 7 (PL 23:346; WEC 3:354) attests the use of candles at
the Gospel in all the Eastern rites even by daylight, as a sign of joy; see Jungmann, *Missarum
Sollemnia*, 1:445.

71 Zerfaß, *Hermeneutik*, 60, 198. Moreover, this accentuates the character of the eucharistic
celebration as an anticipation of the heavenly wedding feast.

72 Madey and Vavanikunnel, *Qurbana*, 144.

73 *Syro-Malabar Qurbana*, 32.

74 Pallath, *Liturgia siro-malabarese*, 55. See Velamparampil, *Word in the Syro-Malabar
Qurbana*, 136–40.

75 Madey and Vavanikunnel, *Qurbana*, 124.

becomes even clearer when one bears in mind the origin of the *rhipidion* in the Eastern court ceremonial that was transposed to Christ.[76]

The Zaire rite calls the Gospel procession the "Enthronement of the Gospel." Before the Alleluia, the Gospel book is shown to the people with a dialogue referring to the Incarnation (Jn 1:14), such that a different herme-neutic is introduced.[77]

The Alexandrian liturgical family does not chant the Alleluia between the proclamation of the reading and the Gospel. Instead, it uses the Trisagion, which is expanded with insertions about the life of Christ (from his birth to his Ascension).[78] In this way, it too leads to the encounter with Christ in the Gospel that is proclaimed.

Preparatory Prayers

Unlike the Roman and Milanese prayer of preparation, in which the priest asks that he himself, as the proclaimer of the Gospel, may receive purity (see Is 6:5–7) and worthiness ("Munda cor *meum*"), some Eastern rites have preparatory prayers addressed to Christ with contents referring to all who hear the Gospel. For example, the Byzantine rite has the follow-ing prayer:

> Make the pure light of Your Divine knowledge shine in our hearts, O loving Master. Open the eyes of our minds that we may understand the message of Your gospel. Instill in us the fear of Your blessed commandments that we may subdue all carnal desires and follow a spiritual way of life, thinking and doing all that pleases You. For You, O Christ our God, are the enlight-enment of our souls and bodies, and we give glory to You… [Trinitarian doxology].[79]

This is prayed silently by the priest (but his intention extends surely to all),[80] while the deacon incenses the altar with the Gospel book, the sanctuary,

---

76 The *rhipidia* originally had a purely practical meaning: they were woven to drive away flies. But they soon became the liturgical honorific symbol of Christ among the seraphim, who are therefore depicted on the fans. See Joseph Braun, *Das christliche Altargerät in seinem Sein und in seiner Entwicklung* (Munich: Hueber, 1932), 642–47.

77 Egbulem, *Rite Zaïrois*, 364.

78 Day, *Eastern Liturgies*, 83, 130–31.

79 Galadza, *Divine Liturgy*, 126.

80 Mateos and Hawkes-Teeples, *Liturgy of the Word*, 226–27. Many manuscripts (even from the 14th/15th centuries) do not have a preparatory prayer of this kind.

and the priest(s), in order to prepare them to hear the Gospel. A prayer with similar content is also found in the Syro-Malankara[81] and Syro-Malabar liturgies.[82] As silent prayers, they have no immediate influence on the faithful's understanding of the proclamation of Scripture, but the petitions for enlightenment or knowledge and for the translation of the Word into our lives show the intention to prepare through prayer the "soil" for the performative effect of the Gospel.

The Coptic and Ethiopian preparatory prayer, which the priest says aloud, alludes to Mt 13:16 ("But blessed are your eyes, because they see, and your ears, because they hear"),[83] thereby establishing the link between the disciples of Jesus and the faithful here and now. This is followed by the request: "May we be made worthy to hear and to do what is written in your holy Gospels, through the prayers of your saints."[84]

Immediate Framing

The introductory greeting, "The Lord be with you" (which corresponds to the risen Christ's salutation "Peace be with you (all)" in the Eastern liturgies), already points to the presence of Christ. The closing formula, *Verbum Domini*, as a subjective genitive, points subtly to the exalted Lord.[85] Moreover, the vocative and the second person address in the acclamation "Glory to you, O Lord" or "Praise to you, Lord Jesus Christ," or similarly in the Byzantine rite, "Glory be to You, O Lord, glory to You," show that Christ himself speaks in the proclamation to those assembled, who now respond to him. The bodily posture of standing (already at the Alleluia) expresses reverence for Christ, who is present in the proclamation of the Gospel. In the Byzantine liturgy, the faithful are explicitly admonished: "Stand aright."[86] In the Maronite liturgy, the deacon invites them to an inner dialogue: "Remain silent, O listeners, for the Holy Gospel is about to be proclaimed to you.

---

81 Madey and Vavanikunnel, *Qurbana*, 33.

82 See *Syro-Malabar Qurbana*, 33.

83 Day, *Eastern Liturgies*, 84, 132.

84 Day, 84 (132).

85 Zerfaß, *Hermeneutik*, 173.

86 John Chrysostom compares the proclamation of Scripture with a decree of the emperor, in order to exhort his hearers to listen reverently (see Reiner Kaczynski, *Das Wort Gottes in Liturgie und Alltag der Gemeinden des Johannes Chrysostomus*, FThST 94 [Freiburg/Br.: Herder, 1974], 73–74; Michel, "Evangelium," 1152).

Listen and give glory and thanks to the Word of the living God."[87] After the proclamation, the people respond: "Praise and blessing to Jesus Christ, our Lord and God, *for giving us his words of life*."[88] The exclamation of the choir or people immediately before the proclamation of the Gospel in the Armenian liturgy is unequivocal and succinct: "God speaks."[89] In terms of biblical hermeneutics, the liturgical framing in the various rites thus emphasizes the presence of Christ, which is also indicated by means of ritual elements.

Ritual Elements

We have already seen in the Gospel procession that the honor shown to the Gospel book is paid to Christ himself. The incensing of the Gospel book attests that it is a symbol of Christ. The Sign of the Cross on brow, mouth, and breast/heart,[90] which is customary only in the Roman and Milanese rites, is meant as a preparation for the encounter with Christ in the Word, "so that the Word of God may enlighten their [the participants'] minds, purify their hearts, and open their lips for the praise of God."[91]

One of the ritual elements is chanting, which is more customary in the Eastern liturgies than in the West,[92] where, in practice—if chanting is employed at all—only the Gospel is chanted. Since amplification systems mean that singing is no longer used in order to achieve audibility in the church, and in daily life a text is hardly ever sung by an individual person, chanting introduces a elevated effect that lends particular emphasis to the text. It is thus clear that chanting can be used, in the first place, as a means of intensifying the solemnity.

Above all, however, it has a hermeneutical importance. The artistic external form bears witness to the high value of the content, and it can penetrate more deeply into those who hear it than a word that is merely spoken. Chanting thus indicates the special character of the Gospel text or the reading and its sacrality/sacramentality as the Word of God. According to *GILM* 17, it is appropriate to sing at least the liturgical framing if the whole Gospel is not

---

87 *Book of Offering*, 17.

88 *Book of Offering*, 17.

89 Day, *Eastern Liturgies*, 39.

90 On the history of the increase of the crosses (first the brow, then the breast, and finally also the mouth and the book), see Tichý, *Proclamation*, 191-97.

91 Praenotanda of the Roman Gospel book (2000), no. 32 (quoted from Tichý, *Proclamation*, 196).

92 Since the audible prayers are likewise sung in the Eastern liturgies, the chanting gives less emphasis to the scriptural texts than is the case in the West.

chanted, since "this is a way of bringing out the importance of the Gospel reading."[93]

After the proclamation, it is customary in the Roman rite in some countries to lift up the Gospel book (or the lectionary), so that an act of displaying emphasizes the words *Verbum Domini*. This, however, is not found in today's liturgical books, and is probably a reflex of the rubric *elevans parumper librum* from the *MRom* 1570/1962,[94] itself doubtless a simple gesture that lifted the book to be kissed.[95] Nevertheless, this kind of act of displaying is certainly appropriate.[96]

The kiss of the book expresses veneration of Christ. At the kiss, the priest says in the Roman rite (but not in the Ambrosian): "Through the words of the Gospel may our sins be wiped away."[97] In the West, only the deacon or priest who proclaims the Gospel kisses the book (or the bishop, when the book is presented to him to be kissed).[98] There is historical evidence attesting to the kiss by the clergy, however, and sometimes also by the people.[99]

The blessing with the Gospel book is also highly expressive.[100] It is customary in the Byzantine[101] and Maronite[102] liturgies after the proclamation of the Gospel, and it is found in the Syro-Malabar liturgy at the introductory greeting by the priest: "Peace + be with you."[103] It was officially introduced into the Roman rite as an optional rite at the solemn pontifical Mass only in 2002.[104]

---

93 *GILM*, 17.

94 Tichý, *Proclamation*, 228.

95 Tichý, 228, 230.

96 See the displaying of the Torah scroll in B.VII.24.2.

97 *Missal*, 525.

98 See *GIRM*, 175; *PLA*, 25. According to MRom 1570, the subdeacon brought the book to the priest (and not only to the bishop) for the kiss (see Tichý, *Proclamation*, 236).

99 Thus, Ordo Romanus I attested the kiss by all the clergy at the papal Mass, and Ordo Romanus V attested the kiss by the faithful too (see Andrieu, *Ordines Romani* 2, 89,217). Further sources in Tichý, *Proclamation*, 232–235; Jungmann, *Missarum Sollemnia*, 1:449–50.

100 See Marco Benini, "The Blessing with the Book of the Gospels. A Recent Adoption from the Byzantine to the Roman Rite," *Antiphon* 24, no. 1 (2020): 50–66.

101 See, e.g., Hieromonk Herman and Vitaly Permiakov, ed., *Hieratikon. Liturgy Book for Priest and Deacon* (South Canaan, PA: St. Tikhon's Monastery, 2017), 107.

102 See *Book of Offering*, 17, 26, 37, and *passim*.

103 Pallath, *Liturgia siro-malabarese*, 55. On the Armenian liturgy, see Day, *Eastern Liturgies*, 36.

104 See *GIRM*, 175.

An interesting process of development shows that this is clearly a recent adoption from the Byzantine liturgy.[105] This gesture was attested for the first time on May 10, 1970, in the papal liturgy for a canonization, at which the same Gospel was read first in Latin and then a second time in Greek. After the Greek-Catholic deacon had read the Gospel in his language, he brought the closed Gospel book to the Pope, who took it in both his hands, kissed it, and then gave the blessing with the book. Further attestations came in 1978, when John Paul I and John Paul II marked the beginning of their pontificates and when they took possession of the Lateran basilica. From 1986 onward, this blessing had been given in all papal Masses that have the Gospel in two languages. From 1988 onward, the Pope blessed with the Gospel book on the Feast of Saints Peter and Paul, at Christmas, and on the Solemnity of Mary the Mother of God, even though the Gospel was not proclaimed in Greek—in other words, after the customary proclamation of the Gospel. From then on, this rite increasingly became a part of the papal liturgy. In the new *Institutio Generalis Missalis Romani* (3rd ed. 2002; and already in the preliminary draft in 2000), bishops too were permitted to give this blessing, because (as inquiries in the Congregation for Divine Worship disclosed) bishops on their own initiative had imitated the papal rite of blessing. The rubrics thus legitimated *post factum* a custom that was already widespread. In the meantime, priests in Italy also appear to be adopting the bishops' rite.[106]

With regard to biblical hermeneutics, the gesture of blessing can be an affirmation that Christ, who is represented here in the symbol of the Gospel book (as in the Gospel procession), desires the proclaimed word of the Gospel to bring blessing in the lives of the hearers. Or, put otherwise, Christ who is present in the proclamation pronounces a blessing (bene-*dicere*) through his Word. The fellowship with Christ that is communicated through the proclamation bestows blessing (see Eph 1:3). This gesture of blessing thus underlines the performative character of the Word of God. It is not simply an additional blessing; rather, it indicates that blessing lies in the encounter with Christ in the Word.

The Roman rubrics do not stipulate where the Gospel book is to be laid after the proclamation,[107] but the symbolic affirmation is important—and thus also hermeneutically significant. If it remains lying open on the ambo,

---

105 On the following section, see Tichý, *Proclamation*, 243–48.

106 Tichý, 247.

107 See *GIRM*, 175: "Lastly, the deacon may carry the Book of the Gospels to the credence table or to another suitable and dignified place." The Praenotanda to the Roman Gospel book (2000) stipulate that the Gospel book is not taken away in the procession at the end of the Mass (no. 37–38; quoted in Tichý, *Proclamation*, 251).

it can suggest that the homily grows out of the Gospel. The option of placing it on the credence table is unsatisfactory, since this looks like getting rid of it. This creates a discrepancy with the solemn Gospel procession, the incensation of the book, etc., hence, *GIRM* 175 suggests bringing it "to another suitable and signified place," which is not specified. In some churches, there is a book rest on the side of the ambo facing the congregation. In the cathedral in Milan, the closed Gospel book is placed on the Gospel side of the altar and is carried back into the sacristy at the end of the Communion rites. In the Byzantine liturgy, the closed Gospel book is replaced on the altar, on which it otherwise always lies. The act of bringing the book back to the altar corresponds to the starting point of the Gospel procession and expresses the unity of the two parts of the Mass as well as the reciprocal relatedness of Word and Eucharist.[108] It is thus also meaningful from the perspective of a biblical hermeneutics. The open book can symbolize the continuing effect of the message that has been proclaimed.

The following tables brings together the numerous individual observations:

	Rom.	Mil.	Zaire	Byz.	Maron.
Proclaimer[109]	D	D	D	D	C
Blessing at reading	+	+	+	+	–
Preparatory prayer	(+)	(+)	(+)	+	–
Call for attention	–	–	+	+	+
The Lord be with you	+	+	–	–	–
Peace be with you (all)	–	–	–	+	+
Praise to you, Christ (or similar)	+	+	+	+	+

108 On this, see B.VIII.29.

109 D = deacon; C = celebrant (priest/bishop); P = priest.

Cross on book / brow/mouth/ heart	+	+	–	–	–
Kiss	+	+	+	Before	–
Blessing with Gospel book	+	–	– ?	+	–
Candles / incense	+	+	+	+	+

	Syro-Malank.	Arm.	Syro-Malab.	Copt.	Ethiop.
Proclaimer[110]	C	D	C	D?	C
Blessing at reading	–	+	–	–	(–)
Preparatory prayer	+	–	+++	+	+
Call for attention	+	+	+	+	–
The Lord be with you	–	–	–	–	+
Peace be with you (all)	+	+	+	+	+
Praise to you, Christ (or similar)	+	+	+	+	+
Cross on book / brow/mouth/ heart	–	–	–	–	–
Kiss	+	–	+	P	all
Blessing with Gospel book	–	+	+	–	–
Candles / incense	+	+	+	+	+

110 D = deacon; C = celebrant (priest/bishop); P = priest.

1.3. Insights Gained from the Comparisons

With regard to biblical hermeneutics, the comparison of the ritual actions has shown, through the liturgical framing, the double character of Scripture as God's Word in the human word. It emphasized (also by means of the prayers) the basic dialogic structure of the proclamation of the Word and its performative effect.

The proclamation of the Gospel appears in all the rites, for several reasons, as the "high point of the Liturgy of the Word."[111] Already the liturgical arrangement shows this with the Gospel as the last of the two to five readings. Clearly, this arrangement is not chronological, since that would require the Acts of the Apostles and the New Testament letters to follow the Gospel with its accounts of the life of the earthly Jesus. Rather, this accentuates the importance of the Gospel; and the ritual elaboration (precious Gospel book with presentation on the altar, procession, singing, candles, incense, standing posture, chanting [in the West], sometimes a more detailed framing and exhortations to the people) illustrates the dignity of the Gospel.

The office of the one who proclaims it also underlines the pre-eminence of the Gospels: as is well known, the Western rites distinguish between the lector for the readings, and the deacon, to whom the Gospel is reserved; some Eastern liturgies reserve it to the presider. The Syro-Malabar rite differentiates even further: the Old Testament reading is read by the lector, the epistle by the deacon, and finally the Gospel by the bishop or priest.[112] This also hints at a different dignity between the Old Testament reading and the New, and this could be understood as devaluing the Old Testament. However, the twofold reading from the law and the prophets speaks against such an interpretation.

In the Roman liturgy, readings from the Old and the New Testaments are treated equally in the ritual; the Ambrosian liturgy makes a differentiation for the reader in the formula used, but not in the dignity of the two readings. In Catholic understanding, the fact that in some rites the bishop preaches, while "only" a deacon proclaims the Gospel, does not entail that the homily has a higher dignity than the Gospel proclamation—for after all, the function of the homily is to expound the Word of God. The "staging" of the Gospel is much more solemn than that of the homily. Therefore, the Gospel is the high point.

---

111 *GILM*, 13, 36; *PLA*, 21–43. See *GIRM*, 60.

112 See also Andreas Heinz, *Licht aus dem Osten. Die Eucharistiefeier der Thomas-Christen, der Assyrer und der Chaldäer mit der Anaphora von Addai und Mari*, Sophia 35 (Trier: Paulinus, 2008), 149.

The elaborate liturgical "staging" of the proclamation of the Gospel is in accordance with what *Dei Verbum* 18 calls the "special preeminence of the Gospels" among all the biblical writings (including those in the New Testament), as "the principal witness for the life and teaching of the incarnate Word." The preeminence of the Gospels can also be seen in the structure of the New Testament canon, since the four Gospels were always placed as a unit at the beginning in the various codices, while Luke's two-volume work was separated, so that Acts, together with the epistles, comes only after the Gospels.[113] The liturgical highlighting of the proclamation of the Gospel also shows that Christ is the high point of revelation and of God's salvation history with human beings.

Moreover, the narrativity of the life of Jesus can explain the liturgical preeminence of the Gospel within the Liturgy of the Word in the Mass. It is through the narrativity that the person of Jesus, with his words and deeds (Incarnation), becomes vivid with a much greater clarity than is possible through the epistolary books of the New Testament, which have a more thematic structure. The contact with the person of Jesus, and the involvement with his life, his dying, and his rising, as these are depicted in the Gospels, can strengthen one's relationship to Christ. Since the liturgical "staging" seeks to express precisely the presence of the risen Christ and the encounter with him here and now—as, for example, acclamations like "Praise to *you*, Lord Jesus Christ" intend to underline—the Gospels are predestined for this task. Their ritual highlighting is therefore logical and corresponds with the content that is proclaimed.

This is all the more the case when one looks at the entire liturgical context of the Mass, in which the presence of Christ in the Liturgy of the Word correlates with his presence in the Eucharist, particularly when one pays attention to the dynamic in the course of the Mass from the Word to the Eucharist.[114] Alexander Zerfaß notes that "the Christ-centeredness of the anamnesis within the Eucharist has consequences for the hermeneutical system of coordinates of the Liturgy of the Word that precedes it," and that accordingly, the special ritual shaping of the proclamation of the Gospel "is thereby legitimated, if not indeed mandatory."[115]

---

113 See Thomas Söding, *Einheit der Heiligen Schrift? Zur Einheit des biblischen Kanons*, QD 211 (Freiburg/Br.: Herder, 2005), 273–76; David Trobisch, *Die Endredaktion des Neuen Testaments. Eine Untersuchung zur Entstehung der christlichen Bibel*, Novum testamentum et orbis antiquus 31 (Fribourg: Universitätsverlag, 1996).

114 See B.VIII.27.

115 Zerfaß, *Hermeneutik*, 116–17.

2. COMPARISON: THE PROCLAMATION
OF THE WORD IN THE SYNAGOGUE

A comparison with the proclamation of Scripture in the Jewish liturgy is instructive. As in the Christian rites, so too in the worship of the synagogue a ritual framework has developed around the scriptural proclamation.[116] Especially after the destruction of the Temple, the synagogue became important as a place for the study of Torah, which attempted to replace the cultic presence of God in the Temple. Initially, it functioned as a house of instruction, but it became more a house of prayer and of liturgy, so that the reading aloud of Torah was inserted into a liturgical event.[117] Our particular interest here, taking the present-day form as our starting point, is the proclamation of the specified section from Torah—the entire Torah is distributed over the year among fifty-four *parashiyot*—in the morning service (*shacharit*) on Sabbath.[118] The section from Torah is accompanied by an appropriate reading from the prophets, the *haftarah*.

The liturgical proclamation of Torah consists of the lifting of the Torah scroll from the shrine, the procession to the raised place of proclamation (*bimah*), the proclamation itself, and finally the replacing of the scroll in the shrine. Ruth Langer has shown in detail that the liturgical framework

---

116 See Ruth Langer, "Sinai, Zion, and God in the Synagogue: Celebrating Torah in Ashkenaz," in *Liturgy in the Life of the Synagogue, Studies in the History of Jewish Prayer*, ed. R. Langer and S. Fine, Duke Judaic Studies Series 2 (Winona Lake: Eisenbrauns, 2005), 121–59; Lawrence A. Hoffman, "Introduction to the Liturgy. The Reading of Torah – Retelling the Jewish Story in the Shadow of Sinai," in *Seder K'riat Hatorah (The Torah Service)*, vol. 4 of *My People's Prayer Book. Traditional Prayers, Modern Commentaries*, ed. L. A. Hoffmann (Woodstock: Jewish Lights Publications, 2000), 1–18. Further bibliography: Ruth Langer, *Jewish Liturgy. A Guide to Research* (Lanham: Rowman & Littlefield, 2015), 126–29.

117 The first witness to a liturgical framework of the reading from Torah seems to be the post-Talmudic tractate Massekhet Seferim, which is dated between the 6th and the 12th century. See Ruth Langer, "From Study of Scripture to a Reenactment of Sinai: The Emergence of the Synagogue Torah Service," *Worship* 72, no. 1 (1998): 43–67, esp. 49, 58.

118 See the list of the fifty-four Torah sections with the accompanying *haftarah* (reading from the prophets) in Andreas Nachama, *Basiswissen Judentum. Mit einem Geleitwort von Rabbiner Henry G. Brandt* (Freiburg/Br.: Herder, 2015), 66–68. On the Simchat Torah feast (Feast of the Joy in Torah) each year, the cycle of readings begins anew. Today's one-year cycle corresponds, with a few divergences, to the Babylonian Talmud, while in Israel a cycle of three-and-a-half years was envisaged. This was suppressed, but was reintroducd in liberal communities from the mid-nineteenth century. See Nachama, 63; Ismar Elbogen, *Jewish Liturgy: A Comprehensive History*, trans. R. P. Scheindlin (New York: Jewish Theological Seminary of America, 1993), 129–49.

presents the reading as a reenactment of God's revelation in the Sinai event.[119] All the denominations in Judaism share this view.

According to the Koren Siddur, which is customarily used in the USA, the lifting of the Torah scroll is followed by various psalm verses that praise the eternal king. In terms of hermeneutics, the introduction to the prayers at the lifting of Torah is most important:

> Whenever the Ark set out, Moses would say, "Arise, LORD, and may Your enemies be scattered. May those who hate You flee before You." [Nm 10:34] For the Torah shall come forth from Zion, and the word of the LORD from Jerusalem [Is 2:3; Mi 4:2]. Blessed is He who, in His holiness, gave the Torah to His people Israel.[120]

This links the proclamation of Torah to three biblical motifs: the gift of Torah on Sinai, the wandering through the wilderness (ark), and finally, the eschatological pilgrimage of the peoples to Zion, from which its instruction goes forth.

The revelation at Sinai and the tent of revelation are already linked in the narrative of the book of Exodus, when the consecration of the tent sanctuary (Ex 40:34–38) alludes linguistically to YHWH's coming on Sinai (Ex 24:15–18), so that the tent of revelation appears as a "wandering Sinai."[121] Jewish liturgy takes this up: the shrine in which the Torah scroll is kept is called "sacred ark," like the Ark of the Covenant in which the tables of the Ten Commandments were kept during the wandering through the wilderness.[122] The curtain before the Torah shrine (parochet) recalls the curtain in the tent sanctuary.[123] Just as the Ark of the Covenant, the sign of YHWH's presence, was lifted up, so now the Torah scroll, which indicates his presence, is lifted up. The procession with the Torah scroll re-stages Israel's wandering through the wilderness and the proclamation of Torah re-stages the

119 See Langer, "Reenactment of Sinai"; Langer, "Sinai, Zion, and God in the Synagogue"; Langer, "Celebrating the Presence of the Torah. The History and Meaning of Reading Torah," in Hoffman, Prayer Book, 19–27.

120 The Koren Siddur, trans. Jonathan Sacks, 2nd ed. (New Milford, CT: OU Press, 2013), 562.

121 Heinz-Günther Schöttler, "'Ex sacra scriptura lectiones leguntur et in homilia explicantur.' Re-Inszenierung, Mimesis und offenes Ereignis," in Franz and Zerfaß, Wort des lebendigen Gottes, 126 with reference to Benno Jakob.

122 See Ex 25:16; Schöttler, "Re-Inszenierung," 125; Gerhard Rouwhorst, "Christlicher Gottesdienst und der Gottesdienst Israels. Forschungsgeschichte, Historische Interaktionen, Theologie," in Theologie des Gottesdienstes. Gottesdienst im Leben der Christen. Christliche und jüdische Liturgie, ed. M. Klöckener, GdK 2,2 (Regensburg: Pustet, 2008), 529.

123 See Ex 26:31–33; Schöttler, "Re-Inszenierung," 125.

revelation at Sinai. At the same time, the vision of Isaiah and Micah brings the eschatological Jerusalem into the picture. Alongside the liturgical mimesis, therefore, the anamnesis emerges as well.

The lifting of the scroll, which is immediately followed by the "Shema Yisrael" prayed in common, and also the ensuing procession in which the precentor carries the scroll to the *bimah,* are marked by the praise of God by the precentor and above all by the congregation:

> Yours, LORD, are the greatness and the power, the glory and the majesty and splendor, for everything in heaven and on earth is Yours. Yours, LORD, is the kingdom; You are exalted as head over all [1 Chr 29:11]. Exalt the LORD our God and bow to His footstool; He is holy. Exalt the LORD our God, and bow at His holy mountain, for holy is the LORD our God [Ps 99:9].[124]

The proclamation is thus inserted into a doxological, and thereby also dialogical, context. During the procession, the faithful touch the Torah scroll with a fringe of the prayer shawl (a *zizit* of the *tallit*) and then kiss the fringe, indicating that everyone has a share in Torah.[125] A positive effect is ascribed even to the act of touching, which is rejected by Reform Judaism.[126]

At the *bimah,* Torah is unclothed—that is, the covering ("Torah shawl") is removed, and it is unrolled. On the Sabbath, seven persons are called one after another to read Torah. This summons is called *aliyah* ("ascent") to the raised *bimah* and is meant to recall Moses' ascent to Mount Sinai.[127] Every section of the reading from Torah is framed by words of blessing (*berakhot*) that praise God for the gift of Torah, thereby establishing a link to Sinai.[128] It must be emphasized that the text from Torah is always chanted. At the end of the reading, the Torah scroll is opened a little further, lifted up, and displayed in such a way that all can see the text themselves. This action is accompanied by hermeneutically interesting words: "This is the Torah that Moses placed before the children of Israel, at the Lord's commandment, by the hand of Moses. [...] It is a tree of life to those who grasp it, and those who uphold it are happy [Prov 3:18]."[129] Here, there is a bridge between the Israelites at

---

124 *Koren Siddur,* 566.

125 See Leo Trepp, *Der jüdische Gottesdienst: Gestalt und Entwicklung,* 2nd ed. (Stuttgart: Kohlhammer, 2004), 46 (similarly when the scroll is lifted from the shrine; see Trepp, 48).

126 See Nachama, *Basiswissen Judentum,* 65.

127 Hoffman, *Prayer Book,* 12.

128 For more detail, see Trepp, *Jüdischer Gottesdienst,* 47.

129 *Koren Siddur,* 576.

the time of Moses and those who hold fast to Torah today, implying their identification with the Israelites at Sinai.

The *haftarah,* with contents related to the Torah reading,[130] is read after the Torah scroll is rolled up and clothed in the shawl. Next, another member of the community, the *maftir,* is summoned to read. The *haftarah* is also framed by *berakhot.* The introductory *berakhah* praises God for choosing the prophets, while the three concluding *berakhot* praise him for leaving none of his words unfulfilled and ask for mercy on Zion and for the coming of the Messiah. Finally, God is thanked for Torah, for the worship service, the prophets, and the Sabbath.[131] The *haftarah* reading is distinguished optically from the Torah reading by the fact that it is read today from a printed book rather than from a scroll, and that no procession takes place. The ritual thus clearly places less emphasis on it. Here there are some parallels to the Liturgy of the Word in the Mass. In synagogue worship, we find analogies to the differentiation between the Gospel book and the lectionary, and to the concordance between the scriptural readings.

After some intercessory prayers, the cantor takes the Torah scroll into his arms again and bears it in procession back to the shrine, accompanied by hymns of praise (Ps 148:13–14 and Ps 29 on the Sabbath or Ps 24 on a weekday).[132] Before the open shrine, there is an allusion to the resting of the Ark of the Covenant during the wandering through the wilderness, with Numbers 10:36 and Psalm 132:8–10, so that there is a correspondence in content between the lifting out and the replacing of Torah:

> When the Ark came to rest, Moses would say: "Return, O LORD, to the myriad thousands of Israel" [Nm 10:36]. Advance, LORD, to Your resting place, You and Your mighty Ark. Your priests are clothed in righteousness, You and Your devoted ones sing in joy. For the sake of Your servant David, do not reject Your anointed one [Ps 132:8-10]. For I give you good instructions; do not forsake My Torah [Prov 4:2]. It is a tree of life to those who grasp it, and those who uphold it are happy [Prov 3:18]. Its ways are ways of pleasantness, and all its paths are peace [Prov 3:17]. Turn us back, O LORD, to You, and we will return. Renew our days as of old.[133]

---

130 Already in Lk 4:16–20, Jesus delivers the reading from the prophet Isaiah, that is, the *haftarah* reading. See also Acts 13:15, 27.

131 Trepp, *Jüdischer Gottesdienst,* 65-67.

132 See *Koren Siddur,* 600. On the various developments with regard to Psalms 24 and 29, see Elbogen, *Jewish Liturgy,* 160. Psalm 24 is particularly appropriate through verses 7–10 (liturgy at the gates), and Psalm 29 underlines the voice of God.

133 *Koren Siddur,* 600. See Trepp, *Jüdischer Gottesdienst,* 47.

The entire rite demonstrates that the Torah scrolls are more than objects bearing a text. They are a medium for the sacred text and announce the presence of God. This is why veneration is shown to them in various forms: they are expensive handwritten products, adorned with valuable shawls and ornaments; they are kept in a nobly furnished shrine, and they may not be touched directly, but only with a pointer (*yad*). On high feast days, important prayers are uttered before the open shrine.[134] All this signals that when we compare the synagogue worship to the Catholic liturgy, we must underscore not only the external parallels of the proclamation of Torah and the Gospel with a procession and a ritual staging, or the relationship between Torah/*haftarah* and Gospel/reading, but also the relationship between Torah and Eucharist.[135] Langer points out that the dramatization of the Torah reading in Ashkhenazi Judaism and the emphasis on the Real Presence in the Eucharist occurred at the same period. "The 'real presence' of God in the host for Christians increasingly finds its parallel in Jewish interaction with the Torah scroll."[136] The shrine can be seen (often in architectural terms too) as analogous to the tabernacle.

The proclamation of the Word makes it clear that more is involved than reading an ancient text aloud. Rather, this is the staging of the Word of God that resounds in the present moment. This means that the anamnesis and the basic dialogic structure have come into view as elements shared with the Christian Liturgy of the Word.

---

134 See Langer, *Jewish Liturgy*, 127.

135 See Clemens Leonhard, "Die Heiligkeit der Heiligen Schrift und Deutungen ihres Status im Rahmen des Synagogengottesdienstes und der Messliturgie," in Franz and Zerfaß, *Wort des lebendigen Gottes*, 169–70, 174, 178–79.

136 Langer, "Sinai, Zion and God in the Synagogue," 139 n. 44.

CHAPTER 25

Hermeneutical Insights

This section has presented the significance of the liturgical context for the interpretation of a scriptural text that is proclaimed or used in prayers, songs, and rites. The primary hermeneutical keys are the occasion of the celebration, the Church year, and the liturgical setting. The phenomenon of intertextuality is particularly important in the relationship of a pericope to other liturgical or biblical texts in one and the same celebration. The order of readings, in turn, influences the understanding of individual pericopes through the division into pericopes and, above all, through the allocation of other scriptural texts.

The embedding of the scriptural readings in ritual and their staging communicate truths that are important for a biblical hermeneutics, such as the presence of God or of Christ in the liturgical proclamation and its dialogic and performative character.[137] The rites, in all their variety, agree on this point, and thereby indicate a fundamental aspect of a liturgical hermeneutics of the Bible. It is precisely the comparison of rites that permits us to underline the elements in common (e.g., the framing of the scriptural texts, or the ritual that highlights the preeminent position of the Gospel) some specific elements (e.g., the pointed affirmation in the Armenian rite: "God speaks"). The comparison highlights the underlying understanding of Scripture in the context of liturgy as the Word of God that goes forth at this moment. This emphasizes the sacrality of Scripture. Some aspects that are only hinted at in the Roman rite, or that do not exist there (such as a blessing at the reading for the lector), are more clearly conscious in other rites. Our look at the synagogue liturgy has allowed us to see the importance of staging, as well as parallels to the Liturgy of the Word.[138] We have frequently touched on theological aspects that we shall discuss more in the next section.

---

137 See B.VIII.28.
138 See B.VII.24.2.

Theological Aspects of the Liturgical Hermeneutics of the Bible

I n keeping with our approach in this study, the theological aspects of a
liturgical hermeneutics of the Bible that we have seen from the observations in Part A will be studied in greater depth in the present section. The
Liturgy is understood as the "realization of the Church's life";[1] in the dic-
tion of the polemical theologian Melchior Cano (1509-1560), it is a *"locus
theologicus."*[2] He coined this term in the course of elaborating his theory of
principles, with the aim of compiling from the ten "places" (or authorities)
theological affirmations that were certain. It is striking that although he did
not include liturgy among the *loci theologici,* he "interpreted, completely as
a matter of course," the Church's worship in all its realizations "as a dimension or element of the ecclesial-apostolic tradition."[3] He thus assigns the

---

1 Julia Knop, *Ecclesia orans. Liturgie als Herausforderung für die Dogmatik* (Freiburg/Br.:
Herder, 2012), 211.

2 Knop, 181-212.

3 Knop, 201. Cano mentions *inter alia* infant baptism, the eucharistic canon, and the veneration
of saints and of images.

Liturgy to the second *locus theologicus,* the *"auctoritas traditionum Christi et Apostolorum,"* which immediately follows Scripture as the first *locus.*[4] Similarly, the patristic authors did not pose the theoretical question whether the Liturgy functions as a *locus* of theological knowledge, because they took it absolutely for granted that it was the "ontological condition that makes theology possible."[5]

In this sense, the basic assumption of the so-called liturgical theology, which was conceptualized by the Orthodox theologian Alexander Schmemann (1921–1983),[6] is that liturgy, understood as *theologia prima,* has a theological significance. We must draw a distinction between the liturgical theology that begins from the Liturgy itself and deduces theological affirmations from it, and the theology of the Liturgy that approaches the Liturgy with criteria and guidelines that come from systematic theology, rather than from the Liturgy itself.[7] The present section takes up the first approach and seeks to bring to light the theological aspects that are linked to the liturgical use of Scripture and that thus constitute an essential dimension of a liturgical hermeneutics of the Bible.

This section has the following structure:

1. We begin with an overview of the functions that Scripture can have in the Liturgy (Chapter 26).

2. The first theological aspect we shall examine, because of its basic centrality, is anamnesis as a making present of God's salvific deeds that are attested in Scripture (Chapter 27).

3. The main focus of the chapter will lie on the sacramentality of the Word. We shall offer a theological justification of the presence of

---

4 Knop, 201–2, 209.

5 Helmut Hoping, "Kult und Reflexion. Joseph Ratzinger als Liturgietheologe," in *Der Logosgemäße Gottesdienst. Theologie der Liturgie bei Joseph Ratzinger,* ed. R. Voderholzer, Ratzinger-Studien 1 (Regensburg: Pustet, 2009), 18.

6 See Alexander Schmemann, *Introduction to Liturgical Theology,* 4th ed. (Crestwood, NY: SVS Press, 1996) [1st ed. 1961]; Aidan Kavanagh, *On Liturgical Theology* (New York: Pueblo, 1992) [1st ed. 1981]; Hoping and Jeggle-Merz, *Liturgische Theologie*; David W. Fagerberg, *Theologia prima. What is liturgical theology?* 2nd ed. (Chicago/Mundelein, IL: Hillenbrand Books, 2004); Irwin, *Context and Text,* passim, esp. 70–120, on the Word of God in the Liturgy 187–239; Helmut Hoping and Birgit Jeggle-Merz, eds. *Liturgische Theologie: Aufgaben systematischer Liturgiewissenschaft* (Paderborn: Schöningh, 2004); Knop, *Ecclesia orans,* 213–55.

7 On this distinction and its opportunities and limitations, see Albert Gerhards and Benedikt Kranemann, *Introduction to the Study of Liturgy,* trans. L. M. Maloney (Collegeville, MN: Liturgical Presss, 2017), 64–68; Hoping, "Kult und Reflexion," 13–19.

God/Christ in the Word. Since sacraments always represent the dialogical event of an encounter, we shall speak of the revelation of God through Scripture and the liturgical response of the human being. We shall also speak of the performative character of Scripture (Chapter 28).

4. The sacramentality of the Word leads to the question of the relationship between Word and sacrament, and in particular, between Word and Eucharist (Chapter 29).

5. The unity of Old and New Testaments is significant for a hermeneutics of the Bible. We shall therefore inquire into liturgical testimonies to the unity of Scripture in the Paschal Mystery. We shall also show how the Liturgy itself functions as "anti-type" of Scripture by actualizing biblical passages in liturgical celebrations (Chapter 30).

6 Finally, we shall treat specifically the pneumatological-epicletic dimension of the Word (Chapter 31).

Since one can observe repeatedly that certain aspects of the liturgical hermeneutics of the Bible are already present embryonically in Scripture itself, we shall, wherever possible, present the testimony of Scripture. Where it is substantially appropriate (and bearing in mind the necessary brevity), we shall also look at the theology of the Word in the patristic writers, with some emphasis on Origen († 253/254) and Ambrose, both of whom played an important role in the formation of the tradition. Above all, however, in keeping with the approach of a liturgical theology itself, we shall investigate the theological implications that are significant for the hermeneutics of the Bible. The panorama that opened up in Part A helps us to keep in view, not only the readings from Scripture, but also the broad spectrum of the use of Scripture.

CHAPTER 26

Functions of Scripture
in the Liturgy

The functions that Scripture can have in a liturgical celebration are broadly varied, as Paul declares: "All Scripture is inspired by God and is useful for teaching, for refutation, for correction, and for training in righteousness" (2 Tm 3:16). According to Romans 15:4, that which was written to give instruction also generates consolation and hope. This was elaborated into the theory of the fourfold meaning of Scripture, which was summarized in the mnemonic:

> Littera gesta docet, quid credas allegoria,
> moralis quid agas, quo tendas anagogia.

> The letter teaches what happened, the allegory what you should believe, the moral sense what you should do, the anagogy whither you should strive.[8]

Scripture, understood in a literal sense, bears witness to the revelation of God that has taken place in history.[9] The literal sense is the basis of the three other senses.[10] The so-called allegorical sense aims at the faith and at the theological interpretation of the historical revelation (*gesta*). The *sensus fidei* brings in a second element, namely, the moral sense as the realization in life of the Scripture that is accepted in faith. The anagogical (or

---

8 A less literal translation in *CCC* 118; quoted in *VD* 37.

9 On this section, see Rudolf Voderholzer, "Der geistige Sinn der Schrift. Frühkirchliche Lehre mit neuer Aktualität," in Voderholzer, *Offenbarung*, 119–50. See also Schwienhorst-Schönberger, "Wiederentdeckung des geistigen Schriftverständnisses," 404–16, esp. 407–8.

10 See Thomas Aquinas, *Summa theologiae*, 1, 1, 10 ad 1: "All other senses of Sacred Scripture are based on the literal" (quoted from *CCC* 116).

eschatological) sense inquires into the relationship between the Word of God and the promised future good things. The spiritual sense, which combines the three senses of Scripture that are additional to the literal sense,[11] thus expounds a scriptural text in its "function" for faith (allegorical), love (moral), and hope (anagogical).

If, then, one single text of Scripture is able *per se* to fulfill several functions when it is expounded, this applies *a fortiori* to Scripture in the framework of the Liturgy, which is additional to the text itself. For, (as the preceding section has demonstrated), the function also depends on the context in which a text stands, or in which it was translated into prayers, songs, or rites. The function of the scriptural reading can therefore vary, depending on whether it is read in the Sunday Mass, in a sacramental celebration, in the Office of Readings, or in the other offices.[12] It was likewise impossible to define one primary function of the Responsorial Psalm.[13] Moreover, Old Testament texts acquire a new function, over and above their original meaning, when they are employed typologically in songs or prayers.[14]

Following Paul Bradshaw's classification,[15] and differentiating it futher, we can distinguish (although not separate) the following functions of the Word of God in the Liturgy.

a) Catechetical function

The proclamation of the Scripture and its other uses in liturgy allow the texts of the Bible to become known and familiar. A catechetical function is always involved here. In view of the narrow choice of pericopes in the *MRom* 1570/1962, the Council Fathers had expressed the wish that "richer fare may be provided for the faithful at the table of God's word,"[16] and thus there was a prominent catechetical motivation in the renewal of the order of readings for the Mass (1969). Explicit aspects of liturgical theology played a rather subordinate role, as the Praenotanda of the *OLM* show: it was only the second edition (1981) that expanded the previous edition (1969) above all

---

11 The twofold meaning of Scripture—literal and spiritual—goes back to the Pauline antithesis between letter and spirit (see 2 Cor 3:6; Voderholzer, "Geistiger Sinn," 136-38).

12 See A.I.

13 See A.II.8.1.

14 See A.III.11; A.IV.14; B.VIII.30.1.

15 See Paul F. Bradshaw, "The Use of the Bible in Liturgy: Some Historical Perspectives," *Studia Liturgica* 22, no. 1 (1992): 36-42.

16 See *SC* 51.

through the three introductory chapters on the theology of the proclamation of the Word. Naturally, the knowledge of Scripture remains an important goal of the order of readings,[17] also after the new edition of the *GILM*, which adheres to this basic pastoral principle.[18] The Office of Readings is oriented even more strongly to this aim. All those who are active in preaching can nourish their ministry from the source of revelation.[19]

It is impossible to overestimate the value of the knowledge of Scripture, if one remembers the celebrated words of Saint Jerome, the great biblical translator: "Ignorance of the Scripture is ignorance of Christ."[20] Like the literal meaning, the communication of knowledge is the fundamental basis of further functions. Nevertheless, it is neither a specific feature of the Liturgy nor its first task.

b) Anamnetic function

Part A has drawn attention many times to the anamnetic function and has shown that making present, here and now, the salvation historically attested in Scripture is a central motif of the liturgical hermeneutics of the Bible. This is not restricted to the scriptural readings on the feast days, which bear witness that the historical basis of the feast is present today. It recurs outside the feasts, and is found in prayers, songs, and rites. Because of its central importance, anamnesis will be the theme of the following chapter (B.VIII.27.).

c) Paracletic or pastoral function

In the third place, Bradshaw mentions the paracletic function. While the catechetical function aims at the cognitive appropriation of Scripture, and the anamnetic function is the one that can most specifically be called "liturgical," the paracletic function addresses the spiritual needs of human beings and can therefore also be called the pastoral function of Scripture. Indeed, Scripture can affirm, encourage, build up, motivate, and console, but also exhort, confront, challenge, and summon to repentance, etc. This is the case first of all with the readings. For example, this function is particularly marked in the readings for funerals, or in the short readings of the Liturgy of the

---

17 See *GILM*, 60–61, 106.

18 See *GILM*, 38, 45, 75–78, 80–81, 83, 88, esp. 58.

19 See *GILH*, 55, 165; A.I.3.1.

20 Jerome, *Commentarius in Isaiam*, Prolegomena (CChr.SL 73:1; *DV* 25): "*Ignoratio enim Scripturarum ignoratio Christi est.*"

Hours in Ordinary Time[21]—and with the homily, which is meant above all to interpret the Scripture with reference to the situation of the participants. The Psalms too can exercise this function through the relation to one's own life. Similarly, the prayers and the central words of the sacraments address their biblical content to the recipients. Nor should we underestimate the ritual signs and actions related to Scripture, such as those in the baptismal liturgy or the Washing of the Feet,[22] which doubtless have a stronger effect than the word that is "merely" heard. It is easy to multiply examples. The characteristic of this function is that one is addressed personally by the word of Scripture, which becomes spiritual nourishment.[23]

d) Meditative function

The meditative function of Scripture deserves a special mention. We have already encountered this as an aspect of the Responsorial Psalm, since it often takes up the words of the reading, sometimes develops its ideas, and serves to interiorize what one has heard. Above all, the refrain can be a meditative element, thanks to the repetition.[24] A meditative use of Scripture is especially typical of the Liturgy of the Hours, since one prays *with* and *on the basis of* the Psalms. Prayer grows from the meditation of the Psalms,[25] and the various situations and emotions of the Psalms reflect one's own life, thus bringing one's life into the presence of God and into prayer.[26]

Through their context in the Liturgy of the Hours, the prayers too have a fundamentally meditative function, so that hearing the Word of God and praying support each other. This means that another function of Scripture is to inspire personal prayer. This applies equally to the short readings, which are read not as a proclamation, but rather as a spiritual impulse. Through their concision and their repetition, they foster familiarity with the Word of God, which is capable of speaking anew in all the variety of existential

---

21 See A.I.5.2.

22 See A.V.

23 See Caesarius of Arles, *Sermo* 6.2–3. (CChr.SL 103:32); *Sermons*, trans. Mary Magdeleine Mueller, Fathers of the Church 31 (Washington, DC: The Catholic University of America Press, 1956), 40: "The light and eternal food of the soul is nothing else but the word of God, without which the soul can neither see nor live. Just as our body dies if it does not receive food, so, too, our soul is killed if it does not receive the word of God."

24 See A.II.8.2.

25 See Ps 1:2: "in lege eius *meditabitur*"; *GILH,* 104.

26 See A.II.9.

situations and experiences.[27] In principle, meditation—often a diffuse concept today—is to be understood first and foremost in the patristic sense as a *ruminatio* (a "chewing the cud," a continuous repetition) of the Word of God, since its goal is the personal interiorization of this Word. It is obvious that the meditative function also promotes a deepening of the spiritual life.

The Liturgy indirectly attests the meditative function of Scripture through the hymns, since their authors composed the poetical texts out of the contemplation of Scripture. They are examples of meditative reflection with the Bible.[28] Something similar applies to many liturgical prayers. The pericope orations are examples of how the Bible becomes the source of prayer.[29]

e) Performative function

When the Word of God is received, it deploys its performative function. In other words, it begins to work in the hearer. Ultimately, this function cannot be separated from the meditative, paracletic-pastoral, or anamnetic functions. Rather, it is a goal inherent in Scripture, which binds all these functions together, and this is why it is mentioned specifically. Scripture makes a significant contribution to the Christian life and to establishing the identity of believers.[30] This function emphasizes the efficacy of the Word and makes it possible to experience its sacramental dimension.[31]

f) Doxological function

Finally, Bradshaw mentions the doxological function.[32] This is obvious in hymnic prayer texts in Scripture, such as the canticles in the Old and New Testaments, and especially in the Psalms (*tehillim* means songs of praise). Augustine could thus say about the inspired psalms: "In order that God may be praised well by human beings, God has praised himself [in the Psalms]."[33] There exists, therefore, a certain closeness to the meditative function. Some

---

27 See A.I.5.

28 See A.IV.14.

29 On this, see A.III.12.

30 See B.IX.36.

31 See B.VIII.28.3.

32 Bradshaw, "Use of the Bible," 42–43.

33 Augustine, *Enarr. in Ps.144,1* (CChr.SL 40:2088): "*Ut bene ab hominibus laudetur Deus, laudavit se ipse Deus.*"

readings in the Liturgy of the Hours likewise have a doxological character.[34] Hymns, chants, and prayers employ Scripture to praise God.

g) Immediate function for the liturgical celebration

Scripture also has another function: to interpret and to shape the Liturgy. For example, Scripture, as an accompanying chant or an interpretative word, makes signs and actions comprehensible.[35] It also has the function of justifying and shaping the feasts in the liturgical year, or the sacraments, as in the reference to James 5 at the beginning of the Anointing of the Sick. This last example makes it clear that Scripture also has a critical function vis-à-vis the Liturgy, as when the tension between the understanding of the Anointing of the Sick as exclusively a preparation for death and the clear statements about illness in James 5 was perceived and finally removed.[36] The criterion for the "correctness" of the songs and prayers is the Word of God. This shows that the Liturgy stands under the criterion of Scripture, which also has a normative function for worship.

---

34 See A.I.5.2; e.g., *Liturgy of the Hours*, 3:681 (Rom 11:33–36); 777-79 (Am 4:14; 5:8, 9b; 9:6).

35 See A.II.7.1 (Psalms, e.g., at the Palm Sunday procession); A.IV.15 (Communion chants), and esp. A.V.

36 See A.I.4.1.

CHAPTER 27

The Anamnesis of Scripture
Making Present God's Salvific Action that Is Attested in the Bible

For liturgical theology, it is impossible to overestimate the importance of anamnesis in the celebration of worship, since anamnesis is the remembrance of God's salvific action that is attested in the Scripture of the Old and New Testaments and that has reached its high point in Jesus Christ—a remembrance that makes this salvific action present today.[37] The studies of "mystery theology" by Odo Casel (1886–1948), which found their reception in the *Constitution on the Liturgy*, have made a decisive contribution here. He wrote that the "Christ-mystery" was made present in the "cult mystery."[38] This fundamental category of the Liturgy includes the way in which liturgy handles Scripture.

1. THE BIBLICAL BASIS OF ANAMNESIS

We begin with a brief look at anamnesis in the Bible. In the Old Testament, the Hebrew root *zkr* ("remember") has a double thrust: the subject who remembers is either God, who remembers his covenant and turns to human beings, or the people of God, who remember God's saving actions, above all in the exodus, and turn to him. Through this remembrance, they preserve their own identity as the people of God.[39] Remembrance is thus

---

37 See Stephan Wahle, *Gottes-Gedenken. Untersuchungen zum anamnetischen Gehalt christlicher und jüdischer Liturgie*, IThS 73 (Innsbruck: Tyrolia-Verlag, 2006).

38 See esp. Odo Casel, *The Mystery of Christian Worship, and Other Writings* (Westminster, MD: Newman Press, 1962); *ALw* 28 (1986) in its entirety is dedicated to Casel.

39 The book of Deuteronomy frequently urges the people not to forget, but to remember the LORD, his saving acts, words, and commandments, the covenant, and also their guilt. See, e.g.,

understood as a mutual relationship, which is ritualized in the annual Passover celebration.

In the New Testament, the mandate to remember given at the Last Supper, "Do this in memory of me" (Lk 22:19; 1 Cor 11:24–25), has been given a clear Christological orientation. The Bible itself already inserts the anamnesis of Christ into a ritual framework.

The biblical anamnesis not only entails making the past present; it also has an eschatological aspect. In the late Old Testament period, there begins a "process of eschatologizing the foundational prehistory,"[40] that is, the expectation of an exodus in the end time as the beginning of the definitive period of salvation. The New Testament knows both a futurist and a realized eschatology because the turn of the ages has already begun in Christ and the kingdom of Christ has already dawned, although, of course, its full realization is still awaited. Since Christ has proleptically brought about the redemption of the world in his dying and rising, the future full realization already reaches into the present day when believers remember the crucified and risen Christ. Christian anamnesis thus unites past and future in the "today" of the liturgical celebration.[41] And since the narrative of Scripture bears witness to the history of God with human beings and proclaims an eternal future in God, the consequence for the Liturgy is that it embraces both the past and the full realization and makes them present in the mode of remembrance.

The "basic structure" of Sacred Scripture is "anamnetic":[42] "anamnesis, memory, and remembrance are not only one theme *in* Scripture, but the *formal definition of the meaning of Scripture* as a whole."[43] And since Scripture not only bears witness to God's encounter with Israel and with the early Church as a historical event, but also opens up the sphere for the encounter with God in the present day, anamnesis is the "leading category that unites" Bible and Liturgy.[44]

Making Scripture present for "today" is central to the Liturgy because its criterion is the way in which Christ himself read and expounded Scripture in the synagogue in Nazareth: "Today this Scripture passage is fulfilled in your

---

Deut 4:9–10, 23; 6:10–12; 8:1–20; 9:7; etc.

40 Meßner, "Wortgottesdienst," 175.

41 See Meßner, "Wortgottesdienst," 176–78; Wahle, *Gottes-Gedenken*, 122–25, 142–43.

42 Georg Steins, "'Hört dies zu meinem Gedächtnis!' Anamnese als Bibel und Liturgie verbindende Leitkategorie," *BiLi* 80, no. 4 (2007): 237.

43 Steins, 241.

44 See Steins, esp. 237.

hearing" (Lk 4:21). The Liturgy follows his call to search all the scriptures on the basis of the "today" of the event that he himself is.[45]

2. THE LITURGICAL REALIZATION OF THE ANAMNESIS OF SCRIPTURE AND WHAT THIS MEANS FOR A LITURGICAL HERMENEUTICS OF THE BIBLE

One particularly striking example of the anamnetic character of the reading of Scripture is the proclamation of the Gospel of the Resurrection on Sunday, the weekly Easter.[46] Egeria's account of her pilgrimage, (probably 381–384), relates that at the early morning Vigil in Jerusalem held every Sunday, it was the bishop himself who proclaimed the Gospel of the Resurrection of Christ. This was the (emotional) high point of the celebration in the Anastasis.[47] The Apostolic Constitutions[48] and the Rule of Benedict[49] bear a similar testimony. Even today, one of the eleven Resurrection Gospels (*eōthina*) is read in the Byzantine Orthros on Sunday.[50]

The new Milanese lectionary (2008) introduced a solemn opening of Sunday in the Vigil Mass on Saturday with the proclamation of a Gospel of the Resurrection.[51] Here, the principal celebrant proclaims at the beginning of the celebration a resurrection Gospel from the altar (not from the ambo), in order to stage liturgically the presence of the risen Lord: just as he once appeared in the midst of the disciples, so too now he appears in the midst of the assembly. Accordingly, the reading begins with the words: "Proclamation of the Resurrection of our Lord Jesus Christ according to N.," and concludes

---

45 See *GILM*, 3; Lk 24:25–27, 44–49.

46 Eusebius, *De solemnitate paschali* 7 (*PG* 24:701) seems to be the earliest known witness to the weekly Easter.

47 See Egeria, *Itinerarium* 24.10 (FontC 20:214–15; WEC 2:342). See Juan Mateos, "La vigile cathédrale chez Égérie," *OCP* 27 (1961) : 286, 291.

48 See *Apostolic Constitutions* 2.59.4 (SChr 320:326; WEC 2:224).

49 See *Regula Benedicti* 11.9 (WEC 4:28). Originally, this most likely referred to a Gospel of the Resurrection. From the early medieval sources onward, it was the Gospel of the Mass. See Reinhard Meßner, "Wortgottesdienst. Historische Typologie und aktuelle Probleme," in Franz and Zerfaß, *Wort des lebendigen Gottes*, 81, 85.

50 See A.I.3.1.2.

51 See *PLA*, 73–75; *Libro delle Vigilie. Secondo il rito della Chiesa di Milano. Riformato a norma dei decreti del Concilio Vaticano II. Promulgato dal Signor Cardinale Angelo Scola, Arcivescovo di Milano e Capo Rito* (Milan: Centro Ambrosiano, 2016), esp. 247–73; Alzati, "Liturgia Vigiliare Vespertina," 112–14.

with the words: "Christ the Lord is risen (in Eastertide: Alleluia, alleluia!)." Where possible, the church bells should ring during the proclamation of the Easter message.

In the solemn form, Mass is joined to the Vespers and a lucernarium. The light can be taken from the Paschal candle and spread from person to person, recalling the Easter Vigil. In practice, the simpler form is more common, in which the resurrection Gospel is proclaimed instead of the Penitential Act. An even simpler form has only a few short verses instead of the entire resurrection Gospel with its ritual staging. The celebrant reads these to the people at the altar after lighting the Paschal candle and the altar candles and a brief introduction. During Lent, the paschal candle is not lit, and instead of the Easter narrative, a Gospel such as the Transfiguration is read.

Since the message of the Resurrection, even in the various narratives, is the same every week, the main point is not the communication of a content that is already well known, but the anamnesis of this content on the day that recalls the Resurrection.

Part A has drawn attention to numerous other examples. The Lenten readings make present the path taken by Jesus to his dying and rising in Jerusalem, so that the believers go with him toward Easter and receive a share anew in the Paschal Mystery of Christ.[52] In the celebrations of the sacraments, the readings clearly show the anamnetic actualization, for example, when Jesus' care for the sick is continued in the anointing, so that there is a concord between the proclamation of the Word and the sacramental action (with prayer).[53] In the readings on saints' feasts, the continuing effect of Scripture in the life of the saints becomes visible, and the saints can be models inspiring us today to translate the Word of God into our own lives.[54] We have likewise drawn attention to the anamnetic function in the short readings of the Liturgy of the Hours (especially in the festal cycles).[55]

All these examples show that the proclamation of Scripture in the Liturgy does not serve only to impart historical information. Rather, it is an effective proclamation here and now of God's saving activity. Even less should one understand anamnesis as a spiritual "time travel" back into the world of the Bible. On the contrary, thanks to the presence of God, who is outside time and is present at every time, the direction is exactly the inverse:

---

52 See A.I.3.2.

53 See A.I.4.

54 See A.I.3.3.

55 See A.I.5.2.

namely, out of the past into the present day. In this way, one becomes in the Liturgy a contemporary of salvation.[56]

The introduction "At that time..." or "In those days ...," which already occurs frequently in the Bible, can be an indicator that the pericope belongs not only to the "historical past, but to the normative time of origin,"[57] which remains significant for today too.

The *GILM* insists from a Christological perspective on the continuation of the work of salvation with regard to the liturgical celebration and to the Word of God: "each recalls the mystery of Christ and each in its own way causes that mystery to be ever present."[58]

Anamnesis is thus not an achievement of the human memory but an act of remembrance on the part of God, who bestows his salvation *hic et nunc* and thereby continues the salvation attested in the Bible and accomplishes it in an analogous manner today. When we ask God to remember what he did in the past (for example, at the beginning of the Good Friday liturgy: "Remember your mercies, O Lord"),[59] this is not done to remind the omniscient God of what he himself has done, but because his remembrance provides salvation for human beings. Naturally, we must open ourselves to what God does, because he respects our freedom. It is obviously important to understand the anamnesis by God and by the human being in personal and relational terms.

The act of making present means that the *content* of Scripture is applied to the contemporary human being and is actualized. It is not only the readings and the homily that help here; anamnesis is the specific form in which the Liturgy as a whole actualizes Scripture.[60] In the liturgical prayers, Scripture is more than an inspirer of formulations. On the one hand, Scripture bears witness to God's saving activity, which is now requested for those gathered for the celebration (of the Mass or the sacrament). On the other hand, it

---

56 Angelus A. Häußling, "Liturgie: Gedächtnis eines Vergangenen und doch Befreiung in der Gegenwart," in Häußling, *Christliche Identität aus der Liturgie. Theologische und historische Studien zum Gottesdienst der Kirche*, ed. M. Klöckener, LQF 79 (Münster: Aschendorff, 1997), 2–10.

57 Zerfaß, *Hermeneutik*, 175.

58 *GILM*, 4–5.

59 *Missal*, 315.

60 The Pontifical Biblical Commission, *Interpretation of the Bible*, 37 (IV, C) emphasizes the Liturgy: "In principle, the Liturgy, and especially the sacramental liturgy, the high point of which is the eucharistic celebration, brings about the most perfect actualization of the biblical texts, for the Liturgy places the proclamation in the midst of the community of believers."

legitimates what the Church does by linking it back to the action of Jesus.[61] For example, as the hymns about the Cross show, the songs not only recall biblical events but relate them to the participants, who see themselves as their addressees in the celebration and respond in grateful praise.[62] Similarly, we noted the anamnetic use of Scripture in the Communion antiphons. When they are taken from the Gospel of the day, a logion of Christ is usually selected and appears thus as a word addressed today to the communicant. The words of the Psalms or the prophets, which can be understood Christologically or eucharistically, make it clear that what the Bible expresses in a text can become concrete experience in the sacramental event of Communion.[63]

The anamnesis of Scripture can also be illustrated through a quotation, since the Liturgy quotes Scripture, whether literally, as in readings and psalms, or in a freer form, as in prayers and songs, or ritually, as in liturgical actions like the Washing of the Feet.[64] In the last case, one can speak of a "ritual quotation." In a literary quotation, an older text is detached from the original *con-text* and inserted into a new one because it appears significant for the new application and brings to light a connection in terms of meaning. Something similar happens in liturgy, when a historical biblical text is inserted into the context of the act of worship and a bridge is constructed across the difference in time.

Since the Christ who is present is the primary actor in the Liturgy, the biblical quotation (literal, free, or ritual) can acquire an anamnetic significance. The liturgical quotation creates presence in the celebration.

Through the Liturgy, therefore, as Augustine says in an Easter homily, the events of Scripture become new (*renovare*) again and again. The celebration (*solemnitas /celebrando*) is not a repetition, but a making present of the unique historical event (*veritas*):

> You know very well that all this happened once. Yet, with the passage of time, the solemnity is renewed as if that were happening again which truth, in so many places in Scripture, declares has happened only once. Nevertheless, truth and the solemnity are not at variance, so that one lies while the other tells the truth. As a matter of fact, what truth declares has actually happened only once, this the solemnity renews as worthy of being celebrated often by pious hearts. Truth reveals what has happened as it

61 See A.III.
62 See A.IV.14.
63 See A.IV.15; B.VIII.30.2.
64 See A.V.17.

actually took place; the solemnity, however, not by re-enacting events, but by dwelling upon them, does not permit the past to pass away.

In a word, "Christ, our Passover, has been sacrificed." [1 Cor 5:7] As He died once who "dies now no more, death shall no longer have dominion over him." [Rom 6:9] Therefore, according to this voice of truth, we say that our Pasch has been sacrificed once and that He will not die again; nevertheless, according to the voice of the feast we say that the Pasch will return each year.[65]

Making present thus means, not that the historical event is renewed and actually takes place today, but that the loving care of God/Christ, which creates salvation and is displayed in the historical event, always goes forth anew.

The liturgical anamnesis makes possible the celebration of salvation in the liturgical year (see Augustine's quotation); in the course of the week, through the remembrance of the Death of Christ on Friday (especially in the Liturgy of the Hours) and his Resurrection on Sunday; and also in the course of the day, since a link is established between scriptural events, especially the Passion, and individual Hours of the Divine Office.

Numerous prayers draw attention to the different temporal levels. The prayer at episcopal ordination from the *Apostolic Tradition* that we examined in Part A showed that the Old and New Testaments are interlaced in language and in content in the anamnesis and are thus seen as a unity. At the same time, the scriptural passages form the basis for the epiclesis for the new bishop, so that a trajectory is drawn from Scripture into "today."[66] The same fundamental principle from paradigms of the Old Testament, via paradigms of the New, down to the "today" of the liturgical celebration, is also found in ordination prayers for priests and deacons, or in the blessing and invocation of God over the baptismal water. The exemplary *tour d'horizon* of salvation history is particularly marked in the Fourth Eucharistic Prayer, which was modeled on the anaphora of Basil: from creation and the fall, God's covenant and the prophets, down to the Christ event "in the fullness of time" (Gal 4:4) and to the bestowing of the Spirit, who continues the work of salvation and is now asked to descend upon the gifts. Anamnesis and epiclesis are joined together, in order to make it clear that God's salvific action in the two-one Bible is the foundation on which we ask for his action, and hence for his "salvation," today. It is striking that what Scripture expressed in the past is

---

65 Augustine, *Sermo*, 220; Augustine, *Sermons on the Liturgical Seasons*, trans. Mary Sarah Muldowney, Fathers of the Church 38 (Washington, DC: The Catholic University of America Press, 1984), 173–74.

66 See A.III.11.

now formulated in the epicletic part in the present tense, since those gathered for the Liturgy stand in the presence of the divine working. The Liturgy employs the totality of salvation history—understood as God's saving action that continually takes place in the Old Testament, in the New Testament, and also "today"—as a key to read Scripture.

The linking of Scripture and today in the liturgical celebration is thus an essential theological aspect of the biblical imprint on the Liturgy, and of the liturgical hermeneutics of the Bible. In the words of Angelus A. Häußling, "The Christian Liturgy is founded in the Bible, not thanks to a plethora of quotations from the Bible, but because, despite calamity [*Unheil*], the history of salvation [*Heil*] is the same in both the Bible and Liturgy. The difference is that it is verified in the Bible, and becomes present when it is recalled in the Liturgy."[67]

As we said in the discussion of the biblical foundation, the anamnesis of Scripture also includes the eschatological future. The Liturgy agrees with Scripture in remembering forward (so to speak): at the close of the liturgical year and on the first Sunday in Advent, the readings present us with the Second Coming of the Lord;[68] the feast of Christ the King is likewise marked by this theme. We frequently find in liturgical prayers a request for the eschatological fulfillment (e.g., in the eucharistic prayers, at the blessing and invocation of God over the baptismal water, and in numerous orations). In the *Exsultet*, we see with particular clarity the union of the various temporal levels (Old Testament—New Testament—"today" of the liturgical celebration—eternity). Signs and rites such as the procession on Palm Sunday[69] and at Candlemas, or the white baptismal garment (see Rev 7:9-17),[70] manifest the eschatological dimension of Scripture and Liturgy. When the canticles from the Book of Revelation are sung at Vespers, a unity is created that looks to the eschatological fulfillment. This becomes even clearer in the Mass *qua* anticipation of the Wedding Feast of the Lamb (Sanctus; "Blessed are those called to the supper of the Lamb").[71] In short, one who takes part in the earthly liturgy shares through a foretaste in the heavenly liturgy,[72] and the eschatological reality irrupts into the here and now of the

---

67 Angelus A. Häußling, "Biblische Grundlegung christlicher Liturgie," in Häußling, *Tagzeitenliturgie*, 310.

68 See *GILM*, 105, 108–9. On the Ambrosian lectionary, see A.I.3.1.2).

69 See also A.II.7.1.b.

70 See A.V.18.

71 *Missal,* 669; Rev 19:9.

72 See *SC* 8.

celebration—although, of course, in the tension between the "already" and the "not yet." In the Liturgy, therefore, the anamnetic dimension of Scripture unfolds in the fusing of the temporal levels, so that what is past becomes present again, and what is future is anticipated.

Thomas Aquinas († 1274) elaborated this temporal structure by means of the Aristotelian triad of cause, form, and goal in relation to the sacraments as means of the sanctification of the human being. "With regard to cause, the sacraments are linked to the *memoria* of the unique suffering of Christ; with regard to form, they have effective force in the presence of those who celebrate them; with regard to goal, they anticipate the as yet unrealized fulfillment."[73] This idea can easily be transposed to the scriptural anamnesis in the Liturgy, which both has human sanctification as its goal and brings this about.[74] The causal basis of the Liturgy is God's biblically attested salvific action in the past, with its high point in the Christ event; formally, the Liturgy is the effective celebration of this salvific action in the present; and in terms of its goal, it is the anticipation of the fulfillment that Scripture promises us.

The anamnetic character of the liturgical use of Scripture can be presented schematically as follows:

Liturgical anamnesis of God's salvific action

Sacred Scripture (OT and NT) — "Today" of Liturgical Celebration — Eschatological Fulfillment

The Liturgy mediates this temporal structure (or the anamnesis) with varying degrees of clarity. The schema "What God did in the past, let him do today" is marked in the prayers and hymns through some signal words. One striking term is "today," which already serves in many special passages

---

73 Josef Wohlmuth, "Vorüberlegungen zu einer theologischen Ästhetik der Sakramente," in Hoping and Jeggle-Merz, *Liturgische Theologie*, 97, based on Thomas Aquinas, *Summa theologiae* 3, 60, 3c.

74 See *SC* 7.

of Scripture to indicate anamnesis.[75] In the Liturgy (not only on feasts), it is not an indication of a date, but refers to the present time. The annual insertion in the canon of the Mass of the Lord's Supper, "that is today,"[76] is particularly striking. It refers, not to Holy Thursday as a day, but rather to the making present of what Jesus anticipated in the Upper Room: namely, his Death and his Resurrection. The same applies to "now," "and now," or "we/us too" (with an explicit reference to the participants).[77] Besides this, parallels drawn between the biblical text and the liturgical celebration can make the anamnesis visible. When the ambo is used for the first time at the consecration of a church, the reading is always the public reading and explanation of the law by the scribe Ezra on a specially erected pulpit (Neh 8:1–4a, 5–6, 8–10).[78] The obvious actualization of this pericope displays in exemplary fashion the fundamental anamnetic dimension of the proclamation of Scripture.

Let us sum up: the importance of the anamnesis is underlined by the fact that we have encountered it both in this section and in the survey of the liturgical use of Scripture in Part A in so many different examples, contexts, and forms of celebration (the Mass, the sacraments, Liturgy of the Hours). The frequent anamnetic use of Scripture guarantees that the Liturgy remains bound to Christ and to the divine salvific action. This ensures that the Church authentically celebrates the God of Jesus Christ. Scripture is thus normative for the Liturgy and for its language; it is, so to speak, the "'mother tongue' of the Liturgy."[79] But a liturgical celebration is more than the recalling of the normative origin. It makes present God's biblically attested salvific action, which simultaneously points to the eschatological fulfillment. Here, the Liturgy employs Scripture, not primarily as a document from the past, but as testimony to God's salvific action in the present, which is addressed to the participants in the celebration of worship. This, of course, is possible only thanks to the sacramentality of the Word.

---

75 "Today" occurs roughly seventy times in Deuteronomy, in order to underline the contemporary relevance of the instructions of God. In Luke too, "today" is employed purposefully (see 2:11; 4:21; 5:26; 19:5, 9; 23:43).

76 *Missal*, 308.

77 See A.III.13 (e.g., the collect at Pentecost; ordination prayer in the *Apostolic Tradition*; and frequently); A.IV.14.2.1 (Romanos).

78 See *Rites*, 2:376.

79 Andreas Redtenbacher, "Biblische Grundlagen liturgischer Bildung: Zur Bedeutung der Bibel für das Verständnis des Gottesdienstes," *HlD* 60, no. 2 (2010): 131.

CHAPTER 28

The Sacramentality of the Word of God

For a liturgical hermeneutics of the Bible, the "sacramentality of the Word" is of central importance.[80] *Verbum Domini* 56 gives it a prominent place and explains it briefly with reference to the Incarnation of the Word and on the analogy of the eucharistic Real Presence. The patristic writers already elaborated the matter itself, that is, the mystery or depth dimension of the biblical Word.[81] Augustine's correlation of word and sign became standard for the Western understanding of the sacraments, although he himself had a much broader understanding of "sacrament" than the seven which became the classic number of sacraments:[82] "The word comes to the element and the sacrament comes into being."[83] The word is necessary for the

80 See Paul Janowiak, *The Holy Preaching: The Sacramentality of the Word in the Liturgical Assembly* (Collegeville, MN: Liturgical Press, 2000); Marco Benini, "Gegenwärtig im Wort. Sakramentalität des Wortes Gottes," in *Liturgie und Bibel: Theologie und Praxis der Verkündigung des Wortes Gottes*, ed. T. Söding and M. Linnenborn (Trier: Deutsches Liturgisches Institut, 2020), 28–52.

81 For example, Origen, *In Numeros Homiliae* 16.9 (*GCS* 30:152) explains that the drinking of the Blood of Christ consists not only in the sacramental rite, but also in the reception of his Word; Origen, *Homilies on Numbers*, trans. T. P. Scheck and C. A. Hall, Ancient Christian Texts (Downers Grove, IL: IVP Academic, 2009), 101.

82 The number seven was first laid down at the Second Council of Lyons in 1274 (see *DH* 860).

83 Augustine, *Trac. in Ioh.* 80.3 (CChr.SL 36:529): "Accedit verbum ad elementum et fit sacramentum." The noun *verbum* can have three meanings: Christ, the Logos, who is the real actor when the sacraments are administered (see *SC* 7); the reading and the "formula of administration"; and/or the prayer that belongs to the sacrament (see Chauvet, *Symbol and Sacrament*, 222).

coming into being of the sacrament, so that he speaks in the same passage of the sacrament as a "visible word" (*visibile verbum*).[84]

A reversal of this argument means that the Word too has an effective sacramental meaning, so that the Word was called an "audible sacrament" (*sacramentum audibile*).[85] In the context of his mystery theology, Odo Casel said that "the scriptural reading in the Liturgy is also in a certain sense a *sacramentum*."[86] It was via the Liturgy that Pius Parsch came to his "great discovery: the Bible is sacramental."[87] Some theologians, from a patristic or dogmatic perspective, have explicitly studied the theology of the Word of God and also thematized its sacramentality.[88] The *GILM* mentions it likewise.[89] The Synod of Bishops on the Word of God expressed the wish to promote theological reflection on the sacramentality of the Word.[90] The first requirement here is a conceptual clarification of "sacramentality." We can assume as consensus that an earthly reality points beyond itself into the divine reality and that the "divine reality" manifests itself "at a concrete place in space and time in a concrete earthly reality, without becoming identical

---

84 Augustine elaborated this idea with regard to the baptismal water, which cleanses only thanks to the word. See also Augustine, *De doctrina christiana* 2.3.4 (CChr.SL 32:34) and Augustine, *Contra Faustum* 19:16 (*CSEL* 25:513).

85 This term is often cited without indicating the source. It is an analogy formed by Gottlieb Söhngen, *Symbol und Wirklichkeit im Kultmysterium*, Grenzfragen zwischen Theologie und Philosophie 4, 2nd ed. (Bonn: Hanstein, 1940), 20. See Walter Kasper, "Wort und Sakrament," in *Martyria, Leiturgia, Diakonia* (FS Hermann Volk), ed. O. Semmelroth (Mainz: Matthias-Grünewald-Verlag, 1968), 280 n. 43. Augustine also employs *sacramentum* for verbal formulations such as the *sacramentum symboli* or the *sacramentum orationis dominicae* (*Sermo* 228.3; *PL* 38:1102).

86 Odo Casel, "The Meaning of the Mystery," in Casel, *Mystery of Christian Worship*, 126.

87 Pius Parsch, *Volksliturgie. Ihr Sinn und Umfang* (Klosterneuburg/Vienna 1940), 261. See Marco Benini, "„Große Entdeckung: Die Bibel ist sakramental." Zu Pius Parschs Wort-Gottes-Theologie und seinen liturgischen Predigten," in *Die Liturgietheologie von Pius Parsch. Klosterneuburger Symposion 2021*, ed. A. Redtenbacher and D. Seper (Freiburg/Br.: Herder, 2022), 174–99.

88 See, e.g., Otto Semmelroth, *Wirkendes Wort. Zur Theologie der Verkündigung* (Frankfurt/M.: Knecht, 1962), 171–81, esp. 173–74; Rolf Gögler, *Zur Theologie des biblischen Wortes bei Origenes* (Düsseldorf: Patmos-Verlag, 1963), 365–80; Leo Scheffczyk, *Von der Heilsmacht des Wortes. Grundzüge einer Theologie des Wortes* (Munich: Hueber, 1966), 264–72. On this, see Janowiak, *Holy Preaching*, 19–64; Alois Moos, *Das Verhältnis von Wort und Sakrament in der deutschsprachigen katholischen Theologie des 20. Jahrhunderts*, KKTS 59 (Paderborn: Bonifatius, 2993); Eisenbach, *Gegenwart Christi*, 502–20.

89 *GILM*, 41: "[…] word that in the celebration becomes sacrament through the Holy Spirit." See also *PLA*, 47.

90 See Eterović, *Parola di Dio*, 631.

with it."[91] It goes without saying that sacramentality is no less essential to revelation (with its high point in Christ as the primal sacrament)[92] than to Church and liturgy.[93] The sacramentality of Scripture thus shares both in the sacramentality of revelation, which is attested by Scripture, and in the sacramentality of the Church, since Scripture came into being in the community of faith, in which the Word of God is handed on and attested.

Our starting point for the following reflections is that in a sacrament, God/Christ is personally present, enters into communication with human beings, and works in them in this way. We shall take three steps: first, we shall reflect on the presence of God/Christ in Scripture. A second point takes up the dialogical encounter through the Word of God. A third illustrates more precisely the performative character of the Word. The reflections begin once again with the liturgical celebration.

1. THE PRESENCE OF GOD/CHRIST IN HIS WORD

As we have already shown in detail, the rites of the Proclamation of the Gospel in the Mass (framing, procession with the Gospel book, etc.) make us most aware of the presence of Christ in the Word. The phrase "The word of the Lord" subtly makes known the presence of God in the readings.[94] This is expressed ritually in every Mass. The bishop articulates it at the consecration of a church when he holds the lectionary aloft before the reading and says: "May the word of God always be heard in this place, as it unfolds the mystery of Christ before you and achieves your salvation within the Church."[95] What can be experienced with the ears is a sign of the presence of God, who makes the building his own.

The rites differentiate between the presence of God in the proclamation of the Word in general and the presence of Christ in the proclamation of the Gospel. However, SC 7 lays down the basic principle of the presence of Christ in all the readings and psalms: "He [Christ] is present in His word, since it is He himself who speaks when the holy scriptures are read in the Church. He is present, lastly, when the Church prays and sings [psalms. Original: *psallit*]."

---

91 Veronika Hoffmann, "Sakramentalität unter dem Vorzeichen des religiösen Pluralismus," *LJ* 65, no. 3 (2015): 159.

92 The first paragraph of *VD* 56 speaks of the *"sacramental* character of revelation" (italics original).

93 See Second Vatican Council, *Lumen Gentium* (November 21, 1964), 1, 9, 48.

94 See B.VII.24.1.

95 *Rites*, 2:376.

Although the Psalms remain hidden in the official English translation of this conciliar text, the Responsorial Psalm and, above all, the Liturgy of the Hours bear witness to Christ's presence in the Word. We must therefore ask how this presence of God and of Christ is to be understood more precisely.

1.1. God's Word in the Human Word: (Liturgical-)Theological Reflections

God reveals himself in such a way that he can be known by the human being. This means that "God speaks to man from within the world, taking man's own experiences as a starting point."[96] God makes use thereby of the means of communication with which the human being himself enters into relation with others: namely, language (although one must, of course, remember that this is an analogy). "The speech of revelation presupposes for its part the speech of God's creation."[97] God thus takes seriously the created reality of human beings by communicating himself and making it possible for us to experience him in the way that is in accord with human beings.

Scripture is the expression, articulated in human words, of such experiences of the encounter with God, so that God speaks in human words. Scripture was already understood within the Old Testament, through rereading, as a word addressed to human beings by God today. The most concentrated correspondence of the divine revelation to the human being occurred in the Incarnation of God, for "the more God reveals himself the more deeply does he conceal himself in men."[98] Accordingly, God no longer only spoke in a human manner;[99] now, he himself has spoken as a human being: "And the Word became flesh" (Jn 1:14).

From this point, the path that leads to the Christian Bible is close at hand.[100] Numerous patristic writers in East and West saw a trajectory from "becoming flesh" to "becoming writing." They explained the presence of God in his Word[101] by saying that the same Word who became flesh has also

---

96 Hans Urs von Balthasar, "God Speaks as Man," in Balthasar, *Verbum Caro*, vol. 1 of *Explorations in Theology* (San Francisco: Ignatius Press, [1958] 1989), 80.

97 Balthasar, 84.

98 Balthasar, 85.

99 See Augustine, *De civitate Dei* 17.6.2. (CChr.SL 48:567): "*Deus* [...] *per hominem more hominum loquitur*" (quoted in *DV* 12).

100 See Roman A. Siebenrock, "Christus-Gegenwart. Von der realen Gegenwart Christi im Wort," *BiLi* 89, no. 3 (2016): 185–84.

101 See Nußbaum, "Gegenwart Gottes/Christi," 72-77; Michael Durst, "Wortkommunion – patristische Grundlagen," *BiLi* 89, no. 3 (2016): 156-67.

become a book. Origen devoted particular attention to elaborating the parallels between "becoming flesh" and "becoming writing."[102] The letters of Scripture correspond to the body of the Incarnate Word and form a covering for the invisible Logos. "For just as there it [the Word of God] was covered with the veil of flesh, so here with the veil of the letters, so that indeed the letter is seen as flesh but the spiritual sense hiding within is perceived as divinity."[103] Origen spoke of the "embodying" (*ensōmatōsis*)[104] of the Word in Scripture as a whole: "Just as Christ came, hidden in a body [...] so too is the entire divine Scripture his embodying, especially [that] of the Old Testament."[105] Ambrose, who (as is well known) took over much of Origen's thinking, wrote: "His body is the traditions of the scriptures."[106] "The discourses of the scriptures are the garments of the Word."[107] Augustine emphasized that the *one* discourse of God is spread out in all the scriptures and that the *one* Word resounds from the mouth of many authors. He explained that the Incarnation made necessary the descent into the small details of human sounds.[108] Jerome, on the other hand, drew a distinction in his Christological exposition of the whole of Scripture between the Gospel, as the body of Christ, and the scriptures, as his teaching.[109]

Other trajectories linking the "becoming writing" and the "becoming flesh" can be seen in the divine-human encounter; in the working of the Spirit both in the Incarnation and in the inspiration of the biblical authors;[110] and in the human reception of the Word in Mary and in the sacred authors. *Dei Verbum* 13 declares: "For the words of God, expressed in human language, have been made like human discourse, just as the word of the eternal Father, when He took to Himself the flesh of human weakness, was in every

---

102 See Gögler, *Theologie des Wortes bei Origenes*, 299–364; Henri de Lubac, *History and Spirit: The Understanding of Scripture According to Origen*, trans. A. E. Nash with J. Merriell (San Francisco: Ignatius Press, 2007), 337–48, 374–84.

103 Origen, *In Lev. hom.* 1.1 (SChr 286:66): Origen, *Homilies on Leviticus*, trans. G. W. Barkley, Fathers of the Church 83 (Washington, DC: The Catholic University of America Press, 1990), 29.

104 Origen, *Comm. in Ioh.* 6.4.4 (SChr 157:150).

105 Origen, *Comm. Ser. in Mat.* 27 (GCS 38:45).

106 Ambrose, *In Luc.* 6.33 (CChr.SL 14:185).

107 Ambrose, *In Luc.* 7.13 (CChr.SL 14:219); Dassmann, *Ambrosius*, 193–223.

108 See Augustine, *Enarr. in Ps.* 103.4 1 (CChr.SL 40:1521).

109 See Jerome, *Trac. in. ps.* 147.14 (CChr.SL 78:337): "*Ergo corpus Iesu Evangelium puto; sanctas scripturas puto doctrinam eius.*"

110 On inspiration, see B.VIII.31.

way made like men." This also makes it clear that God never encounters us through Scripture otherwise than in a mediated way. This preserves both the sovereignty of God and the freedom of the human being.

If the Word of God is not proclaimed literally as in readings or psalms, but is translated in a freer form into prayers, hymns, or rites, the "process of embodying" is raised to a higher level through human formulation, composition, or staging. Here a greater knowledge of the Bible is required, if one is to recognize the Word of God in the human words.

In the various forms, therefore, the divine Word expresses itself in human language so that the Liturgy reflects or continues the incarnational principle: the human words are the "signs" that are bearers of the divine Word here,[111] pointing to it and mediating its presence. Such signs, with their significance that points beyond themselves, correspond exactly to the definition of sacramentality given above, and it is thus not surprising that *Verbum Domini* 56 speaks of the revelation of the incarnate Logos in "the 'sign' of human words and actions" that make it possible to perceive the Word of God.

The presence of Christ in the proclamation of the Gospel, which is the testimony to his earthly life, and in the New Testament readings is obvious, on the basis of the text itself. But our reflections on the Incarnation then prompt the question: How are we to conceive of the presence of Christ in the proclamation of Old Testament readings? Here, the argumentation cannot take its stand on the text itself. Even if, as we have mentioned, Origen called Scripture in its totality the body of the Logos, one must understand *logos* here rather as the divine meaning in Scripture, the meaning that finally became a human being in Christ. In his study of the theology of the Word in Origen, Rolf Gögler writes:

> Since the transcendent divine Logos proclaims himself in the biblical Word and bestows his *parousia* and allows his presence to become an event in the Word that is proclaimed, the Word of Scripture has a sacramental character as the earthly place and the sign, perceptible to the senses, of the presence of the mystery. Down to the last letter and the tiniest comma, Scripture is full of the Logos. It is 'a mountain piled high, a broad ocean of mysteries,' because its deep hidden meaning, its *logos,* is Christ [...]. Through

---

111 It is precisely in this sense that Augustine draws a distinction between the voice and the word that is communicated through the voice, and employs this distinction to interpret the relationship between John the Baptist, as the voice, and Christ, as the eternal Word (see *Sermo* 293.3; PL 38:1328-29; *Liturgy of the Hours*, 3:1487-89).

his meaning (*logos*), the biblical Word is always properly and essentially christo-logical.[112]

Other exaggerated formulations that we occasionally find in the patristic literature cannot simply be adopted today, since an identification *tout court* of Scripture, as the Word of God, with the incarnate Logos fails to do justice either to the Incarnation as a personal and bodily event, or to a differentiated way of looking at the biblical texts. This would amount to an intellectual "imposition" of Christ on these texts.[113] It is indeed true that the Liturgy interprets numerous Old Testament passages in terms of Christ, often following the exegesis in the New Testament and patristic writers. This can be seen with the Psalms[114] or certain passages in the prophets (such as Is 53 on Good Friday), but this is always a matter of individual texts.

Nevertheless, *SC* 7 makes it unmistakably clear that Christ is present in every proclamation of Scripture.[115] The tension is resolved when one combines the reflections on the Incarnation with those on the Paschal Mystery of Christ and on the total liturgical context, since it is not primarily the text or its proclamation that makes Christ present. Rather, the starting point must be the risen Christ, who himself proclaimed the Law, the Prophets, and the Psalms (that is to say, the whole of Scripture) to the disciples on the road to Emmaus,[116] thereby making it his own Word. The textual-substantial level ("*what* referred *to* him in all the scriptures")[117] is complemented by the personal level of the Christ who speaks and expounds the scriptures. As the risen Lord, who is himself outside time and therefore present "today," he is the principal actor in the Liturgy, and thus he is present and active in the act of proclamation too. In the proclamation, the Church, as his Body, lends him (so to speak) its voice, specifically through human readers, but it is Christ

---

112 Gögler, *Theologie des Wortes bei Origenes*, 269–70. Quotation from Origen, *Hom. in Gen.* 91 (*GCS* 29:86; *Homilies on Genesis and Exodus*, 148).

113 One can indeed argue theologically on the basis of the *logos asarkos* (see 1 Cor 10:4; Jn 1:1–13), but a simple identification of Scripture, as the Word of God, with Christ remains problematic.

114 See A.II.

115 The suggestion was made at the Council that the words "especially when the Gospel is proclaimed" should be inserted, but this was not accepted. On the history of the redaction of *SC* 7, see Eisenbach, *Gegenwart Christi*, 152–91, 497–98. In comparison to the corresponding text in the encyclical *Mediator Dei*, 20 of Pius XII (November 20, 1947; *AAS* 39 [1947]: 528), the presence of Christ in the Word was an innovation.

116 See Lk 24:44.

117 Lk 24:27.

himself who proclaims the Word of God. This takes seriously the fact that the words of the Old Testament reading are not originally his own words. But the fact that he makes these words his own and proclaims them on the road to Emmaus entails logically that he is present in the whole of Scripture. It is because he speaks that the whole of Scripture becomes relevant to us today. This argument confirms the affirmation of *SC* 7, although it is not necessary to hear Christ speaking out of the Old Testament reading too. The more obvious way is to hear it as the Word of the Father.

Let us add some information from the history of the redaction of *SC* 7. There was disagreement about whether the presence of Christ should be expanded through the addition "*et explicantur*" to include the homily as well. But the Council Fathers decided to delete these words, because Christ does not speak in the same way in the homily as when Scripture itself is read.[118] However, the encyclical *Mysterium fidei* (1965),[119] the *GILM*,[120] and even more clearly the *Homiletic Directory* speak of the presence of Christ in the homily.[121] This makes it very clear that the presence of Christ cannot depend on the spoken text itself. Rather, Christ, who is already present, wishes to address people today by means of the preacher's words.[122] By analogy, in the case of the words of Scripture, therefore, the wording of the text, which the human authors themselves formulated with the assistance of the Spirit, does not generate the presence of Christ, but rather bears witness to this presence.

At the same time, we cannot ignore the proclaimed text itself, which is canonical in the form that has been handed down to us. In the case of Baptism, the sacrament is indeed brought about not by the water, but by

---

118 Francisco Gil Hellín, *Constitutio de sacra liturgia, Sacrosanctum concilium. Concilii Vaticani II synopsis in ordinem redigens schemata cum relationibus necnon patrum orationes atque animadversiones* (Vatican City: Libreria Editrice Vaticana, 2003), 32–33.

119 See Paul VI, *Mysterium fidei*. Encyclical on the Holy Eucharist (September 3, 1965), 36: "In still another very genuine way, He is present in the Church as she preaches, since the Gospel which she proclaims is the word of God, and it is only in the name of Christ, the Incarnate Word of God, and by His authority and with His help that it is preached."

120 *GILM*, 24 says about the homily: "Christ himself is always present and active in the preaching of his Church." The text refers to documents that speak of the presence of Christ in proclamation outside the Liturgy: the missionary decree of Vatican II, *Ad gentes* (December 7, 1965), 9; Paul VI, *Mysterium fidei*, 36; Paul VI, Apostolic Exhortation *Evangelii nuntiandi* (December 8, 1975), 43.

121 See *Homiletic Directory*, 4: "Christ is present [...] in the preaching of his minister, through whom the same Lord who spoke long ago in the synagogue at Nazareth now instructs his people."

122 See the words of Jesus when he sends out the seventy-two disciples: "Whoever listens to you listens to me" (Lk 10:16).

Christ[123]—and yet, we cannot do without the water. Similarly, the sacramentality of the Word demands respect for the text. Its significance is generated by revelation and by the Incarnation. The kiss and the other signs of reverence for the Gospel book, as well as the worthy design of the lectionary, are all expressions of this respect and of the awareness of the sacramentality of the Word.

The theology of icons can help to illustrate the character of the text as a pointer to the presence of God/Christ. Alexander Schmemann calls the Gospel book "a verbal icon of Christ's manifestation to and presence among us. Above all, it is an icon of his resurrection."[124] He explains this by saying that the same veneration is paid through kiss and incense to the Gospel book as to an icon, and that it is used as a book (and not as a text to be proclaimed) in the Byzantine liturgy at the Anointing of the Sick and the Ordination of a Bishop. In particular, the Gospel book announces the appearing of the risen Lord in the Gospel procession of the Divine Liturgy, when it is carried through the holy doors.[125] Louis-Marie Chauvet speaks more generally of Scripture as an icon of God.[126] Since the icons are "windows" onto the spiritual world, and it is believed that the one depicted on them "shines through" and is present in a personal-relational manner,[127] the icon simultaneously expresses closeness and relatedness, presence and transcendence. The comparison with the icon shows that Scripture, as testimony to revelation, contains that to which it bears witness, but that the divine Word cannot be tied down in a reified manner in the book. "It is, rather, a *being in* that is at the same time linked to a *being above,* and in both of these, the Word of God always remains that which towers above Scripture and transcends it, summoning us again and again to rise up into its mystery."[128]

---

123 See *SC* 7.

124 Alexander Schmemann, *The Eucharist: Sacrament of the Kingdom* (Crestwood, NY: St. Vladimir's Seminary Press, 1988), 71.

125 See Schmemann, 71.

126 See Chauvet, *Symbol and Sacrament*, 217–18. He uses the metaphor of the letter as the "'tabernacle' of the Word" (215).

127 See Christoph Schönborn, *God's Human Face: The Christ-Icon* (San Francisco: Ignatius Press, 1995), 225: "The original is truly present in the icon, but this presence is entirely based on a relationship to a person."

128 Leo Scheffczyk, "Die Heilige Schrift – Wort Gottes und der Kirche," *IKaZ* 30, no. 1 (2001): 53.

1.2. The Analogy to the Presence of Christ in the Eucharist

Verbum Domini 56 presents a second reason for the sacramentality of the Word:

> The sacramentality of the Word can thus be understood by analogy with the real presence of Christ under the appearances of the consecrated bread and wine. By approaching the altar and partaking in the Eucharistic banquet we truly share in the body and blood of Christ. The proclamation of God's word at the celebration entails an acknowledgment that Christ himself is present, that he speaks to us, and that he wishes to be heard. [...] Christ, truly present under the species of bread and wine, is analogously present in the word proclaimed in the Liturgy.

These words suggest that transubstantiation, the model of understanding that was declared to be binding in the case of the Eucharist,[129] should be transferred by analogy to the presence of Christ in the Word. Lothar Lies (1940-2008) expanded the differentiation between the real and the actual presence (Johannes Betz, 1914-1984) to speak of a verbal presence.[130] He understands "Real Presence" in the traditional manner as the presence of Christ in the eucharistic species, and "actual presence" as the presence in action, that is, as the activity of the Christ who is personally present. This activity is mediated by human actions (of the priest or of another person).[131] Lies explains the verbal presence—the presence of Christ in the scriptural readings and in the central words of the sacramental celebrations—by comparing it to the Eucharist:

> When Jesus takes up a profane human word and uses it, he can "transform" this profane-human word to a word that is his own or that speaks about him. He is contained in this word. The word contains his being. We can say that after this transformation, the phonetic sound and the meaning expressed therein are only the accidental envelope, the form, as this is understood, in the proper sense, in the case of the sacramental Eucharist."[132]

---

129 See *DH* 1651–52; see *DH* 1642.

130 See Lothar Lies, "Verbalpräsenz – Aktualpräsenz – Realpräsenz. Versuch einer systematischen Begriffsbestimmung," in *Praesentia Christi* (FS Johannes Betz), ed. Lies (Düsseldorf: Patmos, 1984), 79-100; reprint: Lies, *Mysterium fidei. Annäherungen an das Geheimnis der Eucharistie* (Würzburg: Echter, 2005), 83-107.

131 See Lies, "Verbalpräsenz," 79-84, esp. 83, 91, 96, etc.

132 Lies, 93-94. [Note: The words *wandeln/Wandlung*, translated here as "transform/transformation," are the standard terms in German for the consecration of bread and wine, whereby they become the body and blood of Christ.]

He summarizes as follows: "In the *verbal presence,* Christ transforms our human word into his Word; at the same time, he himself becomes the 'substance' (!) of the word-event, so that our human speaking only represents the accidents. Our word-event not only contains Christ; it is, of its essence, the entire Christ."[133]

With regard to the objective presence, this makes it clear that Christ is not more or less really present in the Word than in the Eucharist, because one cannot conceive of personal presence in a fragmented manner, as if he were present in part or in a varying "concentration." That would be a contradiction in terms. However, a personal presence (even among human beings) demands that the individual subject perceive and receive this presence, and there are thus different degrees in the consciousness of the reality.[134] This makes the *participatio actuosa* in the proclamation of the Word an essential act, if Christ's presence in the Word is to be received.[135] In the reflections on the verbal presence, we are dealing (as in the case of transubstantiation) with a model of understanding. Christ's presence in the Word is to be understood as analogous to the real presence in the Eucharist, but it is not immediately dependent on his presence in the eucharistic species. Its origin lies in the Word of God, or in Christ himself, who communicates himself in the Word. Accordingly, "Scripture is sacramental not by derivation but by essence."[136] The concept of analogy employed in *Verbum Domini* 56, which has been defined as a similarity in the context of a greater dissimilarity,[137] makes it plain that one may not construct here any competition between the presence of Christ in the Word and his presence in the Eucharist. On the contrary, these are related to each other, as we shall discuss below.[138]

2. THE DIALOGICAL EVENT OF ENCOUNTER IN THE WORD

Articles 21 and 25 of *Dei Verbum,* which pay particular attention to the Liturgy, emphasize that God comes to meet human beings in the Liturgy and "speaks with them." The Council quotes the words of Ambrose: "We speak

---

133 Lies, 97 (italics original).

134 See Lies, 95, 98.

135 See B.IX.33.

136 Chauvet, *Symbol and Sacrament,* 213.

137 See *DH* 806.

138 See B.VIII.29.

to Him when we pray; we hear Him when we read the divine saying."[139] In keeping with the fundamentally dialogical character of the Liturgy, Scripture functions here as the revelation of God that goes forth here and now, and also as the basis of the human response. We shall look at this in greater detail in two subchapters. It is precisely in this divine-human event of encounter that we see the sacramentality of the Word and the link to the Incarnation: the divine-human encounter that takes place in the Liturgy has experienced its deepest union in the Incarnation of God in Jesus Christ.

2.1. The Event of Revelation

When we speak of Scripture in the Liturgy as an event of revelation here and now, this is a continuation of what Scripture itself is, since it is the testimony to the revelation that came forth from God and of the human endeavor to understand God.[140] "Revelation" does not mean merely a one-sided imparting of knowledge or communication of truths. It is, rather, God's self-communication, and includes the reception by the human being. Accordingly, it must be understood historically and dialogically, as the event of an encounter. This agrees with the principle that Scripture is employed in the Liturgy not only to impart information; rather, it aims to reach the human being today in an anamnesis that makes him or her a contemporary of God's salvific action.[141] Scripture can be understood as the path of a developing struggle to understand,[142] the path on which revelation has taken place, and this path of understanding continues in liturgy. Liturgy does more than merely create a hermeneutical framework for the understanding of individual pericopes.[143] In this perspective, liturgy is itself the realization of this being *en route* with the living Word in which God encounters the human being and communicates himself, in order that he may be received by the human being.

Scripture itself is not already revelation but is rather the testimony to revelation that came into being over the course of history and that puts

---

139 Ambrose, *De officiis ministrorum* 1.20.88 (*PL* 16:50), quoted in *DV* 25 and *GILH*, 56.

140 See Joseph Ratzinger/Benedict XVI, *In the Beginning: A Catholic Understanding of the Story of Creation and the Fall*, trans. B. Ramsey (Grand Rapids, MI: Eerdmans, 1995), 9: "The Bible is thus the story of God's struggle with human beings to make himself understandable to them over the course of time; but it is also the story of their struggle to seize hold of God over the course of time."

141 See B.VIII.27.

142 See Ratzinger, *In the Beginning*, 9.

143 See B.VII.23.

revelation into writing. What happens in the Liturgy is the inverse process, whereby the written Word that is proclaimed becomes once again a Word that goes forth here and now and addresses human beings. It becomes once again a "*viva vox.*"[144] In the power of the Spirit of God,[145] Scripture can once again become an event of revelation. This means that it is "not simply, as a dead historical book, already God's 'revelation,' which would thus be accessible to, and 'at the disposal' of, every reader (even the profane reader). Rather, it is only in the hands of the living Church in its proclamation that Scripture becomes revelation."[146] For this, the Church's worship, permeated by the Bible, is the privileged *locus.*

The rites framing the proclamation of Scripture[147] and other liturgical texts demonstrate unequivocally that God/Christ is speaking. For example, the antiphon at the invitatory on the feasts of the evangelists Mark and Luke is: "Come, let us worship the Lord who speaks to us through the Gospel."[148] The *GILM* refers to the metaphor employed by Augustine: "The Gospel is the mouth of Christ. He is seated at the right hand of the Father, yet continues to speak on earth."[149] John Chrysostom says explicitly of the readings in the Liturgy: "For when the reader stands up and says, 'Thus says the Lord,' when the deacon stands up and orders everyone to be silent, this is not done in order to honor the one who reads, but to honor him who speaks to everyone through the reader's mouth."[150]

The liturgical tradition has handed on testimonies of this kind, for example, in the influential *Pontificale Romano-Germanicum* (ca. 950): "As the gospel is read Christ speaks with his own mouth to the people ...; the gospel resounds in the church as though Christ himself were speaking to

---

144 See Pontifical Biblical Commission, *Interpretation of the Bible*, 37: "Written text becomes thus living word."

145 See B.VIII.31.

146 Joseph Ratzinger, "Offenbarung und Heilsgeschichte nach der Lehre des heiligen Bonaventura," in Ratzinger, *Offenbarungsverständnis und Geschichtstheologie Bonaventuras. Habilitationsschrift und Bonaventura-Studien,* JRGS 2 (Freiburg/Br.: Herder, 2009), 66–67.

147 See B.VII.24.1.

148 See *Liturgy of the Hours* 3:1782; 4:1492.

149 Augustine, *Sermo* 85.1 (*PL* 38:520), quoted in *GILM*, 4 n. 10. See Augustine, *In Ioh.* 30.1 (CChr.SL 36:289).

150 Chrysostom, *Hom. in 2 Thess.* 3.4 (*PG* 62:484). He continues: "We are only servants; what we proclaim is not our word, but God's Word. Day by day, letters are read aloud that come from heaven." Further texts in Chrysostom: Durst, "Wortkommunion," 159, and esp. Kaczynski, *Wort Gottes bei Chrysostomus,* 34–35.

them."[151] A similar idea can be found in William Durandus' commentary on the Liturgy.[152] There are also early references to God's speaking through the preacher, e.g., in the *Apostolic Tradition*: "If, however, there is an instruction on the Word of God, everyone should prefer to go there because they truly believe that it is God whom they hear in the instructor."[153] This, of course, does not in any way affect the Catholic understanding that the reading from Scripture, as the inspired Word of God, takes precedence over the homily; the liturgical staging shows this clearly. Ultimately, these testimonies are based on the words of Christ himself, which can also be understood with regard to the Liturgy as an event of revelation: "Whoever listens to you listens to me" (Lk 10:16).

The varied use of Scripture that we have seen in Part A shows that the event of revelation in the liturgy is not restricted exclusively to the biblical readings, although these are, of course, particularly suited to this. The Responsorial Psalm too,[154] as a further Old Testament reading (of a special kind) can take on the character of a proclamation that continues the reading(s). But even those Responsorial Psalms that serve more as a meditation or response do justice to the fact that the preceding reading needs a resonance space if it is to be received.

In the Liturgy of the Hours, where the Psalms are a central, independent element, they can be interpreted as an event of revelation, precisely in their oscillation between reading and prayer.[155] When one hears or repeats these words in meditative prayer in the Liturgy, and makes them one's own, a divine-human encounter again takes place on the basis of Scripture. Through their closeness to human life, the Psalms confront the present-day situation of the human being with the collective (prayer-) experience of Israel and of the Church, thereby opening the door to an encounter with God that can bear in itself the character of revelation. It is significant that the Liturgy of the Hours traditionally begins with the invitatory Ps 95 (94), which is a summons to praise that also contains the programmatic verse: "*Today*, listen to the voice of the Lord." Although these words primarily intend to speak of a basic attitude for the new day, the hearing of God's voice certainly also refers to the praying of the Liturgy of the Hours, which begins with the invitatory.

---

151 See *PRG* 99, 18 (Vogel – Elze 1, 334); quoted in *GILM*, 4, n. 10.

152 Durandus, *Rationale divinorum officiorum* 4.24.1 (CChr.CM 140:341).

153 *Apostolic Tradition*, 41 (FontC 1:298; WEC 1:212; see Bradshaw, *Apostolic Tradition*, 194). See also *Didache* 4.1 (FontC 1:109; WEC 1:35).

154 See A.II.8.1.

155 See A.II.9.1.

The Communion antiphon can also been seen as an element in a dialogical event of encounter or revelation (as self-communication), especially when a word directly spoken by Jesus—perhaps recurring as a refrain to the Communion chant—functions as a prompt for meditation in the personal dialogue.[156]

2.2. The Response of the Human Being

In the previous subsection, God's self-communication stood in the foreground. We shall now look at the human side of this dialogical encounter, which encompasses both the response *with* Scripture and the response *to* Scripture. The classical texts here are the Responsorial Psalms that serve as a reaction to the reading (although the concept, which is a translation of *psalmus responsorius,* comes not from its character as a response to the reading, but from the responsorial repetition of the antiphon).[157] Some psalms (or at least some verses) are addressed in the Liturgy of the Hours as a prayer to God. Praying with Scripture includes the canticles and the occasional doxological short readings. Silence and recollection are also important, in order that the Word may "echo," and a conversation between God and the human being may come about. In the apt words of Augustine, "*Verbo crescente, verba deficiunt*"[158] ("When the Word [of God] increases, the words [of men] cease").

In addition to numerous hymns, almost all the liturgical prayers and orations— especially the pericope orations[159] or the orations after the Old Testament readings at the Easter Vigil—show how a prayer arises out of Scripture as an answer. These orations directly illustrate the well-known schema "reading—(psalm-) chant—prayer" (Jungmann),[160] which cannot indeed claim validity in this fundamental quality, as the history of liturgy shows,[161] but which is certainly essential in terms of the theology of liturgy, as SC 33 underlines: "For in the Liturgy God speaks to His people and Christ is still proclaiming His gospel. And the people reply to God both by song and prayer."

---

156 See A.IV.15.

157 See A.II.7.

158 *VD* 66; see Augustine, *Sermo* 288.5 (*PL* 38:1307): "*Quia deficiunt voces crescente verbo.*"

159 See A.III.12.3.

160 See Jungmann, *Liturgy of the Word.*

161 See Meßner, *Einführung,* 184.

There is a theological reason why the answer in prayer *to* Scripture is made *with* Scripture. The human speaking in the Liturgy finds its orientation in God's "speaking" and in his revelation; it answers him *inter alia* with his own words. By drawing from Scripture in its anamnetic-epicletic prayers, the Liturgy becomes the "teacher" of communal and personal prayer.[162]

Naturally, this answer ought not to remain in the context of worship. It must flow into life—and this is the clearest sign of the performative power of the Word.

3. THE PERFORMATIVE CHARACTER OF SCRIPTURE

According to *Verbum Domini* 53 and 56, the sacramentality of Scripture is based on the "performative character" of God's Word. The efficacy of the Word is thus a sign of its sacramentality, and *vice versa*. As "the sacrament is *signum efficax,* so too the Word is *verbum efficax.*"[163]

Verbum Domini takes up here a concept from the speech act theory elaborated by the British philosopher John Langshaw Austin (1911–1960).[164] This essentially states that a speech act contains an immediate consequence of the utterance ("perlocution") and brings about this consequence performatively. But while the concept is modern, the matter itself is already established in Scripture: from the first creation narrative, the efficacy of the Word of God is underlined by means of the Hebrew *dabar*.[165] We often find the conviction that the Word from God's mouth does not return to him empty, but brings about what he wishes and achieves what it was sent out to do (Is 55:11), since it is alive and powerful (Heb 4:12). The Word of his grace has the power to "build you up and give you the inheritance among all who are consecrated" (Acts 20:32). When it is received as the Word of God, it is "at work" in the believers (1 Thes 2:13). Christ's words are "spirit and life"; they are "words of eternal life" (Jn 6:63, 68). A fundamental conviction in the ancient hermeneutics of the Bible was that "the biblical Word has a special power to make itself heard and assert the intended meaning."[166] *Verbum Domini* 53

---

162 On biblical-liturgical spirituality, see B.IX.36.

163 Kasper, "Wort und Sakrament," 280.

164 See John L. Austin, *How to Do Things with Words: The William James Lectures delivered at Harvard University in 1955* (Oxford: Clarendon Press, 1962).

165 See *VD* 53; John 1:3: "All things came to be through the Word, and without the Word nothing came to be."

166 Marschies, "Liturgisches Lesen," 87. Ambrose, *De Noe* 19.70 (CSEL 32/1:464) can serve as an example: "*Evangelium legitur, virtus exit de sermone caelesti*" ("When the Gospel is read, virtue comes forth from heavenly discourse").

sums up: "In salvation history there is no separation between what God says and what he does." This leads over to the Liturgy:

> In the liturgical action too, we encounter his word which accomplishes what it says. By educating the People of God to discover the performative character of God's Word in the Liturgy, we will help them to recognize his activity in salvation history and in their individual lives.

Thus, *Verbum Domini* 53 places these considerations in the context of the celebrations of the sacraments, mentioning specifically the scriptural readings.[167] In speaking of the "unity between gesture and word," it alludes to the central words in the narrower sense, but doubtless also to the prayers that are permeated by Scripture. In the broader context of *Verbum Domini* 53, we should think of both Scripture in the Liturgy as a whole and (especially in view of the final sentence quoted above) of the effect on people's lives of the liturgical use of Scripture. Here, however, we must ask how we are to understand the affirmation that the Word brings about what it says. This may look at first sight like an automatism, but this idea breaks down as soon as the proclamation of salvation is addressed to a concrete situation of suffering, since the discrepancy is too obvious. What, then, does the "performative character" more precisely mean?

Since the Word of God is not a "magical formula," it goes without saying that if it is to be effective, it must be received. The narratives of Jesus' miracles, which mostly have faith as a precondition, show that faith is the presupposition for God's activity.[168] A sacrament presupposes (and strengthens) faith,[169] and the same is true of the Word of God, which (as Augustine put it) is effective "not because it is uttered, but because it is believed."[170] But even where it is received with faith, the proclamation of a healing of the sick certainly does not bring about automatically what the biblical text describes.

A first clarification can be sought in the context of the anamnesis as a making present of the saving action of God/Christ, since here too, we are not to suppose that the biblical situation is duplicated (so to speak) in the contemporary situation and occurs in the same way today as in the past. Rather, it is God's saving care that takes place anew.[171] Most importantly, the

---

167 See A.I.4.

168 See, e.g., Mt 8:13; 15:28; Mk 5:34 par.; 10:52 par.; Lk 7:50; 17:19.

169 See *SC* 59.

170 Augustine, *Trac. in Ioh.* 80.3 with reference to the efficacy of the word at the blessing of the baptismal water (CChr.SL 36:529).

171 See B.VIII.27.2 with the quotation from Augustine; *GILM*, 4.

experience of salvation is always subject to the eschatological reservation, that is, it occurs in the tension between the "already" and the "not yet" of the kingdom of God. The Lord whose presence makes possible the performativity of the Word is at work in the Liturgy—but at the same time, liturgy lives in an eschatological tension towards the full realization.[172]

After having demarcated what the performative character of the Word does not mean, let us now follow the approach of a liturgical theology and look for positive answers supplied by the celebration of the Liturgy itself.

Verbum Domini 53 underlines the effectiveness of the Word in general with reference to the celebration of the sacraments, for it is in fact here that we see with especial clarity that the Church continues the action of Christ that is attested in the Bible (or that he himself acts through the Church) when, for example, the commission to the disciples (Mt 28) is carried out at a baptism. The efficacy of the Word, which is affirmed (for example) in the Byzantine blessing for the deacon when he is to read,[173] or in the words accompanying the handing over of the lectionary at the commissioning of lectors,[174] can be described in several possible complementary "effects."

One first effect is the wakening and deepening of faith. The Liturgy continues what the evangelists already declared to be one goal in their writing ("that you may believe";[175] "that you may realize the certainty of the teachings you have received").[176] It is well known that Paul emphasizes that faith comes from hearing and presupposes the proclamation.[177] In its very sequence—"you may soon receive his word with your ears and profess the faith with your lips"[178]—and the touching first of the ears and then of the mouth, the Ephphetha rite demonstrates the priority of hearing, which is meant to awaken faith. In the initiation of adults, when the creed is handed over to the catechumen, this is done, not by the illustrative rite of giving him

---

172 See also Zerfaß, *Hermeneutik*, 69.

173 See Galadza, *Divine Liturgy*, 126: "[…] that you proclaim the Good News with great power [δυνάμει πολλῇ, Herman and Permiakov, *Hieratikon*, 117]." See B.VII.24.1.2.

174 See *Rites*, 2:106: "Take this book of holy Scripture and be faithful in handing on the word of God, so that it may grow strong in the hearts of his people."

175 Jn 20:21.

176 Lk 1:4.

177 See Rom 10:14–17.

178 *The Order of Baptism of Children. English Translation according to the Second Typical Edition. For Use in the Dioceses of the United States of America* […] (Washington, DC: United States Conference of Catholic Bishops, 2020), 34.

or her a beautifully crafted text of the creed, but by the community's act of declaring the confession of faith.[179]

The Word of God has a catechetical function: it communicates basic knowledge of the faith.[180] But the performative power of the Word surpasses a mere knowledge. Various blessings for the reader emphasize that the Word of God enlightens and consoles the believers and makes them wise.[181] It is a question of an integral edification through the Word.

Another important effect of the Word is the sanctification of the human being. Other blessings for the reader ask that the Word may be profitable for salvation, or that God may let his mercy flow down upon the reader and the hearers.[182] The gesture of blessing with the Gospel book expresses even more clearly the request that the word just proclaimed is to become a blessing through Christ.[183] *Verbum Domini* emphasizes the proclamation of Scripture when a blessing is celebrated, because it "derives its meaning and effectiveness from God's word that is proclaimed."[184] The saving effect is also mentioned at the beginning of the Liturgy of the Word at the consecration of a church: "May the word of God always be heard in this place, as it [...] achieves your salvation within the Church."[185] The power of the Word to impart blessing is also indicated by the solemn blessing and the prayers over the people in the Missal, since these are frequently marked by biblical language, even in the epicletic clauses.[186]

GILM 3 declares emphatically: "the liturgical celebration, based primarily on the word of God and sustained by it, becomes a new event and enriches the word itself with new meaning and power." This formulation indicates that the performative power of the liturgical anamnesis has its origin in God's saving deeds.[187] In particular, the *General Introduction to the Liturgy of the Hours* speaks explicitly of human sanctification as one effect of the Word of God:

---

179 See *Rites*, 1:120–22.

180 See B.VIII.26.a.

181 See B.VII.24.1.

182 See B.VII.23.1.

183 See B.VII.24.1.2.

184 *VD* 63.

185 See *Rites*, 2:376.

186 See *Missal*, 674–87.

187 Se B.VIII.27.

The sanctification of man and the worship of God is achieved in the Liturgy of the Hours by the setting up of a dialogue between God and man, so that "God speaks to his people ... and the people reply to God both by song and by prayer." The saving word of God has great importance in the Liturgy of the Hours, and should be of enormous spiritual benefit for those taking part.[188]

The sanctification thus takes place through the dialogue with God, whose saving Word is literally the foundation of sanctification. The *Introduction* rightly goes on to emphasize the readings, psalms, prayers, and hymns (*SC* 24), because these have a sanctifying effect. A healing[189] or "therapeutic" effect of the Word of God has been linked especially to the Psalms.[190] For example, Ambrose sees Scripture as a medicine against the illnesses of the soul.[191] In principle, the Psalms (especially in the Liturgy of the Hours) take us into the dynamic of the praise of God that is a specific characteristic of the Psalter, and thus lead to God, who brings about sanctification.

This brings us to a second aspect of the performative character of Scripture, namely, its forgiveness of sins. At the end of the proclamation of the Gospel in the Roman rite, the deacon (or priest) prays: "*Per evangelica dicta deleantur nostra delicta*" ("Through the words of the Gospel may our sins be wiped away"[192]). This preserves the conviction that hearing God's Word forgives sins. Although this can be traced back to Jesus' words, "You are already clean through the word that I have spoken to you" (Jn 15:3),[193] there is scarcely any consciousness of this among believers. The power to forgive sins draws attention to the sacramentality of the Word. John Chrysostom understood the classic evening text, Psalm 141 (140), in Vespers (and psalmody in general)

---

188 *GILH*, 4.

189 *VD* 61 underlines "the healing power of the word of God" at the Anointing of the Sick.

190 See Athanasius, *Letter to Marcellinus*, 10 (Gregg, *Athanasius*, 108-09). On Augustine, see Hermann Josef Sieben, "Der Psalter und die Bekehrung der voces und affectus. Zu Augustinus, Conf. IX,4,7-and X,33,49-50," in *"Manna in deserto". Studien zum Schriftgebrauch der Kirchenväter*, ed. Sieben, Edition Cardo 92 (Cologne: Patristisches Zentrum Koinonia-Oriens, 2002), 243-66; Kaczynski, *Wort Gottes bei Chrysostomus*, 104.

191 See Ambrose, *In Ps. 37,7* (CSEL 64:141): "*praeceptis salutaribus repleuit diuinarum seriem scripturarum, quibus infirmitas animae sanaretur*" ("He filled the divine series of scriptures with salutary precepts, by which the infirmity of the soul could be healed").

192 *Missal*, 525.

193 [A literal translation.] See also Eph 5:26.

in this sense, as a sacrament that canceled the sins of the day.[194] For the same reason, Ps 51 (50) became the daily morning psalm, in order that the confession with the words of David might bring about the forgiveness of one's own sins.[195] This idea remains valid even today, when this psalm is prayed every Friday at Lauds, or is prayed as the Responsorial Psalm on Ash Wednesday. Precisely the Ash Wednesday liturgy makes it clear that the Word of God, which is proclaimed in the readings and expounded in the sermon, calls to repentance. Since the liturgical reform, the blessing and distribution of the ashes *follow* the proclamation, in order to show that the repentance is made possible by the summons of the Lord.

One important effect of the Word of God relates to the life of the believers, who "should be instructed by God's word" (*SC* 48), since the proclamation aims at the reception of the Word, which is complete only when it flows into daily living (see Jas 1:22). The homily has an essential task here. According to *Evangelii gaudium,* it "possesses a quasi-sacramental character" as "heart-to-heart communication" between the Lord and his people.[196]

Some readings on saints' days can illustrate the performativity of Scripture, since they were often chosen to fit the *vita,* thereby attesting the unity between Word and life.[197] For example, one who knows the *vita* of Saint Antony the Great (ca. 251–356) and hears Mt 19:16–26 on his feast will remember that Antony heard precisely this Gospel, identified with the rich young man, and at once put the Gospel into practice.[198] When we celebrate the saints, we are reminded again and again of the effectiveness of the Word. The calling of Antony is an extraordinary example; the less spectacular effects are much more common.

Rituals show this too. For example, the Washing of the Feet in the Roman rite is already staged as an action of discipleship, as a response to the Gospel. This action begins in the Liturgy, but it aims at daily living: it is a ritual

194 See Buchinger, "Psalmodie als Sakrament. Johannes Chrysostomus über den täglichen Abendpsalm 140(141)," in Franz und Zerfaß, *Wort des lebendigen Gottes,* esp. 223, 226, 232; Kaczynski, *Wort Gottes bei Chrysostomus,* 103, 253-57. On Ambrose, see Schmitz, *Gottesdienst Mailand,* 347.

195 On the forgiveness of sins in the Liturgy of the Hours (as a form of the *paenitentia quotidiana*), see Meßner, "Feiern der Umkehr und Versöhnung [...]," in Meßner and Kaczynski, *Sakramentliche Feiern I/2,* 78-80.

196 Francis, *Evangelii gaudium,* 142. See *Homiletic Directory,* 4: "Given its liturgical nature, the homily also possesses a sacramental significance."

197 See A.I.3.3.

198 See Athanasius, *Vita Antonii* 2-3 (Gregg, *Athanasius,* 31–32); *VD* 48.

anticipation of what ought to be carried out in our life.[199] This applies even more fundamentally to the Eucharist as the celebration of Christ's Paschal Mystery, which not only is to be made present in the Liturgy but ought also to mark the lives of the baptized. The effect of the Word of God on our life is the clearest sign of its performative power and sacramentality.

---

199 See A.V.17.1.

CHAPTER 29

Reciprocal Relatedness of Word and Sacrament/Eucharist

The preceding chapter has highlighted the sacramentality of the Word. We now take up the question of the relationship between Word and sacrament, and especially between Word and Eucharist. Once again, our starting point is the Liturgy.

1. WORD AND SACRAMENT

Part A has used the Anointing of the Sick[200] as an example to illustrate that the Church anamnetically addresses to the sick person the salvation attested in the pericopes. What the Bible has recorded in words can become an experience in the celebration of the Liturgy,[201] when the one who receives the sacrament understands him/herself as the addressee of Christ's saving action (for example, through identification with persons in Scripture, such as a sick person).[202]

Similarly, Acts 2 is used in the celebration of Confirmation, because the same Spirit who descended on the apostles at that time is now to strengthen the candidates for Confirmation. If the pericope of the wedding feast at Cana (Jn 2:1–11) is read at the celebration of Matrimony, it gives the assurance that if Christ is invited to do so, he will help the bridal couple just as he once did at Cana. In the sacramental celebration, therefore, the Scripture is actualized and concretized in relation to those who receive the sacrament (and to

200 See A.I.4.

201 See B.VIII.30.2.

202 See B.IX.34.

those who participate in the act of worship). The proclamation opens up the salvation-historical sphere for the sacramental event.

This makes it clear, theologically, that the Word of God is (so to speak) the gift that precedes faith.[203] God takes the initiative and addresses the human being. Sacraments are indeed entrusted to the Church in order that it may communicate them. But they are always the gift of God, who turns to us *gratis*, without any human merits: they are first of all his gift. But God demands the response of faith on the part of human beings, in order that a sphere may arise in which he can work in them. This can be seen in the very structure of the sacramental celebrations, where the reading of Scripture illustrates God's preceding act of speaking to us. This reading helps to prepare for the reception of the sacrament; it deepens the faith that is the presupposition of the fruitfulness of the sacrament;[204] and it promotes conscious participation in the celebration. Numerous scriptural texts also point beyond the liturgical action, by showing how those who have received the gift in the sacrament ought to live.[205]

The reading of the Word of God is followed by the celebration of the sacrament in the narrower sense, which is prayer in word and symbolic action. The Church's response to the Word is thus, on the one hand, verbal. The sacramental prayers are profoundly influenced by the Bible and have an anamnetic-epicletic orientation. As we have shown in detail in the case of the Ordination prayer for a bishop,[206] the Church's celebration is rooted in God's saving action, which began with Israel, moved towards its high point in Christ, and is now requested in prayer. We find the same principle in the celebrations of the other sacraments. For example, when the blessing and invocation of God over baptismal water contains three Old Testament and three New Testament paradigms, this is done, not primarily in order to link the specific baptism to biblical events, but rather in order to apply these events to the catechumen, whether they have already been realized in the administration of the sacrament (e.g., forgiveness and a new beginning), or

---

203 See Jürgen Bärsch, "Sakramentenliturgie nach dem Zweiten Vatikanischen Konzil. Anmerkungen und Beobachtungen zu Theologie und Praxis anlässlich des Motu proprio 'Summorum Pontificum' Papst Benedikts XVI. (2007)," in *Weltoffen aus Treue. Studientag zum Zweiten Vatikanischen Konzil*, ed. C. Böttigheimer and E. Naab, Extemporalia 22 (St. Ottilien: EOS-Verlag, 2009), 163–208, at 188–90.

204 See *SC* 59: "They not only presuppose faith, but by words and objects they also nourish, strengthen, and express it; that is why they are called 'sacraments of faith.'"

205 See Nübold, *Schriftlesungen der Sakramente*, 131–32.

206 See A.III.11.

whether they are presented in an eschatological perspective ("rise again to life with him").

On the other hand, when the Church responds to the scriptural reading in the form of a symbolic action, this too has its foundation in Scripture. The symbolic action complements the sacramental prayer, since what is expressed verbally in the prayer is carried out in the symbolic action (e.g., in the rite of water) in a manner perceptible to the senses. At the same time, it is only through the sacramental prayer, or through the Word of God, that the ritual event receives its meaning. God's biblical saving action is continued anamnetically-epicletically into the here and now.

The Word of God is not only proclaimed as a reading in the Liturgy of the Word. It also plays a central role in the celebration of the sacrament in the narrow sense.[207] Because the Word is itself sacramental, and the sacrament is always also verbal, the classical term "Word and sacrament" is (at the very least) insufficiently precise since an antithesis is inappropriate here. It must not be understood merely in the sense of a sequence of two sections, but rather, by emphasizing the "and," as a unity of mutual relatedness and compenetration.[208]

2. WORD AND EUCHARIST

The intimate relationship between Word and Eucharist is already described in the Emmaus pericope (Lk 24:13–35) and in Jesus' discourse about the Bread of Life (Jn 6:22–59).[209] The disciples recognized the risen Lord in the breaking of the bread and noted that their hearts had earlier been set on fire by his words. Experiencing the presence of Christ, first in the word and then in the gesture of breaking the bread, led to recognition. *Verbum Domini* makes the following brief comment on the Bread of Life discourse which has been interpreted both in a eucharistic sense and as referring to the Word of God:[210]

---

207 Already Paul calls the Lord's Supper a proclamation: "For as often as you eat this bread and drink the cup, you proclaim the death of the Lord until he comes" (1 Cor 11:26).

208 It is only in emergencies that one may omit the proclamation of the Word, for example when death is imminent and Baptism, Confirmation, or the Anointing of the Sick is administered without a Liturgy of the Word. The word of Scripture is optional in the sacrament of Penance. Nevertheless, the so-called word of administration always has a biblical imprint.

209 See *VD* 54.

210 See Origen, *Hom. in Numeros* 16.9 (GCS 30:152; *Homilies on Numbers*, 101); Tertullian, *De resurrectione carnis* 37 (PL 2:847).

In the discourse at Capernaum, John's Prologue is brought to a deeper level. There God's *Logos* became flesh, but here this flesh becomes "*bread*" given for the life of the world (cf. Jn 6:51), with an allusion to Jesus' self-gift in the mystery of the cross, confirmed by the words about his blood being given as *drink* (cf. Jn 6:53). The mystery of the Eucharist reveals the true manna, the true bread of heaven: it is God's *Logos* made flesh, who gave himself up for us in the Paschal Mystery.[211]

The Word of God was already perceived as "food" in various passages of Scripture,[212] and the patristic writers very often related this to the Eucharist.[213] For example, Origen wrote:

> You who are accustomed to take part in divine mysteries [*sc.* the Eucharist] know, when you receive the body of the Lord, how you protect it with all caution and veneration, lest any small part fall from it, lest anything of the consecrated gift be lost. For you believe, and correctly, that you are answerable if anything falls from there by neglect. But if you are so careful to preserve his body, and rightly so, how do you think that there is less guilt to have neglected God's word than to have neglected his body?[214]

Origen took the high veneration of the Eucharist and transposed it to the Word. Jerome and Caesarius of Arles made similar statements.[215] Ambrose even spoke of the "wedding feast of the Word."[216] This foundation laid by the Fathers did not disappear completely in the Middle Ages, when (for

---

211 *VD* 54 (italics original).

212 See Dt 8:3 (cited in Mt 4:4 and Lk 4:4); Dt 30:14; Jos 1:8 (LXX / Vulgata: "non recedat volumen legis huius *de ore tuo*"); Ps 119:103; Ez 2:8; 3:1–3; Jer 15:16 (cited in Rev 10:9–10). See Heinz-Günther Schöttler, "'Eingeladen zum Hochzeitsmahl des Wortes' (Ambrosius von Mailand). Überlegungen zur liturgischen Präsenz des Wortes Gottes," *BiLi* 80, no. 1 (2007): 222–24.

213 See Durst, "Wortkommunion," 160–63.

214 Origen, *Hom. in Exodum* 13.3 (*GCS* 29:274); Origen, *Homilies on Genesis and Exodus*, Fathers of the Church: A New Translation 71 (Washington, DC: The Catholic University of America Press, 2010), 380–81.

215 See Jerome, *In Psalmum* 147.14 (CChr.SL 78:337–38; *VD* 56); Caesarius of Arles, *Sermo* 78.2 (CChr.SL 103:323; WEC 4:108).

216 See Ambrose, *De bono mortis* 6.22 (CSEL 32/1:724). See also Jun Nishiwaki, *Ad nuptias verbi. Aspekte einer Theologie des Wortes Gottes bei Ambrosius von Mailand*, TThS 69 (Trier: Paulinus, 2003), 128–29.

example) Thomas à Kempis († 1471) spoke of the two tables (altar and law/ Scripture).[217]

However, above all the Second Vatican Council employed the image of the two tables or one table of the Word and the Body of Christ to affirm their reciprocal relatedness,[218] since the Church distributes the one Bread of Life in Word and Eucharist.[219] This overcomes the depreciation of the Word in comparison to the Eucharist, without reducing the importance of the Eucharist. As we have mentioned, *Verbum Domini* explained the presence of Christ in the Word *inter alia* on the analogy of the Real Presence in the Eucharist.[220] The awareness of the sacramentality of the Word brings the Word in proximity to the Eucharist. Word and Eucharist are ecclesiologically central, since both together build up the Church.[221] Accordingly, the Liturgy—understood as the realization of the Church, the *ecclesia orans*—needs both of these.

The Liturgy itself contributes to this concise historical-theological summary. In addition to the structure of the Mass with its two poles, other elements show that the Liturgy of the Word and the eucharistic celebration are "so closely connected that they form but one single act of worship."[222] In the Byzantine Divine Liturgy, the Little Entrance with the Gospel book and the Great Entrance with the eucharistic gifts have a parallel form, thus demonstrating through their structure the unity and complementarity of the two parts (the Liturgy of the Catechumens and the Liturgy of the Faithful).

There are links in content in the Roman liturgy, such as a eucharistic rereading when the Communion antiphon on occasion takes up the Gospel of the day,[223] or when some prayers after Communion also speak of the Word. For example, the Prayer after Communion on the 23rd Sunday in Ordinary Time says: "you nourish and endow [your faithful] with life through the food of your Word and heavenly sacrament."[224] There is a concrete taking up of the

---

217 Thomas à Kempis, *De Imitatione Christi* 4, 11.

218 See Neuheuser, "Tisch des Wortes und des Brotes," esp. 139–53 (on the patristic and medieval sources of this image Neuheuser, 148–53). *Sacrosanctum Concilium* speaks of two tables (48 and 51), while *Dei Verbum* 21 and *Perfectae caritatis* 6 speak of the one table; *Presbyterorum Ordinis* 18 speaks of "the double table of Sacred Scripture and the Eucharist." *Ad Gentes* 6 mentions the double nourishment through the Word and the eucharistic Bread.

219 See *DV* 21.

220 See *VD* 56; B.VIII.28.1.2.

221 See John Paul II, *Ecclesia de Eucharistia*. Encyclical Letter (April 17, 2003), 1; *VD* 51; De Lubac, *History and Spirit*, 412–15.

222 *GIRM*, 28; see *SC* 56.

223 See A.IV.15.

224 *Missal*, 483.

Gospel on the 1st Sunday in Lent: "that we may learn to hunger for Christ, the true and living Bread, and strive to live by every word which proceeds from your mouth."[225] Similarly, the Prayer after Communion on Saint Matthew's day, which we have discussed, interprets the Gospel with reference to Communion.[226] Some pericopes also have an additional level of eucharistic meaning, whether this is already established in the text itself (as in John 6), or whether this is added by the context of the celebration, e.g., through the Communion antiphon,[227] the Prayer after Communion, or even through a quotation that is always used, such as "Behold the Lamb of God …" (Jn 1:29) or "Lord, I am not worthy …" (Mt 8:8).[228]

From the second edition of the Italian Missal onward, a sentence from the Gospel was selected as Communion antiphon on all the Sundays and feast days, as well as on the weekdays in the festal cycles.[229] The same Christ who worked at that time is now speaking in the Gospel and is present in the Eucharist. At the consecration of a church, the collect prays "that the power of your word and of the sacraments may strengthen" the faithful.[230] The encounter with the eucharistic Lord is thus made additionally concrete through the Word that is proclaimed. This link also makes it clear that the faith necessary for the reception of Communion comes from hearing (Liturgy of the Word). The prayer over the offerings on the Feast of Saint Jerome asks "that, having meditated on your Word, following the example of Saint Jerome, we may more eagerly draw near to offer your majesty the sacrifice of salvation."[231] At the same time, the Eucharist deepens our awareness of the actual presence of Christ in the proclamation of the Word and assists the total acceptance of the Word. We can therefore say that "The Eucharist opens

---

225 *Missal*, 219.

226 See *Missal*, 953; A.III.12.2.

227 See, for Epiphany and the 2nd Sunday after Christmas, A.IV.15.

228 The word of the centurion was used from the tenth century onward as the priest's prayer of preparation. The *RRom* 1614 inserted it into the Communion of the sick, together with the "Behold the Lamb of God." (Fittingly, the prayer said: "My soul shall be *healed*"). Only thereafter was it included in the Roman Mass for the distribution of Communion (see Jungmann, *Missarum Sollemnia*, 2:355-57, 369-73).

229 See A.IV.15.

230 *Missal*, 1221. In Mass formula E for the Church (for the diocese), the collect prays that the faithful may be "gathered together in the Holy Spirit through the Gospel and the Eucharist" (*Missal*, 1242). On the 2nd Sunday in Lent, the collect asks God "to nourish us inwardly by your word" (*Missal*, 226).

231 *Missal*, 962.

us to an understanding of Scripture, just as Scripture for its part illumines and explains the mystery of the Eucharist."[232]

The task of the homily is thus to point out such connecting lines. The *Homiletic Directory* often emphasizes that the Homily, as "part of the Liturgy itself,"[233] must take due account of the liturgical context. In the context of Word and Eucharist, there is an interesting comparison of the homily with the distribution of Communion: "The homily in some sense parallels the distribution of the Lord's Body and Blood to the faithful during the Communion rite. In the homily God's holy Word is 'distributed' for the nourishment of his people."[234] Just as the reception of Communion aims at becoming one with the eucharistic Lord, and in fact only thus becomes a personal encounter (rather than a fleeting contact), so too in the "Word communion"[235] the homily helps people to make their own the Word they have heard. It also has a bracketing function between the proclamation of the Word and the eucharistic celebration since both homily and readings proclaim the same Paschal Mystery that will then be celebrated at the altar.[236] For the homily "must always lead the community of the faithful to celebrate the Eucharist wholeheartedly."[237]

The *GILM* and the numerous examples from the Liturgy mentioned above thus show that the reciprocal relatedness of Word and Eucharist cannot mean playing one off against the other—for there lies a dynamic from Word to Eucharist in the liturgical celebration itself. The Word of God aims precisely to lead us to the Eucharist.[238] As with the Emmaus disciples, the encounter with Christ in the Word opens the door to the encounter with him in the Eucharist.[239] The same Christ is present in both modes of encounter; the difference is the specific fact that Christ is *substantially* present in

---

232 *VD* 55; quoted in *Homiletic Directory*, 54.

233 *SC* 52 (35,2).

234 *Homiletic Directory*, 26.

235 See Nußbaum, "Gegenwart Gottes/Christi," 73 n. 50.

236 See *Homiletic Directory*, 11; *GILM*, 24.

237 *GILM*, 24.

238 See *GILM*, 10; Eisenbach, *Gegenwart Christi*, 553–54.

239 See, e.g., Ambrose, *In Ps. 118*, 15.28 (CSEL 62:345): "You have the apostolic food. Enjoy it, and you will not succumb. Enjoy it first, so that then you may be able to come to the food of Christ, to the food of the Lord's body, to the meal of the sacrament, and to the drink through which the condition of the faithful is intoxicated" (translation following Dassmann, *Ambrosius* 137). In many passages, Ambrose ascribes salvific effects to the Word and to the Eucharist in the same manner, but with the distinction that "the former introduces the encounter with God, while the latter perfects it" (Dassmann, *Ambrosius,* 137).

the Eucharist.[240] Here, we must look more closely at *SC* 7 and its subsequent explanation by the magisterium. As is well known, the *Constitution on the Liturgy* speaks of five modes of Christ's presence, using the adverb *maxime* in the case of the eucharistic species.

In the encyclical *Mysterium fidei* (1965), Paul VI extended this list with examples of the extraliturgical presence of Christ and emphasized the eucharistic presence: "This presence is called 'real' not to exclude the idea that the others are 'real' too, but rather to indicate presence par excellence, because it is substantial [*substantialis*] and through it Christ becomes present whole and entire, God and man."[241] The other modes of Christ's presence (and hence also his presence in the Word) are thus equally real, but since his presence in the Eucharist is substantial, it is given particular emphasis. The Instruction *Eucharisticum mysterium* (1967) gives an ascending list of the modes of Christ's presence, with the Eucharist at the summit.[242]

The question was asked, with regard to *Dei Verbum* 21 ("*Divinas Scripturas sicut et ipsum Corpus dominicum semper venerata est Ecclesia*"), what the "*sicut et*" is in fact saying about the veneration of Scripture and of the body of the Lord. The official English translation is somewhat unclear, the German translation even more so.[243] The "*sicut et*" should be understood in a temporal sense ("as she *also* has venerated the body of the Lord"), not in the sense of an equality of veneration. The Pontifical Commission for the Interpretation of the Decrees of the Second Vatican Council responded, with reference to the documents mentioned above, that veneration is owed to both, but in a different way ("*diverso tamen modo seu ratione*").[244] Also in the perception of the faithful, the presence of Christ is linked in a special measure to the Eucharist, and less to the Word. This is certainly the case because the Eucharist shows and contains the presence of Christ substantially, that is to say, in a visible and abiding manner, and thus corresponds to the human need for signs of transcendence that are especially visible and can be experienced (Holy Communion!).

---

240 See Nußbaum, "Gegenwart Gottes/Christi," 59; Wahle, *Gottes-Gedenken*, 303.

241 Paul VI, *Mysterium fidei*, 39. See Leonhard, *Heiligkeit der Schrift*, 170-74.

242 Congregation of Rites, *Eucharisticum mysterium* (My 25, 1967), 9 and 55.

243 See Marianne Schlosser, "'Ausdruck des Glaubens und Nahrung für ihn' (SC 59). Anmerkungen zur Bedeutung der Sakramente (nicht nur) in Zeiten von Corona," in *Gottesdienst auf eigene Gefahr*, ed. H.-J. Feulner and E. Haslwanter (Münster: Aschendorff, 2020), 73-102, at 99–100.

244 *AAS* 60 (1968): 362. See also Nußbaum, "Gegenwart Gottes/Christi," 69.

Moreover, whereas in the Liturgy of the Word only individual aspects of Scripture can be read aloud each time, the Eucharist is the celebration of the entire mystery of Christ, and therefore adds something to the first part of the Mass. Although both parts involve the encounter with one and the same Christ, the Eucharist makes visible *per se* the risen Christ in his entirety (with his life), while the proclamation can put into words only one small, albeit concrete, part.

This theological argument about concreteness and entirety corresponds in turn to the human capacity for perception. On the one hand, the human being needs that which is concrete, in order to draw close to God. It must be made possible for us to experience the encounter with the fullness, which is greater than the human person, in a specific time and place. In this sense, the proclamation of the Word always directs the focus onto one aspect (or at least, onto individual aspects). On the other hand, this proclamation opens us for the entirety of the Christ event in the celebration of the Eucharist, so that one does not remain at (historical) details that may be completely different from one's own existential situation. Rather, the pericopes are paradigmatic. For example, what is expressed in historical concreteness by narratives of healing is celebrated in the Eucharist, since it binds together into one the many individual details of Scripture. This makes it possible to overcome the distance between the biblical text and one's own situation, because the Eucharist makes present God's comprehensive saving action, which has received its high point in Christ, especially in his dying and rising. The Eucharist brings people into the Paschal Mystery.

The simultaneous relatedness and differentiation are also reflected in church architecture. The ambo and the altar should be related to one another in their artistic form, to demonstrate optically the unity of the two-fold table.[245] Unlike the altar, however, the ambo is not a symbol of Christ, and is neither kissed nor incensed—it is the Gospel book that receives these two gestures. We should also consider the form of a place for the Word of God also outside the liturgical celebration. *Verbum Domini* 68 approves of "a visible place of honor inside the temple," but "without prejudice to the central place proper to the tabernacle." This distinction is comprehensible in the light of what we have said up to this point, because Christ's presence in the Word is not linked materially to the book. It is linked instead to the liturgical act of proclamation.

These arguments will have made it clear that, for theological reasons, it is precisely the reciprocal relatedness of Word and Eucharist, with their

---

245 See *VD* 68; *GIRM*, 309; Benini, "Ambo," 33.

inherent dynamic, that forbids an equalization as if the two modes of Christ's presence were ultimately interchangeable. In anthropological terms too, hearing and seeing,[246] understanding and tasting, intellectual and sensuous perception complement each other. As in everyday life, they cannot be played off against each other in the Liturgy, if worship is to address the various dimensions of the human being.

---

246 Patrick Prétot, "Vatican II – nouvelle appréciation de la Parole de Dieu," in *Présence et rôle de la Bible dans la liturgie*, 225. Prétot emphasizes the correct relationship between hearing and seeing, and points out (simplifying, but not incorrectly) that the visual was privileged in the aftermath of the Council of Trent in the Baroque period and in the Counter-Reformation display of splendor, whereas after Vatican II, hearing was given a higher position than seeing.

CHAPTER 30

The Unity of Scripture in the Paschal Mystery of Christ

The New Testament clearly attests to both the abiding significance of "Scripture," that is to say, of the Old Testament, and to the newness of the Christ event, which does not abolish Scripture, but fulfills it.[247] When the New Testament became established and canonical, the disputes with Marcion († ca. 160), the Manichees, and others who rejected the Old Testament led to an insistence on the unity of the Testaments as the basis of the Christian hermeneutics of the Bible.[248] Patristic and medieval theologians, who were aware that there were numerous biblical authors, took for granted the unity of Scripture, because it had one divine author.[249] They took over from the New Testament the *interpretatio christiana* of the Old, which (for example) Ambrose formulated as follows: "Christ is the true interpreter of Scripture."[250]

---

247 See Mt 5:17; 12:40–42; Lk 24:27; Jn 5:39, 46; Heb 1:1–2; 1 Pt 1:10–12. See Söding, *Einheit der Schrift*, passim, esp. 389-97.

248 See, e.g., Rudolf Voderholzer, *Die Einheit der Schrift und ihr geistiger Sinn. Der Beitrag Henri de Lubacs zur Erforschung von Geschichte und Systematik christlicher Bibelhermeneutik*, Sammlung Horizonte; Neue Folge 31 (Einsiedeln: Johannes, 1998), 71-85, esp. 71-73. There is also a canonical framework within the Bible that connects Rev 22 to Gn 1-3.

249 See Ludger Schwienhorst-Schönberger, "Einheit und Vielheit. Gibt es eine sinnvolle Mitte des AT?" in *Wieviel Systematik erlaubt die Schrift? Auf der Suche nach einer gesamtbiblischen Theologie*, ed. F. L. Hossfeld, QD 185 (Freiburg/Br.: Herder, 2001), 48–49.

250 Ambrose, *In Luc.* 7.50 (CChr.SL 14:230): "scripturae verus interpres Christus." See Thomas Graumann, *Christus interpres. Die Einheit von Auslegung und Verkündigung in der Lukaserklärung des Ambrosius von Mailand*, PTS 41 (Berlin: De Gruyter, 1994), esp. 200-203, 255-75; Viktor Hahn, *Das wahre Gesetz. Eine Untersuchung zur Auffassung des Ambrosius von Mailand vom Verhältnis der beiden Testamente*, MBTh 33 (Münster: Aschendorff, 1969).

1. THE LITURGICAL TESTIMONY
TO THE UNITY OF SCRIPTURE

For a liturgical hermeneutics of the Bible it is, of course, particularly interesting to see how the Liturgy defines the relationship between the Old and the New Testaments and how it realizes in the celebration the unity of which the *GILM* speaks in a programmatic declaration: "Christ himself is the center and fullness of all of Scripture, as he is of the entire Liturgy."[251] The following presentation discusses three variants of this relationship, which become more and more open: the promise-fulfillment schema; typology;[252] and more generally, the links and correspondences in form or in substance.

Promise – Fulfillment

This schema holds that the Old Testament text itself already contains a promise that finds its fulfillment in the New Testament, that is to say, in the Christ event, as this is articulated in some so-called fulfillment quotations in the Gospels.[253] This schema is a firm fixture in the Liturgy, above all in Advent and Christmastide.[254]

A direct fulfillment is not always expressed in the Gospel, as we see, e.g., in the vision of peace from Isaiah 11 on the 2nd Sunday in Advent A. This does indeed point to the Messiah's realm of peace, but the *de facto* fulfillment is hoped for only in the eschaton.[255] This makes it clear that the "promise" belongs not only to the Old Testament, nor the "fulfillment" wholly to the

---

251 *GILM*, 5.

252 Exegetes evaluate typology (including promise–fulfillment) in various ways. Söding, *Einheit der Schrift*, 353–54: "This category [promise-fulfillment] is often criticized today. A closer examination shows that although it is often misunderstood, it provides an important orientation in the relationship between the two Testaments." The Pontifical Biblical Commission, *Interpretation of the Bible*, 37 calls typology one path (among others) of the interpretation of Scripture, a path suggested by the Liturgy.

253 The so-called fulfillment quotations in the Gospels not only have recourse to texts that contain a promise in the strict sense (a messianic or other promise of salvation). They are also in part to be understood in the sense of a typology (see the following section b in the text). The conceptual pair "promise-fulfillment" is found in combination in the Bible only at Acts 13:32–33.

254 See, e.g., Is 7:14 – Matt 1:23 on the 4th Sunday in Advent A, or Is 9:1–6 – Lk 2:1–14 at Midnight Mass on Christmas. The readings thematize the future salvation, the coming of God, or (more concretely) the hoped-for Messiah (see Nübold, *Perikopenordnung*, 293–301; *GILM*, 93-95, although without the concept of "typology").

255 Ambrose used the triad *umbra-imago-veritas* to describe these three steps (see Hahn, *Gesetz*, 207-23, 488, 491, 498–99, etc.).

New, since the Christ event is itself also "promise," and we still await his second coming in glory.[256] We are reminded of this precisely by readings and prayers on the 1st Sunday in Advent—but also by every Mass ("until you come again"). The promise-fulfillment schema is found not only in the order of readings, but also in the various psalms understood in a messianic-prophetic sense,[257] as well as in numerous hymns[258] and chants of this period. Similarly, a number of Communion antiphons transport Old Testament promises and proclaim that these have been fulfilled in Christ.[259] Explicit promises of this kind are rather rare in the other periods of the liturgical year.

Typology

The concept of typology[260] (in the narrower sense) is understood here as an anticipatory image (τύπος): a correspondence is found in the New Testament to an Old Testament reality (events, things, persons). Unlike the case of a promise in which a text must already itself point into the future, this need not be the case with typology. The correspondence becomes comprehensible only on the basis of the retrospective from the New Testament antitype. We already find typology in the many comparisons between Old Testament leaders and Jesus in the Gospels, or in Paul's Adam-Christ typology.[261]

In the order of readings, we find this (for example) in the Song of the Suffering Servant on Good Friday, on Corpus Christi (manna, blood of the Sinai covenant, Melchizedek), or occasionally on Marian feasts,[262] but also on the Sundays in Ordinary Time.[263] This arrangement can appear problematic, if what we hear is simply the "outdoing" of the Old Testament reading by the Gospel reading.[264] The typological arrangement is used in the Ambrosian

---

256 See Söding, *Einheit der Schrift*, 355, 358, etc.

257 See, e.g., on Ps 24 in Advent and Christmastide, A.II.7.1a.

258 See, e.g., the hymn *Corde natus ex parentis* by Prudentius (January 1), esp. the 4th stanza (*Liturgy of the Hours*, 1:410).

259 See A.IV.15.

260 On the difficult differentiation between typology and allegory, see Voderholzer, *Einheit der Schrift*, 465-67; Stuart George Hall, "Typologie," *TRE* 34 (2002): 208-24.

261 See Rom 5:14: "Adam [...] is the type [τύπος] of the one who was to come."

262 E.g., the parallel between Eve and Mary on December 8; further examples (above all from the Byzantine liturgy, in which the typological interpretation plays an important role on Marian feasts) in A.I.3.3.

263 See examples in Nübold, *Perikopenordnung*, 292.

264 See, e.g., the multiplication of loaves by Elisha and by Jesus (17th Sunday in Ordinary Time).

lectionary even more strongly than in the OLM.[265] In the Office of Readings too, Old Testament readings are frequently explained typologically, with New Testament references, in the patristic readings or in the responsories.[266]

In addition to promoting knowledge of the Bible, one can see here the attempt to draw on the spiritual sense of Scripture[267] in order to make the texts bear stronger spiritual fruit. The Christological interpretation of the Psalms as *vox de Christo* or as *vox Christi ad patrem* is likewise a form of typology, because the content of the psalm or the one who prays the psalm is an anticipatory image of Christ.[268] The best known example is Ps 22 (21) as the Responsorial Psalm on Palm Sunday or in the Liturgy of the Hours on Good Friday and at Daytime Prayer on Friday of the 3rd week.[269] The Ordination prayers also show that a typological relationship is posited between the offices and ministries in the people of Israel and the ecclesial *ordo*.[270]

Part A also showed the important value of typology through the examples of the Western and especially the Eastern hymns about the Cross.[271] The hymnographers use this means as a matter of course—and so does the Liturgy. Some antiphons and numerous troparia imprint, through their repetition, a typological interpretation of a particular passage in Scripture.[272] Precisely in the poetry, but also in the order of readings, one is struck by the variety in the evidential character, which covers a spectrum from keyword associations to theological connections.

---

265 See *PLA*, 79; Magnoli, *Certa unità tematica*, 84–85. One interesting example is Genesis 18 (the three men who visit Abraham) as a typological anticipatory image of the triune God, on Trinity Sunday C.

266 See, e.g., the parallels between David and Christ in *Liturgy of the Hours*, 3:438–442. See in general Häußling, "Bibel in der Liturgie der Tagzeiten," 99–100.

267 See B.VIII.26.

268 See A.II.7.

269 See *Liturgy of the Hours*, 2:468-70, 1464-66.

270 On the prayers at episcopal Ordination, see A.III.11. The Roman prayer at priestly ordination states in clearly typological terms that "Already in the earlier covenant offices arose [...] which were a shadow of the good things to come" (*Ordination of a Bishop*, 87). The Levites are a typological anticipatory image of the deacons; see *Ordination of a Bishop*, 140 (ordination prayer); *Missal*, 354 (*Exsultet*).

271 See A.IV.14.

272 For example, an antiphon at Vespers on January 1 makes an explicit typological reference: "By your miraculous birth from the Virgin you have fulfilled the Scriptures: like a gentle rain falling upon the earth you have come down to save your people. O God, we praise you." (*Liturgy of the Hours*, 1:477, 491; see Jgs 6:36–40).

Links/Correspondences in Form or in Substance

In addition to typology, the Liturgy has more general ways of expressing the unity of the two Testaments. The order of readings sometimes selects the Old Testament reading on the Sundays in Ordinary Time because it is cited in the Gospel. This makes us conscious of the quotation as such (with its immediate context), and thereby of the fact that the New Testament takes up the Old anew. Or else, the choice may be intended to provide necessary background information. In terms of biblical hermeneutics, this shows that the New Testament can be understood only through knowledge of the Old.

In other cases, the Old Testament reading was chosen for its content, in order to complement the Gospel. This can demonstrate the richness of Scripture and the reciprocal relatedness of the two Testaments.[273] *PLA* 79 speaks appropriately here of the "theological, spiritual, or moral thematic convergence." The order of readings thus also helps to make us aware of the unity of the two-one Bible. In addition to the combination of the texts, the arrangement of the Old Testament readings in Lent in the Roman rite also underlines this unity, when the *tour d'horizon* of important stages in salvation history closes on the 5th Sunday with the prophets, and then on Palm Sunday with the Song of the Suffering Servant, understood Christologically.[274] There is also a very clear transition from the Old Testament to the New in the Ambrosian order of readings in the period after Pentecost, with its three sections.[275]

The Responsorial Psalm also mediates the union between the two Testaments, since it has a bracket function in its structure and sometimes in its content, when it casts a thematic bridge between the first reading and the Gospel, or when it was chosen for its appropriateness to the period in the liturgical year. If a New Testament refrain is chosen for the psalm, it allows the psalm to appear in a new light and unobtrusively creates a dialogue between the Testaments.[276] The same clearly occurs in the Liturgy of the Hours through the combination of New Testament antiphons and the Psalms. Above all, the Christological interpretation of a psalm, such as we find especially on feasts or as a possibility in the Liturgy of the Hours, underlines the compenetration of the two parts of the Bible.[277]

---

273 See Nübold, *Perikopenordnung*, 288–93.

274 See A.I.3.2.2.

275 See A.I.3.1.2.

276 See A.II.8.

277 See A.II.7 and A.II.9.

The Roman prayer at episcopal Ordination[278] (and in a similar manner, other central liturgical prayers)[279] displays clearly the interlacing of Old and New Testament anamnesis.[280] Without constructing a continuous trajectory (which is not found in Scripture itself), the Liturgy displays the unity of the Testaments based on the continuity of God's salvific action. This touches the category of "salvation history," which also finds expression in the hymns about the Cross that we have discussed (Fall – Redemption on the Cross),[281] and, of course, the examples can easily be multiplied. The combinations attest both a harmonious relationship between the two Testaments and their Christological orientation, which the liturgical context demands.[282]

These observations show that the unity of the two Testaments is not in the least attested only in the (recent)[283] order of readings.[284] Rather, it is clearly rooted more broadly in the Liturgy, and the chants and prayers, many of which come from the tradition, demonstrate this diachronically. There is no lack of examples that highlight the similarities and the continuity, but most of the links can be understood only on the basis of the New Testament (as antitype); the starting point for the interpretation is the Christ event, which in turn receives an additional interpretation by the Old Testament. In Augustine's memorable words, "In the Old Testament the New lies hidden, and the Old lies open in the New."[285]

Ritual acts described above also show both unity and differentiation. The structure of the Liturgy of the Word in the Roman Sunday Mass, with two Old Testament readings (including the Psalm)[286] and two New Testament readings, makes clear that the two parts of the Bible belong together.[287]

---

278 See A.III.11.1.

279 To take an example that has not been presented hitherto, see the Prayer for the Consecration of the Chrism (*Rites*, 1:335–38).

280 See B.VIII.27.2.

281 See A.IV.14.

282 See A.IV.15.

283 Today's Western orders of readings have recourse to the tradition on feasts (and in the festal cycles).

284 Meaningful links continually occur between readings that were not consciously selected in view of each other (e.g., on the weekdays in Ordinary Time). This demonstrates the unity of Scripture in an even deeper sense.

285 Augustine, *Quaestionum in Heptateuchum libri VII* 2.73 (CChr.SL 33:106): "*et in vetere novum lateat, et in novo vetus pateat.*"

286 On the Psalm as reading, see A.II.8.1.

287 Even when there is only one reading on weekdays, and this is taken from the New Testament, the Old Testament nevertheless remains present through the Psalm. The

In the West, these are proclaimed at the same place, the ambo. This is even clearer in the two Old Testament readings (Torah and prophets) and the two New Testament readings (Paul and Gospel) in the Syro-Malabar rite. Other Eastern rites have an Old Testament deficit.[288] In the Roman rite, the Old and New Testament readings, both of which are contained in the lectionary, are "staged" in the same way, while the ritual highlighting of the Gospel and the use of the Gospel book in the Mass emphasize the special place of Christ in Scripture.

For a liturgical hermeneutics of the Bible we see that the liturgical celebration takes for granted that the two Testaments belong together, and that Scripture finds its unity in the Christological orientation or (to put it very briefly) in the Paschal Mystery of Christ.[289] The orientation of the reading of the Old Testament to Christ, and hence the explicitly Christological interpretation of some passages, are obviously present in Christian worship, which of its nature is the celebration of Christ's Paschal Mystery. This is particularly true in the Mass, thanks to the eucharistic context.[290]

Behind this, as one can already see in the New Testament, lie both the consciousness of the identity of the one God who acts in history and creates salvation, and the conviction of faith that the eschatological fullness of salvation is in Christ.[291] The Liturgy expresses the unity of Scripture by linking the Old and New Testaments. However, this unity is to be understood, not as the sum of individual links, but more fundamentally, on the basis of God's salvific action with its high point in Christ, that is to say, from the Paschal Mystery.[292]

The *Constitution on the Liturgy* first introduces the concept of the Paschal Mystery, which had been coined by the mystery theology of Odo Casel

---

Ambrosian rite knows two Old Testament readings on weekdays in Advent and Lent (see A.I.3.1.4).

288 See B.VII.24.1.1; A.I.3.1.4.

289 Ambrose, *Explanatio Psalmi* 1.33 (CSEL 64:28–30) expresses the unity of the Testaments in Christ through a metaphor: "Drink the Old Testament first, in order that you may drink the New as well. If you do not drink the former, you will not be able to drink the latter either. [...] Drink both chalices, therefore, that of the Old and that of the New Testaments, for in both, it is Christ that you drink. [...] Drink this Word, but drink it in its own order, first the Old Testament, and then hasten to drink it in the New Testament too" (quoted also in *PLA*, 11).

290 See Zerfaß, *Hermeneutik*, 129.

291 See Söding, *Einheit der Schrift*, 350–51; *GIRM*, 57.

292 See also *GILM*, 66; *VD* 57.

(mentioned above), in the context of salvation history (*SC* 5),[293] when it presents Christ's dying and rising as the high point of God's salvific action. Only then does it describe the Liturgy itself as the celebration of the Paschal Mystery of Christ: "the Church has never failed to come together to celebrate the Paschal Mystery: reading those things 'which were in all the scriptures concerning him' (Lk 24:27)."[294] In the perspective of salvation history, the Liturgy is explained by means of Scripture, because it is the celebration of that which is attested in Scripture. This, however, means conversely that since the Liturgy makes present Christ's life, dying, and rising as the center of the Christian faith, it is only logical to look from this center at salvation history and to understand Scripture.

A centering on the Paschal Mystery of Christ does not, of course, mean that every passage in the Bible must be interpreted in terms of Christ. This is shown by the facts that an Old Testament *lectio semicontinua* is envisaged on the weekdays in Ordinary Time without any conscious orientation to the Gospel of the day, or that one can meditate on the Psalms in their literal sense, and hence without a Christological interpretation, in the Liturgy of the Hours.[295] The Liturgy does not cover up the plurality of the individual writings and of their themes, especially since the recent orders of readings attempt to let a "more representative portion" (*SC* 51: "*praestantior pars*") be heard. Occasional formulations and arrangements that let the Old Testament appear merely as a shadow of the New are, however, problematic. With regard to the understanding of Scripture in the Liturgy, we can speak (in Jürgen Werbick's words) of a "hermeneutics centering on the Christ event," which, however, also tolerates a "decentering through non-christological interpretations of biblical traditions" that "cannot simply be exploited Christologically."[296]

---

293 Today, one would no longer use the misleading language of *SC* 5, which describes "the wonderful works of God among the people of the Old Testament" as "but a prelude to the work of Christ the Lord in redeeming mankind."

294 *SC* 6. See Simon A. Schrott, *Pascha-Mysterium. Zum liturgietheologichen Leitbegriff des Zweiten Vatikanischen Konzils*, Theologie der Liturgie 6 (Regensburg: Pustet, 2014), here esp. 265-78, 496; on the Paschal Mystery and Scripture Schrott, 445–46 and *VD* 55, 57.

295 See A.II.9.2.

296 Jürgen Werbick, "Bibel Jesu und Evangelium Jesu Christi: Systematisch-theologische Perspektiven," *BiLi* 70, no. 3 (1997): 216–17.

2. THE LITURGICAL ACTIONS
AS "ANTITYPE" OF SCRIPTURE

The Liturgy does not limit itself to showing the unity of Scripture; as the celebration of the Paschal Mystery, it brings the participants themselves into the sphere of Scripture, since the liturgical actions are an "antitype" of Scripture. Ambrose understood typology not only in the sense described above, where an Old Testament event or person as type is interpreted with regard to a New Testament event or person as antitype. He made a link not only from the Old Testament to the New, but from Scripture as a whole into the present day, in order to relate "the biblical salvation history to the personal salvation history of the faithful."[297] It is of particular interest here to note that he employed passages from the New Testament, and especially from the Old, to explain the Rites of Initiation. He saw these passages as anticipatory images of the sacraments, so that the sacramental life of the Church became an additional antitype to numerous scriptural texts.[298] In his mystagogical catecheses,[299] for example, Ambrose interpreted Naaman's healing through dipping into the Jordan (see 2 Kgs 5:1–14) as an image of Baptism in sanctified water.[300] Origen likewise interpreted Joshua's crossing of the Jordan in relation to initiation, and explained its meaning for the baptized: "All this is fulfilled in you in a mystical sense."[301]

Some typological explanations may seem artificial today, but it is important for a liturgical hermeneutics of the Bible to hold fast to what we emphasized with regard to the anamnesis of Scripture: namely, that the salvation attested in the Bible is realized ever anew in the celebration of the Liturgy. This is why there is a profound inherent connection between Bible and Liturgy. Jean Daniélou wrote:

---

297 Christoph Jacob, "Zum hermeneutischen Horizont der Typologie: Der Antitypos als Prinzip ambrosianischer Allegorese," in Richter and Kranemann, *Christologie der Liturgie*, 108; Christoph Jacob, *"Arkandisziplin", Allegorese, Mystagogie. Ein neuer Zugang zur Theologie des Ambrosius von Mailand*, Theophaneia 32 (Frankfurt/M.: Hain, 1990), 176–79.

298 See Jacob, *"Arkandisziplin"*, esp. 180–96; Hahn, *Gesetz*, 387–405. For a differentiated criticism of Jacob, see Graumann, *Christus interpres*, 244–50.

299 On the various accentuations in the use of Scripture in the mystagogical catecheses, see Enrico Mazza, *Mystagogy: A Theology of Liturgy in the Patristic Age*, trans. M. J. O'Connell (New York: Pueblo, 1989).

300 See Ambrose, *De sacramentis* 1.13–15 (FontC 3:86–89; WEC 2:43).

301 Origen, *Hom. in librum Iesu Nave* 4.1 (GCS 30:304–5).

The sacraments are conceived in relation to the acts of God in the Old Testament and the New. God acts in this world [...]. God creates, judges, makes a covenant, is present, makes holy, delivers. These same acts are carried out in the different phases of the history of salvation. There is, then, a fundamental analogy between these actions. The sacraments are simply the continuation in the era of the Church of God's acts in the Old Testament and the New. This is the proper significance of the relationship between Bible and the Liturgy. The Bible is a sacred history; the Liturgy is a sacred history.[302]

This connection can be seen again and again in the liturgical texts themselves. For example, the *Exsultet* interprets the crossing of the Red Sea in relation to the night of Baptism, which "sets Christian believers apart from worldly vices and from the gloom of sin, leading them to grace and joining them to his holy ones."[303] In a brief but similar form, some of the orations after the readings at the Easter Vigil connect the Old Testament pericopes to the Resurrection of Christ and the liturgical act of Baptism.[304] In the Roman canon, the Church prays that God may receive the gifts as he did with Abel, Abraham, and Melchizedek. What God did when he received their sacrificial gifts,[305] becomes the anticipatory image leading to the prayer that God might now look down in grace and reconciliation at the eucharistic sacrifice and accept it. In other words, the anticipatory image and the present-day action involve the same procedure: "It ought to become clear to everyone who takes part today in the Liturgy that one takes one's place in a procession of praise of God that comes from the depths of the centuries, from Abel and Abraham."[306]

The Communion antiphons, especially in Advent and Christmastide, choose verses from the prophets or from psalms understood in a messianic sense, which have their "fulfillment" not only in Jesus of Nazareth (that is to say, in the New Testament), but above all, in the Christ who is present and

---

302 Jean Daniélou, "The Sacraments and the History of Salvation," in *The Liturgy and the Word of God*, ed. A. G. Martimort (Collegeville, MN: Liturgical Press, 1959), 28.

303 *Missal*, 641. The same idea is also found at the blessing of the baptismal water (*Missal*, 377), in Ambrose (see *de sacramentis* 1.12 [FontC 3:86–87; WE 2:43]), and in other patristic writers.

304 See especially the prayers after the 2nd (Gn 22), 3rd (Ex 14), 4th (Is 54), and 6th (Bar 3–4) readings: *Missal*, 365–67. In keeping with this understanding, all the Old Testament readings in the preconciliar *Missale Romanum* were called "*prophetia*," irrespective of the biblical book from which they were taken (see MRom 1570, 265–76).

305 See *Missal*, 641.

306 Lohfink, "AT und Liturgie," 5.

is now received sacramentally.[307] The Liturgy as "fulfillment" of Scripture comes into sight on Corpus Christi too, when the Gospel of the multiplication of the loaves (Lk 9:11b-17) is read in Year C. The occasion of the celebration makes it more than obvious that we should connect the bread in the Gospel to the eucharistic Bread, so that the multiplication of the loaves as the type finds its antitype in the eucharistic celebration and thus happens anew (so to speak).[308] All these examples, which are very close to anamnesis,[309] express once again the relatedness of Word and sacrament/Eucharist.[310] They point to an inherent reason for the interlacing of Scripture and Liturgy: namely, to Christ, who is the protagonist in the Liturgy and the interpreter of Scripture who "expounds his own self in the writings of the Old and New Testaments."[311]

These examples bring us to another important aspect of the liturgical hermeneutics of the Bible: namely, that the Liturgy makes it possible to *experience* Scripture, by presenting the Word of God in the context of a celebration in which the faithful themselves can take part. In short, liturgy *does* what the Scripture *says*.[312] The Liturgy not only communicates Scripture cognitively but deals with it holistically and in a celebration. In his *Mystagogical Catecheses*, Cyril of Jerusalem pursues the idea that the anticipatory Old and New Testament images (*typoi*) of the event of Baptism have become something now experienced in the celebration. He begins by stating:

> Long have I desired to address you concerning these spiritual and heavenly mysteries. But because I well know that the eye is better than the ear, I awaited the present occasion so as to find you, *from your own experience,* ever more open to my words.[313]

---

307 See A.IV.15. and A.IV.16. Communion antiphons from the New Testament, especially when they are taken from the Gospel (or the Gospel of the day), can acquire an actualization, so that the Liturgy can appear here too as the antitype of Scripture.

308 The eucharistic interpretation of the multiplication of the loaves is also found frequently in art, for example, in the Church of the Multiplication at Tabgha, where a floor mosaic before the altar depicts a basket with only four loaves, with the intention of suggesting that the fifth loaf is on the altar and will be distributed in Communion.

309 See B.VIII.27.

310 See B.VIII.29.

311 Benedikt Kranemann, "Bibel und Liturgie in Wechselbeziehung. Eine Perspektivensuche vor historischem Hintergrund," *BiLi* 80, no. 4 (2007): 212.

312 See also Paul De Clerck, "Débat final: Réactions d'un auditeur catholique," in *Dans les compositions liturgiques, prières et chants,* vol. 2 of *Liturgie, interprète de l'écriture,* ed. C. Braga and A. Pistoia, BEL.S 191 (Rome: CLV-Edizioni Liturgiche, 2003), 277-81, at 280.

313 Cyril, *Mystagogicae catecheses* 1.1 (FontC 7:95; WEC 2:326), italics added.

He believes that it is only a person's own experiences that make it possible to understand the rites and the biblical texts; the interpretation makes sense only after the event. Baptism in fact allows one to experience what Paul has described in Romans 6.[314] The Ephphetha rite takes one bodily and spiritually into the underlying pericope. The white baptismal garment is the vivid translation of a number of scriptural passages.[315] The Emmaus narrative is made present in every celebration of the Mass. Accordingly, what was established in the Bible, and what *could* be immediately experienced at the time of Jesus, is made visible, and capable of being experienced, today too, in the liturgical celebration. Pope Leo the Great († 461) expressed this in eloquent words that have often been quoted: "What was visible in our Savior has passed over into his mysteries [*sacramenta*]."[316] Naturally, "*sacramenta*" in the vocabulary of the early centuries referred, not to the (seven) sacraments, but to the divine dimension of earthly reality, and it was widely used as a synonym for the "*mysteria*" of the Liturgy. Ildefons Herwegen wrote in pointed terms about the relationship between Bible and Liturgy: "Liturgy is a unique, wonderful situation, and the only effective event in which one can experience Sacred Scripture and make its vital content flowing and fruitful."[317]

314 See in general A.I.4.2.

315 See A.V.18.

316 *Sermo* 74.2 (CChr.SL 138A: 457; *CCC* 115).

317 Herwegen, "Heilige Schrift in der Liturgie," 17.

The Pneumatological-Epicletic Dimension of the Word of God

W e have scarcely touched upon this point on the pneumatological dimension, to which we now devote a separate chapter. This belongs necessarily to the anamnesis and to the sacramentality of the Word,[318] as well as to the actualization of the Word in the celebration of the sacraments, as an antitype to Scripture. It permeates the celebration of worship as a whole, as the later addition to the text of *SC* 6 states: "through the power of the Holy Spirit."[319] This also refers to the reading of Scripture, mentioned earlier in the text. A liturgical hermeneutics of the Bible must therefore investigate the relationships between Scripture and Pneuma in the Liturgy.

The doctrine of inspiration is, naturally, fundamental here.[320] The Holy Spirit inspired the sacred writers, breathing on them in such a way that, while using their human capabilities, they wrote down in their own words what was revealed by God.[321] Inspiration theologically grounds God's Word in human words, and the unity of this Word through one and the same

---

318 See *GILM*, 41: "the word that in the celebration becomes sacrament *through the Holy Spirit*"; *GILM*, 4: "The word of God constantly proclaimed in the Liturgy is always, then, a living and effective word *through the power of the Holy Spirit*" (italics added).

319 See Kaczynski, "*Sacrosanctum Concilium*," 65; Gil Hellín, *Constitutio*, 29. On the Holy Spirit in the Constitution on the Liturgy, see Jakob Baumgartner, "Locus ubi Spiritus Sanctus floret. Eine Geist-Epiklese im Wortgottesdienst?" *FZPhTh* 23, no. 1/2 (1976): 114–15.

320 See Helmut Gabel, *Inspirationsverständnis im Wandel. Theologische Neuorientierung im Umfeld des Zweiten Vatikanischen Konzils* (Mainz: Matthias-Grünewald-Verlag, 1991).

321 See *DV* 11; 2 Tm 3:15–16. ("Scripture inspired by God"); 2 Pt 1:21 ("moved by the Holy Spirit"). See also Acts 28:25 ("Well did the Holy Spirit speak to your ancestors through the prophet Isaiah").

divine inspirer and author.[322] But inspiration is not only a historical process at the writing of the Bible. It is also something that happens today, something that continues to have an effect at the proclamation, exposition, or liturgical implementation of Scripture, while at the same time linking what the Church does today (in liturgy) to the origin in which the Spirit was at work.[323] The same Spirit who inspired the biblical authors now works by making, through his activity, the human words of the proclamation words in which God/Christ is present. According to Odo Casel, Christ, or God's saving activity, is "pneumatologically present"[324] through the proclamation. The *PLA* underlines that the Holy Spirit brings about the presence of God / Christ in the Word and is the guarantee of effective communication in the act of worship.[325] The Holy Spirit makes possible the dialogical event of encounter in the Word. The Praenotanda to the Roman Gospel book have the following pregnant formulation: "Out of the power of the Spirit who bestows life, the written word is made alive, and the mystery of salvation is carried out anew."[326]

It is interesting that these ideas have scarcely found any immediate expression in the liturgical celebration within the framework of the Liturgy of the Word. The pericope orations of the Italian *Missal* are an exception, since they often request the aid of the Holy Spirit, in order to be able to grasp and fulfill what the scriptural readings say.[327] Historically, one can point to the sermon service at which the antiphon *Veni sancte Spiritus* could precede

---

322 See Cyril, *Lenten Catecheses* 17.5 (*PG* 33:975–76); The Works of Saint Cyril of Jerusalem, trans. Leo P. McCauley and Anthony A. Stephenson, Fathers of the Church 64, vol. 2 (Washington, DC: The Catholic University of America Press, 1970), 99–100: "There is not one Spirit in the Law and Prophets and another in the Gospels and the Apostles; it is one and the same Holy Spirit, the author of the divine Scriptures in the Old and the New Testaments" (see also. 4.16; 16.4).

323 Gabel, *Inspirationsverständnis*, 302 emphasizes, against a purely historical understanding, that the theology of inspiration ought more meaningfully to be understood "as speaking about the special relationship of Scripture to the Spirit" because this includes also the "working of the Spirit today as an integral component of the 'inspiration' of Scripture."

324 Odo Casel, "Mysteriengegenwart," *JLw* 8 (1928): 209. See also Casel, "The Meaning of the Mystery," 149: "In preaching, and even more in the Word proclaimed within the Liturgy in the Gospel, the saving action of Christ is made *present in the Spirit [pneumatisch gegenwärtig]*." See, with reference to a Vigil reading, Casel, 158: "this act [of creation] becomes once more a *Spiritual presence* in our midst" (italics original).

325 See *PLA*, 9.

326 No. 18 (see Tichý, *Proclamation*, 300).

327 34 out of 156 orations mention the Holy Spirit in the text of the oration itself, before the doxology. See A.III.12.3.

the reading of the scriptural text (in the vernacular) and the sermon.[328] At any rate, the theology of the Liturgy must bear in mind that the proclamation of the inspired readings of Scripture is itself a place where the Holy Spirit works.[329]

The Psalms also belong in this context. Numerous early Christian texts bear witness to the conviction that the Spirit of God speaks out of the Psalms,[330] and the *GILH* too refers to the Holy Spirit in the recitation of the Psalms: "that Spirit who inspired the psalmists and is present to devout men and women ready to accept his grace."[331] A trajectory is drawn here from the inspiration to today's prayer.

The working of the Holy Spirit through Scripture is expressed more clearly in the prayers, especially at the celebrations of the sacraments, since they have recourse to Scripture and often ask for the Holy Spirit. Our example, the prayer at episcopal ordination, showed that Scripture supplies not only the content of the anamnetic part—which could scarcely be otherwise—but also the epicletic part, so that the request for the working of the Holy Spirit is concretized in several tasks of the bishop, all taken from Scripture.[332] The prayer also requests that Scripture (or the passages that are specifically evoked) may become effective thanks to the working of the Spirit. Indeed, the performative character of the Word has its origin in the working of the Spirit. This allows us to speak here of an epicletic dimension of the Word.

The Word of God in the Liturgy has an essentially anamnetic character,[333] and it likewise contains an epicletic element, since the epicletic element in the Liturgy must not be restricted to the sacramental celebrations alone, and still less to the few explicit requests for the sending of the Spirit. Rather,

---

328 See Jungmann, *Missarum Sollemnia*, 1:461. For examples in the Reformed tradition, see Baumgartner, "Geist-Epiklese im Wortgottesdienst," 137–42; Chauvet, *Symbol and Sacrament*, 226.

329 See also Acts 10:44: "While Peter was still speaking these things, the Holy Spirit fell upon all who were listening to the word." Ambrose once introduced a scriptural quotation from Ps 24 (23):4 as follows: "Today, the Holy Spirit has declared through the voice of the youthful reader..." (*De Excessu Fratris* 1.61. CSEL 73:240–41).

330 See Hansjörg Auf der Maur, *Das Psalmenverständnis des Ambrosius von Mailand. Ein Beitrag zum Deutungshintergrund der Psalmenverwendung im Gottesdienst der Alten Kirche* (Leiden: Brill, 1977), 313. Buchinger, "Älteste Psalmenhomilie," 291–92, 98. On the inspiration of the Psalms in relation to the other scriptures, see Athanasius, *Letter to Marcellinus* 2.9 (Gregg, *Athanasius*, 101, 106–7).

331 *GILH*, 104; see also, 100.

332 See A.III.11.

333 See B.VIII.27.

the epicletic element has a fundamental significance for Christian worship as the sphere where the Spirit of God is at work, although this is brought to light in varying degrees, depending on the celebration and the element. This means that the event of the Word in the Liturgy also has an epicletic dimension. The proclamation and, more generally, the liturgical actions are thus not an autonomous activity on the part of the Church, but are always the gift of God, brought about by the Spirit.

The Word in the Liturgy shares in the basic anamnetic-epicletic structure of the Liturgy, so that the Word of God in the celebration of worship itself becomes a living, anamnetic-epicletic event. At the same time, however, the inspired Word brings this fundamental structure *ab intra* into the Liturgy, in two ways: first, it prescribes for the celebration of the Liturgy the content of the remembrance, and secondly, it mediates a power that creates salvation, inspires, and shows the path to be taken here and now, a power that emanates from the Word. Accordingly, while it is possible to distinguish anamnesis and epiclesis conceptually and intellectually in the Liturgy, as in the Word of God too, they are ultimately inseparable.[334] This likewise demonstrates the close theological relationship between Scripture and Liturgy, which goes deeper than biblical quotations or allusions, but has its foundation in the essence of Scripture and of Liturgy.

The pneumatological-epicletic dimension finally leads us, after our customary summary of the hermeneutical insights gained, to the next chapter about the liturgical reception of Scripture. For inspiration is not related exclusively to the genesis of Scripture. Origen pointed out long ago that the same Spirit who was at work in the biblical authors is now at work in the reader and interpreter too.[335] In addition to the inspired author, there is thus also the "inspired reader"[336] or hearer. *GILM* 9 emphasizes: "The working of the Holy Spirit is needed if the word of God is to make what we hear outwardly have its effect inwardly."[337]

---

334 This is also indicated by the verbal link between anamnesis and epiclesis (as, e.g., in the prayer at episcopal ordination in the *Apostolic Tradition*; see A.III.11.1.).

335 See Helmut Gabel, "Inspiration. III. Theologie- und dogmengeschichtlich. IV. Systematisch-theologisch," in *LThK*, vol. 5 (Freiburg/Br.: Herder, 1996) 536 with reference to *Origenes. Peri Archon/De principiis*, praef. 4; *hom. in Jer* 39.1; *hom. in Ez* 2.2.

336 See Ulrich H. J. Körtner, *Der inspirierte Leser. Zentrale Aspekte biblischer Hermeneutik*, Sammlung Vandenhoeck (Göttingen: Vandenhoeck & Ruprecht, 1994).

337 See *GILM*, 4, 47.

CHAPTER 32

Hermeneutical Insights

I n accordance with liturgical theology,[338] this section has looked at the celebration of worship itself to see what theological aspects it contributes to a liturgical hermeneutics of the Bible. Here, it was necessary to look first at the functions of Scripture, because these too have an effect on the understanding of the text. Since a biblical text has several functions (the fourfold sense of Scripture), it can have not only the fundamental catechetical function in the Liturgy, but also a paracletic-pastoral, a meditative, a performative, and/or a doxological function as well. In relation to the liturgical celebration itself, Scripture can also have an interpretative, foundational, or critical function, so that it also is normative for the Liturgy.[339]

The anamnesis (remembrance) of God's saving deeds is already attested clearly in the Old Testament (*zkr*) and the New ("Do this in memory of me"), and establishes a substantial link between Bible and Liturgy.[340] In agreement with the biblical understanding, and in continuity with it, the liturgical anamnesis does not mean "time traveling" back into the history of Israel or of the early Church, but rather making present God's saving deeds, which are documented in Scripture, in the "today" of the liturgical celebration in such a way that the past is re-presented and the eschatological fulfillment is anticipated. The Liturgy employs the totality of salvation history, that is to say, "Old Testament—New Testament—today," or "Scripture—today—fulfillment" as the key to interpret Scripture; this is illustrated by numerous prayers (such as the Fourth Eucharistic Prayer). The example of the proclamation of the Gospel of the Resurrection on Sunday shows that this is not simply a matter of historical information. Through the anamnesis, the participants in the Liturgy become contemporaries of salvation. Accordingly, the Liturgy

---

338 On this, see the introduction to this section B.VIII.

339 See B.VIII.26.

340 See B.VIII.27.1.

understands and employs Scripture, not primarily as a document of the past, but as testimony to the Christ who is present and to God's saving activity.[341]

For a liturgical hermeneutics of the Bible, awareness of the "sacramentality of the Word" (*VD* 56), of its depth dimension, is central: God himself is present and at work in his Word in the power of the Spirit. The rites of the proclamation of the Word in the Mass announce that, in the proclamation of Scripture, God or Christ is speaking to the hearers, for God spoke to the human being in a human way—especially in Jesus Christ, who became a human being—and he continues to do so.

Numerous patristic writers interpreted the "becoming writing" as a continuation of the Incarnation, thereby explaining the presence of *Christ* in the Word. This patristic affirmation, prominently taken over in *SC* 7, prompted the question of his presence in Old Testament texts. The starting point here cannot be the text itself, since although the entire Old Testament (especially when the prophets are given their place at the end) has an openness to Christ, only a few passages can be immediately understood as referring to him. The growing sensitivity to the Old Testament as also the Sacred Scripture of Judaism forbids a fundamental Christian "colonization." Rather, our thinking must begin from the risen Christ, who proclaims and interprets the Scriptures as he did with the Emmaus disciples. The text, or the proclamation, thus does not generate his presence, but bears witness to it. Respect for the canonical text is born of the awareness of its sacramentality and manifests this sacramentality. The presence of God/Christ in the Word can also be illustrated by the theology of icons, which takes equal account of closeness and of distance.[342]

On the analogy of the real presence of Christ in the Eucharist, one can speak of a "verbal presence" (Lothar Lies) of Christ in the Word, which argues in a similar manner that a transubstantiation occurs: Christ transforms the human word into his own Word and himself becomes the subject of the word-event, while the human sounds are the accidents. Christ's presence in the Word is just as real as in the Eucharist, but there are varying degrees in the consciousness of reality.[343]

This involves a revelation that goes forth anew and aims at reception by the human being and at his or her response. The dialogical character of the Liturgy and the understanding of Scripture as an event of revelation compenetrate each other as two sides of the same coin. The Liturgy

341 See B.VIII.27.2.

342 See B.VIII.28.1.1.

343 See B.VIII.28.1.2.

strengthens the awareness that Scripture is the medium of the encounter with God, whose Word comes to meet us in human words through the proclamation (or in other liturgical implementations), and to whom the human being responds, in part with the words of Scripture itself.[344] Scripture is thus understood as alive and active. Through the anamnesis brought about by the Spirit, Scripture becomes anew the event of salvation, and unfolds—while respecting human freedom and the eschatological reservation—a performative power that supports faith, builds up the human being, forgives sins, accomplishes salvation, and is meant to leave its mark on daily living.[345] Scripture must be understood in personal and relational terms, especially when it is employed in the Liturgy as a divine-human event of encounter. In other words, it is sacramental.

The emphasis on the sacramentality of the Word means that one must rethink the traditional conceptual pair "Word and sacrament." The liturgical celebration shows that the sacramental celebration in the narrower sense of the term is also structured verbally: the reading, which presents God's prevenient speaking, elicits the word of response in prayer and signs, especially in the sacramental prayer and in the symbolic action (with accompanying words), both of which bear the imprint of the Bible and are, in part, a ritual translation of the anamnetic readings. If, then, the Word is sacramental and the sacrament is verbal, the "and" that unites them must be emphasized: Word *and* sacrament are related to each other in their structure and content, so that they form one inherent complementary unity, in which, of course, one can differentiate between Word and sacrament in their specific characteristics.[346] The Mass contains a dynamic from the Word to the Eucharist, because one and the same Paschal Mystery is first proclaimed in the Word and then enacted sacramentally. As with the disciples of Emmaus, the Word (always as a concrete pericope) sheds light on the eucharistic event (the celebration of the entire Christ), while at the same time, the Eucharist opens the door to the understanding of Scripture. The concreteness and the totality have need of each other.

Although the same Christ is really present in the Word and in the Eucharist, the special characteristic of the latter is that he is present in the Eucharist substantially, and hence also abidingly and visibly. The relatedness and the inherent dynamic forbid an equalization, as if Word and Eucharist were ultimately interchangeable. Anthropological reasons also mean that we need

344 See B.VIII.28.2.

345 See B.VIII.28.3.

346 See B.VIII.29.1.

both modes of the presence of Christ, since the Liturgy seeks to correspond to both hearing and understanding, on the one hand, and seeing and tasting, on the other—to the human perception through both the intellect and the senses.[347]

The Old Testament and the New are combined in the Liturgy in the Order of Readings, the prayers and the chants, as well as through the schema promise—fulfillment, through typology, or connections in content and in form. This combination communicates to the participants the insight into the unity of the two Testaments in the Paschal Mystery (an insight that is important for biblical hermeneutics) and their orientation to Christ.[348] The Liturgy not only creates a bridge from the Old Testament to the New, but also extends this from Scripture to today's liturgical celebration, which thus becomes the "antitype" of Scripture (Ambrose). By *doing* what Scripture *says*, the Liturgy makes it possible to experience Scripture.[349]

Finally, we have illustrated the pneumatological dimension of the Word in the Liturgy in connection with inspiration. This was not only important in the genesis of Scripture, but is equally something that happens today, since the same Spirit who worked in the sacred authors makes Christ/God present today in the Word, makes possible the dialogical encounter, generates the performative effect of the Word, and inspires the hearers. The Word thus also possesses an epicletic dimension in the celebration of worship. Indeed, like the Liturgy itself, it is an anamnetic-epicletic event—and this once again shows the intimate relationship between Scripture and Liturgy.[350] The Spirit of God also makes us ready to receive the Word. We shall now turn to this theme.

347 See B.VIII.29.2.
348 See B.VIII.30.1.
349 See B.VIII.30.2.
350 See B.VIII.31.

The Reception of Scripture in the Celebration of the Liturgy

After looking at the theological aspects, we shall now turn to the reception of Scripture within the Liturgy (as distinguished from other concepts of reception). In other words: What does the participant in Liturgy receive from Scripture, and how does it reach him or her? Two elements interact here: from the perspective of liturgical studies the *participatio actuosa*, and from the perspective of literary studies reception theory, which has increasingly found a place in theology too.[1]

In literary studies, reception theory,[2] as an interaction between text and reader, draws attention to two insights. First, there is the openness of historical texts to differing and new interpretations, depending on the individual recipient in his or her various contexts. Umberto Eco underlines that the

---

1 For biblical studies, see, e.g., Braulik, "Rezeptionsästhetik," esp. 525–28; for dogmatics, see, e.g., Rudolf Voderholzer, "'Die Heilige Schrift wächst irgendwie mit den Lesern' (Gregor der Große). Dogmatik und Rezeptionsästhetik," in Voderholzer, *Offenbarung*, 151–69.

2 On the first orientation, see Heinz Antor, "Rezeptionsästhetik," in *Metzler Lexikon Literatur- und Kulturtheorie. Ansätze – Personen – Grundbegriffe*, ed. A. Nünning, 5th ed. (Stuttgart: J. B. Metzler, 2013), 650–52 (with bibliography); Hans Robert Jauß, "Rezeption und Rezeptionsästhetik," *HWP* 8 (1992): 996–1004; Rainer Warning, ed., *Rezeptionsästhetik. Theorie und Praxis*, UTB 303, 2nd ed. (Munich: Fink, 1979).

author hands over to the reader an "open work," "a work to be completed,"[3] because the reader collaborates on the interpretation.[4] The understanding is influenced by one's life experience and culture, but it is not arbitrary, since it is guided by the interplay of empty or indeterminate passages and commentaries in the text.[5] Secondly, therefore, the reader has a central part to play in the reception of a text. The literary scholar Wolfgang Iser draws attention to the "act of reading" and emphasizes that in the act of writing, the author already has in mind the role of the implicit reader,[6] which should be adopted by a concrete reader in order to discover the potential of meaning in the text that the author offers. Reader-response criticism in American literary scholarship has highlighted similar insights.[7] We can therefore say that "The greatest revolution in modern hermeneutics is the discovery of the reader."[8] This brief overview of literary studies makes it clear that reflections on reception theory also belong essentially to a liturgical hermeneutics of the Bible, although in the case of the reception of Scripture in the context of worship, one must bear in mind not so much the reader, as the hearer.

The present section begins with:

1. The reception of Scripture (by the individual and by the Church) as an act of active participation in liturgy (Chapter 33).

---

3 Umberto Eco, *The Open Work*, trans. A. Cancogni (Cambridge, MA: Harvard University Press, 1989), 19.

4 Hans-Georg Gadamer, *Truth and Method*, trans. J. Weinsheimer and D. G. Mashall, 2nd ed. (London, New York: Continuum, 2006), 296 underlined that "[t]he real meaning of a text" is not exhausted in the meaning of the author and of his original public, but goes beyond this, so that "understanding is not merely a reproductive but always a productive activity as well." Accordingly, he emphasizes the *Wirkungsgeschichte* ("history of effect": see Gadamer, 298-306), because the concrete understanding of a text is always (unconsciously) influenced by the interpretations that are taken over from the history of its effect (see Gadamer, 298–99). See also Voderholzer, "Rezeptionsästhetik," 156.

5 See Umberto Eco, *The Role of the Reader: Explorations in the Semiotics of Texts*, Advances in semiotics (Bloomington, IN: Indiana University Press, 1981).

6 See Wolfgang Iser, *The Act of Reading: A Theory of Aesthetic Response* (Baltimore: Johns Hopkins University Press, 1978); Iser, *The Implied Reader: Patterns of Communication in Prose Fiction from Bunyan to Beckett* (Baltimore: Johns Hopkins University Press, 1974); Eco, *Role of the Reader*.

7 See Jane P. Tompkins, ed., *Reader-Response Criticism: From Formalism to Post-Structuralism* (Baltimore: Johns Hopkins University Press, 1980); Elizabeth Freund, *The Return of the Reader: Reader-Response Criticism* (London/New York: Routledge, 2003). See, with transposition to the Liturgy, Janowiak, *Holy Preaching*, 129-59.

8 Oeming, "Verborgene Nähe," 193. See Oeming, *Contemporary Biblical Hermeneutics*, 75-112, esp. 75-77.

2. The identification with biblical characters that the participant in the Liturgy cites in the first person (Chapter 34).
3. How reception includes a cognitive, content-related aspect, that is to say, how Scripture is received and remains in one's memory (Chapter 35).
4. An exploration of a spiritual aspect that aims at a Christian identity nourished by Scripture and by the Liturgy (Chapter 36).

CHAPTER 33

The Reception of Scripture as an Act of *Participatio Actuosa*

J ust as a human word must be received by one's counterpart, so too the Word of God, in accordance with the event of a dialogical revelation and encounter,[9] demands a resonance in the hearer, who must make it his or her own. Reception does not in the least occur automatically. It is a conscious act of "active participation"[10] in the Liturgy. The *participatio actuosa* must not be misunderstood as a "pastoral method" of involving the faithful in worship. On the contrary, it "is demanded by the very nature of the Liturgy" (*SC* 14) and is a central principle of the celebration of worship.[11] It is also highly important for the way in which we encounter the Word of God, because it makes it possible truly to receive it.

Participation, with regard to Scripture, includes both interior and exterior acts.[12] The ritual actions are first of all physical: through bodily postures (sitting, standing), acclamations, singing, seeing, and above all hearing, but also through silence, the faithful take part in the proclamation of the Word.

9 See B.VIII.28.2.

10 See Mark Searle, *Called to Participate. Theological, Ritual, and Social Perspectives*, ed. B. Searle and A. Y. Koester (Collegeville,MN: Liturgical Press, 2006); Marco Benini, "Andrea Pozzos Deckenfresco von Sant'Ignazio in Rom und die tätige Teilnahme an der Liturgie der Kirche," in *"Dein Antlitz, Herr, will ich suchen!". Selbstoffenbarung Gottes und Antwort des Menschen* (FS Michael Schneider), ed. T. Kremer, Koinonia – Oriens 55 (Münster: Aschendorff, 2019), 421–41.

11 If the Liturgy is the celebration and the making present of the Paschal Mystery, and hence seeks to draw people into the dying and rising of Christ, it must aim at participation in this celebration. The very frequency with which this is mentioned in *SC* demonstrates the importance of this formal principle of the liturgical renewal: the *"participatio actuosa"* is mentioned thirteen times, and the text speaks twenty-eight times of *"participare"* / *"participatio."*

12 See *SC* 19; 99; 110.

Participation in the Liturgy begins through external, bodily behavior, but this aims to lead us to an internal sharing. Since the Word in the Liturgy has a sacramental character,[13] the external event and the internal realization belong together, and only in this way make possible a holistic participation that is in accord with both the human being in one's perceptive faculty and with the Word of God, which seeks to bear fruit in the hearer. By making us aware of the importance of God's Word, the ritual actions promote our attentiveness and aid an interior reception of the Word, which ideally addresses the hearer genuinely and flows into a reflection on what has been heard. Reception naturally also makes demands of the quality of the public reading or singing, and profits from an aesthetically attractive staging of the proclamation of the Word, as well as from the mystagogical communication of its theological aspects. Since the Liturgy is the celebration of the Church, and individual and communal participation complement one another, we shall look in what follows at the reception of Scripture both by the individual and in the ecclesial community.

1. RECEPTION AS THE ACT OF THE INDIVIDUAL

Reception theory emphasizes the collaboration of the reader and the act of reading itself. An initial act of the *participatio actuosa* for the Liturgy thus consists in the conscious hearing of a scriptural text (or of a text bearing the imprint of the Bible). Hearing has different conditions from reading, where one can pause for reflection if something is unclear or go back and read a section of the text again. In reading, the text as a whole lies before one's eyes. In hearing, however, it has a point-by-point orientation. Depending on how it is read aloud, a text that is heard can make an impact that differs from a text that one personally reads. This is why one can experience again and again in the Liturgy that while a biblical text is read aloud, one perceives different aspects from those one had noticed when reading it personally beforehand. Or (on the other hand) one may simply fail to hear some words or ideas that have been read aloud.

After hearing, the second step of reception is understanding, which is likewise an essential act of participation in worship and can take different forms in different persons. But not only is hearing the presupposition of understanding; conversely, only a certain degree of understanding makes a conscious hearing possible.

---

13 See B.VIII.28.

What applies to one single text is immensely expanded in the case of the intertextual references that the attentive hearer can establish in one's head when several biblical texts are read aloud in the Liturgy of the Word. If one has noticed that the Responsorial Psalm (usually) has a reference to the preceding reading (deepening an idea in it, formulating a response, etc.), one will consciously listen carefully to see where a connection can be found. The refrain that is repeated by the congregation can play a supporting role here.[14] In an analogous way, the perception of intertextual relationships between the readings and other liturgical texts or hymns chosen for their suitability is an act of interior participation. Although it is relatively easy to recognize that the Gospel of the day is taken up again in the Communion antiphon, here too conscious, active participation is required, if one is to interpret the text spiritually or to actualize it in relation to Holy Communion.[15] Such acts are not primarily the fruit of an intellectual endeavor. If one is accustomed to play one's role consciously, they automatically take place performatively (so to speak).[16] This means that, as with participation in the Liturgy as a whole, reception has both an active and a passive-receptive side.[17]

Reception is a living process. Reception theory has made us newly aware of something that Gregory the Great († 604) summed up as follows in a homily on Ezekiel, on the basis of his own experience of reflecting on Scripture: "*Divina eloquia cum legente crescunt*" – "The divine words grow with the reader, for each one understands them more deeply, the more deeply one penetrates them."[18] Spiritual growth is accompanied by an increase in the understanding of Scripture, since Gregory sees this as a dynamic reality that condescends to the level of the reader and assimilates itself to him or her.[19] This can also be experienced in the Liturgy, especially in the regularly recurring short readings or psalms in the Liturgy of the Hours, which speak

---

14 See A.II.8.

15 On this, see A.IV.15.

16 See also B.VIII.28.3.

17 The concept of *participatio* in classical Latin already has a passive-receptive character and is also understood in 1 Cor 10:16–17 ("The bread that we break, is it not a participation [*participatio*/κοινωνία] in the body of Christ?"), in the First Eucharistic Prayer ("*ex hac altaris participatione*"), and in some prayers after Communion in the Roman Mass, as a participation in God's gift. It was only in the Motu Proprio *Tra le sollecitudini* of Pius X (1903) that the concept also acquired an active meaning, which was taken up through the liturgical movement and made its way into *SC*.

18 Gregory, *Homiliae in Ezechielem prophetam* 1.7.8 (CChr.SL 142:87). See *VD* 30.

19 See Stephan Ch. Kessler, *Gregor der Große als Exeget. Eine theologische Interpretation der Ezechielhomilien*, IThS 43 (Innsbruck: Tyrolia, 1995), 252–53.

differently each time, depending on one's own situation. Over the course of time, there is a growth in the words of Scripture in the sense that one and the same text accumulates subjective connotations for the individual, and sometimes also evokes earlier connotations.

The liturgical reception of Scripture is linked to specific individual presuppositions. This begins with the interests and expectations generated by one's personal existential situation. If, for example, one is confronted by a person's death, affirmations about dying and rising (not only in the readings) will be perceived with greater clarity. In addition to a basic openness, one condition of which is a person's attitude to Church and to religion, reception frequently presupposes biblical knowledge, since the subtle allusions in prayers and hymns will be heard only by one who knows the Bible. Familiarity with the Bible is thus a component of competence with regard to the celebration.[20] A lack of scriptural knowledge entails considerable difficulties in understanding the Liturgy.

Reception theory indicates that the indeterminate passages in a text open the door to the possibility of differing interpretations. The Liturgy also gives the hearer freedom about how to hear a biblical text, to understand it, and to make it bear fruit. It is interesting here that, while a liturgy often points to one possible path of understanding, it does not insist on this. In the Liturgy of the Hours, for example, the antiphons on a feast day color the Psalms in such a way that they suggest a corresponding (usually Christological) interpretation, but the individual is not in the least obliged to follow this. The introit antiphon on Easter Sunday, from Ps 139: "I have risen (*Resurrexi*), and I am with you ...," is the classic example here. It suggests an interpretation with particular clarity, while however leaving it open. It is obvious that the key word *Resurrexi* has determined the choice of text, with the unambiguous hint that this psalm verse should be understood as *vox Christi ad patrem*.[21] The same applies to the Responsorial Psalm at the Easter Vigil and on Easter Sunday, the classic Easter Psalm 118, which includes the words "I shall not die, I shall live." However, the Christological interpretation is not expressed in the text of the introit, nor in the Psalm—it is up to the hearer to understand it in this way. Harald Buchinger sums up: "The poetry proper to the Roman tradition lies in the simultaneity of an unambiguous allusion

20 See Harald Buchinger, "Mehr als ein Steinbruch? Beobachtungen und Fragen zur Bibelverwendung in der römischen Liturgie," *BiLi* 82, no. 1 (2009): 24. On the other hand, taking part in the celebration itself intensifies this kind of competence, since the biblical texts are continually repeated in the Liturgy, and one's familiarity with them grows.

21 See A.II.7.2.

and an openness about its acceptance."[22] This differs from the Byzantine liturgy, which directly specifies a Christologization of the psalms through the numerous stichira or troparia, when for example the words "Christ is risen from the dead" are inserted countless times in the Easter Vigil.[23] Here, the reception by the individual is especially conditioned by the ecclesial community.

2. THE CHURCH AS A COMMUNITY OF RECEPTION

It is very important today to look at the individual and at the personal existential relevance of Bible and Liturgy. However, the Liturgy is always the celebration of the Church, and hence first and foremost a community celebration.[24] Similarly, the Bible is not primarily a book for individual edification and private reading, but the book of the Church. This is true with regard to its genesis, since it was only thanks to the ecclesial process of reception that writings were admitted to the canon (and public reading aloud in the Liturgy played a central role here).[25] Moreover, canonical texts are "public and normative texts of a reading community. The implied ideal recipient is not, as in the modern novel, an individual in one's sitting room, but the listening community of reception in its liturgical assembly."[26] This can be seen in Scripture itself, when, for example, we read in Colossians 4:16: "And when this letter is read before you, have it read also in the church of the Laodiceans, and you yourselves read the one from Laodicea."[27] The horizon of a book

---

22 Buchinger, "Mehr als ein Steinbruch," 23.

23 See Buchinger, "Lebensraum des Wortes," 205 n. 90.

24 See SC, 26.

25 See bibliography in the Introduction 1.

26 Dieter Böhler, "Der Kanon als hermeneutische Vorgabe biblischer Theologie. Über aktuelle Methodendiskussionen in der Bibelwissenschaft," *ThPh* 77, no. 2 (2002): 178 n. 35. In his concluding homily at the Synod of Bishops on the Word of God (October 26, 2008), Benedict XVI declared that in the Liturgy "it appears that the Bible is a book of the people and for the people: a heritage, a testament consigned to readers so that the salvation history witnessed in the text becomes concrete in their own lives. There is therefore a vital, reciprocal relationship of belonging between the people and the book: the Bible remains a living book with the people as its subject who read it. The people cannot exist without the book, because in it they find their reason for being, their vocation and their identity. This mutual belonging between people and Sacred Scripture is celebrated in every liturgical assembly" (https://www.vatican.va/content/benedict-xvi/en/homilies/2008/documents/hf_ben-xvi_hom_20081026_conclusione-sinodo.html [retrieved 2/21/2022]). See also Chauvet, *Symbol and Sacrament*, 209: "The Community Writes Itself in the Book It Reads."

27 See Böhler, "Kanon," 178 n. 35; Dt 31:10–11; Neh 8; Rev 1:3.

is broadened for the present day when it is admitted to the canon and read aloud at liturgy. For example, it is clear that Paul's Letter to Philemon, with its request about Philemon's slave Onesimus, was, in its original intention, primarily a personal letter; however, it was elevated to a testimony of faith for the Church.[28] Reception in the community of the Church, and *a fortiori* in the horizon of worship, shows us that Scripture is indeed the Word of God. "In the hearing of God's word the Church is built up and grows."[29]

One can also explain the reception of Scripture by the Church from the perspective of cultural anthropology.[30] The sociologist Maurice Halbwachs (1877-1945)[31] introduced the collective memory into the discourse of the cultural sciences and showed that the individual with one's "individual memory" (biography, experiences, etc.) is integrated into a group or society, and exists only in this manner. This is why the individual memory has a social character and is conditioned *inter alia* by the so-called "collective memory." The Egyptologist Jan Assmann subsequently developed this concept.[32] He draws a distinction between the "communicative memory" and the "cultural memory." The former contains the events of (one's personal) daily living, which are narrated orally. If these are not documented in writing, they fade after no later than three to four generations and are replaced by new events. The cultural memory, on the other hand, mediates the original story (or stories) that are the foundation of the identity of a group or society. Even if these lie far back in the past, they are authoritative for its self-understanding. Cultural memory "possesses a normative and formative quality."[33] This, of course, requires specific forms of remembering that lie outside everyday communication. In order to maintain the cultural memory in existence, a

---

28 See Böhler, 168, with further examples.

29 *GILM*, 7.

30 Liturgical studies frequently draw on this cultural-anthropological explanation with regard to anamnesis. See Zerfaß, *Hermeneutik*, 9-11.

31 See Maurice Halbwachs, *On Collective Memory*, trans. L. A. Coser, Heritage of Sociology Series (Chicago: The University of Chicago Press, 1992).

32 See Jan Assmann, *Cultural Memory and Early Civilization: Writing, Remembrance, and Political Imagination*, trans. D. H. Wilson (Cambridge,/New York: Cambridge University Press, 2011).

33 Jan Assmann, "Der zweidimensionale Mensch: Das Fest als Medium des kollektiven Gedächtnisses," in *Das Fest und das Heilige. Religiöse Kontrapunkte zur Alltagswelt*, ed. J. Assmann in collaboration with T. Sundermeier, Studien zum Verstehen fremder Religionen 1 (Gütersloh: Gütersloher Verlagshaus, 1991), 13-30, at 22.

"ceremonial communication" is needed, with rites that stage it again and again, and with the dimension of the feast.[34]

A link can be made here to the Bible and the Liturgy. In this terminology, Scripture is the document of the "cultural memory" that is staged and remembered through the Liturgy in such a way that it is relevant to today and keeps alive the identity of the Church as a community of faith. Through the liturgical anamnesis of Scripture in the proclamation, but also in the other forms such as prayer, hymns, and rites, the original event—the revelation of God in the history of salvation with human beings—is kept alive, so that it becomes the foundation that creates the identity of today's Church as a community of faith. From this perspective, liturgy, with its dimension of the "feast" (celebration), and the ritual staging of Scripture, which differs from everyday communication, are absolutely necessary for ecclesial identity.

The distinction mentioned above between the individual and the collective memory (and in turn between the communicative and the cultural memory) can shed light on the relationship between the individual and the communal reception of Scripture. The individual believer no doubt remembers in his or her individual memory those stories or statements in Scripture that have addressed him or her personally (also in the celebration of the Liturgy), or that have left their mark on the personal journey of faith.[35] Besides this, the Church has a collective memory of Scripture at hand that can leave its mark on the participant in the Liturgy, even if particular passages do not cross over as such into one's individual memory. Taking up Assmann's differentiation, we could say that the communicative memory, which is primarily transmitted orally and covers only a limited time span, stands for the memories of those experiences of faith that have been transmitted in the family or the local community, and that in their own way have mediated aspects of Scripture. The cultural memory—the Bible—is "kept going"[36] for the Church as a community of faith in the Liturgy (in the variety of the different celebrations) and is offered to the individual to be received, even if the individual certainly cannot assimilate the totality of it.

Far from devaluing reception by the individual, this places it in a larger context that transcends the individual. When, for example, the Psalms are prayed in the Liturgy of the Hours, there may indeed be a difference between the mood in a psalm and one's own personal situation. But the fact that one is praying, not only in one's own name, but also in the name of the Church,

---

34 See Assmann, 24.

35 See B.IX.35.

36 Assmann, "Der zweidimensionale Mensch," 24.

makes possible the personal reception of the Psalm in one's prayer.[37] More-over, interpretations of scriptural passages are handed on over the centuries in the Liturgy, so that (unlike a homily that is tied to one particular period) they acquire a certain official and normative character. This is the case with the mostly patristic texts in the Office of Readings, which (according to *GILH* 163) are "an authentic interpretation of the word of God," or with the hymns that transmit in poetic language traditional expositions of Scripture. As the example of the hymns about the Cross has shown,[38] hymns can draw attention to aspects that would surely not occur automatically to one who prays today—such as seeing the Passion and Cross of Christ as a triumph. The Liturgy also mediates typological interpretations of Old Testament texts, which have their origin in the context of the spiritual exposition of Scripture in earlier times.[39]

The variety of horizons of understanding in the tradition and in the present day need not necessarily be a disadvantage. This can be an enrich-ment, since if the Liturgy were allowed to verbalize only what is immediately obvious to every single person, this would lead to its impoverishment. In principle, each person must understand something, but certainly not every-thing, of any high-quality text—and liturgical texts must be of high quality, for the simple reason that it must be possible to repeat them.[40] The Liturgy, through its repetition of the texts, can also bring about a broadening of the theological field of vision, thanks to liturgical tradition.

Difficulties arise, of course, when metaphors are employed that are no longer comprehensible and that must first be made plausible through expla-nations (or more generally, through instruction in the Bible and the Liturgy). Here, one must take into account the form of worship and the intended participants. This touches on fundamental hermeneutical questions, with their opportunities and their limitations—questions that affect eighteenth-century hymns just as much as the biblical texts themselves.

It is clear that the Church has a breadth in its liturgical reception of Scripture that goes beyond what the individual can assimilate. The Church's experience of faith and of the scriptures is, simply, larger, and this means that it can enrich the individual who shares in the Liturgy in the Church's experi-ence. This brings out the added value of the ecclesial reception. At the same time, not everything that an individual deduces from a scriptural passage,

---

37 See A.II.9.2; *GILH*, 108.

38 See A.IV.14.

39 See B.VIII.30; A.IV.16.

40 See Böhler, "Liturgiam authenticam," 214.

even if it is meaningful and legitimate for him or her, can be the Church's interpretation. The reception by the Church is thus a kind of "quality control" that protects against subjectivism and objectifies the interpretation, while the Liturgy also gives room for one's personal reception.

CHAPTER 34

First-Person Role Identification

We have seen at several points in Part A the first-person role identification (Angelus A. Häußling)[41] as a means of the reception of Scripture, when the Liturgy suggests, either through the context or immediately in the first-person singular, that one should identify with a biblical person and take on his or her role. This helps to grasp that one is the addressee of the saving action attested in the Bible and enables him or her to become contemporary with salvation. This hermeneutical "method" is, collectively or individually, an act of the active participation by the faithful, which can also be found in Jewish exegesis and liturgy.[42] The first-person quotation is ultimately biblical, as we see in the tax collector in the Temple, who quotes the great penitential prayer of David, Psalm 51, and thereby takes on his role.[43]

The Sunday Gospels of Lent in the Roman and Ambrosian rites present "models" of faith (the Samaritan woman, the deaf and mute man, Martha), with whom the hearer can identify personally on one's own pilgrimage toward Easter. For example, by referring to oneself Jesus' question to Martha: "Do you believe this?" one may answer with her: "Yes, Lord, I have come to believe that …" (Jn 11:26–27).[44] The example of the Anointing of the Sick showed how the various Gospel texts (historically selected on the basis of the gender of the sick person) help the sick to empathize with the sufferers in the Bible, to adopt their attitude of trust, and to ask through Jesus Christ

---

41 See Häußling, "Liturgie: Gedächtnis eines Vergangenen"; Häußling, "Bibel in der Liturgie der Tagzeiten," 96-100.

42 Examples are the identification in the Passover celebration with the Israelites who were liberated from Egypt, or with the Israelites at Sinai when Torah is proclaimed (see B.VII.24.2).

43 See Häußling, "Biblische Grundlegung," 306; Lk 18:13.

44 See A.I.3.2.2.

that they themselves may be healed.[45] When the hearers identify with the biblical persons, this role identification supports the meditative reception of the readings, while also making them aware that the pericopes also speak anamnetically[46] both of and to those who take part today. In Häußling's terminology, "The use of the words of Sacred Scripture in the 'salvation-historical, identifying' sense and the meditative-internalizing use complement and confirm each other."[47]

Besides this, role identification can permit rites with a biblical character to unfold a deeper meaning. For example, at the Washing of the Feet on Holy Thursday, the identification with the disciples (especially by means of the accompanying chants) seeks to motivate the participants to grasp the charge given by the Lord himself and to fulfill it.[48] The priest's role identification when he speaks the words of institution is a special case here.

The adoption of a first-person role in songs often occurs. Here, we think of the three Gospel canticles that are recited every day, the *Benedictus*, *Magnificat*, and *Nunc dimittis*, especially because "their psalmodic form, the deep personal involvement of the speakers, and the intensity of the original situation of salvation"[49] make an identification easy. Those who pray share in the salvation that Zechariah, Mary, and Simeon experienced, and that remains valid down through the ages. In a similar way, we praise God with Daniel 3 because we identify with those who in their confession of faith in the true God experienced his saving intervention in their distress. This likewise became a paradigm for later generations, so that this canticle is prayed at Lauds every Sunday as a testimony of faith and an expression of hope in God's power.[50]

The role identification is even clearer at the Sanctus. Those who celebrate the Eucharist take over the threefold "Holy!" of the seraphim (Is 6:3 and Rev 4:8) and are already, thanks to the role identification, participants in the heavenly liturgy. In the Byzantine Divine Liturgy, the role identification is mentioned explicitly in the Hymn of the Cherubim (cherubikon): "Let us who mystically represent the cherubim and sing the Thrice-holy Hymn to

---

45 See A.I.4.1.

46 See B.VIII.27.

47 Häußling, "Bibel in der Liturgie der Tagzeiten," 98.

48 See A.V.17.1.

49 Häußling, "Liturgie: Gedächtnis und Befreiung," 6.

50 See Häußling, "Bibel in der Liturgie der Tagzeiten," 97. The use of Dn 3 on Sunday shows that the paradigm of rescue by God is interpreted here with regard to the raising of Jesus from the dead too.

the life-giving Trinity, now lay aside all cares of life. That we may receive the King of all, escorted invisibly by ranks of angels. Alleluja, alleluja, alleluja."[51]

In contrast, role identification is found rather seldom in the Communion antiphons. An example is when they address Christ with the words of a biblical person, such as Martha's confession, quoted above (Jn 11:27),[52] or when the Magi appear on the feast of the Epiphany as the *typos* of the communicants.[53]

The first-person role identification is particularly important for the hermeneutics of the Psalms. The guiding question for the patristic exposition of the Psalms, as Hilary of Poitiers († 368) put it in the introduction to his *Commentary on the Psalms*, was "*ex cuius persona vel in quem*" a psalm is spoken, (or to put it more simply: who is speaking to whom?).[54] The first question is decisive: Who is the speaker, who is joined by the one who prays these words in the first person today? In the classic psalm of repentance, 51 (50), one can identify with David, the sinner who received forgiveness.[55] A special form of role identification is the Christologization, especially the interpretation of a psalm as *vox Christi*, which is important for the hermeneutics of the Psalms and their liturgical reception (precisely on feast days).[56]

The role identification with narrative texts shows that a first-person formulation is not necessary, but it is certainly helpful. For a liturgical hermeneutics of the Bible, it is particularly interesting and significant when a cantor or the congregation in the first person makes their own a psalm that must unambiguously be understood Christologically because of its context.[57] Our example is taken from the First Vespers of Palm Sunday. The antiphon to the first Psalm is a first-person logion of Jesus, spoken immediately before his arrest (see Mk 14:49), expanded with a reference to the ensuing path of suffering: "Day after day I sat teaching you in the temple and you did not lay hands on me. Now you come to scourge me and lead me to the cross."[58] The

---

51 Galadza, *Divine Liturgy*, 222. See Taft and Parenti, *Grande ingresso*, 155-84, 199-206.

52 See 7th Sunday in Ordinary Time (*Missal*, 467), or on the feast of Saint Martha (*Missal*, 910).

53 See A.IV.15; *Missal*, 189.

54 Hilary, *Tractatus super psalmos* 1.1 (CSEL 22:19). See Rondeau, *Commentaires patristiques du Psautier*, 2:7.

55 See also Häußling, "Liturgie: Gedächtnis und Befreiung," 7.

56 See A.II.8.

57 See Buchinger, "Mehr als ein Steinbruch," 24.

58 *Liturgy of the Hours*, 2:1208.

liturgical context suggests that Psalm 119:105–112, otherwise usually prayed in the Psalter of the second week and likewise formulated in the first person, can also be understood as words of Christ about his Passion, since numerous verses (italicized here) point in this direction:

> [105] Your word is a lamp for my steps * and a light for my path.
>
> [106] I have sworn and have made up my mind * to obey your decrees.
>
> [107] *Lord, I am deeply afflicted:* * by your word give me life.
>
> [108] Accept, Lord, the homage of my lips * and teach me your decrees.
>
> [109] *Though I carry my life in my hands,* * I remember your law.
>
> [110] *Though the wicked try to ensnare me,* * I do not stray from your precepts.
>
> [111] Your will is my heritage for ever, * the joy of my heart.
>
> [112] *I set myself to carry out your will* * *in fullness,* for ever.[59]

Jesus' teaching in the Temple, mentioned in the antiphon, could also find an echo in God's "word" / "decrees" / "law" / "precepts." The psalm also draws attention to Jesus' endurance (vv. 107, 109–10) and already to Easter motifs (vv. 111–12: "for ever" / "heritage" / "joy"). The decisive point is that the one who now prays this psalm can identify its "I" with the "I" of Jesus and/or with one's own "I," so that the psalm supplies words both for the meditative "empathy" with Jesus' interior disposition before his death and for one's own path as a follower of the crucified and risen Christ.

The second psalm too can be understood along these lines. The antiphon is taken from the third Song of the Suffering Servant ("The Lord God is my help; no shame can harm me" [Is 50:7]),[60] so that it is read on Palm Sunday as speaking of Christ, especially since the same text is proclaimed as the first reading at Mass that day. Together with Psalm 16, especially vv. 10–11 ("For you will not leave my soul among the dead [...]. You will show me the path of life"), this generates a subtle look ahead to Easter, which also resonates in the canticle from Philippians 2:6–11 (vv. 9–11) that follows.[61] Here too, the one who prays can hear Jesus speaking in the psalm and know that he/she is led, in Jesus' footsteps, on the path that leads through affliction to life. This double hermeneutics of the Psalms gently makes clear to the one who prays that one is repeating the words of Jesus' "I," and imitating the Lord who has gone before him. One confesses that one is a Christian and is strengthened

---

59 *Liturgy of the Hours,* 2:1209.

60 *Liturgy of the Hours,* 2:1210.

61 The same text is also read as the second reading at Mass on Palm Sunday and draws attention to the Paschal Mystery in its entirety.

in one's Christian identity by praying the Psalms. Repeating Jesus' words in prayer leads to imitating him in one's life.

It is precisely this openness, which leaves it up to the one who prays to decide in whose person one wishes to speak the text, and the fact that one activitates this mechanism in one's own head (*participatio!*), that makes this hermeneutical procedure even more attractive. If, however, a psalm already has a strong Christological imprint, such as Psalm 22 (21), the Responsorial Psalm on Palm Sunday, with its refrain: "My God, my God, why have you forsaken me?", one will probably stay (perfectly legitimately) with the meditative contemplation of the life of Jesus to a greater degree than when one prays Psalm 119 at First Vespers of that day.

The same hermeneutical phenomenon occurs more rarely on saints' days, when an antiphon consists of first-person words of a saint and is followed by an "I-psalm." For example, on the feast of Saint Lawrence (August 10), the first antiphon at Lauds takes up the following Psalm 63 (62) literally and expands it biographically: "My soul clings to you, my God, because I endured death by fire for your sake."[62] The Psalm is placed on his lips, so to speak, and the one who prays repeats it after him. This suggests that, just as Lawrence prayed this psalm, so we too are praying it today. On the feast of the Conversion of Saint Paul, first-person words of Paul are combined to form antiphons that are now recited by the one who prays.[63] Other examples could be mentioned.[64] The role identification is made easier by the absence (often, although not always) of an introductory clause such as "Lawrence said," which would leave the words more firmly in the past.

The Responsorial Psalm occasionally supports a role identification, for example on the 3rd Sunday of Easter C, after the reading about the interrogation of Peter and the other apostles before the Sanhedrin, from which they depart full of joy, despite or because of the shame they have suffered (Acts 5:27b-32, 40b-41). The Responsorial Psalm meditates on the joy in praising God, which is mentioned only briefly in the pericope. Like the psalm itself,

---

62 *Liturgy of the Hours*, 4:1307. An analogous procedure is employed on the feasts of Our Lady of Sorrows (4:1403) and Saint Stephen (1:1258).

63 See *Liturgy of the Hours*, 3:1320, 1324, 1327.

64 See also Saint Polycarp ("For eighty-six years I have served Jesus ..."; *Liturgy of the Hours*, 3:1398); Peter and Paul (3:1500, 1503, 1508); the apostle Thomas (3:1518, 1520), Mary Magdalene (3:1545), Augustine (4:1358), Francis (4:1468), Ignatius of Antioch (4:1492–93), Luke (4:1500), Martin (4:1555), Andrew (4:1589), the Immaculate Conception (1:1222), Lucy (1:1245), and the evangelist Mark (2:1789). The links between antiphon and Psalm are not equally evident in all these examples.

the refrain is in the first person:[65] "I will praise you, Lord, for you have rescued me." Cantor and congregation can thus recite the psalm in the role of the apostles, meditating on their situation. Yet the context of the Easter season also makes it possible to understand the psalm as speaking about Christ, who has arisen out of the depths of death, and hence to identify with him (as the apostles themselves did). At the same time, a door is opened to bring one's own experiences of this kind into the singing of the psalm.

These numerous examples demonstrate not only the frequency with which role identification is employed as a means of the liturgical hermeneutics of the Bible, but also its various facets. Role identification always establishes a bridge between the biblical text and the recipients, both by helping them to enter personally into the text and thus understand it better, and by applying the text anamnetically to those who hear or pray it.

---

65 Many refrains are formulated in the first person (see A.II.8.2).

CHAPTER 35

Cognitive Reception:
The "Relief" of the Bible Generated by the Liturgy

U p to this point, we have concentrated on the mode of reception; now we shall focus on the result of the reception. This includes first of all a cognitive aspect that asks about the contents of Scripture that are received through the celebration of the Liturgy. Although today (unlike in the past) everyone has access to the Bible, the Liturgy remains the place where most Christians receive Scripture. Accordingly, what is heard in worship is centrally important for their knowledge of the Bible.

We can put the question in metaphorical form: What "relief of the Bible" is generated in the faithful through the Liturgy? Depending on the frequency of attendance at worship, this may be a high, low, or sunken relief. One who goes to church only at particular feasts, such as Christmas, hears only a few "peaks." One who takes part in the Liturgy every Sunday hears more, and one who attends weekday Mass will hear even more. A person who prays the principal Hours penetrates more deeply; the Office of Readings further consolidates this. Over the course of time, at least ideally, the depth of knowledge is accompanied also by a growth in understanding. To employ the metaphor of the relief, contact surfaces and contours increase.

The liturgical reform has greatly improved the order of readings in terms of quantity.[66] From a cognitive perspective, of course, the abridged versions are counterproductive. By way of contrast, the Ambrosian lectionary in 2008 increased the length of the readings at Mass even further, through the length of the individual pericopes and the introduction of two Old Testament readings on the weekdays of Advent and Lent.[67]

---

66 See A.I. The fact that every weekday has its own readings is a recent phenomenon.

67 On this, see A.I.3.1.2 and A.I.3.1.4.

1. THE RELATIONSHIP BETWEEN THE "LITURGICAL BIBLE" AND THE CANONICAL BIBLE

What is the relationship between the "liturgical Bible" and the canonical Bible, that is to say, between what a participant in the Liturgy receives in comparison to the Bible as whole? This concrete question is highly important for a liturgical hermeneutics of the Bible. The sheer amount of text means that the aim cannot be completeness. In addition to this, the primary goals of the act of worship are not didactic.[68] Scripture also contains pericopes of varying importance, so that it is justifiable to make a selection. It is particularly interesting to note which parts of the Gospels, "the principal witness for the life and teaching of the incarnate Word, our savior" (*DV* 18), are included in the order of readings, and which are left out. Elmar Nübold has drawn up a list of twenty-five "important" pericopes that are not found in the *OLM* on Sundays and public feast days.[69] His starting point was not the four Gospels in their entirety; his criterion for "important" was whether the pericopes were included in drafts for the *OLM* or other orders of readings.[70] Although he attempts to achieve a certain objectivity, his evaluations naturally remain subjective.

If one goes beyond this list and compares the Gospels that are proclaimed with the four canonical Gospels, one notices that there are also other passages and verses that are not read on a Sunday,[71] presumably because they were regarded as "difficult" texts. These were avoided on Sundays and solemnities "for pastoral reasons." *GILM* 76 specifies: "The difficulties may be objective, in that the texts themselves raise complex literary, critical, or exegetical problems; or, at least to a certain extent, the difficulties may lie in the faithful's ability to understand the texts." Additionally, a verse is occasionally omitted if it is "unsuitable pastorally or involves truly difficult problems."[72] Despite what is often supposed, these difficulties occur not only in the Old Testament, but also in Paul and the Gospels. One prominent example of the omission of a verse for reasons of content is the Gospel of the Easter Vigil B,

---

68 See B.VIII.26.

69 Nübold, *Perikopenordnung*, 203–17 mentions, e.g., Mt 19:10–12 (logion about eunuchs), Mk 8:14 (hardened hearts of the disciples, who are worried because they have forgotten bread), Mk 9:14–29 par. (unsuccessful attempt by the disciples to heal), Jn 1:43–51 (Jesus calls Nathanael), Jn 5:19–25 (important text on realized eschatology in John).

70 See Nübold, *Perikopenordnung*, 203.

71 See the helpful list of the Mass readings: https://dli.institute/wp/praxis/schriftstellen-verzeichnis-fuer-die-lesungen-der-messe/ (retrieved 05/19/2021).

72 *GILM*, 77.

Mk 16:1–7, which omits v. 8 (the original concluding verse of Mark) about the disciples, who "fled from the tomb, seized with trembling and bewilderment. They said nothing to anyone, for they were afraid." Clearly, such a conclusion to the Gospel in the Easter Vigil was felt to be unsuitable; in the Ambrosian liturgy, Mk 16:1–8a is used as one of the Gospels of the Resurrection in the Sunday Vigil Mass, so that the reading contains the disciples' fear, but not their silence.[73]

It is not irrelevant to the liturgical reception of the Bible that Jesus' cries of woe are avoided on Sunday, with the exception of those in Luke's Sermon on the Plain (Lk 6:24–26; 6th Sunday in Ordinary Time C). Other cries of woe,[74] and the more drastically formulated reproaches of the Pharisees and scribes, are heard only on weekdays.[75] This means that the Sunday liturgy communicates a picture of Jesus that is slightly different from the picture in the Gospels.

There are, however, also texts in the Gospels that have in principle been excluded from the Liturgy. For a better understanding, especially in the case of more difficult texts from the Synoptics, for example on the end times, the evangelist who formulated the text more easily was preferred.[76] The omissions mean not only that small details from the special material of each evangelist are missing (for example, we never learn from the Liturgy that the disciples of Jesus baptized in the Jordan during Jesus' lifetime).[77] Entire sections of the Gospel of John, such as Jn 7:3–9, 11–24, 31–36, are not included in the order of readings.[78] Other sections were presumably

73 On this, see further information in A.I.3.1.2.

74 The cries of woe upon the seducer (Mt 18:7 not in the Liturgy; Lk 17:1), upon Chorazin and Bethsaida (Mt 11:21; Lk10:13), and upon the Pharisees and scribes (Mt 23:13–27; Lk 11:42–52) are present in the weekday order of readings. The cry of woe upon the pregnant women in the distress of the end time, which has a different content from these cries, is not read at Mass (Mt 24:19; Mk 13:17).

75 See Mt 23:13–32 from Monday to Wednesday of week 21 in Ordinary Time; Lk 11:37–54 from Tuesday to Thursday of week 28 in Ordinary Time.

76 For example, we do not find the pericope about the peak of distress (Mt 24:15–28; Mk 13:14–23), but Luke's eschatological discourse is read completely in the 34th week. This means that the "desolating abomination" (Mt 24:15; Mk 13:14 – see Dn 9:27; 11:31; 12:11) is avoided, as well as the exclamation "Let the reader understand" in Mark, which Matthew already seems to have found too cryptic. He expanded it with the reference to Daniel.

77 See Jn 4:1–2.

78 Only a small group hears Jn 7:14–18 at the commissioning of lectors. Other texts that are missing include Jn 10:19–21; Jn 12:17–19 (which one could have included without any problems on Palm Sunday); Jn 12:34–36 (read only at Votive Masses of the Cross and at the blessing of a chalice and ciborium); Jn 12:37–43 (synoptic parallels are included).

excluded in order to avoid transporting an anti-Jewish understanding, since Jesus' harsher confrontations (Jn 8:43–50 and 15:22–25) are never read in the Liturgy, although "the Jews" here are the authorities in Jerusalem at that time and those with whom Jesus was in conflict—not the entire people, to which he himself belonged.[79] The clear words spoken by Jesus on this topic (Jn 8:44: "You belong to your father the devil"; 15:24: "They have seen and hated both me and my Father") probably led to the omission of these passages. This supposition is strengthened by the omission of Mt 12:33–37 (especially 34!) and 23:33–36. The Liturgy allows John the Baptist to use the term "brood of vipers,"[80] but Jesus is not allowed to use the same term against the Pharisees (Mt 23:33: "You serpents, you brood of vipers, how can you flee from the judgment of Gehenna?"). The selection on Sunday can be justified by the argument that there is insufficient place for all the texts, but this cannot be asserted about the weekdays, where it would certainly have been possible to find a place for these pericopes.[81]

It is interesting here to compare how the new Milanese lectionary (2008) tackles these texts. Here, both Johannine passages are found even on Sundays: John 8, in keeping with tradition, on the Sunday of Abraham (3rd Sunday in Lent, every year),[82] and John 15:24–27 on Trinity Sunday. The two Matthean pericopes are read in the continuous reading from Matthew on the weekdays in Advent.[83] *PLA* 81–82, which is formulated with a clear recourse to *GILM* 76–77, speak of omissions for pastoral reasons, which, however, are "reduced to a minimum."[84]

In the case of the Gospels, one can present strong arguments both for and against the omissions; however, one must be aware of the hermeneutical consequences entailed by these decisions. A gradation that distinguishes between Sundays and weekdays makes sense also with regard to the participants. If one opts "for pastoral reasons" for deliberate omissions, one can avoid elements of confusion for both hearers and preachers. One could argue here that it is more fruitful for the faithful to concentrate the attention on central passages than to have to deal with less important—and more difficult—passages.

---

79 See Pontifical Biblical Commission, *Jewish People*, 77–78.

80 See Mt 3:7 on 2nd Sunday in Advent A (Lk 3:7 in Masses for Reconciliation).

81 It was probably felt desirable in 1969 to avoid an excessively harsh image of God.

82 See A.I.3.2.1.

83 Thursday of 2nd week and Saturday of 5th week (although the latter occurs seldom, because the week before Christmas, from December 17 onwards, has proper texts).

84 *PLA*, 81.

One must, however, ask: Is not Jesus being "censored" here, so to speak, perhaps in order that the testimony of the Liturgy may make him appear nicer, less harsh? Is it legitimate for the picture of Jesus generated by the celebration of the Liturgy to be anything other than completely identical with the picture that the reading of the Gospels shows us? That would mean that the Liturgy communicates an image of God that is somewhat different from the Gospels' image—no small problem for a liturgical hermeneutics of the Bible. The same considerations apply to the omission of the so-called "imprecatory" psalms and the corresponding verses in other psalms.[85]

While these observations concern above all those who want to draw deeply on the "relief of the Bible," the question of reception in liturgical praxis touches on an even more relevant problem. If fewer and fewer people attend church regularly, what does this mean for the order of readings—given that a continuous reading, by its very concept, presupposes a continuous reception? An order of readings prevents the subjective selection of particular favorite passages, by presenting a wide spectrum of the message of Jesus and the Word of God, and this makes an order of readings absolutely necessary. But at the same time, a fixed continuous reading means that those who attend worship at longer intervals necessarily encounter pericopes that may be less relevant to their own lives. Of course, much also depends on the homily and not only on the proclamation texts. However, here we must ask: Is it in fact possible for an order of pericopes that is the same everywhere in the world to correspond to today's pastoral situations locally, in the various countries? Or would flexible additional orders of readings be necessary, with an even more elementary arrangement that focused more strongly on the participants (e.g., in family Masses)?[86] Here, one would have to weigh the opportunities against the risks (such as a one-sided selection). The present study, which concentrates on the fundamental issues, can only indicate these questions and problems.

2. MNEMOTECHNICAL CONDITIONS

With regard to reception by the hearers, we must take note, not only of the order of readings – that is to say, which biblical texts are proclaimed— but also of what actually remains in their memory. Insights of the human

---

85 See A.II.9.2.

86 Already at the international liturgical study sessions before the Second Vatican Council, mission territories had demanded greater flexibility in the order of readings (see Schmitt, *Liturgische Studientreffen*, 355).

sciences about cognitive reception, such as those applied in the media reception research, are helpful here.[87] Simplifying, we may say that there are three memory systems:[88] *first*, the sensory register (the echoic or ultra-short-term memory), which has a high capacity and receives very briefly the information supplied by the senses; *second*, the working memory (short-term memory), which retains information consciously received at one particular point in time; and *third*, the long-term memory, which stores in the so-called semantic memory knowledge of the world or of facts (here also knowledge of the Bible). In the case of a text that is heard, this means, ideally, that the sound impulses received in the sensory register are selectively chosen in the working memory for further processing and are aligned with the information from the long-term memory; resources of attentiveness are employed for this purpose, depending on the difficulty of the specific task. The incoming information thus acquires a significance and a meaning and can then be stored in the long-term memory (comparable to an associative network of numerous linked memory contents). In the act of remembering, the network of the long-term memory is scanned for specific information; linked memory contents are transferred back into the working memory and thus reactivated.[89] "It is now assumed that the storing of such memory contents takes place on the basis of verbal and visual codes. Sensory information and concrete sentences tend more to be stored as images, while abstract sentences tend rather to be encoded verbally."[90]

When we apply this last point to the reception of Scripture in the Liturgy, it explains the mnemotechnical differences in the textual genres that one knows from one's own experience: a narrative text from the Gospels or the Old Testament, or a metaphor (e.g., the vine and the branches) sticks more easily in the memory than a pericope in Paul with rather abstract theological ideas. The greater the number of associative links that already exist, the easier it is to remember a memory content. This means that the memorability of a

---

87 On this, see Helena Bilandzic, *Medienrezeptionsforschung*, UTB 4003 Kommunikationswissenschaft, Psychologie, Soziologie (Konstanz: UVK Verlag, 2015), 29–48.

88 On what follows, see Bilandzic, 31–32; Annemarie Frick-Salzmann, "Gedächtnissysteme," in *Gedächtnistraining. Theoretische und praktische Grundlagen*, ed. H. Schloffer, E. Prank, and A. Frick-Salzmann (Heidelberg: Springer, 2010), 34–43; Franz J. Schermer, *Lernen und Gedächtnis*, Grundriss der Psychologie 10; Kohlhammer-Urban-Taschenbücher 559, 5th ed. (Stuttgart: Kohlhammer, 2014), 142–68, and specifically on the semantic memory, 169–99.

89 See Bilandzic, *Medienrezeptionsforschung*, 45.

90 Werner Stangl, "Semiotisches Gedächtnis," in *Online Lexikon für Psychologie und Pädagogik*. http://lexikon.stangl.eu/3128/semantisches-gedachtnis/ [2012; retrieved 02/21/22]. See in greater detail Schermer, *Lernen und Gedächtnis*, 156–58, 189–92.

text increases in accordance with the previous understanding and with its integration into already-existing and organized knowledge (the so-called schemas and scripts in the long-term memory).[91]

Cognition research highlights various factors for the lasting imprinting on the memory.[92] The first step is the careful reception of information. Applied to the Liturgy, this means attentiveness during the proclamation, which is also connected to the so-called "arriving" in the liturgical celebration and to recollection in the opening part of the Mass. The importance of repetition is obvious, since the process of reception entails a scanning of knowledge stored in the long-term memory, which it then reactivates. Besides this, the generating of units of knowledge, that is to say, the recognition of connections, plays an important role. From the perspective of liturgical studies, this could speak in favor of the formation of consonant formulas and for the use of the Responsorial Psalm, which is coordinated with the reading(s).[93] When contents are also linked to emotions, their memorability is enhanced. This means that the relatedness of a pericope to one's own experience, for example in the form of a role identification that is "covered" by one's life, helps one to remember a biblical passage better. It goes without saying that these observations are also relevant to the homily, which likewise makes a significant contribution to the memorizing of biblical knowledge, and thus to its spiritual reception.

91 See Schermer, *Lernen und Gedächtnis*, 192–96.

92 See Bilandzic, *Medienrezeptionsforschung*, 45–47.

93 Franz too argues in similar terms, on the basis of the psychology of understanding: *Wortgottesdienst*, 276–280. See B.VII.23.2.

CHAPTER 36

Spiritual Reception
The Habitat of the Word
that Is Opened Up in the Liturgy

The use of Scripture in liturgy not only promotes the knowledge of the Bible, but also seeks to "promote a warm and living love for Scripture" (SC 24). The Emmaus disciples show that while knowledge is indeed the foundation, it is not the decisive factor: they knew all the information about the Resurrection of Jesus and were able to report it correctly,[94] but they still lacked "understanding." The Word had first to find the path "from the head to the heart," to be interiorized, and to become experience. This is why a liturgical hermeneutics of the Bible, the holistic understanding of Scripture, also includes spiritual reception. This can be more variable in individuals than cognitive reception. This makes it impossible to offer an unambiguous academic description; all we can do here is to indicate basic lines.

The concept of "spirituality," which is hard to define precisely, not only contains a purely spiritual dimension, but covers the whole of Christian existence in its relationship both to God and to daily living. Michael Plattig describes spirituality as "the continuous transformation of a human being who responds to the call of God."[95] Since the Word of Scripture goes forth

---

94 See Lk 24:21b-24.

95 Michael Plattig, "Was ist Spiritualität?" in *Spiritualität in der sozialen Arbeit*, ed. M. Lewkowitcz and A. Lob-Hüdepohl (Freiburg/Br.: Lambertus, 2003), 12-32, at 13. Hans Bernhard Meyer, "Gottesdienst und Spiritualität," in Klöckener, *Theologie des Gottesdienstes*, 168 presents a "descriptive definition of the matter" that emphasizes first and foremost the ecclesial aspect. He understands a lived Christian spirituality "in terms of form, as the realization of the life of the Church and of its members; and in terms of content, as the response, expressed in a life based on faith, to God's saving act through Christ in the Holy Spirit, mediated ecclesially (through *martyria, leiturgia,* and *diakonia*)." Meyer, 270: "Without liturgy, there is no spirituality that deserves to be called Christian."

in the Liturgy as God's call here and now, Liturgy and Bible are closely interwoven sources of spirituality. The Liturgy helps us to perceive and receive Scripture as a spiritual resource for one's own life.[96] It opens up for believers a "sphere of experience marked by the Bible [...], which they are to enter, to bring to life, and to dwell in."[97] A liturgical spirituality, one that grows out of the celebration of worship,[98] is also a biblical-liturgical spirituality because the Liturgy is so profoundly marked by the Bible. For, according to Benedict XVI, the Liturgy is "the privileged setting in which God speaks to us" (*VD* 52) and "a great school of spirituality."[99] It teaches us by way of example how Scripture can be received and made spiritually fruitful.

As Part A showed in the case of the Lenten readings, Scripture presents figures who believed, and thereby serves as spiritual nourishment on one's own path of faith.[100] In principle, individual inspirations can be received when one hears a biblical text and its exposition in the homily, which plays a central role for the spiritual reception. In keeping with the dual orientation of spirituality to God and to daily living, it is especially those biblical passages and ideas that help to integrate faith and daily living, and hence are perceived to be relevant to life, that are particularly suitable for a spiritual reception.[101]

It is impossible to prize too highly the criterion of subjective relevance for the reception of Scripture, since in late-modern society a fact does not appear significant because it is in the Bible; it appears relevant only when the subjects evaluate it as relevant to themselves. Role identification[102] can be helpful here because the relationship of a biblical passage to the hearer and to his or her existential situation thereby comes to light. One's own experiences of God are compared with those that are expressed in the biblical readings. In part, there is a process of verification,[103] so that the hearer subjectively confirms the text to be true and recognizes the working of God in his or her

---

96 Paul VI said, with regard to the new order of readings: "Sacred Scripture will be regarded by all as an abiding foundation of spiritual life" (*Missal*, 15).

97 Buchinger, "Lebensraum des Wortes," 206.

98 See Meyer, "Gottesdienst und Spiritualität," 278.

99 Benedict XVI, *General Audience*, September 29, 2010: https://www.vatican.va/content/benedict-xvi/en/audiences/2010/documents/hf_ben-xvi_aud_20100929.html (retrieved 08/23/2022).

100 See A.I.3.2.

101 The short readings in the Liturgy of the Hours in Ordinary Time seem to have been chosen especially as practical impulses for the day (see A.I.5.2).

102 See B.IX.34.

103 See Häußling, "Biblische Grundlegung," 304.

own life. In part, the biblical texts challenge one to acknowledge the biblical text as a criterion that provides orientation and as a communication of the divine will. And in part, the texts are confusing, when a text (initially) remains incomprehensible, or indeed appears as a provocation, because it contradicts one's own experiences. The Bible functions as what one might call a "spiritual memory"[104] that "stores" the various paths taken by human beings with God (including turning to him and away from him) and makes these accessible for today in the Liturgy in a normative manner. One's own experiences can thus be broadened and reflected upon together with the experiences of the people of Israel and of the Church.

The liturgical prayers, (pericope-) orations, and often the hymns show how prayer is formed out of Scripture, and thus contain numerous examples of a spiritual reception of the Bible.[105] Above all, the Psalms can enrich one's own prayer in its content and form.[106] When the Psalter is prayed again and again in the Liturgy of the Hours, it becomes a "school that leads to the contemplation of God," since it teaches "the language of familiar contact with him."[107] Individual verses can become one's own prayer, or can give birth to this prayer, while other verses are left aside. Just as a bird (to use Balthasar Fischer's image) flaps its wings and then glides effortlessly until it regains momentum with a new flap of its wings for the next stretch, so the one who prays, at a specific word or verse, can make an attentive link between the Psalm and one's own situation (that is like flapping the wings). He is certain that this will carry him across those passages where a psalm says little to him, or where his thoughts still remain with that specific word.[108] At another time, the wings can flap at another passage (or the same one) in the same psalm, with an intensity that varies in accordance with the situation, thereby meshing together the psalm and one's own experience of life. One's own life

---

104 This expression is modeled on Assmann's *Cultural Memory* (see B.IX.1.2).

105 See A.III and IV.

106 See A.II.9.1.

107 Aimé-Georges Martimort, "Vom Beten der Psalmen im Stundengebet," in *Gott feiern. Theologische Anregung und geistliche Vertiefung zur Feier von Messe und Stundengebet* (FS Theodor Schnitzler), ed. J. G. Plöger (Freiburg/Br.: Herder, 1980), 384–94, at 389.

108 See Balthasar Fischer, "Dienst des Lobes – Dienst der Fürbitte. Zur Spiritualität des Stundengebetes," in Fischer, *Frömmigkeit der Kirche. Gesammelte Studien zur christlichen Spiritualität*, ed. A. Gerhards and A. Heinz, Hereditas 17 (Bonn: Borengässer, 2000), 204-15, at 211; Fischer, "Christological Interpretation," 234, where he employs this metaphor for the Christological interpretation of individual verses. The image of flying over "unsuitable" verses should not be understood in a negative sense. In a similar way, a concentration on one (or several) ideas in the texts of the readings usually has a positive effect on the spiritual reception.

can be discovered between the lines of the breviary and brought to God. The objective exterior of the Word of God needs a subjective interior, in order that "heart and voice may be one."[109]

It is legitimate for the spiritual reception to take on very personal traits here, and to be time-conditioned, since it is not like a commentary that must give explanations that are as general as possible. It is precisely this kind of reception that means that a text, even after it has been used frequently, does not become boring or stale. This reception bears witness to the spiritual riches of the Word of God, which grows along with the one who reads it.[110] Even in the context of worship, the biblical-liturgical spirituality remains something personal, which, however, is "linked to the Church which celebrates its faith publicly and in common."[111] The psalms are accompanied by a self-transcendence into the prayer of the Church, and hence into prayer for others, and this too is a spiritual enrichment.[112]

We conclude this chapter with a text by Ephrem the Syrian († 373), who describes the Word of God as an inexhaustible spring of life. These thoughts can also be applied to the Liturgy, which is (so to speak) the vessel that draws up water from this spring:

> Lord, who can comprehend even one of your words? We lose more of it than we grasp, like those who drink from a living spring. For God's word offers different facets according to the capacity of the listener, and the Lord has portrayed his message in many colors, so that whoever gazes upon it can see in it what suits him. Within it he has buried manifold treasures, so that each of us might grow rich in seeking them out.
>
> The word of God is a tree of life that offers us blessed fruit from each of its branches. It is like that rock which was struck open in the wilderness, from which all were offered spiritual drink. As the Apostle says: "They ate spiritual food and they drank spiritual drink." (1 Cor 10:3–4)
>
> And so whenever anyone discovers some part of the treasure, he should not think that he has exhausted God's word. Instead he should feel that this is all that he was able to find of the wealth contained in it. Nor should he say that the word is weak and sterile or look down on it simply because this portion was all that he happened to find. But precisely because he could not capture it all he should give thanks for its riches.

---

109 *Regula Benedicti* 19; *SC*, 90; *GILH*, 19.

110 See *Gregory, Homiliae in Ezechielem prophetam* 1,7,8 (CChr.SL 142:87); B.IX.33.

111 Meyer, "Gottesdienst und Spiritualität," 278.

112 See A.II.9.2.

Be glad that you are overwhelmed, and do not be saddened because it has overcome you. A thirsty man is happy when he is drinking, and he is not depressed because he cannot exhaust the spring. So let this spring quench your thirst, and not your thirst the spring. For if you can satisfy your thirst without exhausting the spring, then when you thirst again you can drink from it once more; but if when your thirst is sated the spring is also dried up, then your victory would turn to your own harm. Be thankful then for what you have received, and do not be saddened at all that such an abundance still remains. What you have received and attained is your present share, while what is left will be your heritage. For what you could not take at one time because of your weakness, you will be able to grasp at another if you only persevere. So do not foolishly try to drain in one draught what cannot be consumed all at once, and do not cease out of faintheartedness from what you will be able to absorb as time goes on.[113]

---

113 *Ephrem, Commentarium in Diatessaron* 1.18-19 (SChr 121:52–53; *Liturgy of the Hours,* 3:199–200).

CHAPTER 37

Hermeneutical Insights

With our starting point in the reception theory elaborated in literary studies, which draws attention to the reader as the recipient
of a text, the reception of a biblical text, with its intertextual
references, in the Liturgy was presented as an act of the *participatio actuosa*
of the individual. This involves individual presuppositions such as interests
determined by a person's biography or biblical knowledge that may be necessary in order to understand allusions. One attractive aspect of the liturgical hermeneutics of the Bible is that the Roman liturgy in particular, while
clearly guiding the interpretation (e.g., in the Christological interpretation of
a text from the Psalms), leaves it up to the freedom of the individual whether
or not one actually does note the references and undertake for oneself the
suggested interpretations.[114]

In the Liturgy, Scripture is always read in the reception community of
the Church, which produced the canon of the Bible and makes us aware in
the liturgical celebration that it is the word of God (and thus a normative
text). The Church maintains here, with its interpretations acquired from the
tradition, and with its experience of faith and of Scripture, a breadth that
transcends the individual, but in which he or she receives a share.[115]

An important hermeneutical means that can often be employed is the
first-person role identification. This helps to empathize meditatively with
the biblical persons (and thereby to understand the text better), and to
relate anamnetically to oneself the salvation that is attested in these persons.
The psalms formulated in the first-person singular, which can be given a
clearly Christological interpretation by their context (antiphons, liturgical
year), suggest an identification with Christ, whose prayer one thus repeats
after him. Similar phenomena are sometimes found on feasts of saints. The

---

114 See B.IX.33.
115 See B.IX.33.2.

quotation that takes on a role, which occurs also in chants like the *Sanctus* or the *Magnificat*, always establishes in its various facets a bridge between the biblical text and the recipient.[116]

The Liturgy communicates contents of the Bible in an incidental manner, so that a "relief of the Bible" with varying depths comes into being in the mind of the recipient, depending on the frequency of one's participation in worship. Even in the case of the Gospels, the "liturgical Bible," that is to say, the part of Scripture that is proclaimed in worship, is not identical to the canonical Bible on account of the omissions that have been undertaken for pastoral reasons. This leads to the hermeneutically problematic situation whereby liturgy mediates a picture of Jesus and of God that differs somewhat from the Gospels. The question of an order of readings for those who attend church at irregular intervals is pastorally more urgent, since a continuous reading cannot "function" for them. In the cognitive reception of the Bible, we must also pay attention to mnemotechnical conditions.[117]

Since the primary goals of the Liturgy are not didactic, the cognitive reception of Scripture is continued by the spiritual reception. The Liturgy opens up a "habitat of the Word" into which one enters in the celebration. One's own experiences of God can be compared with those of Scripture, which is a "spiritual memory" that presents the various paths God has taken with human beings; and ideally, one's experiences can be verified. Scripture in the Liturgy, and the Psalms in particular, also function as a "school of prayer," promoting a biblical-liturgical spirituality that contains legitimate personal traits and is at the same time linked to the faith of the Church.[118]

116 See B.IX.34.
117 See B.IX.35.
118 See B.IX.36.

PART C

Insights and Perspectives: Liturgical Approach

This brief closing part does not seek to summarize all the details of the present study, especially since concise "Hermeneutical insights" chapters are included at the end of each section. Rather, in a first point, we shall bring together the central themes that run through the various observations and reflections. We shall then briefly indicate some aspects of a liturgical hermeneutics of the Bible. This will point, by way of a summary, to the "liturgical approach" to Scripture,[1] which implicitly runs through the entire study as a path of access and understanding that is in accord with the Bible itself. Secondly, prompted by the theme of this book, we shall indicate possible links between biblical and liturgical scholarship.

---

1 Here there is a conceptual analogy to the "canonical approach" of biblical scholarship.

CHAPTER 38

Bringing the Insights Together

Taken as a whole, this study clearly presents the eminent significance of Sacred Scripture for the Liturgy. *SC* 24 puts this into eloquent words, and Part A illustrates by means of examples how Scripture permeates every area of liturgy. However, the links between Scripture and Liturgy go beyond the immediate use of the Bible in readings and Psalms, in the biblical allusions in the texts of prayers and hymns, or in the ritual staging of some pericopes. The fundamental fact that the formation of the canon, as a phenomenon of the reception by the synagogue or by the Church, is due in no small measure to the liturgical reading aloud of the scriptures in question[2] suggests that the reciprocal theological interrelatedness goes much deeper.

Here, we must mention, first of all, the anamnesis that is proper to both Bible and Liturgy.[3] Scripture is essentially more than a historical source or testimony to an earlier (and hence vanished) time. Both Testaments contain the exhortation to remember the saving deeds of God, so that they may thus be kept alive as a history of the origins that is relevant to the present day.[4] This injunction is carried out in hearing and reading Scripture, so that Scripture is at the service of the encounter with God. Liturgy (both Christian and Jewish)[5] has the same goal in its dealings with Scripture. It is well known that anamnesis is a central leading category of liturgy. It does not transpose us back into a "then" of the history of Israel or the life of Jesus; on the contrary, a movement in the opposite direction dwells in liturgy. God's presence, which transcends time, makes it possible for the Liturgy to proclaim in the liturgical "today" his saving activity, which took place "then." The Liturgy bestows a

---

2 See B.IX.33.2 and Introduction 1.

3 See B.VIII.27 with frequent recourse to A.

4 See B.VIII.27.1. For example, Hebrews 11 points to the Old Testament witnesses of faith, and leads in this way to Jesus, "the leader and perfecter of faith."

5 See B.VII.24.2.

participation in this activity. The hermeneutical means of first-person role identification, which occurs frequently in the Liturgy, helps us to empathize with the biblical persons and thereby to recognize Scripture as a personal word of salvation for the present day.[6] At the same time, both Scripture and Liturgy also look to the eschatological fulfillment, in the tension between "already" and "not yet." The Liturgy celebrates what the Scripture contains paradigmatically or by way of anticipation. The temporal concept "Scripture—today—fulfillment" reminds us: We are a part of "salvation history," of God's action in time, which both Scripture and Liturgy testify to, the one in the past, the other in the present. God's salvific action, however, is ultimately the same.[7]

The sacramentality of the Word makes us particularly aware of the connection between the Bible and Liturgy.[8] This theological concept denotes the performative presence of God or of Christ, brought about by the Spirit in his Word, his speaking through the human words both of the sacred writers and of the one who proclaims the Word. This means that the word of Scripture is not a dead letter or merely a bearer of information. Rather, it possesses a deeper dimension that bears witness to the divine presence, which is both personal and dynamic, and aims at the encounter with the hearers and readers.[9] The Liturgy too, understood as the celebration of the Paschal Mystery and the realization of Christ's priestly ministry,[10] lives from the presence of God/Christ, mediates this, and allows us to experience it. This is why the Liturgy is the answer to the prevenient call of God, which acquires a visible expression in the proclamation of Scripture. The understanding of Scripture as an event of revelation, which also includes its reception, and the dialogical character of the Liturgy permeate and strengthen each other.

The sacramentality of the Word draws our attention to the close reciprocal dependency between Word and sacrament.[11] The Word is sacramental, and the sacraments of the Church are structured verbally; indeed, sign and word together constitute the sacrament. This places an emphasis on the "and": the structural and substantial unity of Word *and* sacrament also makes clear, in a wider sense, the inherent connection between Bible and Liturgy. This is highlighted in the understanding of the Liturgy as the antitype

---

6 See B.IX.34.

7 See Häußling, "Biblische Grundlegung," 310 and B.VIII.27.2.

8 See B.VIII.28.

9 See B.VI.22.

10 See *SC* 6–7, and passim.

11 See B.VIII.29.

of Scripture, because one can experience with the senses in liturgy what Scripture expresses verbally. The Word of Scripture can become an experience in the celebration of the Liturgy, as the biblical salvation is realized ever anew in those who participate in worship.[12]

The pneumatological-epicletic dimension of the Word likewise demonstrates the closeness of Scripture and Liturgy,[13] since the same Spirit who inspired the sacred writers in the composition of the biblical books (and the later editors who wrote the continuation of the texts) now makes Scripture alive in the Liturgy. The Holy Spirit brings about the verbal presence of God/Christ in the Word, makes possible the dialogical encounter, and mediates the performative power of the Word. Together with the anamnetic character of which we have spoken above, the Word in the Liturgy is an anamnetic-epicletic event, just as the Liturgy itself in its basic structure is an anamnetic-epicletic event. In the celebration of worship, the Word shares in this basic structure. At the same time, Scripture prescribes for the Liturgy the content of the anamnesis and mediates through the Spirit a saving power that "inspires" the hearer too.

The inherent interweaving of Bible and Liturgy finds many expressions. Louis-Marie Chauvet makes this point in a metaphor: "The Bible is in the Liturgy as a fish in water."[14] If the theological relationship is as close as we have affirmed, thanks to both the genesis of the canon and in today's celebration, and indeed, if Scripture itself implies that the Church is a community of reception,[15] it follows that a liturgical hermeneutics of the Bible is a meaningful and appropriate approach, not only on the part of liturgical scholarship, but also from the perspective of biblical theology. A "liturgical approach" to Scripture is thus in accord with Scripture itself. We have presented as a thesis in the Introduction to the present study what *Verbum Domini* 52 demands: namely, that a "faith-filled understanding of sacred Scripture must always refer back to the Liturgy."[16] In the course of our investigations, this approach has been demonstrated by means of examples (Part A) and structured systematically (Part B). We review the arguments briefly here.

We now offer a concise summary of the hermeneutical implications of such a "liturgical approach" or, in keeping with the title of this study, the

---

12 See B.VIII.30.2.

13 See B.VIII.31.

14 Chauvet, "What makes Liturgy biblical?," 127. The content of this image may be indeterminate, but it expresses how natural the inherent interweaving of Bible and Liturgy is.

15 See B.IX.34.

16 *VD* 52. See Introduction 2; esp. B.VI.21.

essential characteristics of a liturgical hermeneutics of sacred Scripture, by presenting some insights in the manner of key words.

(1.) The Liturgy understands Scripture, not primarily as a document of the past, but as the current and living Word of God, perceived as a Word of revelation that was spoken in history yet remains valid or (more precisely) that goes forth ever anew.[17] It is testimony to the risen Christ who is present, who expounds and proclaims the Word of God. This becomes particularly clear at the proclamation of the Gospel, but as the Emmaus pericope shows, it applies to the whole of Scripture.[18]

The rites of the proclamation of the Word, despite the differences in detail in East and West, all agree that God/Christ himself is present in his Word and speaks to his people. This agreement among the rites, as well as the parallel to the proclamation of Torah in the synagogue liturgy, indicate that this is an essential characteristic of the liturgical hermeneutics of the Bible. A look at the ritual elements (B.VII.24) together with the theological aspects (B.VIII) makes it obvious that the "staging" is not merely a decorative (and hence dispensable) ritual framing of the Word. Rather, it is the expression and the translation of the theological insights that Scripture is an event of revelation and that the Liturgy is a dialogical event of encounter. This means that the ritual dimension of the proclamation of the Word has the important function of transporting hermeneutical concerns. Aesthetics is at the service of theological hermeneutics. It promotes the correct understanding of Scripture and lends support to its proclamation.

(2.) The Liturgy understands and uses Scripture as a medium of the encounter with God, both in the katabatic sense (especially in the proclamation of the Word) and in the anabatic sense, above all when Scripture forms prayers and hymns, calls for a response, or at once supplies this response with a word from Scripture. The Liturgy serves here as a bridge between the biblical text and the participants, for example, when the Responsorial Psalm (with the refrain) refers to the reading(s) and also to the community that sings;[19] when the homily seeks to link the Word that is proclaimed and our daily lives; when a psalm in the Liturgy of the Hours is close to life and permits one's personal situation to flow into the prayer;[20] when the Liturgy suggests a role identification with a biblical person or with Christ;[21] when prayers transport a biblical text into the present time according to the schema "as in

17 See B.VIII.27.2.

18 See B.VIII.28.1.

19 See A.II.8.2.

20 See A.II.9.

21 See B.IX.34.

the past, so also today";[22] when hymns do not simply narrate a biblical text again, but interpret it with reference to the community;[23] when scriptural passages are ritualized and carried out in liturgical signs and actions.[24] Many other possibilities can be mentioned. The fundamental point for the Liturgy is to bring specific passages from Scripture to the participants in the celebration by anamnesis and to open up, via the biblical testimony, a space where they can experience the salvific encounter with God.[25]

(3.) A liturgical hermeneutics of the Bible also shows how the Liturgy itself functions as interpreter of Scripture, by means of the order of readings that establishes an intertextual communication between various biblical texts; by linking the biblical texts to other liturgical texts; or by contributing a pre-understanding through the liturgical year and the occasion of the celebration. The Liturgy thus locates Scripture in the context of the celebration and interprets it thereby. One can speak of a liturgical interpretation of Scripture, when, for example, liturgical texts such as antiphons, pericope orations, hymns, etc., emphasize certain aspects or display these in a special light, while passing over other aspects. This amounts to a significant interpretation of the scriptural texts.[26] At the same time, the Bible allows us to understand the Liturgy.[27]

(4.) The Liturgy presupposes as a matter of course the unity of Scripture,[28] and displays a clear Christological orientation in its hermeneutics.[29] We see this, for example, in the order of readings (traditionally on feasts, and recently also on other days),[30] in the Christological exposition of the Psalms,[31] and in some prayers[32] and chants.[33] Here, the Liturgy takes

22 See A.III; A.III.12.1 (Pentecost collect).

23 See A. IV; A.IV.14.1.2.

24 See A.V.

25 See also B.IX.36.

26 See B.VII.23.

27 The interpretations are reciprocal since the Liturgy is itself marked by Scripture. Numerous liturgical actions are interpreted either by biblical accompanying chants or by interpretative words from the Bible (see A.V), or, on an even more fundamental level, have grown out of the Scripture (e.g., the scriptural texts of the Church year).

28 See B.VIII.30.

29 One illustration of this is the fact that many relationships between the Old Testament and the New can be understood only on the basis of Christ.

30 See A.I.3.1.1; A.I.3.1.4; B.VII.23.

31 See A.II (especially 7 and 9).

32 See A.III.11.1; A.III.11.3.

33 See A.IV.14; A.IV.15; A.IV.16.

up the Christian interpretation of the Old Testament that is already found in the New Testament and in the patristic writers, who have influenced the liturgical exposition to some extent. A basic hermeneutic attitude of this kind is logical for the Liturgy, which is the celebration of the Paschal Mystery of Christ; but the Roman rite, more than other rites, leaves the individual freedom whether or not to accept the Christological interpretation that it presents.[34]

(5.) When we look at the present study from a diachronic perspective, we see that every age brings its own hermeneutics into the Liturgy. On the one hand, the Liturgy transports in numerous prayers (e.g., from the *Apostolic Tradition*)[35] and hymns (beginning with Ambrose) traditional material that has stood the test of time. Thereby, the Liturgy also transports positions taken by their authors or compilers with regard to biblical hermeneutics. On the other hand, the recent Western orders of readings, or the distribution of the Psalms in the Liturgy of the Hours today, are equally marked by specific hermeneutical and theological prior decisions; these are the product of their own historical period, and they exclude other possibilities. This means that an ideal, perennially valid order of readings cannot exist. A liturgical hermeneutics of the Bible (like other hermeneutics of Scripture) thus displays both constant elements and time-conditioned elements. Moreover, the comparison of rites in Part A showed that, while overarching common elements certainly exist (such as the use of typology),[36] the Roman and the Byzantine traditions also posit theological-spiritual accents that diverge in part, for example, by referring to different passages in Scripture.[37]

(6.) A liturgical approach to Scripture is no purely theoretical matter. Ultimately, it is oriented to a biblical-liturgical spirituality that receives Scripture in prayer and in celebration as the Word of God, and that attempts to translate it into life. The goal, by means of the repetition of the celebration, is the formation of a Christian identity that is nourished by the Bible and the Liturgy.[38]

---

34 See B.IX.33.

35 See A.III.11.1.

36 See B.VIII.30.1.

37 See, e.g., A.I.3.2.3 (the title "Messiah" in the Byzantine order of readings in Lent); A.III.11.3 (differing biblical passages in the prayer at episcopal ordination). A different liturgical understanding, especially with regard to mimesis, has led to different forms of the rite of the Washing of the Feet (see A.V.17).

38 See B.IX.36.

CHAPTER 39

Perspectives
Bridges Between Biblical
and Liturgical Scholarship

The extremely close relationship between Bible and Liturgy, which we have described above, prompts the question of how the respective academic disciplines relate to each other. A "liturgical approach" to Scripture opens up a field of dialogue between the two theological disciplines that is rewarding for both of them. As its theme suggests, the present study understands itself as a contribution and a stimulus to the conversation between biblical and liturgical scholarship.

More than thirty years have passed since Balthasar Fischer argued that one must pay closer attention to the interdisciplinary connections,[39] since both disciplines have tended in the course of history rather to lead parallel lives.[40] Simple considerations of methodology meant that exegesis, with its primarily historical-critical orientation that inquired into the original intention of the texts in their historical conditions and connections, had scarcely any interest in the liturgical reception. In recent decades, the so-called canonical exegesis[41] has come on the scene.[42] This expounds the final text synchronously in the context of the entire canon and emphasizes the unity of Scripture. The *Constitution on Divine Revelation (Dei Verbum* 12)

---

39 See Balthasar Fischer, "Liturgiegeschichte und Exegesegeschichte. Interdisziplinäre Zusammenhänge," *JbAC* 30 (1987): 5-13. See, from the perspective of biblical studies, Édouard Cothenet, *Exégèse et liturgie*, Lectio divina 133 (Paris: Les Éditions du Cerf, 1988).

40 For a review of the history, see also Oeming, "Verborgene Nähe," 182-89, 196-97.

41 See, e.g., Steins, *Kanonisch-intertextuelle Studien zum AT*; Böhler, "Kanon"; Thomas Hieke, "Alles Auslegungssache. Methodisch-hermeneutische Erwägungen zur Kontextualisierung biblischer Auslegung," *BN* 140 (2009): 95-110.

42 See Ralf Rothenbusch, "Historisch oder kanonisch? Zum exegetischen Methodenstreit 50 Jahre nach Dei Verbum," *HerKorr* 69, no. 6 (2015): 316-20.

had already vaguely hinted[43] that both orientations of exegesis are necessary and justified, and indeed that they should complement one another; this is explicitly highlighted in *Verbum Domini* 34 with recourse to the conciliar text.[44] Since canonical exegesis also takes account of the reception of a text in the community of interpretation and of "the continuously enacted drawing upon a potential of meaning,"[45] it seems that the "large-scale weather pattern"[46] in biblical studies is changing. The emphasis lies, not on reconstructing as unambiguously as possible the original historical meaning of a text, but on the text's openness to various meanings.[47] This comes very close to the liturgical use and exposition of Scripture, so that a window of dialogue opens up between biblical and liturgical scholarship. Bearing in mind the plurality of approaches and methodologies in contemporary biblical studies, not only canonical exegesis but also the study of the history of reception[48] can display points of contact with liturgical studies, since (to take one example) the proclamation of the exodus from Egypt (Ex 14) in the Easter Vigil has made a profound impact on the Christian exposition of the text.

---

43 See Norbert Lohfink, "Der weiße Fleck in Dei Verbum 12," in Lohfink, *Studien zur biblischen Theologie*, 78–96; Thomas Söding, "Theologie mit Seele. Der Stellenwert der Schriftauslegung nach der Offenbarungskonstitution Dei Verbum," in *Erinnerung an die Zukunft. Das Zweite Vatikanische Konzil*, ed. J. H. Tück (Freiburg/Br.: Herder, 2012), 423–48, esp. 425–26, 436–38; Ludger Schwienhorst-Schönberger, "Zwei antagonistische Modelle der Schriftauslegung in Dei Verbum?", in Tück, *Erinnerung an die Zukunft*, 449–61.

44 "Only where both methodological levels, the historical-critical and the theological, are respected, can one speak of a theological exegesis, an exegesis worthy of this book." See also Benedict XVI, *Jesus of Nazareth* 1, xvii–xx. He had already discussed this theme in 1968: In *Dei Verbum*, we find "the affirmation of the historical-critical method and the affirmation of the exposition on the basis of the tradition, of the Church's faith, peaceably alongside one another. But this double affirmation conceals the antagonism of two fundamental attitudes that, both in their origin and in their goal, undoubtedly run in opposite directions" (Joseph Ratzinger, "Die Bedeutung der Väter für die gegenwärtige Theologie," *ThQ* 148, no. 8 (1968): 260). *VD* 57 recommends the "canonical interpretation" for the lectionary.

45 Egbert Ballhorn, "Das historische und das kanonische Paradigma in der Exegese," in *Der Bibelkanon in der Bibelauslegung. Methodenreflexionen und Beispielexegesen*, ed. E. Ballhorn and G. Steins (Stuttgart: Kohlhammer, 2007), 9–30, at 22. Canonical exegesis has taken up impulses from the reception theory in literary studies (see the Introduction to B.IX).

46 Georg Steins, "Kanon und Anamnese. Auf dem Weg zu einer Neuen Biblischen Theologie," in Steins, *Kanonisch-intertextuelle Studien*, 61.

47 See Ludger Schwienhorst-Schönberger, "'Eines hat Gott gesagt, zweierlei habe ich gehört' (Ps 62,12). Sinnoffenheit als Kriterium einer biblischen Theologie," in *Wie biblisch ist die Theologie?*, ed. M. Ebner, JBTh 25 (Neukirchen-Vluyn: Neukirchener Theologie / Vandenhoeck & Ruprecht, 2010), 45–61, at 51–54; Schwienhorst-Schönberger, "Einheit statt Eindeutigkeit. Paradigmenwechsel in der Bibelwissenschaft?," *HerKorr* 57, no. 8 (2003): 412–17.

48 See Oeming, *Contemporary Biblical Hermeneutics*, 77–85.

Two examples will show the openness of the texts to various meanings and present the connection between the liturgical use and an inner-biblical process of updating and interpretation. The first example concerns the psalms; we have already seen it above.[49] A psalm can take on different connotations already within the Old Testament re-reading in the various redactions of the Psalter. The messianic redaction of the Psalter is one important factor for the New Testament reception, since it offers a bridge from the text itself to the Christological interpretation. This understanding of the psalms was further developed by the patristic writers and can be applied as a hermeneutical instrument in the Liturgy, as our investigation of the liturgical use of Psalm 24 clearly showed.

A similar reception of the text-immanent movement itself, which points beyond the original situation, can be seen in the first reading of Midnight Mass at Christmas, Isaiah 9:1–6. Oeming writes that this text has been updated several times: "In the course of the updating process, a word of consolation addressed to the northern kingdom is expanded to become a pacifist messianism that embraces the whole world."[50] One may question the reconstruction of the hypothetical stages of the textual development; but the messianic understanding opens the text to further interpretations. The canonical exposition of Scripture places this promise of salvation in the content of the Bible as a whole and links it to Christ, in accordance with Matthew 4:14–16.[51] And this is what the Liturgy does too: when this prophetic text is proclaimed at Christmas, the liturgical use takes up the text-immanent movement and "updates" it (so to speak) for those assembled, who are celebrating the birth of Christ, the definitive savior. In both examples, in the Psalms and in Isaiah 9, the Liturgy thus updates the path of the inner-biblical (messianic) interpretation, although of course it is not the genesis of the text that is relevant to the Liturgy, but the canonical final text.

The concept of intertextuality in literary studies[52] leads us to pay attention to contextualization. In canonical exegesis, the first and privileged context is the biblical canon itself, so that biblical texts are correlated with and illuminate each other, both within the Old Testament and within the New, as well as between the two Testaments. This is exactly what an order of readings does when it combines several pericopes in one and the same celebration: Old Testament texts (first reading and psalm) are combined with each other

49 See A.II. Introduction and Chapter 7.

50 Oeming, "Verborgene Nähe," 199.

51 Is 8:23b–9:3 and Mt 4:12–23 are paired on the 3rd Sunday in Ordinary Time A.

52 See B.VII.23.

and then with the New Testament texts. The order of readings often draws our attention to relationships between reading and Gospel, which exegesis (both historical-critical and canonical) likewise studies.[53] The dialogue of the texts and of the two Testaments also occurs in the Liturgy of the Hours, for example, when psalms and canticles and readings from both Testaments come together. In particular, the responsories often display interesting links.[54] In the past, the typological relationships and interpretations that are frequently employed by the Liturgy (following in the footsteps of expositions of Scripture in the early Church) were often viewed with a very critical eye, but it appears that there is a more differentiated judgment today.[55]

The contextualization of the scriptural texts can also go beyond the Bible, so that biblical and liturgical texts can be combined. Scripture can also be linked to the liturgical year, to the occasion of a particular celebration (e.g., the Zacchaeus pericope [Lk 19:1–10] at the dedication of a church) or a rite (e.g., Jn 1:29, "Behold the Lamb of God," with Holy Communion), etc.[56] Scriptural texts often acquire an additional meaning in the Liturgy in this way—a meaning that does indeed go beyond the intention of the original affirmation, but is not in the least arbitrary.[57] Especially passages which the biblical text keeps undetermined or "open" in their meaning are often "filled" by the liturgical context.[58]

The decontextualizations and recontextualizations of Scripture that are undertaken by the Liturgy appear legitimate in the light of the canonical and reception-theoretical orientations in biblical scholarship. In general, the liturgical use of Scripture, and thereby also its hermeneutics, now appear in a positive light, so that Manfred Oeming can speak of the "hidden closeness of exegetical and liturgical hermeneutics," which must be "unearthed" anew:[59]

---

53 For example, on December 19, the annunciation of the birth of the Baptist (Lk 1:5–25) is preceded by a text on which Luke has worked, namely, the annunciation of the birth of Samson (Jgs 13:2–7, 24–25a).

54 See B.VIII.30.1.

55 See B.VIII.30.1.

56 See B.VII.23.1; B.VIII.29.2.

57 The criterion remains the agreement with the Church's faith, and thus with the totality of Scripture, since the *regula fidei* is not imposed externally, as an alien reality, upon Scripture. Rather, it grows out of Scripture itself. See Ludger Schwienhorst-Schönberger, "'Damit die Bibel nicht ein Wort der Vergangenheit bleibt' – Historische Kritik und geistige Schriftauslegung," in *Gottes Wort in Menschenwort. Die eine Bibel als Fundament der Theologie* (FS Norbert Lohfink), ed. K. Lehmann and R. Rothenbusch, QD 266 (Freiburg/Br.: Herder, 2014), 183.

58 See B.IX. (Introduction) and, as an example, Ps 24 (A.II.7).

59 See Oeming, "Verborgene Nähe," esp. 196–203, at 197.

"We need a modern hermeneutics that grasps the plurality of meanings of the texts and opens these up, a hermeneutics that is capable of establishing a new bridge between exegesis and liturgy. And this would do justice in a new manner to both the patristic and the Jewish traditions."[60] On this point, Thomas Hieke writes:

> There is a perfectly "natural" connection between exegesis and liturgical studies. In the Liturgy, no matter what its color or confession may be, the Bible has from the very beginning been more than just read. It is *read aloud,* it is performed, it is celebrated, and as the "Word of the living God," the dead printer's ink comes to life in the celebrating community and irrupts into the context of the people who are assembled. This too is exposition of sacred Scripture, not only through reading and sermon, but also through song, music, and dance. This procedure, which has unfolded an immense cultural variety in the course of history, must be accompanied and reflected upon by academic theology, and this is a great common project of exegesis and liturgical studies.[61]

These may be solitary voices (although others could be mentioned), and each theological discipline may for the time being work in its own field; but we should indicate bridges that have already been constructed, where interdisciplinary work has borne fruit, as well as possible perspectives.

On the one hand, liturgical studies can profit from biblical studies, from which liturgical scholars have learned to examine more precisely how one deals with liturgical texts, and especially with the biblical texts in the Liturgy, and have applied in many cases what they have learned. This input helped greatly in the post-conciliar promotion of the Word of God and in the renewal of the order of readings. Biblical science can help us to examine critically how far the selection and combination of scriptural texts in the liturgical formulas is meaningful, or to see what alternatives exist. It is interesting that the Milanese order of readings (2008) reacted to criticism of the *OLM* with regard to the intrinsic value of the Old Testament, and also paid greater hermeneutical attention to this intrinsic value in the period after

60 Oeming, 202.

61 Hieke, "Auslegungssache," 102 (italics original). See also Hieke, 103. [The words translated here as: "Word of the living God" are spoken by the reader in the German-language Mass at the end of the readings from the Old and New Testaments.]

Pentecost.[62] The distribution of the Psalms in the Liturgy of the Hours also shows how current exegetical trends flowed into the Liturgy.[63]

On the other hand, liturgical studies can provide impulses for the interdisciplinary conversation and for biblical studies. Publications, conferences, and university teaching can only profit from this.[64]

The Liturgy is an important testimony to the Church's dealings with Scripture and is thus "lived" biblical hermeneutics. As the Liturgy is *theologia prima,* so too it mediates a *hermeneutica prima.*[65] Since it is in the context of liturgy that most of the faithful encounter the Bible, biblical scholarship gains a meaningful relationship to praxis when it pays attention to the liturgical context.

We should ask whether a liturgical hermeneutics of the Bible can also supply inspiration for the present-day discussion of methodologies, in particular to the question of the relationship between historical-critical and canonical exegesis.[66] Since Scripture is both a reality that has come into being historically and a canonical reality, one cannot play one off against the other, or simply juxtapose them (and still less, see the relationship as antagonistic).[67] Ludger Schwienhorst-Schönberger makes the case for "an integration of the historical-critical exegesis into the model of the traditional ecclesial hermeneutics of the Bible."[68] First of all, this would acknowledge the insights of historical-critical scholarship; at the same time, "the scriptural hermeneutics of the tradition, with the emphasis on the spiritual meaning of Scripture," corresponds "in a congenial manner to the personal-dynamic understanding of revelation."[69] This would do justice both to the polysemy

---

62 See A.I.3.1.2 and A.I.3.1.4.

63 See A.II.9.2.

64 The author has experienced this mutual enrichment in two seminars on "Psalms in exegetical and liturgical interpretation" and especially in the summer school "Understanding the Bible from the Liturgy" for international students in Trier (2022).

65 Alexander Deeg, "Hermeneutica prima. Eine evangelische Wahrnehmung von Marco Beninis 'Liturgische Bibelhermeneutik. Die Heilige Schrift im Horizont des Gottesdienstes'," *LJ* 70, no. 4 (2020): 259–68.

66 See Rothenbusch, "Historisch oder kanonisch?".

67 See Rothenbusch, 320; VD 35.

68 Schwienhorst-Schönberger, "Historische Kritik und geistige Schriftauslegung," 177. See Schwienhorst-Schönberger, "Wiederentdeckung des geistigen Schriftverständnisses," 422; Lohfink, "Der weiße Fleck," 96: the "much fuller hermeneutics of the early period." This position does not find a general consensus.

69 Schwienhorst-Schönberger, "Wiederentdeckung des geistigen Schriftverständnisses," 405; see Schwienhorst-Schönberger, 423.

and to the unity of Scripture.[70] However the relationship of these two orientations in exegesis may be conceived in the future, it would make sense to pay attention to a liturgical hermeneutics of the Bible, since it not only hands on traditional elements of the patristic hermeneutics and translates them for "today," but also integrates more recent considerations in the liturgical reforms. Georg Steins points to anamnesis, or "the anamnetic reading of the Bible," as a bridge between biblical exposition and the Liturgy.[71] A certain parallel to the complementary functions of historical-critical and canonical exegesis, and to the connection between the verbal and the spiritual exposition of Scripture, can also be seen in the different functions of Scripture in the Liturgy, which are likewise complementary.[72]

Another point of contact is the acceptance in exegesis of the approach from reception theory because this approach is put into practice in the Liturgy *qua* place of reception of Scripture. This involves a liturgical rereading or exposition of Scripture—what Georg Braulik calls "a kind of liturgical exegesis"[73]—when many prayers, orations, chants, or rites explicitly refer to particular biblical passages and explain these (e.g., the Preface about the Samaritan woman on the 3rd Sunday in Lent),[74] interpreting them with regard to the participants. The liturgical context often becomes the framework for the interpretation of particular pericopes.[75] Interest in the history of exposition seems in recent years to have increased noticeably among biblical scholars,[76] so that some commentaries also take up the reception of the biblical texts in patristic literature and the history of reception. With a few exceptions, however,[77] they have seldom or never looked at the liturgical

---

70 See Schwienhorst-Schönberger, 404–06.

71 See Steins, "Brücken zwischen Bibelauslegung und Liturgie," esp. 141–44.

72 See B.VIII.26.

73 Braulik, "Rezeptionsästhetik," 527: "Intertextuality concerns not only the literary context, but also the situative context in which a text is received. For us today, the liturgy is certainly the most important place of tradition and reception, where the writings of the Bible, and especially the Old Testament Psalms, are read, heard, prayed, and thereby brought into relation to our situation. Reception theory therefore ultimately justifies us in undertaking a kind of liturgical exegesis."

74 See *Missal*, 238.

75 See, e.g., B.VII.23.1; C.38; A.III.12.2.

76 See Schwienhorst-Schönberger, "Historische Kritik und geistige Schriftauslegung," 70.

77 See, e.g., Charles A. Bobertz, *The Gospel of Mark: A Liturgical Reading* (Grand Rapids, MI: Baker Academic, 2016). This commentary makes the basic assumption that the Gospel was written primarily for the liturgical assembly, and that this is how it is to be appropriately understood. See Bobertz, "A Prolegomena to a Ritual/Liturgical Reading of Mark's Gospel,"

reception. Since, however, the liturgical interpretations are very widespread and are acknowledged by the Church as "official" (so to speak), this ought to be taken account of in an academic context too. It would therefore be a desirable enrichment, and indeed highly necessary in the case of some texts, if biblical commentaries were to take up the reception in the Liturgy,[78] since this is a decisive influence on numerous texts. At the same time, this would clearly promote the conversation between biblical and liturgical scholarship, from which both would profit.

---

in *Reading in Christian Communities. Essays on Interpretation in the Early Church*, ed. C. A. Bobertz and D. Brakkem (Notre Dame, IN: University of Notre Dame Press, 2002), 174-87.

78 Böhler, *Psalmen, 1-50* also discusses the liturgy.

Closing Words

On September 30, the feast of Saint Jerome, an important biblical translator and commentator, Matthew 13:47–52 is proclaimed as the Gospel at Mass (when the sanctoral readings are used). It concludes with a question Jesus puts to his disciples:

"Do you understand all these things?" They answered, "Yes." And he replied, "Then every scribe who has been instructed in the kingdom of heaven is like the head of a household who brings from his storeroom both the new and the old."

The choice of this Gospel for Jerome is certainly appropriate, since he himself declared in the prologue to his commentary on Isaiah that these verses were the criterion of his own exposition of Scripture.[79] He wanted to imitate the head of the household who brought out of his treasure both the new and the old, and to expound Isaiah in this way—Isaiah who, when he spoke about Christ, was prophet, apostle, and evangelist.[80] Jerome thus universalized the Matthean passage, a text originally referring to the disciples and to Jesus' parables, and transposed it to the fundamental understanding of Scripture.

If one joins Jerome in interpreting the words of Jesus, "Do you understand *all these things*?" as speaking of the whole of Scripture, this is ultimately a matter of the hermeneutics of the Bible. There can scarcely be any doubt that "the new" means Jesus' message about the kingdom of God, while "the

---

79 See Wilfried Hagemann, *Wort als Begegnung mit Christus. Die christozentrische Schrift-auslegung des Kirchenvaters Hieronymus*, TThS 23 (Trier: Paulinus, 1970); Ludger Schwien-horst-Schönberger, "Hieronymus als Gesprächspartner einer zeitgemäßen Bibelwissenschaft," in *Hieronymus als Exeget und Theologe. Interdisziplinäre Zugänge zum Koheletkommentar des Hieronymus*, ed. E. Birnbaum and L. Schwienhorst-Schönberger, EThL Bibliothea 268 (Leuven: Peeters, 2014), 273-98.

80 See Jerome, *Commentarius in Isaiam*, Prolegomena (CChr.SL 73:1; *Liturgy of the Hours*, 4:1447-49).

old" can be understood to mean Scripture.[81] We are not far here from seeing "the new" as the New Testament and "the old" as the Old Testament.

From today's perspective, we can ask: Is the so-called New Testament still genuinely new? Is it not ultimately, like the so-called Old Testament, thousands of years old? The impulses from the liturgical hermeneutics of the Bible could inspire us to a further interpretation of "the new and the old." Although Scripture, in its historical dimension, is in fact "the old," it is celebrated continually in the Liturgy as a relevant and living Word. In Liturgy, Scripture is always both "the old" *and* "the new." It is made present in the liturgical "today,"[82] and forms a rich storehouse for the Church, which brings forth treasures from it in the celebration of the Liturgy.

In this sense, the old question of Christ, "Do you understand all these things?", becomes a word that challenges us ever anew, since (changing the wording of *SC* 7 slightly) he himself puts this question when this Gospel is read in the Church. A liturgical hermeneutics of the Bible sketches an answer: the celebration of the Liturgy is a tried and proven way for the Church to understand how to become a disciple of the kingdom of heaven thanks to Bible and Liturgy, and thus, like the apostles, to grow into a "yes" that embraces the whole of one's person.

---

81 The fact that "the new" is mentioned first is striking, when we bear in mind Matthew's interest in the continuity with "the old" (see 5:17).

82 On this, see B.VIII.27.

Bibliography

Sources are listed by category and then alphabetically.

LITURGICAL SOURCES

Western Liturgical Sources

Ceremonial of Bishops. Revised by Decree of the Second Vatican Council and Published by the Authority of Pope John Paul II. Collegeville, MN: Liturgical Press, 1989.

Hymni ad usum in Liturgia Horarum. Redacti a Marco Benini cum praefatione episcopi Eystettensis Dr. Gregorii Mariae Hanke OSB, edited by Bischöfliches Seminar Eichstätt. 2nd ed. Eichstätt: Bischöfliches Seminar, 2007.

Andrieu, Michel, ed. *Les Ordines Romani du haut Moyen Âge.* 5 vols. SSL 11.23–24.28–29. Louvain: Spicilegium Sacrum Lovaniense, 1931–1961.

Lezionario Ambrosiano secondo il rito della Santa Chiesa di Milano. Riformato a norma dei decreti del Concilio Vaticano II promulgato dal Signor Cardinale Dionigi Tettamanzi […]. 7 vols. Milan: ITL Arcidiocesi di Milano, 2008–2009.

Liber sacramentorum romanae aeclesiae ordinis anni circuli […]. Sacramentarium Gelasianum, edited by L. C. Mohlberg. RED.F 4. 3rd ed. Rome: Herder, 1981.

Libro delle Vigilie. Secondo il rito della Chiesa di Milano. Riformato a norma dei decreti del Concilio Vaticano II. Promulgato dal Signor Cardinale Angelo Scola, Arcivescovo di Milano e Capo Rito. Milan: Centro Ambrosiano, 2016.

Liturgia Horarum iuxta ritum Romanum. Editio typica altera. Officium Divinum ex Decreto Sacrosancti Oecumenici Concilii Vaticani II instauratum auctoritate Pauli PP. VI promulgatum. 4 vols. Vatican City: Liberia Editrice Vaticana, 2000.

Liturgy of the Hours according to the Roman Rite. 4 vols. New York: Catholic Book Publishing, 1975/76.

Messale Ambrosiano secondo il rito della Santa Chiesa di Milano. Riformato a norma dei decreti del Concilio Vaticano II. Promulgato dal Signor Cardinale Giovanni Colombo. 2nd ed. Milan: Centro Ambrosiano di Documentazione e Studi Religiosi, 1986.

Messale Romano riformato a norma dei decreti del Concilio Vaticano II e promulgato da Papa Paolo VI e riveduto da Papa Giovanni Paolo II. 3rd ed. Rome: Fondazione di Religione Santi Francesco d'Assisi e Caterina da Siena, 2020.

Missale Ambrosianum juxta ritum Sanctae Ecclesiae Mediolanensis. Editio quinta post typicam. Milan: Daverio, 1954.

Missale Gothicum (Vat. Reg. lat. 317), edited by L. C. Mohlberg. RED.F 5. Rome: Herder, 1961.

Missale Romanum. Editio princeps (1570). Edizione anastatica, Introduzione e Appendice, edited by M. Sodi and A. M. Triacca. MLCT 2. Vatican City: Editrice Vaticana, 1998 [MRom 1570].

Missale Romanum ex decreto sacrosancti œcumenici Concilii Vaticani II instauratum, auctoritate Pauli Pp. VI promulgatim. Editio typica. Vatican City: Typis Polyglottis Vaticanis, 1970 [MRom 1970].

Missale Romanum ex decreto sacrosancti Oecumenici Concilii Vaticani II instauratum auctoritate Pauli PP. VI promulgatum Ioannis Pauli PP. II cura recognitum. Editio typica tertia. Vatican City: Typis Vaticanis, 2002 [MRom 2002].

Monastisches Stundenbuch für die Benediktiner des deutschen Sprachgebietes. Authentische Ausgabe für den liturgischen Gebrauch. 3 vols. St. Ottilien: EOS, 1–2 vol.: 2nd ed., 1993. 3rd vol.: 3rd ed., 2011.

Opening Prayers. Scripture-related Collects for Years A, B and C from the Sacramentary. The ICEL Collects. Norwich: Canterbury Press, 1999.

The Order of Baptism of Children, English translation according to the Second Typical Edition, for use in the dioceses of the United States of America. Washington, D.C.: United States Conference of Catholic Bishops, 2020.

Ordo Hebdomadae Sanctae instauratus. Editio typica. Vatican City: Typis Polyglottis Vaticanis, 1956.

Ordo initiationis Christianae adultorum. Rituale Romanum ex decreto sacrosancti oecumenici concilii Vaticani II instauratum auctoritate Pauli pp. VI promulgatum. Editio typica. Vatican City: Typis Polyglottis Vaticanis, 1972.

Le Pontifical Romano-Germanique du dixième siècle, edited by C. Vogel and R. Elze, 3 vols. StT 226–27, 269. Vatican City: Biblioteca Apostolica Vaticana, 1963, 1966, 1972.

The Rites of the Catholic Church as Revised by the Second Vatican Ecumenical Council. Prepared by International Commission on English in the Liturgy, 2 vols. New York: Pueblo, 1990–1991.

Rites of Ordination of a Bishop, of Priests, and of Deacons. 2nd typical ed. Washington, D.C.: United States Conference of Catholic Bishops, 2003.

Rituale Romanum. Editio princeps (1614). Edizione anastatica, Introduzione e Appendice, edited by M. Sodi and J. J. Flores Arcas. MLCT 5. Vatican City: Libreria Editrice Vaticana, 2004.

The Roman Missal. Renewed by Decree of the Most Holy Second Ecumenical Council of the Vatican, Promulgated by Authority of Pope Paul VI and Revised at the Direction of Pope John Paul II. English Translation according to the Third Typical Edition. Collegeville, MN: Liturgical Press, 2013.

Sunday Celebration of the Word and Hours. Approved by the National Liturgy Office for Use in Canada. Ottawa, Ontario: Publications Service, Canadian Conference of Catholic Bishops, 1995.

Byzantine Liturgical Sources

Ἀνθολόγιον τοῦ ὅλου ἐνιαυτοῦ περιέχον καθημερινὴν Ἀκολουθίαν ἐκ τοῦ Ὡρολογίου, τῆς Παρακλητικῆς καὶ τῶν Μηναίων (ἀπὸ τῆς Α΄ Σεμπτεμβρίου μέχρι τῆς ἀρχῆς τοῦ Τριῳδίου). Rome 1967.

Anthologhion di tutto l'anno. Contenente l'ufficio quotidiano dall'Orológhion, dal Paraklitikí e dai Minéi. 4 vols. Rome: Lipa Edizioni, 1999–2000.

Εὐχολόγιον τὸ Μέγα. Athens: Παπαδημητρίου, 1992.

Galadza, Peter, ed. *The Divine Liturgy. An Anthology for Worship.* 2nd ed. Ottawa: Metropolitan Andrey Sheptytsky Institute of Eastern Christian Studies, 2005.

Herman, Hieromonk and Vitaly Permiakov, eds. *Hieratikon. Liturgy Book for Priest and Deacon.* South Canaan, PA: St. Tikhon's Monastery, 2017.

Mateos, Juan, ed. *Le Typicon de la Grande Église. Ms. Sainte-Croix no 40, Xe siècle.* 2 vols. OCA 165–66. Rome: Pontificum Institutum Orientalium Studiorum, 1962–1963.

Parenti, Stefano and Elena Velkovska, eds. *L'Eucologio Barberini gr. 336. Seconda edizione riveduta. Con traduzione in lingua italiana.* BEL.S 80. Rome: CLV-Edizioni Liturgiche, 2000.

The Order of Episcopal Naming, Presentation, Profession, Ordination, and Enthronement: A Supplement for the Divine Liturgy of Our Holy Fathers John Chrysostom and Basil the Great. Pittsburgh: Byzantine Seminary Press, 2013.

Triode de carême. Translated by D. Guillaume. 3rd ed. Parma: Diaconie apostolique, 1997.

Eastern non-Byzantine Liturgical Sources

Book of Offering according to the Rite of the Antiochene Syriac Maronite Church: According to the Bkerke 2005 Edition. Approved by the Maronite Bishops of the English-Speaking Eparchies of Australia, Canada and the United States of America and Promulgated by the Maronite Patriarch (s.l., 2012).

Day, Peter D. *Eastern Christian Liturgies: The Armenian, Copic, Ethiopian and Syrian Rites: Eucharistic Rites with Introductory Notes and Rubrical Instructions.* Shannon: Irish University Press, 1972.

Findikyan, Daniel, ed. *The Divine Liturgy of the Armenian Church. With Modern Armenian and English Translations, Transliteration, Musical Notation, Introductions and Notes.* New York: St. Vartan Press, 2000.

Madey, Johannes and Georg Vavanikunnel, eds. *Qurbana oder die Eucharistiefeier der Thomaschristen Indiens.* Paderborn et al.: Sandesanilayam, 1968.

The Occasional Services. Vol. 3 of *The Great Book of Needs.* Translated by St. Tikhon's Monastery. South Canaan, PA: St. Tikhon's Monastery Press, 1999.

The Order of the Syro-Malabar Qurbana, edited by Commission for Liturgy, Major Archiepiscopal Curia Mount St. Thomas. Kochi, India: Don Bosco IGACT, 2005.

Pallath, Paul, ed. *La liturgia eucaristica della Chiesa siro-malabarese.* RivLi / Quaderni 3/1. Padua: Messaggero, 2000.

Jewish Liturgical Sources

The Koren Siddur. Translated by J. Sacks. 2nd ed. New Milford, CT: OU Press, 2013.

FURTHER SOURCES

Ambrose. *De bono mortis.* CSEL 32/1:701–53.

———. *De Excessu Fratris.* CSEL 73:207–325.

———. *De Noe.* CSEL 32/1:411–97.

———. *De officiis ministrorum.* PL 16:18–184.

———. *De sacramentis.* FontC 3. WEC 2:40–69.

———. *Explanatio Psalmi.* CSEL 64.

———. *Expositio Evangelii secundum Lucam.* CChr.SL 14.

The Apocryphical Gospels: Texts and Translations, edited by B. D. Ehrman and Z. Plešee. New York: Oxford University Press, 2011.

Apostolic Constitutions. SChr 320, 329, 336. WEC 2:217–84.

Apostolic Tradition. FontC 1:141–313. WEC 1:193–214. Bradshaw, Paul F., et al. *The Apostolic Tradition. A Commentary.* Hermeneia. Minneapolis: Fortress Press, 2002.

Athanasius. *The Life of Antony and the Letter to Marcellinus.* Translated by R. C. Gregg. New York: Paulist, 1980.

Augustine. *Contra Faustum.* CSEL 25:249–797. WEC 3:9–10.

———. *De Civitate Dei.* CChr.SL 47–48.

———. *De doctrina christiana*. CChr.SL 32.

———. *Enarrationes in psalmos*. CChr.SL 35–40. WEC 3:29–32.

———. *Tractatus in Iohannem*. CChr.SL 36.

———. *Quaestionum in Heptateuchum libri VII*. CChr.SL 33.

———. *Sermons on the Liturgical Seasons*. Translated by M. S. Muldowney. The Fathers of the Church 38. Washington, D.C.: The Catholic University of America Press, 1984.

Benedict. *Rule*. WEC 4:27–37.

Caesarius of Arles. *Sermons*. Translated by M. M. Mueller. The Fathers of the Church 31. Washington, D.C.: The Catholic University of America Press, 1956.

John Cassian, *De institutis coenobiorum*. SChr 109. WEC 3:163–175.

Chrysostom. *Hom. in 2 Thess*. PG 62:467–500.

Cyril. *The Works of Saint Cyril of Jerusalem*. Translated by L. P. McCauley and A. A. Stephenson. The Fathers of the Church 64. Vol. 2. Washington, D.C.: The Catholic University of America Press, 1970.

———. *Mystagogicae catecheses*. FontC 7. WEC 2:326–37.

Didache. FontC 1:25–139. WEC 1:31–41.

Durandus. *Rationale divinorum officiorum*. CChr.CM 140.

Egeria. *Itinerarium:* McGowan, Anne and Paul F. Bradshaw. *The Pilgrimage of Egeria. A New Translation of the Itinerarium Egeriae with Introduction and Commentary*. Collegeville, MN: Liturgical Press, 2018.

Ephrem. *Commentarium in Diatessaron*. SChr 121.

Eusebius. *De solemnitate paschali*. PG 24:693–706.

Gregory. *Homiliae in Ezechielem prophetam*. CChr.SL 142.

Hilary. *Tractatus super psalmos*. CSEL 22.

Jerome. *Commentarius in Isaiam*. CChr.SL 73–73A.

———. *Contra Vigilantium*. PL 23:339–358. WEC 3:354–55.

———. *Tractatus in librum psalmorum*. CChr.SL 78.

Justin. *Apologiae*. FontC 91. WEC 1:65–69.

Origen. *Commentarius in Iohannem*. SChr 120, 157, 222, 290, 385.

———. *Commentariorum series in Mathaeum*. GCS 38.

———. *Homilia in librum Iesu Nave*. GCS 30:286–463.

———. *Homilies on Leviticus*. Translated by G. W. Barkley. The Fathers of the Church 83. Washington, D.C.: The Catholic University of America Press, 1990.

———. *Homilies on Numbers*. Translated by T. P. Scheck and C. A. Hall. Ancient Christian Texts. Downers Grove, IL: IVP Academic, 2009.

———. *Homilies on Genesis and Exodus,* The Fathers of the Church: A New Translation 71. Washington, D.C.: The Catholic University of America Press, 2010.

Kontakia of Romanos, Byzantine Melodist. 1: *On the Person of Christ,* edited by M. Carpenter. Columbia: University of Missouri Press, 1970.

Romanos le Mélode. Hymnes. Introduction, texte critique, traduction et notes, edited and translated by J. Grosdidier de Matons. 5 vols. SChr 99, 110, 114, 128, 283. Paris: Éd. du Cerf, 1964–1981.

Romanos Melodos. Die Hymnen, edited and translated by J. Koder. 2 vols. Bibliothek der griechischen Literatur 62.64. Stuttgart: Hiersemann, 2005–2006.

Tertullian. *De resurrectione carnis.* PL 2:791–886.

Thomas Aquinas. *Summa theologiae.*

Thomas à Kempis. *The Imitation of Christ,* edited by P. G. Zomberg. Rockland: Dustan Press, 1985.

MAGISTERIUM

Benedict XVI. Postsynodal Apostolic Exhortation *Verbum Domini.* September 30, 2010.

Congregation of Rites, *Eucharisticum mysterium.* May 25, 1967.

Congregation for Divine Worship and the Discipline of the Sacraments. *Homiletic Directory.* June 29, 2014.

———. Decree *In Missa in Cena Domini.* January 6, 2016.

Documents on the Liturgy 1963–1979: Conciliar, Papal and Curial Texts, edited and translated by T. C. O'Brien. Collegeville, MN: Liturgical Press, 1982.

Enchiridion biblicum. Documenta ecclesiastica sacram scripturam spectantia, edited by The Pontifical Biblical Commission. 4th ed. Naples et al.: d'Auria, 1965.

Francis. Apostolic Exhortation *Evangelii Gaudium.* November 24, 2013.

———. Motu proprio *Aperuit illis.* September 30, 2019.

John Paul II. *Ecclesia de Eucharistia.* Encyclical Letter. April 17, 2003.

The Liturgy Documents: A Parish Resource, edited by D. Lysik. 4th ed. Vol. 1. Chicago: Liturgy Training Publications, 2004.

Paul VI. Apostolic Exhortation *Evangelii nuntiandi.* December 8, 1975.

———. *Mysterium fidei.* Encyclical on the Holy Eucharist. September 3, 1965.

Pius XII. *Mediator Dei.* November 20, 1947.

Pontifical Biblical Commission. *The Interpretation of the Bible in the Church.* Vatican City: Libreria Editrice Vaticana, 1993.

———. *The Jewish people and their sacred scriptures in the Christian Bible.* Vatican City: Libreria Editrice Vaticana, 2002.

———. *Inspiration and Truth of Sacred Scripture.* Collegeville, MN: Liturgical Press, 2014.

Vatican Council II. *Sacrosanctum Concilium.* December 4, 1963.

———. *Lumen Gentium.* November 21, 1964.

———. *Perfectae caritatis.* October 28, 1965.

———. *Dei Verbum.* November 15, 1965.

———. *Ad Gentes.* December 7, 1965.

———. *Presbyterorum Ordinis.* December 7, 1965.

STUDIES

Alföldi, Andreas. *Die monarchische Repräsentation im römischen Kaiserreiche: Mit einem Register von Elisabeth Alföldi-Rosenbaum.* Darmstadt: Wissenschaftliche Buchgesellschaft, 1970.

Alzati, Cesare. *Il Lezionario della chiesa Ambrosiana. La tradizione liturgica e il rinnovato "ordo lectionum".* MSIL 50. Vatican City: Libreria Editrice Vaticana, 2009.

———. "Il Libro della Liturgia Vigiliare Vespertina." *Ambrosius* 85 (2009): 107–22.

———. *Ambrosianum mysterium. La chiesa di Milano e la sua tradizione liturgica.* Archivio Ambrosiano 81. Milan: Ambrosiana, 2000.

Antor, Heinz. "Rezeptionsästhetik." In *Metzler Lexikon Literatur- und Kulturtheorie. Ansätze – Personen – Grundbegriffe,* edited by A. Nünning, 5th ed., 650–52. Stuttgart: J.B. Metzler, 2013.

Assmann, Jan. *Cultural Memory and Early Civilization: Writing, Remembrance, and Political Imagination.* Translated by D. H. Wilson. Cambridge, New York: Cambridge University Press, 2011.

———. "Der zweidimensionale Mensch: das Fest als Medium des kollektiven Gedächtnisses." In *Das Fest und das Heilige. Religiöse Kontrapunkte zur Alltagswelt,* edited by J. Assmann in collaboration with T. Sundermeier, Studien zum Verstehen fremder Religionen 1, 13–30. Gütersloh: Gütersloher Verlagshaus, 1991.

Auf der Maur, Hansjörg. *Das Psalmenverständnis des Ambrosius von Mailand. Ein Beitrag zum Deutungshintergrund der Psalmenverwendung im Gottesdienst der Alten Kirche.* Leiden: Brill, 1977.

———. *Feiern im Rhythmus der Zeit 1. Herrenfeste in Woche und Jahr.* GdK 5. Regensburg: Pustet, 1983.

———. "Feste und Gedenktage der Heiligen." In *Feiern im Rhythmus der Zeit II/1,* edited by P. Harnoncourt and H. Auf der Maur, GdK 6,1, 65–357. Regensburg: Pustet, 1994.

Austin, John L. *How to Do Things with Words: The William James Lectures delivered at Harvard University in 1955.* Oxford: Clarendon Press, 1962.

Baldovin, John F. *The Urban Character of Christian Worship. The Origins, Development and Meaning of Stational Liturgy*. OCA 228. Rome: Pontificium Institutum Studiorum Orientalium, 1987.

Ballhorn, Egbert. "Kontext wird Text. Die Psalmen in Forschungsgeschichte, in biblischer Zeit und in christlicher Liturgie." *BiLi* 77, no. 3 (2004): 161–70.

———. "Das historische und das kanonische Paradigma in der Exegese." In *Der Bibelkanon in der Bibelauslegung. Methodenreflexionen und Beispielexegesen*, edited by E. Ballhorn and G. Steins, 9–30. Stuttgart: Kohlhammer, 2007.

Balthasar, Hans Urs von. "God Speaks as Man." In Balthasar, *Verbum Caro*. Vol 1 of *Explorations in Theology*, 69–93. San Francisco: Ignatius Press, [1958] 1989.

Bärsch, Jürgen. "Sakramentenliturgie nach dem Zweiten Vatikanischen Konzil. Anmerkungen und Beobachtungen zu Theologie und Praxis anlässlich des Motu proprio ‚Summorum Pontificum' Papst Benedikts XVI. (2007)." In *Weltoffen aus Treue. Studientag zum Zweiten Vatikanischen Konzil*, edited by C. Böttigheimer and E. Naab, Extemporalia 22, 163–208. St. Ottilien: EOS-Verlag, 2009.

———. *Liturgie im Prozess: Studien zur Geschichte des religiösen Lebens*, edited by M. Benini et al. Münster: Aschendorff, 2019.

Barsotti, Divo. *Il mistero cristiano e la parola di Dio*. Firenze: Fiorentina, 1953.

Baumgartner, Jakob. "Locus ubi Spiritus Sanctus floret. Eine Geist-Epiklese im Wortgottesdienst?" *FZPhTh* 23, no. 1/2 (1976): 112–45.

Baumstark, Anton. *Liturgie comparée. Principes et méthodes pour l'étude historique des liturgies chrétiennes*. Reviewed by B. Botte. 3rd ed. Collection Irénikon. Chevetogne et al.: Éditions de Chevetogne, 1953.

Beatrice, Pier Franco. *La lavanda dei piedi. Contributo alla storia delle antiche liturgie cristiane*. BEL.S 28. Rome: Edizioni Liturgiche, 1983.

Becker, Hansjakob and Reiner Kaczynski, eds. *Liturgie und Dichtung. Ein interdisziplinäres Kompendium*. PiLi 1–2. 2 vols. St. Ottilien: EOS, 1983.

Benini, Marco. "Hilfsmittel für Prediger: Zum neuen Homiletischen Direktorium." *Gottesdienst* 49, no. 7 (2015): 53–55.

———. "Johannes Eck als achtsamer Liturge. Sein Ingolstädter Pfarrbuch als liturgiehistorische Quelle unter besonderer Berücksichtigung der szenischen Liturgie des Osterfestkreises." *ALw* 57 (2015): 72–95.

———. *Die Feier des Osterfestkreises im Ingolstädter Pfarrbuch des Johannes Eck*. LQF 105. Münster: Aschendorff, 2016.

———. "Andrea Pozzos Deckenfresko von Sant'Ignazio in Rom und die tätige Teilnahme an der Liturgie der Kirche." In *„Dein Antlitz, Herr, will ich suchen!". Selbstoffenbarung Gottes und Antwort des Menschen* (FS Michael Schneider), edited by T. Kremer, Koinonia - Oriens 55, 421–41. Münster: Aschendorff, 2019.

———. "Der Ambo – „Tisch des Gotteswortes" (SC 51)." In *„Zeichen und Symbol überirdischer Wirklichkeit": Liturgische Orte und ihre künstlerische Gestaltung: Eine*

Festschrift für den Künstler Friedrich Koller, edited by S. Kopp and J. Werz, 25–33. Regensburg: Pustet, 2019.

———. "The Blessing with the Book of the Gospels. A Recent Adoption from the Byzantine to the Roman Rite." *Antiphon* 24, no. 1 (2020): 50–66.

———. "Gegenwärtig im Wort. Sakramentalität des Wortes Gottes." In *Liturgie und Bibel: Theologie und Praxis der Verkündigung des Wortes Gottes*, edited by T. Söding and M. Linnenborn, 28–52. Trier: Deutsches Liturgisches Institut, 2020.

———. *Liturgische Bibelhermeneutik. Die Heilige Schrift im Horizont des Gottesdienstes*. LQF 109. Münster: Aschendorff, 2020.

———. "Liturgical Actions: Anamnesis and/or Mimesis of Sacred Scripture? Exemplified by the Rite of Footwashing (Holy Thursday) and Ephphetha (Baptismal Liturgy)." *Worship* 95, no. 1 (2021): 34–50.

———. "„Große Entdeckung: Die Bibel ist sakramental." Zu Pius Parschs Wort-Gottes-Theologie und seinen liturgischen Predigten." In *Die Liturgietheologie von Pius Parsch. Klosterneuburger Symposion 2021*, edited by A. Redtenbacher and D. Seper, 174–99 (Freiburg/Br.: Herder, 2022).

Berger, Rupert et. al., eds. *Gestalt des Gottesdienstes: Sprachliche und nichtsprachliche Ausdrucksformen*. GdK 3. 2nd ed. Regensburg: Pustet, 1990.

Bertonière, Gabriel. *The Sundays of Lent in the Tridion [sic!]. The Sundays Without a Commemoration*. OCA 253. Rome: Pontificium Institutum Studiorum Orientalium, 1997.

Bevilacqua, Giulio, ed. *Miscellanea liturgica in onore di Sua Eminenza il Cardinale Giacomo Lercaro, arcivescovo di Bologna, presidente del "Consilium" per l'applicazione della costituzione sulla sacra liturgia*. 2 vols. Rome et al.: Desclée de Brouwer, 1966–1967.

Biblia patristica. Index des citations et allusions bibliques dans la littérature patristique, edited by Centre d'Analyse et de Documentation Patristiques. 7 vols. Paris: Centre National de la Recherche Scientifique, 1975–2000.

Bilandzic, Helena et al. *Medienrezeptionsforschung*. UTB 4003 Kommunikationswissenschaft, Psychologie, Soziologie. Konstanz: UVK Verlag, 2015.

Bishops' Committee on the Liturgy. "Newsletter 23, February 1987." In *Thirty-Five Years of the BCL Newsletters 1965–2000*, 1043–44. Washington, D.C.: United States Conference of Catholic Bishops, 2004.

Bizău, Ioan. "Les psaumes et leur interprétation dans le rituel orthodoxe de la consécration de l'Eglise." In Braga and Pistoia, *Liturgie, interprète de l'écriture* 2, 131–67.

Blanchard, Yves-Marie. "Interdépendance entre la formulation du Canon biblique chrétien et la lecture liturgique." In *Présence et rôle de la Bible dans la liturgie*, edited by M. Klöckener et al., 69–93. Fribourg: Academic Press, 2006.

Bobertz, Charles A. "A Prolegomena to a Ritual/Liturgical Reading of Mark's Gospel." In *Reading in Christian Communities. Essays on Interpretation in the Early Church*, edited by C. A. Bobertz and D. Brakke, 174–87. Notre Dame, IN: University of Notre Dame Press, 2002.

———. *The Gospel of Mark: A Liturgical Reading*. Grand Rapids: Baker Academic, 2016.

Böhler, Dieter. "Der Kanon als hermeneutische Vorgabe biblischer Theologie. Über aktuelle Methodendiskussionen in der Bibelwissenschaft." *ThPh* 77, no. 2 (2002): 161–78.

———. "Anmerkungen eines Exegeten zur Instructio quinta 'Liturgiam authenticam." *LJ* 54, no. 4 (2004): 205–22.

———. "Vom einsamen Murmeln des Gerechten zum Jubelchor der ganzen Schöpfung. Was es bedeutet, im Stundengebet nicht nur Psalmen, sondern den Psalter zu beten." *Notitiae* 44, no. 503–504 (2008): 416–34.

———. *Psalmen 1–50*. HThKAT. Freiburg/Br. et al.: Herder, 2021.

Bonneau, Normand. *The Sunday Lectionary: Ritual Word, Paschal Shape*. Collegeville, MN: Liturgical Press, 1998.

Bormann, Claus V. "Hermeneutik: I. Philosophisch-theologisch." In *TRE 25*, edited by G. Krause and G. Müller, 108–37. Berlin: De Gruyter, 1995.

Botte, Bernard. "Das Weihesakrament nach den Gebeten des Weiheritus." In *Das apostolische Amt*, edited by J. Guyot, 13–33. Mainz: Matthias-Grünewald, 1961.

———. "L'ordination de l'évêque." *MD* 98 (1969): 113–26.

Bouhot, Jean-Paul. "Le choix des lectures liturgique dans l'église romaine: quelques exemples." In *Präsenz und Verwendung der Heiligen Schrift im christlichen Frühmittelalter. Exegetische Literatur und liturgische Texte*, edited by P. Carmassi, Wolfenbütteler Mittelalter-Studien 20, 239–249. Wiesbaden: Harrasowitz, 2008.

Bradshaw, Paul F. *Ordination Rites of the Ancient Churches of East and West*. New York: Pueblo Publication, 1990.

———. "The Use of the Bible in Liturgy: Some Historical Perspectives." *Studia Liturgica* 22, no. 1 (1992): 35–52.

———. "From Word to Action: The Changing Role of Psalmody in Early Christianity." In *Like a Two-Edged Sword. The Word of God in Liturgy and History* (FS Canon Donald Gray), edited by M. R. Dudley, 21–37. Norwich: Canterbury Press, 1995.

———., et al. *The Apostolic Tradition. A Commentary*. Hermeneia. Minneapolis: Fortress Press, 2002.

———. *Rites of Ordination. Their History and Theology*. A Pueblo book. Collegeville, MN: Liturgical Press, 2013.

Braga, Carlo and Alessandro Pistoia, eds. *Dans les compositions liturgiques, prières et chants*. Vol 2 of *La liturgie, interprète de l'écriture*. BEL.S 126. Rome: CLV-Edizioni Liturgiche, 2003.

Braschi, Francesco. "Libro II. Mistero della Pasqua." *Ambrosius* 85 (2009): 161–99.

Braulik, Georg and Norbert Lohfink, eds. *Osternacht und Altes Testament. Studien und Vorschläge: Mit einer Exsultetvertonung von Erwin Bücken.* ÖBS 22. Frankfurt/M. et al.: Lang, 2003.

———., eds. *Liturgie und Bibel: Gesammelte Aufsätze.* ÖBS 28. Frankfurt/M. et al.: Lang, 2005.

———. "Christologisches Verständnis der Psalmen – schon im Alten Testament?" In Richter and Kranemann, *Christologie der Liturgie*, 57–86.

———. "Psalter und Messias. Zum christologischen Verständnis der Psalmen im Alten Testament und bei den Kirchenvätern." In Braulik and Lohfink, *Liturgie und Bibel*, 481–502.

———. "Rezeptionsästhetik, kanonische Intertextualität und unsere Meditation des Psalters." In Braulik and Lohfink, *Liturgie und Bibel*, 523–47.

———. *L'esegesi anticotestamentaria e la liturgia: Nuovi sviluppi negli ultimi decenni.* Leiturgia – Lectiones Vagagginianae 5. Assisi: Cittadella Editrice, 2014.

Braun, Joseph. *Das christliche Altargerät in seinem Sein und in seiner Entwicklung.* Munich: Hueber, 1932.

Browe, Peter. "Mittelalterliche Kommunionriten." *JLw* 15 (1941): 23–66.

Brucker, Ralph. "'Wer ist der König der Herrlichkeit?' Ps 23[24] Text, Wirkung, Rezeption." In *Die Septuaginta – Text, Wirkung, Rezeption. 4. Internationale Fachtagung veranstaltet von Septuaginta Deutsch (LXX.D) [...],* edited by W. Kraus and S. Kreuzer, WUNT 325, 405–29. Tübingen: Mohr Siebeck, 2014.

Bruylants, Placide. *Les oraisons du Missel Romain. Texte et histoire.* Études liturgiques 1. 2 vols. Louvain: Centre de Documentation et d'Information Liturgiques, 1952.

Bruni, Vitaliano. *I funerali di un sacerdote nel rito bizantino. Secondo gli eucologi manoscritti di lingua greca.* Publications of the Studium Biblicum Franciscanum. Collectio minor 14. Jerusalem: Franciscan Printing Press, 1972.

Buchinger, Harald. "Die älteste erhaltene christliche Psalmenhomilie. Zu Verwendung und Verständnis des Psalters bei Hippolyt." *TThZ* 104, no. 2 and 4 (1995): 125–44, 272–98.

———. "Zur Hermeneutik liturgischer Psalmenverwendung. Methodologische Überlegungen im Schnittpunkt von Bibelwissenschaft, Patristik und Liturgiewissenschaft." *HlD* 54, no. 3 (2000): 193–222.

———. "Mehr als ein Steinbruch? Beobachtungen und Fragen zur Bibelverwendung in der römischen Liturgie." *BiLi* 82, no. 1 (2009): 22–31.

———. "Lebensraum des Wortes. Zur Bibelverwendung der römischen Liturgie am Beispiel ihrer Gesänge." *LJ* 62, no. 3 (2012): 181–206.

———. "Pentekoste, II. Alte Kirche. III. Zusammenfassende Interpretation." *RAC* 27 (2015): 94–108.

———. "Pentekoste, Pfingsten und Himmelfahrt. Grunddaten und Fragen zur Frühgeschichte." In *Preaching after Easter. Mid-Pentecost, Ascension, and Pentecost in*

Late Antiquity, edited by R. W. Bishop et. al, Supplements to Vigiliae Christianae 136, 15–84. Leiden: Brill, 2016.

———. "Psalmodie als Sakrament. Johannes Chrysostomus über den täglichen Abendpsalm 140(141)." In Franz and Zerfaß, *Wort des lebendigen Gottes*, 221–40.

Buchinger, Harald and Clemens Leonhard, eds. *Liturgische Bibelrezeption.* Forschungen zur Kirchen- und Dogmengeschichte 108. Göttingen: Vandenhoeck & Ruprecht, 2021.

Bugnini, Annibale and Carlo Braga, eds. *Ordo Hebdomadae Sanctae instauratus. Commentarium […].* BEL.H 25. Rome: Edizioni Liturgiche, 1956.

Bugnini, Annibale. *The Reform of the Liturgy, 1948-1975.* Translated by M. J. O'Connell. Collegeville, MN: Liturgical Press, 1990.

Carmassi, Patrizia. *Libri liturgici e istituzioni ecclesiastiche a Milano in età medioevale. Studio sulla formazione del lezionario ambrosiano.* LQF 85. Münster: Aschendorff, 2001.

Casel, Odo. "Mysteriengegenwart." *JLw* 8 (1928): 145–224.

———. "The Meaning of the Mystery." In O. Casel. *The Mystery of Christian Worship, and Other Writings*, 97–165. Westminster, MD: Newman Press, 1962.

Cernokrak, Nicolas. "La narratologie liturgique byzantine selon les péricopes dominicales du Grand Carême de l'évangile de saint Marc." In Triacca and Pistoia, *Liturgie, interprète de l'écriture* 1, 183–200.

Chauvet, Louis-Marie. "What makes Liturgy biblical? – Texts." *SL* 22, no. 2 (1992): 121–133.

———. *Symbol and Sacrament: A Sacramental Reinterpretation of Christian Existence.* Collegeville, MN: Liturgical Press, 1995.

Chronz, Tinatin. *Die Feier des Heiligen Öles nach Jerusalemer Ordnung mit dem Text des slavischen Codex Hilferding 21 der Russischen Nationalbibliothek in Sankt Petersburg sowie georgischen Übersetzungen palästinischer und konstantinopolitanischer Quellen. Einführung – Edition – Kommentar.* JThF 18. Münster: Aschendorff, 2012.

Cothenet, Édouard. *Exégèse et liturgie.* Lectio divina 133. Paris: Les Éditions du Cerf, 1988.

Crnčević, Ante. *Induere Christum. Rito e linguaggio simbolico-teologico della vestizione battesimale.* BEL.S 108. Rome: CLV-Edizioni Liturgiche, 2000.

Dalferth, Ingolf U. *Die Kunst des Verstehens: Grundzüge einer Hermeneutik der Kommunikation durch Texte.* Tübingen: Mohr Siebeck, 2018.

Daniélou, Jean. "The Sacraments and the History of Salvation." In *The liturgy and the Word of God*, edited by A. G. Martimort, 21–32. Collegeville, MN: Liturgical Press, 1959.

Daschner, Dominik. "Meditation oder Antwort – Zur Funktion des Antwortpsalms." *HlD* 48, no. 2, no. 3 (1994): 131–53, 200–220.

Dassmann, Ernst. "Die Bedeutung des Alten Testamentes für das Verständnis des kirchlichen Amtes in der frühpatristischen Theologie." In Dassmann, Ämter und Dienste in den frühchristlichen Gemeinden, Hereditas 8, 96–113. Bonn: Borengässer, 1994.

———. *Ambrosius von Mailand. Leben und Werk.* Stuttgart: Kohlhammer, 2004.

De Clerck, Paul. "L'usage de l'Ecriture dans les prières d'ordination des liturgies byzantine, gallicane et romaine." In *Ordination et ministères,* edited by A. M. Triacca and A. Pistoia, BEL.S 85, 107–17. Rome: CLV-Edizioni Liturgiche, 1996.

———. "Débat final: Réactions d'un auditeur catholique." In *Dans les compositions liturgiques, prières et chants,* vol. 2 of *Liturgie, interprète de l'écriture,* edited by C. Braga and A. Pistoia, BEL.S 126, 277–81. Rome: CLV-Edizioni Liturgiche, 2003.

———. "L'«Ordo lectionum missae» de l'Église romaine." In *Présence et rôle de la Bible dans la liturgie,* edited by M. Klöckener, 239–51. Fribourg: Academic Press, 2006.

Deeg, Alexander. *Das äußere Wort und seine liturgische Gestalt: Überlegungen zu einer evangelischen Fundamentalliturgik.* Arbeiten zur Pastoraltheologie, Liturgik und Hymnologie 68. Göttingen: Vandenhoeck & Ruprecht, 2012.

———. "Heilige Schrift und Gottesdienst. Evangelische Überlegungen zur Bibel in der Liturgie – oder: SC 24 als ökumenisches Projekt." In Franz and Zerfaß, *Wort des lebendigen Gottes,* 49–70.

———. "Hermeneutica prima. Eine evangelische Wahrnehmung von Marco Beninis »Liturgische Bibelhermeneutik. Die Heilige Schrift im Horizont des Gottesdienstes«." *LJ* 70, no. 4 (2020): 259–68.

De Lubac, Henri. *History and Spirit: The Understanding of Scripture According to Origen.* Translated by A. E. Nash with J. Merriell. San Francisco: Ignatius Press, 2007.

De Zan, Renato. "Bible and Liturgy." In *Introduction to the Liturgy,* vol. 1 of *Handbook for Liturgical Studies,* edited by A. J. Chupungco, 33–51. Collegeville, MN: Liturgical Press, 1997.

———. *Unius verbi Dei multiplices thesauri. La lettura liturgica della bibbia. Appunti per un metodo.* BEL.S 196. Rome: CLV-Edizioni Liturgiche 2021.

Dumas, Antoine. "Les sources du nouveau missel romain." *Notitiae* 7, no. 60–63, 65, 68 (1971): 37–42, 74–77, 94–95, 134–36, 276–80, 409–10.

Durst, Michael. "Wortkommunion – patristische Grundlagen." *BiLi* 89, no. 3 (2016): 156–67.

Dyer, Joseph. "The Desert, the City and Psalmody in the Late Fourth Century." In Gallagher, *Western Plainchant,* 11–43.

Eco, Umberto. *The Role of the Reader: Explorations in the Semiotics of Texts.* Advances in semiotics. Bloomington, IN: Indiana University Press, 1981.

———. *The Open Work.* Translated by A. Cancogni. Cambridge, MA: Harvard University Press, 1989.

Egbulem, Chris Nwaka. *The "Rite Zairois" in the Context of Liturgical Inculturation in Middle-Belt Africa Since the Second Vatican Council.* Washington, D.C.: ProQuest Dissertations Publishing, 1989.

Eisenbach, Franziskus. *Die Gegenwart Jesu Christi im Gottesdienst: Systematische Studien zur Liturgiekonstitution des II. Vatikanischen Konzils.* Mainz: Grünewald, 1982.

Elberti, Arturo. *La liturgia delle ore in Occidente. Storia e teologia.* Collana teologia liturgica. Rome: Ed. Dehoniane, 1998.

Elbogen, Ismar. *Jewish Liturgy: A Comprehensive History.* Translated by R. P. Scheindlin. New York: Jewish Theological Seminary of America, 1993.

Eterović, Nikola, ed. *La parola di Dio nella vita e nella missione della Chiesa: XII assemblea generale ordina-ria del sinodo dei vescovi: Esortazione apostolica postsinodale Verbum Domini.* Sinodo dei vescovi 2. Vatican City: Libreria Editrice Vaticana, 2011.

Fagerberg, David W. *Theologia prima. What is liturgical theology?* 2nd ed. Chicago/Mundelein, IL: Hillenbrand Books, 2004.

Fiedrowicz, Michael. *Psalmus vox totius Christi. Studien zu Augustins "Enarrationes in Psalmos."* Freiburg/Br. et al.: Herder, 1997.

Fischer, Balthasar. *Die Psalmen als Stimme der Kirche. Gesammelte Studien zur christlichen Psalmenfrömmigkeit* (FS Balthasar Fischer), edited by A. Heinz. Trier: Paulinus, 1982.

———. "Christliches Psalmenverständnis im 2. Jahrhundert." In Fischer, *Psalmen als Stimme der Kirche*, 85–102.

———. "Die Psalmenfrömmigkeit der Martyrerkirche." In Fischer, *Psalmen als Stimme der Kirche*, 15–35.

———. "Liturgiegeschichte und Exegesegeschichte. Interdisziplinäre Zusammenhänge." *JbAC* 30 (1987): 5–13.

———. "Christological Interpretation of the Psalms seen in the Mirror of the Liturgy." *QL* 71, no. 3 (1990): 227–35.

———. "Formen der Verkündigung" In Berger, *Gestalt des Gottesdienstes*, 77–93.

———. *Redemptionis mysterium. Studien zur Osterfeier und zur christlichen Initiation,* edited by A. Gerhards und A. Heinz. Paderborn et al.: Schöningh, 1992.

———. "Die Auferstehungsfeier am Ostermorgen. Altchristliches Gedankengut in mittelalterlicher Fassung." In Fischer, *Redemptionis mysterium*, 13–27.

———. "Der patristische Hintergrund der drei großen johanneischen Taufperikopen von der Samariterin, der Heilung des Blindgeborenen und der Auferweckung des Lazarus am dritten, vierten und fünften Sonntag der Quadragesima." In Fischer, *Redemptionis mysterium*, 172–85.

———. "Dienst des Lobes – Dienst der Fürbitte. Zur Spiritualität des Stundengebetes." In Fischer, *Frömmigkeit der Kirche. Gesammelte Studien zur christlichen Spiritualität,* edited by A. Gerhards and A. Heinz, Hereditas 17, 204–15. Bonn: Borengässer, 2000.

Fischer, Balthasar and Helmut Hucke. "Poetische Formen." In Berger, *Gestalt des Gottesdienstes*, 180–219.

Fontaine, Gaston. "Commentarium ad Ordinem Lectionum Missae." *Notitiae* 5, no. 47 (1969): 256–82.

Franz, Ansgar, ed. *Streit am Tisch des Wortes? Zur Deutung und Bedeutung des Alten Testaments und seiner Verwendung in der Liturgie.* PiLi 8. St. Ottilien: EOS, 1997.

————. *Wortgottesdienst der Messe und Altes Testament: Katholische und ökumenische Lektionarreform nach dem II. Vatikanum im Spiegel von Ordo Lectionum Missae, Revised Common Lectionary und Four Year Lectionary: Positionen, Probleme, Perspektiven.* PiLi.S 14. Tübingen/Basel: Francke, 2002.

Franz, Ansgar and Alexander Zerfaß, eds., *Wort des lebendigen Gottes. Liturgie und Bibel* (FS Hansjakob Becker). PiLi 16. Tübingen: Narr Francke Attempto, 2016.

Freund, Elisabeth. *The Return of the Reader: Reader-Response Criticism.* London/New York: Routledge, 2003.

Frick-Salzmann, Annemarie. "Gedächtnissysteme." In *Gedächtnistraining. Theoretische und praktische Grundlagen,* edited by H. Schloffer, E. Prank and A. Frick-Salzmann, 34–43. Heidelberg: Springer, 2010.

Fuchs, Guido. "Theologie der Eucharistie im Spiegel eucharistischer Gesänge." *ALw* 31, no. 3 (1989): 313–41.

Füglister, Notker. "Vom Mut zur ganzen Schrift. Zur vorgesehenen Eliminierung der sogenannten Fluchpsalmen aus dem neuen römischen Brevier." *StZ* 184 (1969): 186–200.

————. "Die Verwendung und das Verständnis der Psalmen und des Psalters um die Zeitenwende." In *Beiträge zur Psalmenforschung. Psalm 2 und 22,* edited by J. Schreiner, Forschung zur Bibel 60, 319–84. Würzburg: Echter, 1988.

Gabel, Helmut. *Inspirationsverständnis im Wandel. Theologische Neuorientierung im Umfeld des Zweiten Vatikanischen Konzils.* Mainz: Matthias-Grünewald-Verlag, 1991.

————. "Inspiration. III. Theologie- und dogmengeschichtlich. IV. Systematisch-theologisch." In *LThK,* vol. 5, 535–41. Freiburg/Br.: Herder, 1996.

Gadamer, Hans-Georg. *Truth and Method.* Translated by J. Weinsheimer and D. G. Mashall. 2nd ed. London, New York: Continuum, 2006.

Gallagher, Sean, ed. *Western Plainchant in the First Millennium. Studies in the Medieval Liturgy and its Music.* Aldershot et al.: Ashgate, 2003.

Gerhards, Albert and Benedikt Kranemann. *Introduction to the Study of Liturgy.* Translated by L. M. Maloney. Collegeville, MN: Liturgical Press, 2017.

Getcha, Job. "Le système des lectures bibliques du rite byzantin." In Triacca and Pistoia, *Liturgie, interprète de l'écriture* 1, 25–56.

————. *The Typikon Decoded. An Explanation of Byzantine Liturgical Practice.* Orthodox Liturgy Series 3. Yonkers, NY: St Vladimir's Seminary Press, 2012.

Gil Hellín, Francisco. *Constitutio de sacra liturgia, Sacrosanctum concilium. Concilii Vaticani II synopsis in ordinem redigens schemata cum relationibus necnon patrum orationes atque animadversiones.* Vatican City: Libreria Editrice Vaticana, 2003.

Gögler, Rolf. *Zur Theologie des biblischen Wortes bei Origenes.* Düsseldorf: Patmos-Verlag, 1963.

Graumann, Thomas. *Christus interpres. Die Einheit von Auslegung und Verkündigung in der Lukaserklärung des Ambrosius von Mailand*. PTS 41. Berlin et al.: De Gruyter, 1994.

Grisar, Hartmann. *Das Missale im Lichte römischer Stadtgeschichte. Stationen, Perikopen, Gebräuche*. Freiburg/Br.: Herder, 1925.

Groen, Bert. "Die Krankensalbung im orthodoxen Griechenland." *LJ* 45, no. 3 (1995): 178–82.

Groen, Basilius J. and Christian Gastgeber, eds. *Die Liturgie der Ostkirche. Ein Führer zu Gottesdienst und Glaubensleben der orthodoxen und orientalischen Kirchen*. 2nd ed. Freiburg/Br. et al.: Herder, 2013.

Grosdidier de Matons, José. *Romanos le Mélode et les origines de la poésie religieuse à Byzance*. Beauchesne religions. Paris: Beauchesne, 1977.

Gusmer, Charles W. *And You Visited Me: Sacramental Ministry to the Sick and the Dying*. Collegeville, MN: Pueblo, 1990.

Gussone, Nikolaus. "Der Codex auf dem Thron. Zur Ehrung des Evangelienbuches in Liturgie und Zeremoniell." In Neuheuser, *Wort und Buch*, 191–232.

Gy, Pierre-Marie. "La théologie des prières anciennes pour l'ordination des évêques et des prêtres." *RSPhTh* 58 (1974): 599–617.

Hagemann, Wilfried. *Wort als Begegnung mit Christus. Die christozentrische Schriftauslegung des Kirchenvaters Hieronymus*. TThS 23. Trier: Paulinus, 1970.

Hahn, Viktor. *Das wahre Gesetz. Eine Untersuchung der Auffassung des Ambrosius von Mailand vom Verhältnis der beiden Testamente*. MBTh 33. Münster: Aschendorff, 1969.

Halbwachs, Maurice. *On Collective Memory*. Translated by L. A. Coser. Heritage of Sociology Series. Chicago: The University of Chicago Press, 1992.

Hall, Stuart George. "Typologie." *TRE* 34 (2002): 208–24.

Hallit, Joseph. "La croix dans le rite byzantin. Histoire et théologie." *Parole de l'Orient* 3, no. 2 (1972): 261–311.

Hanssens, Jean Michel. *Institutiones liturgicae de ritibus orientalibus*. 4 vols. Rome: Pontificae Universitatis Gregorianae, 1930–32.

Haunerland, Winfried. "Die Fußwaschung am Gründonnerstag – Evangelienspiel oder Nachfolgehandlung?" *LJ* 48, no. 2 (1998): 79–95.

———. "„Lebendig ist das Wort Gottes" (Hebr 4,12). Die Liturgie als Sitz im Leben der Schrift." *ThPQ* 149, no. 2 (2001): 114–24.

Häußling, Angelus A. "Verkündigung in den Tageshoren." *LJ* 13, no. 2 (1963): 92–98.

———. "Liturgie: Gedächtnis eines Vergangenen und doch Befreiung in der Gegenwart." In Häußling, *Christliche Identität aus der Liturgie. Theologische und historische Studien zum Gottesdienst der Kirche*, edited by M. Klöckener et al., LQF 79, 2–10. Münster: Aschendorff, 1997.

———. "Die Bibel in der Liturgie der Tagzeiten." In *Präsenz der Schrift im Frühmittelalter*, edited by P. Carmassi, Wolfenbütteler Mittelalter-Studien 20, 299–322. Wiesbaden: Harrassowitz, 2008.

———. "Die Psalmen des Alten Testamentes in der Liturgie des Neuen Bundes." In Richter and Kranemann, *Christologie der Liturgie*, 87–102.

———. *Tagzeitenliturgie in Geschichte und Gegenwart. Historische und theologische Studien*, edited by M. Klöckener. 2nd ed. LQF 100. Münster: Aschendorff, 2017.

———. "Biblische Grundlegung christlicher Liturgie." In Häußling, *Tagzeitenliturgie*, 302–10.

Heid, Stefan. "Kreuz." *RAC* 21 (2006): 1099–1148.

Heinz, Andreas. *Licht aus dem Osten. Die Eucharistiefeier der Thomas-Christen, der Assyrer und der Chaldäer mit der Anaphora von Addai und Mari.* Sophia 35. Trier: Paulinus, 2008.

Herwegen, Ildefons. "Die Heilige Schrift in der Liturgie der Kirche." *LiZs* 3, no. 1 (1930/31): 8–17.

Hieke, Thomas. "Alles Auslegungssache. Methodisch-hermeneutische Erwägungen zur Kontextualisierung biblischer Auslegung." *BN* 140 (2009): 95–110.

Hoffman, Lawrence A., ed. *Seder K'riat Hatorah (The Torah Service).* Vol. 4 of *My People's Prayer Book. Traditional Prayers, Modern Commentaries.* Woodstock: Jewish Lights Publications, 2000.

———. "Introduction to the Liturgy. The Reading of Torah – Retelling the Jewish Story in the Shadow of Sinai." In Hoffman, *Prayer Book*, 1-18.

Hoffmann, Veronika. "Sakramentalität unter dem Vorzeichen des religiösen Pluralismus." *LJ* 65, no. 3 (2015): 155–71.

Hollaardt, Augustinus. "Sens, contenu et formes du chant de communion." *QL* 78, no. 1 (1997): 5–15.

Hoping, Helmut. "Kult und Reflexion. Joseph Ratzinger als Liturgietheologe." In *Der Logos-gemäße Gottesdienst. Theologie der Liturgie bei Joseph Ratzinger*, edited by R. Voderholzer, Ratzinger-Studien 1, 12–25. Regensburg: Pustet, 2009.

Hoping, Helmut and Birgit Jeggle-Merz, eds. *Liturgische Theologie: Aufgaben systematischer Liturgiewissenschaft.* Paderborn et al.: Schöningh, 2004.

Höslinger, Anton W. "Bibel und Liturgie." In *Liturgie lernen und leben – zwischen Tradition und Innovation. Pius-Parsch-Symposion 2014*, edited by A. Redtenbacher, PPSt 12, 225–234. Freiburg/Br. et al.: Herder, 2015.

Höslinger, Norbert and Theodor Maas-Ewerd, eds. *Mit sanfter Zähigkeit: Pius Parsch und die biblisch-liturgische Erneuerung.* Schriften des Pius-Parsch-Instituts Klosterneuburg 4. Klosterneuburg: Pius–Parsch–Institut, 1979.

Hossfeld, Frank-Lothar and Erich Zenger, eds. *Psalm 1–50.* Vol. 1 of *Die Psalmen. Kommentar zum Alten Testament mit der Einheitsübersetzung.* Die neue Echter-Bibel. Altes Testament 23,1. Würzburg: Echter, 1993.

Huglo, Michel. "Le Répons-Graduel de la Messe. Evolution de la forme. Permanence de la fonction." In *Chant grégorien et musique médiévale*, edited by M. Huglo, Variorum Collected Studies Series 814, 53–73. Aldershot et al.: Ashgate, 2005.

Hunger, Herbert. "Romanos Melodos. Überlegungen zum Ort und zur Art des Vortrags seiner Hymnen. Mit anschließender kurzer Strukturanalyse eines Kontakions (O 19. SC 35 = Maria unter dem Kreuz)." *ByZ* 92, no. 1 (1999): 1–9.

Huonder, Vitus. *Die Psalmen in der Liturgia Horarum*. Studia Friburgensia 74. Freiburg/ Schweiz: Universitätsverlag, 1991.

Irwin, Kevin W. *Context and Text. A Method for Liturgical Theology. Revised Edition.* Collegeville, MN: Liturgical Press, 2018.

Iser, Wolfgang. *The Implied Reader: Patterns Communication in Prose Fiction from Bunyan to Beckett*. Baltimore: Johns Hopkins University Press, 1974.

———. *The Act of Reading: A Theory of Aesthetic Response.* Baltimore: Johns Hopkins University Press, 1978.

Jacob, Christoph. *„Arkandisziplin", Allegorese, Mystagogie. Ein neuer Zugang zur Theologie des Ambrosius von Mailand.* Theophaneia 32. Frankfurt/M.: Hain, 1990.

———. "Zum hermeneutischen Horizont der Typologie: Der Antitypos als Prinzip ambrosianischer Allegorese." In Richter and Kranemann, *Christologie der Liturgie*, 103–11.

Janeras, Sebastià. "I vangeli domenicali della resurrezione nelle tradizioni liturgiche agiapolita e bizantina." In *Paschale mysterium. Studi in memoria dell'Abate Prof. Salvatore Marsili (1910–1983)*, edited by G. Farnedi, StA 91, AnLi 10, 55–69. Rome: Abbazia S. Paolo, 1986.

Janowiak, Paul. *The Holy Preaching: The Sacramentality of the Word in the Liturgical Assembly.* Collegeville, MN: Liturgical Press, 2000.

Jauß, Hans Robert. "Rezeption und Rezeptionsästhetik." *HWP* 8 (1992): 996–1004.

Jeanes, Gordon and Bridget Nichols, eds. *Lively Oracles of God. Perspectives on the Bible and Liturgy.* Collegeville, MN: Liturgical Press, 2022.

Jeffery, Peter. *A New Commandment. Toward a Renewed Rite for the Washing of Feet.* Collegeville, MN: Liturgical Press, 1992.

———. "Mandatum Novum Do Vobis. Toward a Renewal of the Holy Thursday Footwashing Rite." *Worship* 64, no. 2 (1990): 107–41.

———. "Monastic Reading and the Emerging Roman Chant Repertory." In Gallagher, *Western Plainchant*, 45–103.

Jilek, August. *Initiationsfeier und Amt. Ein Beitrag zur Struktur und Theologie der Ämter und des Taufgottesdienstes in der frühen Kirche (Traditio Apostolica, Tertullian, Cyprian).* EHS 23/130. Frankfurt/M. et al.: Lang, 1979.

Jörns, Klaus-Peter. "Liturgie – Wiege der Heiligen Schrift? " *ALw* 34, no. 3 (1992): 313–32.

Jungmann, Josef Andreas. *Gewordene Liturgie: Studien und Durchblicke.* Innsbruck et al.: Rauch, 1941.

———. *The Mass of the Roman Rite: Its Origins and Development (Missarum Sollemnia).* 2 vols. Translated by F. Brunner. New York: Benzinger, 1951–1955.

———. *Liturgy of the Word.* Translated by H. E. Winstone. Collegeville, MN: Liturgical Press, 1966.

Kaczynski, Reiner. *Das Wort Gottes in Liturgie und Alltag der Gemeinden des Johannes Chrysostomus.* FThSt 94. Freiburg/Br. et al.: Herder, 1974.

———. "Die Psalmodie bei der Begräbnisfeier." In Becker and Kaczynski, *Liturgie und Dichtung* 2, 795–835.

———. "Die Feier der Krankensalbung." In Meßner and Kaczynski, *Sakramentliche Feiern* I/2, 241–343.

———. "Theologischer Kommentar zur Konstitution über die heilige Liturgie Sacrosanctum Concilium." In *Theologischer Kommentar zum Zweiten Vatikanischen Konzil* 2, 1–227. *Herders Theologischer Kommentar zum Zweiten Vatikanischen Konzil,* edited by P. Hünermann and B. J. Hilberath, 5 vols. Freiburg/Br. et al.: 2004–2006.

Kannookadan, Pauly. *The East Syrian Lectionary. An Historico-Liturgical Study.* Rome: Mar Thoma Yogam, 1991.

Kasper, Walter. "Wort und Sakrament." In *Martyria, Liturgy, Diakonia* (FS Hermann Volk), edited by O. Semmelroth, 260–85. Mainz: Matthias-Grünewald-Verlag, 1968.

Kavanagh, Aidan. *On Liturgical Theology.* New York: Pueblo Publ. Co., 1992.

Kessler, Stephan C. *Gregor der Große als Exeget. Eine theologische Interpretation der Ezechielhomilien.* IThS 43. Innsbruck et al.: Tyrolia, 1995.

Kleinheyer, Bruno. "Ordinationen und Beauftragungen." In *Sakramentliche Feiern II,* edited by B. Kleinheyer et al. GdK 8, 7–65. Regensburg: Pustet, 1984.

Klöckener, Martin. "Bibel und Liturgie: Anmerkungen zu ihrer inneren Beziehung nach dem apostolischen Schreiben „Verbum Domini"." *LJ* 62, no. 3 (2012): 157–80.

Klöckener, Martin et al., ed. *Theologie des Gottesdienstes. Gottesdienst im Leben der Christen. Christliche und jüdische Liturgie.* GdK 2,2. Regensburg: Pustet, 2008.

Kniazeff, Alexis. "Le lecture de l'Ancien et du Nouveau Testament dans le rite byzantin." In *La prière des heures,* edited by K. Bezobrazov and B. Botte, 201–51. Paris: Éditions du Cerf, 1963.

Knop, Julia. *Ecclesia orans. Liturgie als Herausforderung für die Dogmatik.* Freiburg/Br. et al.: Herder, 2012.

Körtner, Ulrich H. J. *Der inspirierte Leser. Zentrale Aspekte biblischer Hermeneutik.* Sammlung Vandenhoeck. Göttingen: Vandenhoeck & Ruprecht, 1994.

———. *Einführung in die theologische Hermeneutik.* Einführung Theologie. Darmstadt: Wissenschaftliche Buchgesellschaft, 2006.

Kötting, Bernhard. "Fußwaschung." *RAC* 8 (1972): 743–77.

Koutsouras, Gerasimos. "Koinonikon. The Hymnological Kontext of Holy Communion." *Phronema* 21 (2006): 61–82.

Kranemann, Benedikt. "Liturgie nach den Grundsätzen der Vernunft und der Heiligen Schrift: Überlegungen zur Prägung der Liturgie des deutschen Aufklärungskatholizismus durch die Bibel." *ALw* 37, no. 1 (1995): 45–67.

———. "Bibel und Liturgie in Wechselbeziehung. Eine Perspektivensuche vor historischem Hintergrund." *BiLi* 80, no. 4 (2007): 205–17.

———. "Wort Gottes in der Liturgie." *LJ* 63, no. 3 (2013): 167–83.

Kunzler, Michael. "Darsteller des wahren Hirten (Μιμητὴς τοῦ ἀληθινοῦ Ποιμένος). Zugänge zum Wesen des Weiheamtes am Beispiel der byzantinischen Bischofsweihe." In *Manifestatio Ecclesiae. Studien zu Pontifikale und bischöflicher Liturgie* (FS Reiner Kaczynski), edited by W. Haunerland et al., StPaLi 17, 15–36. Regensburg: Pustet, 2004.

Langer, Ruth. "From Study of Scripture to a Reenactment of Sinai: The Emergence of the Synagogue Torah Service." *Worship* 72, no. 1 (1998): 43–67.

———. "Celebrating the Presence of the Torah. The History and Meaning of Reading Torah." In Hoffman, *Prayer Book*, 19–27.

———. "Sinai, Zion, and God in the Synagogue: Celebrating Torah in Ashkenaz." In *Liturgy in the Life of the Synagogue. Studies in the History of Jewish Prayer*, edited by R. Langer and S. Fine, Duke Judaic Studies Series 2, 121–59. Winona Lake, IN: Eisenbrauns, 2005.

———. *Jewish Liturgy. A Guide to Research*. Lanham et al.: Rowman & Littlefield, 2015.

Lathrop, Gordon W. *Saving Images: The Presence of the Bible in Christian Liturgy*. Minneapolis: Fortress Press, 2017.

Leclercq, Henri. "Communion (rite et antienne de la)." *DACL* 3 (1914): 2427–36.

Lengeling, Emil Joseph. "Liturgia Horarum. Die Lesungen und Responsorien im neuen Stundengebet." *LJ* 20, no. 4 (1970): 231–49.

Leonhard, Clemens. "Die Heiligkeit der Heiligen Schrift und Deutungen ihres Status im Rahmen des Synagogengottesdienstes und der Messliturgie." In Franz and Zerfaß, *Wort des lebendigen Gottes*, 149–80.

Lies, Lothar. "Verbalpräsenz – Aktualpräsenz – Realpräsenz. Versuch einer systematischen Begriffsbestimmung." In *Praesentia Christi* (FS Johannes Betz), edited by L. Lies, 79–100. Düsseldorf: Patmos, 1984; reprint: L. Lies, *Mysterium fidei. Annäherungen an das Geheimnis der Eucharistie*, 83–107. Würzburg: Echter, 2005.

Lingas, Alexander. "The Liturgical Place of the Kontakion in Constantinople." In *Liturgy, Architecture and Art of the Byzantine World: Papers of the XVIII International Byzantine Congress (Moscow, 8–15 August 1991) and Other Essays Dedicated to the Memory of Fr. John Meyendorff*, edited by C. C. Akentiev, Byzantinorossica 1, 50–57. St. Petersburg: Byzantinorossica, 1995.

Lohfink, Norbert. "Altes Testament und Liturgie: Unsere Schwierigkeiten und unsere Chancen." *LJ* 47, no. 1 (1997): 3–22.

———. "Was wird anders bei kanonischer Schriftauslegung? Beobachtungen am Beispiel von Psalm 6." In Lohfink, *Studien zur biblischen Theologie*, 263–93.

———. "Zur Perikopenordnung für die Sonntage im Jahreskreis." In Braulik and Lohfink, *Liturgie und Bibel*, 199–224.

———."Psalmengebet und Psalterredaktion." In Braulik and Lohfink, *Liturgie und Bibel*, 437–59.

———. "Der weiße Fleck in Dei Verbum 12." In Lohfink, *Studien zur biblischen Theologie*, 78–96.

Lohfink, Norbert, ed. *Studien zur biblischen Theologie*. Stuttgarter biblische Aufsatzbände 16. Altes Testament. Stuttgart: Katholisches Bibelwerk, 1993.

Lossky, André. "La cérémonie du lavement des pieds. Un essai d'étude comparée." In *Acts of the International Congress Comparative Liturgy Fifty Years After Anton Baumstark (1872–1948) [...]*, edited by R. F. Taft and G. Winkler, OChrA 265, 809–32. Rome: Pontificio Istituto Orientale, 2001.

———. "Lavement des pieds et charité fraternelle : L'exemple du rite byzantin." In Triacca and Pistoia, *Liturgie et charité fraternelle*, 87–96.

Magnoli, Claudio. "Il Lezionario Ambrosiano per i tempi liturgici." *RivLi* 96, no. 4 (2009): 487–507.

———. "Il quadro generale e le scelte qualificanti." *Ambrosius* 85, no. 1 (2009): 79–95.

———. "Il Lezionario ambrosiano a norma dei decreti del Concilio Vaticano II." In *L'omelia [...]*, edited by P. Chiaramello, BEL.S 160, 243–65. Rome: CLV-Edizioni Liturgiche, 2012.

———. "*Una certa unità tematica. Il n. 79 delle «Premesse» al Lezionario ambrosiano.*" In *Sacrificium et canticum laudis. Parola, eucaristia, liturgia delle ore, vita della Chiesa (FS Manlio Sodi)*, edited by D. Medeiros, Pontificia Academia Theologica. Itineraria 10, 79–88. Vatican City: Libreria Editrice Vaticana, 2015.

Margoni-Kögler, Michael. *Die Perikopen im Gottesdienst bei Augustinus. Ein Beitrag zur Erforschung der liturgischen Schriftlesung in der frühen Kirche*. SÖAW.PH 810. Vienna: Verlag der Österreichischen Akademie der Wissenschaft, 2010.

Markschies, Christoph. "Liturgisches Lesen und Hermeneutik der Schrift." In *Patristica et Oecumenica* (FS Wolfgang A. Bienert), edited by P. Gemeinhardt, Marburger Theologische Studien 85, 77–88. Marburg: Elwert, 2004.

Martimort, Aimé-Georges. "Fonction de la Psalmodie dans la Liturgie de la Parole." In Becker and Kaczynski, *Liturgie und Dichtung* 2, 837–56.

———. "Vom Beten der Psalmen im Stundengebet." In *Gott feiern. Theologische Anregung und geistliche Vertiefung zur Feier von Messe und Stundengebet* (FS Theodor Schnitzler), edited by J. G. Plöger, 384–94. Freiburg/Br. et al.: Herder, 1980.

Mateos, Juan. "La vigile cathédrale chez Égérie." *OCP* 27 (1961): 281–312.

Mateos, Juan and Steven Hawkes-Teeples. *The Liturgy of the Word*. Vol. 1 of *A History of the Liturgy of St. John Chrysostom*. Fairfax, VA: Jack Figel, Eastern Christian Publications, 2016.

Mayer, Hans Bernhard. "Gottesdienst und Spiritualität." In Klöckener, *Theologie des Gottesdienstes*, 159–279.

Mazza, Enrico. *Mystagogy: A Theology of Liturgy in the Patristic Age*. Translated by M. J. O'Connell. New York: Pueblo, 1989.

McKinnon, James. "Desert Monasticism and the Later Forth-Century Psalmodic Movement." In *Temple, Church Fathers and Early Western Chant*, edited by J. McKinnon, Variorum Collected Studies Series 606, 505–21. Aldershot et al.: Ashgate, 1998.

———. "The Forth-Century Origin of the Gradual." In *Temple, Church Fathers and Early Western Chant*, edited by J. McKinnon, Variorum Collected Studies Series 606, 91–106. Aldershot et al.: Ashgate, 1998.

———. *The Advent Project. The Later-Seventh-Century Creation of the Roman Mass Proper*. Berkeley: University of California Press, 2000.

Melzl, Thomas. *Die Schriftlesung im Gottesdienst: Eine liturgiewissenschaftliche Betrachtung*. Leipzig: Evangelische Verlagsanstalt, 2011.

Meyendorff, Paul. *The Anointing of the Sick*. Orthodox Liturgy Series 1. New York: SVS Press, 2009.

Meßner, Reinhard. "Feiern der Umkehr und Versöhnung. Mit einem Beitrag von Robert Oberforcher." In Meßner and Kaczynski, *Sakramentliche Feiern I/2*, 9–240.

———. *Einführung in die Liturgiewissenschaft*. 2nd ed. UTB 2173. Paderborn et al.: Schöningh, 2009.

———. "Der Wortgottesdienst der Messe als rituell inszenierte Christusanamnese." *HlD* 66, no. 3 (2012): 171–85.

———. "Wortgottesdienst. Historische Typologie und aktuelle Probleme." In Franz und Zerfaß, *Wort des lebendigen Gottes*, 73–110.

Meßner, Reinhard and Reiner Kaczynski, eds. *Sakramentliche Feiern*. Vol. I/2, Feiern der Umkehr und Versöhnung. GdK 7,2. Regensburg: Pustet, 1992.

Meßner, Reinhard et al., eds. *Bewahren und Erneuern. Studien zur Meßliturgie* (FS Hans Bernhard Meyer). IThS 42. Innsbruck et al.: Tyrolia, 1995.

Michel, Otto. "Evangelium." *RAC* 6 (1966): 1107–60.

Moos, Alois. *Das Verhältnis von Wort und Sakrament in der deutschsprachigen katholischen Theologie des 20. Jahrhunderts*. KKTS 59. Paderborn: Bonifatius, 1993.

Nachama, Andreas et al. *Basiswissen Judentum. Mit einem Geleitwort von Rabbiner Henry G. Brandt*. Freiburg/Br. et al.: Herder, 2015.

Navoni, Marco. "Colori liturgici." In *Dizionario di liturgia ambrosiana*, edited by M. Navoni, 147–48. Milan: NED, 1996.

Neuheuser, Hanns Peter, ed. *Wort und Buch in der Liturgie: Interdisziplinäre Beiträge zur Wirkmächtigkeit des Wortes und Zeichenhaftigkeit des Buches.* St. Ottilien: EOS, 1995.

Neuheuser, Hanns Peter. "Das Bild vom Tisch des Wortes und des Brotes: Kernaussagen der Liturgiekonstitution zum Verhältnis von Wortliturgie und Eucharistiefeier." In Neuheuser, *Wort und Buch*, 133–69.

———. "Wortliturgie und Bibellektüre – Zur Prävalenz der liturgischen Wortverkündigung vor dem privaten Bibelstudium." *LJ* 60, no. 1 (2010): 21–40.

Nicklas, Tobias. "Zum Verhältnis von Liturgie und Neuem Testament: Rezeption oder Kreation." In *Liturgische Bibelrezeption. Dimensionen und Perspektiven interdisziplinärer Forschung / Liturgical Reception of the Bible. Dimensions and Perspectives of Interdisciplinary Research*, ed. H. Buchinger and C. Leonhard, 39–56. Göttingen: Vandenhoeck & Ruprecht, 2022.

Nishiwaki, Jun. *Ad nuptias verbi. Aspekte einer Theologie des Wortes Gottes bei Ambrosius von Mailand.* TThS 69. Trier: Paulinus, 2003.

Nocent, Adrien. "Les deuxièmes lectures des dimanches ordinaires." In *EO* 8 (1991): 125–36.

———. *Le renouveau liturgique. Une relecture.* Le point théologique 58. Paris: Beauchesne, 1993.

———. "Eine »kleine Geschichte am Rande«. Zum Lektionar für die Messe der ›gewöhnlichen‹ Sonntage." In Franz, *Streit am Tisch des Wortes*, 649–57.

Nübold, Elmar. *Entstehung und Bewertung der neuen Perikopenordnung des römischen Ritus für die Meßfeier an Sonn- und Festtagen.* Paderborn: Bonifatius, 1986.

———. "Das Alte Testament in der gegenwärtigen Perikopenordnung – Offene Wünsche." *LJ* 47, no. 3 (1997): 174–89.

———. "Der Stellenwert des Alten Testaments in der nachvatikanischen Liturgiereform unter besonderer Berücksichtigung der Meßperikopen der Sonn-und Festtage." In Franz, *Streit am Tisch des Wortes*, 605–17.

Nußbaum, Otto. "Von der Gegenwart Gottes/Christi im Wort der Schriftlesungen und zur Auswirkung dieser Gegenwart auf das Buch der Schriftlesungen." In Neuheuser, *Wort und Buch*, 65–92.

Oeming, Manfred. *Contemporary Biblical Hermeneutics: An Introduction.* Translated by J. F. Vette. New York: Ashgate, 2006.

———. "Die verborgene Nähe. Zum Verhältnis von liturgischer und exegetischer Schrifthermeneutik (mit besonderer Berücksichtigung des Alten Testaments in der christlichen Predigt)." In Franz and Zerfaß, *Wort des lebendigen Gottes*, 181–203.

Old, Hughes Oliphant. *The medieval Church.* Vol. 3 of *The Reading and Preaching of the Scriptures in the Worship of the Christian Church.* Grand Rapids, MI: Eerdmans, 1999.

Otranto, Giorgo. *Esegesi biblica e storia in Giustino (Dial. 63–84).* QVetChr 14. Bari: Istituto di Letteratura Cristiana Antica, 1979.

Pacik, Rudolf. "Der Antwortpsalm." *LJ* 30, no. 1 (1980): 43–66.

Pahl, Irmgard. "Die Stellung Christi in den Präsidialgebeten der Eucharistiefeier." In Meßner, *Bewahren und Erneuern*, 92–113.

Parsch, Pius. *Wie halte ich Bibelstunde?* Edited by. F. Röhrig. 2nd ed. Klosterneuburg: Pius–Parsch–Institut, 1957.

Parenti, Stefano. "Care and Anointing of the Sick in the East." In *Sacraments and Sacramentals*. Vol 4 of *Handbook for Liturgical Studies*, edited by A. J. Chupungco, 161–69. Collegeville, MN: Liturgical Press, 2000.

Parenti, Stefano and Elena Velkovska. "La croce nel rito bizantino." In *La croce nella Liturgia*. Vol. 3 of *La Croce. Iconografia e interpretazione (secoli I – inizio XVI)*, edited by B. Ulianich, 55–74. Napoli: Elio de Rosa, 2007.

Pecklers, Keith F. *The Genius of the Roman Rite. On the Reception and Implementation of the New Missal*. Collegeville, MN: Liturgical Press, 2009.

Petrynko, Oleksandr. *Der jambische Weihnachtskanon des Johannes von Damaskus. Einleitung, Text, Übersetzung, Kommentar*. JThF 15. Münster: Aschendorff, 2010.

Plank, Peter. "Der byzantinische Begräbnisritus." In *Liturgie im Angesicht des Todes. 1: Judenttum und Ostkirchen I: Texte und Kommentare*, edited by H. Becker and H. Ühlein, PiLi 9, 773–819. St. Ottilien et al.: EOS, 1997.

———. "Der byzantinische Begräbnisritus." In *Liturgie im Angesicht des Todes. 2: Judentum und Ostkirchen II: Übersetzungen, Anhänge und Register*, edited by H. Becker and H. Ühlein, PiLi 10, 1279–1313. St. Ottilien et al.: EOS, 1997.

Plattig, Michael. "Was ist Spiritualität?" In *Spiritualität in der sozialen Arbeit*, edited by M. Lewkowicz and A. Lob-Hüdepohl, 12–32. Freiburg/Br.: Lambertus, 2003.

Poirot, Eliane. "La fête du saint prophète Elie dans la liturgie byzantine." *EO* 9 (1992): 173–200.

Power, David N. *"The Word of the Lord." Liturgy's Use of Scripture*. Maryknoll, NY: Orbis Books, 2001.

Praßl, Franz Karl. "Psallite sapienter. Gedanken zur Auswahl von Meßgesängen." In Meßner, *Bewahren und Erneuern*, 252–63.

Prétot, Patrick. "Vatican II – nouvelle appréciation de la Parole de Dieu." In *Présence et rôle de la Bible dans la liturgie*, edited by M. Klöckener et al., 205–25. Fribourg: Academic Press, 2006.

Prieur, Jean-Marc. "„Le Seigneur a régné depuis le bois". L'adjonction chrétienne au Psaume 95, 10 et son interprétation." In *Rois et reines de la Bible au miroir des Pères*, Cahiers de Biblia patristica 6, 127–40. Strasbourg: Univ. Marc Bloch, 1999.

———. *Das Kreuz in der christlichen Literatur der Antike*. TC 14. Bern et al.: Lang, 2006.

Pugliesi, James F. *Epistemological Principles and Roman Catholic Rites*. Vol. 1 of *The Process of Admission to Ordained Ministry. A Comparative Study* (A pueblo book). Collegeville, MN: Liturgical Press, 1996.

Quasten, Johannes. "The Garment of Immortality. A Study of the „Accipe vestem candidam"." In Bevilaqua, *Miscellanea Lercaro* 1, 391–401.

Rahner, Hugo. *Symbole der Kirche. Die Ekklesiologie der Väter.* Salzburg: Müller, 1964.

Ratzinger, Joseph. "Die Bedeutung der Väter für die gegenwärtige Theologie." *ThQ*, 148, no. 3 (1968): 257–82.

Ratzinger, Joseph / Benedict XVI. *In the Beginning: A Catholic Understanding of the Story of Creation and the Fall.* Translated by B. Ramsey. Grand Rapids, MI: Eerdmans, 1995.

———. *Jesus of Nazareth.* 1: *From the Baptism in the Jordan to the Transfiguration.* Translated by A. Walker. New York: Doubleday, 2007.

———. "Offenbarung und Heilsgeschichte nach der Lehre des heiligen Bonaventura." In Ratzinger, *Offenbarungsverständnis und Geschichtstheologie Bonaventuras. Habilitationsschrift und Bonaventura-Studien*, JRGS 2, 52–417. Freiburg/Br. et al.: Herder, 2009.

———. *Jesus of Nazareth.* 2: *From the Entrance into Jerusalem to the Resurrection.* San Francisco: Ignatius Press, 2011.

Redtenbacher, Andreas. "Biblische Grundlagen liturgischer Bildung: Zur Bedeutung der Bibel für das Verständnis des Gottesdienstes." *HlD* 60, no. 2 (2010): 122–36.

Reemts, Christiana. "Psalm 23. Öffnet ihm die Tore." In *Die Psalmen bei den Kirchenvätern. Psalm 1–30*, edited by T. Heither and C. Reemts, 361–73. Münster: Aschendorff, 2017.

Reijners, Gerardus Quirinus. *The Terminology of the Holy Cross in Early Christian Literature As Based Upon Old Testament Typology.* Nijmegen: Dekker & van de Vegt, 1965.

Richter, Klemens. "Zum Ritus der Bischofsordination in der „Apostolischen Überlieferung" Hippolyts von Rom und davon abhängigen Schriften." *ALw* 27, no. 17/18 (1975/76): 7–51.

Richter, Klemens and Benedikt Kranemann, eds. *Christologie der Liturgie. Der Gottesdienst der Kirche – Christusbekenntnis und Sinaibund.* QD 159. Freiburg/Br.: Herder, 1995.

Rondeau, Marie-Josèphe. *Les commentaires patristiques du Psautier (IIIe – Ve siècles).* 2 vols. OCA 219–20. Rome: Pontificium Institutum Studiorum Orientalium, 1982–1985.

Rose, André. "„Attollite portas, principes, vestras…". Aperçus sur la lecture chrétienne du Ps. 24 (23) B." In Bevilaqua, *Miscellanea Lercaro* 1, 454–78.

———. *Les psaumes. Voix du Christ et de l'Église.* Bible et vie chrétienne. Référence. Paris: Lethielleux, 1982.

———. "Sous-Titres psalmiques de la 'Liturgia Horarum'." In *Mens concordet voci […]* (FS Aimé-Georges Martimort). Paris: Desclée, 1983, 679–90.

———. "Le chant de communion en divers rites chrétiens." In Triacca and Pistoia, *Liturgie et charité fraternelle*, 19–30.

Rosso, Stefano. *La celebrazione della storia della salvezza nel rito bizantino. Misteri sacramentali, feste e tempi liturgici.* MSIL 60. Vatican City: Libreria Editrice Vaticana, 2010.

Rothenbusch, Ralf. "Historisch oder kanonisch? Zum exegetischen Methodenstreit 50 Jahre nach Dei Verbum." *HerKorr* 69, no. 6 (2015): 316–20.

Rouwhorst, Gerard. "Christlicher Gottesdienst und der Gottesdienst Israels. Forschungsgeschichte, Historische Interaktionen, Theologie." In Klöckener, *Theologie des Gottesdienstes*, 491–572.

Scagnelli, Peter John. *Creativity within Continuity. The ICEL Scriptural Collects*. ProQuest Dissertations Publishing, 2003.

Schäfer, Thomas. *Die Fußwaschung im monastischen Brauchtum und in der lateinischen Liturgie. Liturgiegeschichtliche Untersuchung*. TAB I. Abt. 47. Beuron: Beuroner Kunstverlag, 1956.

Schattauer, Thomas H. "The Koinonicon of the Byzantine Liturgy: An Historical Study." *OCP* 49 (1983): 91–129.

Scheffczyk, Leo. *Von der Heilsmacht des Wortes. Grundzüge einer Theologie des Wortes*. Munich: Hueber, 1966.

———. "Die Heilige Schrift – Wort Gottes und der Kirche." *IKaZ* 30, no. 1 (2001): 44–57.

Scheiding, Oliver. "Intertextualität." In *Gedächtniskonzepte der Literaturwissenschaft. Theoretische Grundlegung und Anwendungsperspektiven*, edited by A. Erll and A. Nünning, Media and Cultural Memory 2, 53–72. Berlin et al.: De Gruyter, 2005.

Schermer, Franz J. *Lernen und Gedächtnis*. Grundriss der Psychologie 10. Kohlhammer-Urban-Taschenbücher 559. 5th ed. Stuttgart: Kohlhammer, 2014.

Schlosser, Marianne. "„Ausdruck des Glaubens und Nahrung für ihn" (SC 59). Anmerkungen zur Bedeutung der Sakramente (nicht nur) in Zeiten von Corona." In *Gottesdienst auf eigene Gefahr*, edited by H.-J. Feulner and E. Haslwanter, 73–102. Münster: Aschendorff, 2020.

Schmemann, Alexander. *Introduction to Liturgical Theology*. 4th ed. Crestwood, New York: SVS Press, 1996 [1st ed. 1961].

———. *Great Lent: A School of Repentance. Its Meaning for Orthodox Christians*. Crestwood, NY: St. Vladimir's Seminary Press, 1974.

———. *The Eucharist: Sacrament of the Kingdom*. Crestwood, NY: St. Vladimir's Seminary Press, 1988.

Schmidt, Herman A. P. *Hebdomada sancta*. 2: *Fontes historici, commentarius historicus*. Rome et al.: Herder, 1957.

Schmitt, Siegfried. *Die internationalen liturgischen Studientreffen 1951–1960. Zur Vorgeschichte der Liturgiekonstitution*. TThS 53. Trier: Paulinus, 1992.

Schmitz, Josef. *Gottesdienst im altchristlichen Mailand. Eine liturgiewissenschaftliche Untersuchung über Initiation und Meßfeier während des Jahres zur Zeit des Bischofs Ambrosius († 397)*. Theophaneia 25. Bonn: Hanstein, 1975.

Schnabel, Nikodemus C. "Die liturgische Verehrung der Heiligen des Alten Testaments in der lateinischen Kirche. Ein vergessenes Desiderat der Konzilsgeneration." In *Liturgies in East and West. Ecumenical Relevance of Early Liturgical Development. Acts of the International Symposium Vindobonense I, Vienna, November 17-20, 2007*, edited by H.-J. Feulner, ÖSLS 6, 319–31. Münster: Lit-Verlag, 2013.

Schönborn, Christoph. *God's Human Face: The Christ-Icon*. San Francisco: Ignatius Press, 1995.

Schöttler, Heinz-Günther. "„Eingeladen zum Hochzeitsmahl des Wortes" (Ambrosius von Mailand). Überlegungen zur liturgischen Präsenz des Wortes Gottes." *BiLi* 80, no. 1 (2007): 217–36.

———. "„Ex sacra scriptura lectiones leguntur et in homilia explicantur". Re-Inszenierung, Mimesis und offenes Ereignis." In Franz and Zerfaß, *Wort des lebendigen Gottes*, 111–47.

Schrott, Simon A. *Pascha-Mysterium. Zum liturgietheologischen Leitbegriff des Zweiten Vatikanischen Konzils*. Theologie der Liturgie 6. Regensburg: Pustet, 2014.

Schulz, Hans-Joachim. "Liturgie, Tagzeiten und Kirchenjahr des byzantinischen Ritus." In *Handbuch der Ostkirchenkunde* 2, edited by W. Nyssen et al., 30–100. Düsseldorf: Patmos, 1989.

Schürmann, Heinz. "Das apostolische Kerygma als Interpretationshilfe für das vierfache Evangelium. Konsonante Episteln für die Sonntage im Jahreskreis." In *Surrexit dominus vere. Die Gegenwart des Auferstandenen in seiner Kirche* (FS Johannes Joachim Degenhardt), edited by J. Ernst and S. Leimgruber, 173–87. Paderborn: Bonifatius, 1996.

———. "Konsonante Episteln für die Sonntage im Jahreskreis. Eine Vergleichstabelle mit Reformvorschlägen zum Ordo Lectionum Missae" In *Schrift und Tradition* (FS Josef Ernst), edited by K. Backhaus and F. G. Untergaßmair, 395–441. Paderborn: Schöningh, 1996.

Schwienhorst-Schönberger, Ludger. "Einheit und Vielheit. Gibt es eine sinnvolle Mitte des AT?" In *Wieviel Systematik erlaubt die Schrift? Auf der Suche nach einer gesamtbiblischen Theologie*, edited by F.-L. Hossfeld, QD 185, 48–87. Freiburg/Br et al.: Herder, 2001.

———. "Einheit statt Eindeutigkeit. Paradigmenwechsel in der Bibelwissenschaft?" *HerKorr* 57, no. 8 (2003): 412–17.

———. "„Eines hat Gott gesagt, zweierlei habe ich gehört" (Ps 62,12). Sinnoffenheit als Kriterium einer biblischen Theologie." In *Wie biblisch ist die Theologie?*, edited by M. Ebner, JBTh 25, 45–61. Neukirchen-Vluyn: Neuenkirchener Theologie/ Vandenhoeck&Ruprecht, 2010.

———. "Wiederentdeckung des geistigen Schriftverständnisses. Zur Bedeutung der Kirchenväterhermeneutik." *ThGl* 101, no 3 (2011): 402–25.

———. "Zwei antagonistische Modelle der Schriftauslegung in Dei Verbum?" In Tück, *Erinnerung an die Zukunft*, 449–61.

———. " „Damit die Bibel nicht ein Wort der Vergangenheit bleibt" – Historische Kritik und geistige Schriftauslegung." In *Gottes Wort in Menschenwort. Die eine Bibel als Fundament der Theologie* (FS Norbert Lohfink), edited by K. Lehmann and R. Rothenbusch, QD 266, 177–201. Freiburg/Br. et al.: Herder, 2014.

———. "Hieronymus als Gesprächspartner einer zeitgemäßen Bibelwissenschaft." In *Hieronymus als Exeget und Theologe. Interdisziplinäre Zugänge zum Koheletkommentar des Hieronymus*, edited by E. Birnbaum and L. Schwienhorst-Schönberger, EThL Bibliotheca 268, 273–98. Leuven et al.: Peeters, 2014.

Searle, Mark. *Called to Participate. Theological, Ritual, and Social Perspectives*, edited by B. Searle and A. Y. Koester. Collegeville, MN: Liturgical Press, 2006.

Semmelroth, Otto. *Wirkendes Wort. Zur Theologie der Verkündigung*. Frankfurt/M.: Knecht, 1962.

Seremak, Jerzy. *Psalm 24 als Text zwischen den Texten*. ÖBS 26. Frankfurt/M. et al.: Peter Lang, 2004.

Sieben, Hermann Josef. "Der Psalter und die Bekehrung der voces und affectus. Zu Augustinus, Conf. IX,4,7–11 und X,33,49–50." In *"Manna in deserto". Studien zum Schriftgebrauch der Kirchenväter*, edited by H. J. Sieben, Edition Cardo 92, 243–66. Cologne: Patristisches Zentrum Koinonia-Oriens, 2002.

———. *Schlüssel zum Psalter. Sechzehn Kirchenvätereinführungen von Hippolyt bis Cassiodor*. Paderborn et al.: Schöningh, 2011.

Siebenrock, Roman A. "Christus-Gegenwart. Von der realen Gegenwart Christi im Wort." *BiLi* 89, no. 3 (2016): 185–94.

Sodi, Manlio. *La parola di Dio nella celebrazione eucaristica. The Word of God in the Eucharistic Celebration: Tavole sinottiche – Synoptic Tables*. MSIL 7. Vatican City: Libreria Editrice Vaticana, 2000.

Söding, Thomas. *Einheit der Heiligen Schrift? Zur Theologie des biblischen Kanons*. QD 211. Freiburg/Br. et al.: Herder, 2005.

———. "Theologie mit Seele. Der Stellenwert der Schriftauslegung nach der Offenbarungskonstitution Dei Verbum." In Tück, *Erinnerung an die Zukunft*, 423–48.

Söhngen, Gottlieb. *Symbol und Wirklichkeit im Kultmysterium*. Grenzfragen zwischen Theologie und Philosophie 4. 2nd ed. Bonn: Hanstein, 1940.

Stangl, Werner. "Semiotisches Gedächtnis." In *Online Lexikon für Psychologie und Pädagogik*. http://lexikon.stangl.eu/3128/semantisches-gedachtnis/ [2012; retrieved 02/21/22].

Steins, Georg. " „Hört dies zu meinem Gedächtnis!" Anamnese als Bibel und Liturgie verbindende Leitkategorie." *BiLi* 80, no. 4 (2007): 236–43.

———. "Kanon und Anamnese. Auf dem Weg zu einer Neuen Biblischen Theologie." In Steins, *Kanonisch-intertextuelle Studien*, 61–85.

———. *Kanonisch-intertextuelle Studien zum Alten Testament*. Stuttgarter Biblische Aufsatzbände 48. Altes Testament. Stuttgart: Katholisches Bibelwerk, 2009.

———. "Wort des lebendigen Gottes: Neue Brücken zwischen Bibelauslegung und Liturgie." In Steins, *Kanonisch-intertextuelle Studien*, 131–44.

Szövérffy, Josef. *Hymns of the Holy Cross. An Annotated Edition with Introduction*. Medieval Classics 7. Brookline, MA et al.: Classical Folia Editions, 1976.

Taft, Robert F. *The Liturgy of the Hours in East and West: The Origins of the Divine Office and its Meaning for Today*. 2nd ed. Collegeville, MN: Liturgical Press, 1993.

———. *The Precommunion Rites*. Vol. 5 of *A History of the Liturgy of St. John Chrysostom*. OCA 261. Rome: Pontificium Institutum Studiorum Orientalium, 2000.

———. "Anton Baumstark's Comparative Liturgy Revisited." In *Comparative Liturgy Fifty Years after Anton Baumstark (1872–1948). Acts of the International Congress. Rome, 25–29 September 1998*, edited by R. F. Taft and G. Winkler, OCA 265, 191–232. Rome: Pontificio Istituto Orientale, 2001.

Taft, Robert F. and Stefano Parenti. *Storia della liturgia di S. Giovanni Crisostomo*. 2: *Il grande ingresso. Edizione italiana rivista, aggiornata e ampliata*. Analekta Kryptopherrēs 10. Grottaferrata: Monastero Esarchico, 2014.

Tichý, Radek. *Proclamation de l'Évangile dans la messe en occident. Ritualité, histoire, comparaison, théologie*. StA 168. Rome: Pontificio Ateneo S. Anselmo, 2016.

Tompkins, Jane P. *Reader-Response Criticism: From Formalism to Post-Structuralism*. Baltimore: Johns Hopkins University Press, 1980.

Treitinger, Otto. *Die oströmische Kaiser- und Reichsidee nach ihrer Gestaltung im höfischen Zeremoniell*. 2nd ed. Darmstadt: Wissenschaftliche Buchgesellschaft, 1956.

Trepp, Leo. *Der jüdische Gottesdienst: Gestalt und Entwicklung*. 2nd ed. Stuttgart: Kohlhammer, 2004.

Triacca, Achille M. and Alessandro Pistoia, eds. *Liturgie et charité fraternelle*. BEL.S 101. Rome: CLV-Edizioni Liturgiche, 1999.

———. *Les lectures bibliques pour les dimanches et fêtes*. Vol 1 of *Liturgie, interprète de l'écriture*. BEL.S 119. Rome: CLV-Edizioni Liturgiche, 2002.

Trobisch, David. *Die Endredaktion des Neuen Testaments. Eine Untersuchung zur Entstehung der christlichen Bibel*. Novum testamentum et orbis antiquus 31. Fribourg: Universitätsverlag, 1996.

Tück, Jan Heiner, ed. *Erinnerung an die Zukunft. Das Zweite Vatikanische Konzil*. Freiburg/Br. et al.: Herder, 2012.

Turner, Paul. *Words without Alloy. A Biography of the Lectionary for Mass*. Collegeville, MN: Liturgical Press, 2022.

Valli, Norberto. "Libro I – Mistero dell'Incarnazione." *Ambrosius* 85 (2009): 123–59.

———. "«Redemptionis enim nostrae magna mysteria celebramus». Il ciclo de tempore nella liturgia ambrosiana." *RivLi* 96, no. 4 (2009): 508–30.

van Tongeren, Louis. *Exaltation of the Cross. Toward the Origins of the Feast of the Cross and the Meaning of the Cross in Early Medieval Liturgy*. LC 11. Leuven et al.: Peeters, 2000.

Velamparampil, Cyrus. *The Celebration of the Liturgy of the Word in the Syro-Malabar Qurbana. A Biblico-Theological Analysis.* Oriental Institute Publications 194. Kottayam: Oriental Institution of Religious Studies, 1997.

Velkovska, Elena. "Funeral Rites according to Byzantine Liturgical Sources." *DOP* 55 (2001): 21–51.

Verheul, Ambroos. "Les psaumes dans la prière des heures hier et aujourd'hui." *QL* 71, no. 3/4 (1990): 261–95.

Voderholzer, Rudolf. *Die Einheit der Schrift und ihr geistiger Sinn. Der Beitrag Henri de Lubacs zur Erforschung von Geschichte und Systematik christlicher Bibelhermeneutik.* Sammlung Horizonte. Neue Folge 31. Einsiedeln et al.: Johannes, 1998.

———. *Offenbarung. Tradition und Schriftauslegung. Bausteine zu einer christlichen Bibelhermeneutik.* Regensburg: Pustet, 2013.

———. "Der geistige Sinn der Schrift. Frühkirchliche Lehre mit neuer Aktualität." In Voderholzer, *Offenbarung,* 119–50.

———. "„Die Heilige Schrift wächst irgendwie mit den Lesern" (Gregor der Große). Dogmatik und Rezeptionsästhetik." In Voderholzer, *Offenbarung,* 151–69.

———. "Zum Verständnis von „traditio/paradosis" in der Frühen Kirche. Unter besonderer Berücksichtigung der „Regula fidei"." In Voderholzer, *Offenbarung,* 105–18.

Vogüe, Adalbert de. "Psalmodier n'est pas prier." *EO* 6 (1989): 7–32.

Wahle, Stephan. *Gottes-Gedenken. Untersuchungen zum anamnetischen Gehalt christlicher und jüdischer Liturgie.* IThS 73. Innsbruck et al.: Tyrolia-Verlag, 2006.

Ward, Anthony. "The Orations after the Readings at the Easter Vigil in the 2000 '*Missale Romanum*'." *EL* 123, no. 4 (2009): 460–507.

Ward, Anthony and Cuthbert Johnson, eds. *The Prefaces of the Roman Missal. A Source Compendium with Concordance and Indices.* Rome: Tipografia Poliglotta Vaticana, 1989.

Warning, Rainer, ed. *Rezeptionsästhetik. Theorie und Praxis.* UTB 303. 2nd ed. Munich: Fink, 1979.

Werbick, Jürgen. "Bibel Jesu und Evangelium Jesu Christi: Systematisch-theologische Perspektiven." *BiLi* 70, no. 3 (1997): 213–18.

West, Fritz. *The Comparative Liturgy of Anton Baumstark.* Joint Liturgical Studies 31. Bramcote: Grove Books, 1995.

———. *Scripture and Memory: The Ecumenical Hermeneutic of the Three-Year-Lectionaires.* A Pueblo Book. Collegeville, MN: Liturgical Press, 1997.

———. "A Reader's Guide to the Methodological Writings of Anton Baumstark." *Worship* 88, no. 3 (2014): 194–217.

Weinert, Franz-Rudolf. *Christi Himmelfahrt, neutestamentliches Fest im Spiegel alttestamentlicher Psalmen. Zur Entstehung des römischen Himmelfahrtsoffiziums.* Diss.T 25. St. Ottilien: EOS, 1987.

Wieland, Georg. "Hermeneutik: I. Begriff und Geschichte." In *LThK*, vol. 5, 1–3. Freiburg/Br.: Herder, 1996.

Wohlmuth, Josef. "Vorüberlegungen zu einer theologischen Ästhetik der Sakramente." In Hoping and Jeggle-Merz, *Liturgische Theologie*, 85–106.

Zenger, Erich. "Von der Psalmenexegese zur Psalterexegese." *BiKi* 56, no. 1 (2001): 8–15.

———. "„Du thronst auf den Psalmen Israels" (Ps 22,4). Von der Unverzichtbarkeit der jüdischen Psalmen im christlichen Wortgottesdienst." In *Wie das Wort Gottes feiern? Der Wortgottesdienst als theologische Herausforderung*, edited by B. Kranemann and T. Sternberg, QD 194, 16–40. Freiburg/Br. et al.: Herder, 2002.

Zerfaß, Alexander. *Auf dem Weg nach Emmaus: Die Hermeneutik der Schriftlesung im Wortgottesdienst der Messe*. PiLi.S 24. Tübingen/Basel: Narr Francke Attempto, 2016.

Zerfaß, Rolf. "Die Rolle der Lesung im Stundengebet." *LJ* 13, no. 3 (1963): 159–67.

———. *Die Schriftlesung im Kathedraloffizium Jerusalems*. LQF 48. Münster: Aschendorff, 1968.

Scriptural Index

OLD TESTAMENT

NEW TESTAMENT

Index of Magisterial Documents

Index of Authors / People (deceased)

Index of Subjects